To my [illegible]
Ther[illegible]
met hartelige groeten
Y. L. Wu
5/1/97, [illegible], Palo Al[illegible]

吴元黎

Occasional Papers/Reprint Series in Contemporary Asian Studies

All contributions (in English only) and communications should be sent to:

Professor Hungdah Chiu, University of Maryland School of Law,
500 West Baltimore Street, Baltimore, Maryland 21201-1786, USA.

All publications in this series reflect only the views of the authors.

While the editor accepts responsibility for the selection of materials to be published, the individual author is responsible for statements of facts and expressions of opinion contained therein.

Subscription is US $30.00 per year for 6 issues (regardless of the price of individual issues) in the United States and $35.00 for Canada or overseas. Checks should be addressed to OPRSCAS.

Tel.: (410) 706-3870
Fax: (410) 706-4045

Price for single copy of this issue: US $35.00 (paper back).
$45.00 (hard cover)

ISSN 0730-0107
ISBN 0-925153-52-4 (paper back)
ISBN 0-925153-53-2 (hard cover)

TIANANMEN TO TIANANMEN
CHINA UNDER COMMUNISM
1947-1996

After Delusion and Disillusionment
A Nation at a Crossroads

by

Yuan-Li Wu

TIANANMEN TO TIANANMEN: CHINA UNDER COMMUNISM 1947-1996

*Yuan-Li Wu**

TABLE OF CONTENTS

* Professor Emeritus of Economics, University of San Francisco; Consultant, Hoover Institution, Stanford University.

Chapter V ECONOMIC DEVELOPMENT AFTER SOCIALIZATION – BUT FOR WHAT?

Chapter VI ONCE MORE IN TRANSITION AFTER MAO: FROM HUA TO DENG

CHAPTER VIII THE 1989 TIANANMEN CRISIS AND AN UNFINISHED REFORM AGENDA

CHAPTER IX EXTERNAL RELATIONS AND NATIONAL POLICY GOALS: THE PRC BETWEEN TWO SUPERPOWERS (1949-1964)

CHAPTER X EXTERNAL RELATIONS AND NATIONAL POLICY GOALS: COUNTER-CONTAINMENT AND OPPORTUNISM

CHAPTER XI EXTERNAL RELATIONS AND NATIONAL POLICY GOALS: TOWARD RESTRUCTURING

CHAPTER XII EXTERNAL RELATIONS AND NATIONAL POLICY GOALS: SOURCES OF CAPITAL AND LEARNING TO KNOW ONE'S NEIGHBORS

FOREWORD ONE

by
D.W.Y. Kwok
Professor of History, University of Hawaii

If revolution, as distinguished from upheaval and dynastic change, means a fundamental rearrangement of the ways by which a state and society is organized, Chinese history has witnessed only three such major shifts: in 221 B.C., in 1911, and in 1949. In all three revolutions, legalism was somehow involved, with legalism viewed as a preference for laws above moral standards, of government by laws over government by man. In 221 B.C., legalism was installed. The state of Ch'in not only defeated six other hegemonic contenders for the imperial legacy of a disintegrated Chou empire, but also unified China. This unification introduced the fact and theory of a unified bureaucratic state, with a province-district division of China that still stands in essential outline today. It was a revolution from the "feudal" and ritual arrangements of power and territory which characterized the Chou rule of China. Along with an institutionalized Confucianism established during the Han which followed the Ch'in, this legalist grid for state and society prevailed during the next two thousand years in China.

In 1911, legalism was overthrown by the revolution led by Sun Yat-sen in favor of a republic, believed by the Chinese revolutionaries of the time to be the most forward form of political organization, inspired as they were by the French and American examples. But the following decades saw China grappling with modern democratic forms and aspirations. In the intellectual realm, science and democracy became the catchwords for intellectual and political revolutions respectively. In politics, the warlord decades gave way to protracted struggles between the Nationalists and the Communists for supremacy, both parties formed on Leninist principles of political organization and action in the early 1920s. Adding to all this internal struggle was a lingering heritage of an imperialist presence which emboldened as much as compromised a nationalism at times positive, sometimes negative, but always restive and strident. Japanese aggression in China in many ways was an extension of this imperialism, even if it assumed an anticolonial rationale in such slogans as "East Asia Co-Prosperity Sphere."

Legalism returned to China in 1949 with the Communist Revolution. A centralized bureaucratic state returned to China with a program of positive laws that contravened customs and moral restraints. Yet, this revolution took place in the century of democratic aspirations. The interpretation, therefore, of this mid-century Chinese revolution has been spirited since its founding. There is little need to question whether the two-thousand year tradition of unified imperial rule or the forty years of the 1911 Republic of imperfect democracy have had the stronger influence on the course of Chinese communism during the second half of the twentieth century. The quizzical nature of the new state and society can be seen in the following way.

On October 1, 1959, more than half a million civilian and military personnel passed in review at Tiananmen Square celebrating a decade of socialist construction and massive economic, political and social transformations. The buoyant spirit was that of a people who had "stood up," as Chairman Mao Zedong had proclaimed atop the parapet facing Tiananmen Square ten years earlier at the founding of the People's Republic of China on October 1, 1949. Nineteen fifty-nine represented the completion of the first decade of improbable achievements. China had in that period fought the combined forces of the United Nations to a standstill in Korea, established diplomatic relations which saw China emerge as the leader of the Third World, and exceeded all expected quotas in heavy industry production.

October 1, 1969, marked a drastically different decade, and national day observances at Tiananmen Square were subdued, muted, and confusing. China was three years into the Great Proletarian Cultural Revolution. The decade began with the disastrous consequences of the Great Leap Forward (with its attendant three years of severe famine), intraparty struggles that presaged as well as introduced the Cultural Revolution, and the dissolution of diplomatic relations that left China with Albania as its only friend.

October 1, 1979, came three years after the formal end of the Cultural Revolution. National day was again observed, but in reduced scale. The decade preceding 1979 had seen mostly cataclysmic events: domination by and eventual downfall of the Gang of Four in the Cultural Revolution; and, the deaths of Zhou Enlai, Zhu De, and Mao Zedong in 1976, with the Tangshan earthquake in between. Coming out of the stupefaction of the Cultural Revolution, China showed the first stirrings of hope and optimism that accompanied her resumption of relations with the world. In the midst of this decade, the visit of Richard Nixon to China was of historic importance to United States-China relations.

October 1, 1989, was to have been a celebration to match the fanfare and buoyancy of the 1959 observations. The decade following the opening of China brought a new rush of energy and ideas into the Chinese body politic, now known as the Deng Xiaoping era, during which China regained her considerable world stature through both internal development and external reciprocities. Yet, Tiananmen Square on October 1 was quiet, scrubbed clean and bedecked with flowers. Movements in the square were sedate, observed and guarded. Four months earlier the square had seen Chinese youth who told, through peaceful demonstrations, the world of their longing for science and democracy. In historical irony, that was the same voice heard in Beijing seventy years earlier, in May 1919.

By national day on October 1, 1999, Hong Kong will have already reverted to China for two years, and Macao to follow in two months time. The decade resonates with counterpunctal cadences of nationalism, human rights and East-West rectitudes, as well as with question as to whether economics or politics should command.

This portraiture of China dramatizes the importance of China's transformation during the second half of the twentieth century, as the adjustment to modernity of this populous and long-lived state and society seizes the imagination everywhere. Of the three revolutions in Chinese history, two occurred in the twentieth century. In the twentieth century, we may add the Nationalist Revolution (viewed by some as a continuation of the 1911 Revolution) and the Great Proletarian Cultural Revolution (if it qualifies as a revolution). However viewed, these were events which affected inescapably the political, economic, social, and cultural lives of not only Chinese, but in varying degrees the world as well. The 1911 Revolution overthrew a two-thousand year old polity and society and ushered in the expectations for science and democracy (standing for intellectual and political resolutions); the Nationalist Revolution in 1926-28 aimed at ridding China of warlordism and imperialist presence, presumably fulfilling the earlier revolution envisaged by Sun Yat-sen; and, the Communist Revolution in 1949, broader than the previous two in all aspects, but perhaps most intensely in the social aspect, came close to changing human nature in its attempt at total communization. The scope and nature of this revolution presaged the Great Proletarian Cultural Revolution, a massive turning inward upon China and Chinese themselves. None escaped the personality cult of Mao; few were able to withstand the assault by the masses upon the dignities of the person. In this sense, the lofty ideals of 1949 seemed truncated by the events of 1969, a short twenty years into supposed revolutionary union of the century. By 1989, the government turned on its own people and fired into their midst, quashing their voices.

Yet, China stands today, to many observers, only as a strong economy, enjoying a rate of growth reportedly faster and greater than any other nation, with the potential of its markets exerting a magnetic effect on the world's industries and businesses. The country seeks entry into world trade bodies and economic councils, while resenting external attention on its internal treatment of its own people whose ideas and ideals are shared with the world. The world has entered China, by force or by invitation, throughout the twentieth century. China's own search for a comfortable stance in the world has been anxious and unrequited as her tumultuous events of the twentieth century indicate. Viewing China at the end of the twentieth century and the beginning of the twenty-first demands the viewer to be historically informed.

Professor Yuan-li Wu's current volume, *Tiananmen to Tiananmen*, is a work about China during the last fifty years of the twentieth century written with the interpretive and analytical insight of a lifetime devoted to the study of the Chinese political economy. Students of modern China are already informed by Professor Wu's meticulous research scholarship. The current work, however, is more than scholarship; it is scholarship with the benefit of reflection. In the tradition of a P.P.E. education (politics, philosophy, and economics) in London, Professor Wu narrates, queries, and probes in his elegant prose the complex changes wrought in China. The reader finds in this work elucidation of the myriad events, episodes, policies and personages in modern Chinese history and encounters a wry realism borne of keen observation and historical sensibility.

FOREWORD TWO

by
Richard L. Walker
Ambassador-in-Residence, University of South Carolina

In the 1990s the grim realities of the Maoist era in China were becoming manifest for the attentive public, many of whom had been awash in the tides of praise for "unparalleled and formidable" achievements attributed to the "Great Helmsman," as Mao was called. Surely today some China specialists are embarrassed by their earlier rhapsodic paeans for Maoist rule. The author of this work, Yuan-li Wu, is not one of those. Western contributors to the Mao cult maintained their faith in his positive contributions and greatness even up through the mid-1980s. For example, a group of fifteen China specialists was gathered at Columbia University while the Cultural Revolution was still in progress (its toll in deaths and destruction is still not completely measured), to assess the conditions in the Middle Kingdom. Given recent revelations, their observations seem today almost a parody. Almost all of the fifteen authors heaped praise on the Chinese model which they opined might serve as a guide for the United States in solving our own domestic and foreign policy problems. They extolled China's educational programs (this while education was under siege there), the Chinese system of law and penology (which in many respects was surpassing the horrors of Stalin's gulags), Beijing's approach to ecology (we now know this was disastrous), and even treatment of minorities (Tibetans apparently never had it so good, we were told).

After nearly a half century of Communist rule in China, more balanced appraisal today can only conclude that the price was much too high for all the Chinese people and for a world which seeks decency and cannot accept Mao Zedong beliefs and formulas asserting that violence and war are great schools. We now know he was not the great genius whom the hagiographers, including Western Specialists with their China romancing claimed him to be. The cult of personality deranged Stalin and the results proved to be an embarrassment to his many supporters in the West. That warning was apparently not heeded by all too many scholars and journalists who failed to dig beneath the surface glitter of praise for Mao and the claimed achievements of the "People's Republic". We now know, for instance, that many of the works attributed to Mao, whose poems and writings proclaimed that he would be the greatest ruler in all of Chinese history, were acutely ghost-written. Thus, his much-discussed piece "On Contradictions" turns out to have been cribbed from a Soviet middle-school textbook with some illustrations from the Chinese scene added. Court flatterers wrote other works for which he took credit.

Throughout the Communist era, including the drive to power of the Mao-led Chinese Communist Party, China's historical traditions, its internal disparities, its strategic position, and its manifold problems have all pointed to the centrality of economic issues and the failures of the Soviet-inspired model of economic planning for rural and urban development. That centrality has often been inadequately woven into the survey volumes on China under Communism.

This is one reason why Yuan-li Wu's book is very important; he is a rigorously trained economist who from the outset understood the long-range futility and agony for China when it attempted to follow the Soviet model for development. Yuan-li Wu brings to bear on this volume a rich lifetime of scholarship that has stood the test of time. But he has kept actively up to date with the recently published memoirs and notes of some of the leaders in Communist China who have been revealing the extent of intraparty struggling during and after Mao's long reign Economic Chinese czars like Bo Ibo's and Chen Yun's works are now available; so too are the observations of Li Xiannian and Nie Rongzhen; and there is the account of Mao's doctor, Li Zhisui, which fortunately has been generally available in English as well as in the original Chinese.

But Dr. Wu's book is important for other reasons. It examines the interaction between military-strategic factors for China as well as the personal political dynamics of decision-making under and after Mao. Wu's service in the U.S. Department of Defense as a Deputy Assistant Secretary in the Office of International Security Affairs has helped his portrayal of the manner in which Mao's searching for military great power status, including atomic club membership, wreaked havoc on an economy that was not prepared to sustain the Chairman's demands. The author's background enables him to bring out for us interesting details on practical logistic problems, many of which continue, for the PRC.

Since this careful scholar was never misled by the parade of statistics designed for propaganda purposes in Beijing, he is able to point out clearly the enormity of the mistakes made during the Mao era. In a condensed but admirably clear manner he dissects the two enormous calamities, the Great Leap forward and the Cultural Revolution. And, refreshingly, he minces no words about Mao and his harebrained schemes, observing that Mao's patterns "only tended to accentuate the importance of economic realities." With more than adequate illustrative material, the reader of this book will join Yuan-li Wu in concluding that on matters so important for a sustained future of development for China the Chairman was indeed an ignoramus.

The author of this significant volume has condensed an unprecedented wealth of complexities into a neatly organized pattern that yields answers to many of the questions we would have about the strange half-century course for China under Communism with two symbolic peaks enacted at Tiananmen, first in 1949 when Mao proclaimed that "China has stood up" and then almost 40 years later in 1989 when leaders, still believing in Mao's doctrine that "political power grows out of the barrel of a gun" carried out a massacre that was seen round the world on television screens. The ideology had failed, and China was searching for the right path to take. Wu's analysis of this situation "again at the crossroads" sets us to thinking of some of his Nobel-laureate mentors.

Every reader will want to reread and ponder the meaning of Chapter XIII after going through this thorough condensation of China's paths of economic and political development and then of foreign policy behavior. Dr. Wu faces up to the question of why the Chinese people would have put up with the tyrant Mao for so long. It was indeed a "costly dictatorship". After reading this condensed answer, we hope that an elaboration on this theme will be the subject for another volume to follow from this rigorous analytical scholar.

Professor Yuan-li Wu's distinguished service and his extraordinary background have made it fortunate for me to become his friend and co-worker over many years. We began our studies of and attention to the political development of China during World War II and have had occasions to work together in the decades following. I naturally expected a balanced and solid account, and I was not disappointed. I have managed to see some associations of events and to gain new insights into the problems and development in China, as will every reader of this significant contribution to the often too-voluminous literature on the Middle Kingdom. So much has now been written about the China of Mao and about the Chairman himself, the confused reader can get almost any assessment from whatever perspective he wants. But Yuan-li's volume reflects the sort of solid and penetrating analysis we should all seek.

PREFACE

The nature and contents of this book are fully explained in Chapter I. It remains for me to note here in the Preface why I wish to write this book and why I think I have something to say that readers may wish to know.

As the book proceeds, it will soon be clear that as long as Mao Zedong was alive, the People's Republic of China did not offer the Chinese people what he originally said it would. Even after Mao left the scene, Deng Xiaoping's reform program also failed to satisfy what many Chinese apparently wanted and thought Deng's "reform and openness" were going to offer. The 1989 crisis came as a great shock. But nearly a decade later, today in 1996, China still stands at the crossroads although Chinese communism is no longer what it was.

My wish to write this book stems from my concern about what lies ahead and returning to the same point for a new start may not be possible. My concern is that different paths lead from this point and some alternatives may not be any better than Mao's original choice even though a return to the Maoist past can be ruled out for the near future. Apart from poor alternative choices, there are also signs that suggest China may be on an irregular orbit of development. Chinese history may repeat itself in certain aspects even though it will not repeat itself fully. The current PRC is a great deal larger in size compared to the time of the Opium War a century and a half ago. It is also militarily a great deal stronger in relative power in the world than in the 1840s. Therefore, China's choice for its own future cannot but be treated seriously by other nations as a factor which will affect their own future. This is why I think I have something worthwhile to offer my readers.

My own continuous study of Chinese affairs, involving research, travel and other activities, including a stint in the U.S. government, began before the establishment of the People's Republic of China in 1949. The scope of these studies has convinced me that we cannot fully understand Chinese Communist policy and especially Mao Zedong's major decisions without considering the interactions of political, military, economic and psychological factors, each acting as both cause of, and constraint on, the others. For some of my readers, many years have passed since the 1940s and some of the relevant events may no longer be within quick recall.

Since this is a personal interpretation of contemporary Chinese history, a few reminiscences may not be out of place. They will help explain some of my thoughts and opinions.

It was at the London School of Economics (L.S.E.), during World War II, that I earned both undergraduate and graduate degrees. There I had Friedrich A. Hayek, later a Nobel Laureate, for my thesis advisor. My tutors in the undergraduate years were W. Arthur Lewis, Nicholas Kaldor and Hayek. Because of the war, L.S.E. was physically located in Cambridge University, which opened its doors to all London students, thus giving us access to the Cambridge faculty, including both John Maynard Keynes and the redoubtable Mrs. Joan Robinson. But the most remarkable aspect of this English influence was the truly free reign of academic tolerance. Among the many stimulating seminars and writings from which I benefited greatly were those of Harold Laski, whose arguments in support of Labor Party ideas could not have been more eloquent than his devotion to the concept of freedom. Hayek and Laski were particularly helpful in shaping my own outlook. After the war, in 1946, I had the good fortune of benefiting from association with Simon Kuznets, then in Pennsylvania. Through Kuznets, who headed the first post-World War II research project on China, based in New York City, under the auspices of the Republic of China's National Resources Commission, I began to work on China's postwar economy. I also had the unusual opportunity in 1946 of attending many of Ludwig von Mises' seminars at New York University's Graduate School of Business, thus obtaining a glimpse of the intellectual beginnings of non-collectivist thinking in pre-Hitlerian Europe.

When the "Chinese Volunteers" crossed the Yalu to go to Kim Il Sung's aid in the Korean War and Stanford Research Institute (SRI) entered the field of Chinese studies, I was afforded the opportunity to participate in the first major Chinese research project at SRI; here I devoted full time to a very wide-ranging reading on China, thanks to the voluminous library collection of the Hoover Institution at Stanford University. These experiences led me to several decades of both teaching in economic theory and research on a vast range of topics on China, not to mention extensive travels in Europe and East and Southeast Asia and the Pacific. All this, especially during the last quarter century, constituted in a sense preparation for this volume, apart from the benefits of what I had learned from my three Nobel mentors (Arthur Lewis and Kuznets also received the Nobel Prize in Economics.)

Finally, it was my good fortune that back in Peiping (Beijing today) in a *hutung* (alley) to the northeast of the Drum Tower, my parents had in the late 1920s put me under the care of a hard-driving and conscientious tutor who taught me the basic Chinese classics. In addition, my mother daily oversaw my homework in the evening. This rigorous old-fashioned Chinese training, combined later with my free-ranging studies in war-time England and in the United States and Europe, has stood me in good stead and enabled me to make profitable use of some of the vast intellectual resources of U.S. institutions, especially through the Hoover Institution. It is here in my California home that I have finally had time to contemplate some of the perplexing issues of China's development, which I had hoped to participate in resolving more directly five decades ago.

Twice in the past there was a chance that this book would never have been written. Once in 1946, when the fate of Manchuria in Northeast China bordering on the then USSR had not yet been sealed by Soviet occupation troops, I was asked to join an economic survey team there. I was in New York City at the time and could not immediately leave for China. Had I accepted the assignment, I am not sure whether I could have gotten out of Manchuria before the evacuation a year later. Again, in early 1947, before the resumption of full-scale Civil War in China, I was asked by U.S. Ambassador to the Republic of China, Dr. Leighton Stuart, whether I would be interested in teaching at Yenching University in Peking (Beijing). Had I accepted his gracious invitation, I would have had difficulty in getting out when the city was surrendered to the Communists' People's Liberation Army. Or had I weathered the initial period of Communist rule, thanks to Guo Moruo's advice to Mao noted later in this volume, there would have been a strong likelihood that I too would have fallen victim to Mao's Anti-Rightist campaign of 1957.

I have Connie Ann Jacobi, my wife of more than 55 years, to thank in both instances for making the right choice. If it had not been for her painful experience in Nazi Germany and courage to leave it, all alone and at a tender age, for freedom in Great Britain, I am not sure that I could have cut loose so decisively from a Chinese past filled with happy childhood memories. Her help to me over the years has gone immeasurably beyond the sacrifices required of a writer's spouse. My studies and diverse personal experiences in China-watching, for longer than the People's Republic of China has been in existence, have in turn given me an unshakeable moral obligation to tell all who will listen what I think has happened in China during the last half century under the Chinese Communists. All this accounts for this volume.

I do not at all claim that my interpretation of mainland China's recent history is the final word. But it does contain certain less widely-known and interconnected facts and some novel thinking. I hope new reports will present a far better picture of China's future and that greater optimism about present-day China will turn out to be justified.

ACKNOWLEDGMENTS

Several persons have done me the great favor of reading through painstakingly all or mostly the chapters of this study and given me their comments in detail. They are professors D.W.Y. Kwok (Hawaii), Taling Lee (Southern Connecticut), Jan Prybyla (Penn State), Richard L. Walker (South Carolina) and Richard Y. C. Yin (George Washington) whose observations based on years of experience and scholarship have either jolted my memory or have led my mind to fruitful new paths that might otherwise have escaped me. These benefits to me go beyond mere facts and theories.

At a different level, it is quite impossible for me to thank adequately the innumerable persons whose guidance, knowledge, and ideas have helped me over the past fifty years in accumulating all the facts and arriving at all the interpretations that have gone into this volume. Needless to say, included among these persons are some whose views are at variance with my own. For, as Confucius said in *Shu Er* (*Analects*, Book VII, Chapter 21), when one walks along with two others, one should learn from both, the one because of the person's correct ideas, the other because of the person's mistaken ones, so as better to avoid them. In recent years especially, many thoughtful Chinese persons in and outside China, some of whose names appear in this book, have shared their knowledge and insights with me, some through their memoirs, others through private talks and interviews. I hope that, if only from a purely intellectual point of view, they will allow me to express my thanks in this anonymous way.

As for the final preparation of the manuscript, I wish in particular to mention Chen Ying-hsiu, Tsai Jui-jung, and Yu Woan-yu whose immense help has been indispensable. And in Mrs. Julie Lee Wei I have found an able and perceptive editor to whom thanks are due perhaps from my English-reading public no less than from myself.

NOTE ON TRANSLITERATION

Renditions of all Chinese proper names in this book are in the Wade-Giles system of transliteration if they originate in the Republic of China (Taiwan). Otherwise the Pinyin system employed in the PRC is used. In some instances, because both systems have appeared in the media over a long period, both romanizations are presented, at least for the first time. Our criterion is to minimize confusion for the reader. Transliteration of reference titles and authors' names follows the same practice: (1) Wade-Giles for Taiwan and pre-Communist publications and titles and authors published in Hong Kong; (2) Pinyin for PRC publications and authors.

CHAPTER I

FROM TIANANMEN 1949 TO TIANANMEN 1989

I. NATIONAL RENEWAL: HOPE OR PROMISE?

Triumph

On October 1, 1949 Mao Zedong stood atop Tiananmen (the Gate of Heavenly Peace) in Beijing to proclaim the birth of a new China. Barely five months earlier, the world was thunderstruck when the communist People's Liberation Army captured Shanghai, the nation's foremost economic center, and Nanjing (Nanking), the capital of the Republic of China (ROC). Mao Zedong (also Mao Tsetung) had come to the ancient capital of Beijing (Peking) to proclaim the establishment of a new "People's Republic of China" (PRC) and to convene the first People's Consultative Conference. His proclamation was simultaneously a declaration of victory of the Chinese Communist Party (CCP) over the Kuomintang (KMT or Nationalist Party) and of the People's Liberation Army (PLA) over the government forces under Chiang Kai-shek in the Civil War that had resumed in 1947. All this happened only four years after the surrender of Japan in World War II.

Many of the spectators at Tiananmen that day had come with great enthusiasm and expectation. Others more likely came to celebrate the end of the uncertainty of war and to witness what some thought was another "dynastic" change and the crowning of a new emperor. Of course, among those who did not come were doubtless a great number who were resigned to their fate or too frightened to be seen in public, even though the ROC government then temporarily in Canton under the nominal presidency of Acting President Li Tsung-jen was still attempting to retain a foothold on the Chinese mainland. The Chinese Communist Party's political victory and Mao's enormous personal triumph seemed quite final. In proclaiming the rise of a new China, Mao made a promise to the Chinese people on October 1, 1949. Will the "new China" be worth the celebration? The people of Beijing hoped for the best.

Tiananmen as Symbol

The choice of Tiananmen as the venue for the official mass meeting with Mao Zedong at center stage was fraught with a historical symbolism that could not have escaped Mao.[1]

Under the Manchu Dynasty the capital city of Beijing consisted of two parts[2]: an Outer City and a walled Inner City (see map). The Outer City was built adjacent to the Inner City, supporting the latter, as it were, as a wider base to the south. The Inner City in turn enclosed the Imperial City, the walls of which had been mostly torn down before Mao's time. And inside the Imperial City was the Forbidden City, containing the former imperial palaces and grounds as well as some administrative offices. The Forbidden City sat on a north-south vertical axis. A series of halls for the Emperor's use, including audiences to foreign envoys, stood one after another along this vertical axis.

At the base of the vertical axis immediately inside the Forbidden City is the Imperial Hall of Supreme Harmony. South of this hall stands *Wumen* (the Meridian Gate, *men* meaning "gate"), the first of a series of gates which shield the imperial halls and offices from the outside world; the second gate, separating the Forbidden City from the rest of the Imperial City, is *Tiananmen* (Tian An Men, Heaven Peace Gate, or Gate of Heavenly Peace). Thus Tiananmen is the main gate leading from the center of power to the country and world outside. Symbolically it is where the Chinese emperor could come into contact spiritually with his subjects.

One can well imagine how Emperor Qianlong (1711-99), seated on his throne at the center of the Forbidden City and scoffing at Britain's offer to trade, could look through the southern Gate of Heavenly Peace with total self-satisfaction, secure in the knowledge that all the subjects of his vast dominion, down to the shores of the South China Sea, were basking in the immense beneficence of his rule.

Under his communist regime, Mao had the area outside Tiananmen leveled, rebuilding the square into a vast parade ground. Perhaps he had in mind the Red Square of Moscow, only a

---

1. Mao had compared himself to emperors of the Han and T'ang dynasties, and above all to the First Emperor of the Ch'in dynasty, dismissing them all as far inferior to himself. See Chapter III below. The Ch'in dynasty emperor (whose tomb has become a major tourist site near present-day Xian) was famous in Chinese history both for his unification of the "Warring Kingdoms" and for burying alive many dissident scholars.

2. See Nigel Cameron and Brain Brake, *Peking, A Tale of Three Cities* (New York: Harper and Row, 1965), for maps and photos of the city.

great deal larger. A mausoleum was later built here to house his remains, for the benefit of those who wished to pay him homage, again after the style of his Soviet "patron saint," Vladimir Lenin. To Mao, therefore, Tiananmen was a symbol of power, imperium and glory, both in the context of Chinese history and in the eternity of Marxist utopianism.

One can even better appreciate the symbolism of the Gate of Heavenly Peace if one recalls that there is on the northern side of the Forbidden City a *Dianmen* (Di An Men, Earth Peace Gate), Gate of Earthly Peace. Dianmen and Tiananmen suggested that eternal peace was to prevail both in heaven and on earth. The mandate from Heaven must be in accord with the same divine will that must be simultaneously carried out on earth, so that humans ruled from the Forbidden City may enjoy a tranquil and happy life. However, *Di*anmen never enjoyed the prominence of Tiananmen. On the map it barely survives as a landmark between the drum and bell towers and the coal hill where the last Ming emperor hanged himself when the rebel forces of General Li Zicheng entered the city in 1644.

Mandate Lost

Not quite forty tumultuous years had gone by after October 1, 1949, when, in the early hours of June 4, 1989, People's Liberation Army tanks and heavily armed soldiers and members of the security police, all sworn to "serve the people," were ordered by top Chinese Communist Party officials (their identities concealed up to this writing in 1996) to clear Tiananmen Square of unarmed student demonstrators who had occupied it for several weeks to demand government reform.[3]

---

3. Historically, Tiananmen became a politically symbolic site long before the 1949 and 1989 events cited here. The May Fourth Movement (1919), a landmark of China's modernization effort, had Tiananmen in the background. The Manchurian warlord Chang Tso-lin left his mark there too in the 1930s. During his Cultural Revolution period, Mao gave audience to selected Red Guards at Tiananmen. Later students registered their remembrance of PRC Premier Zhou Enlai on April 5, 1976, sparking a violent suppression at the same site. Thus, the Gate of Heavenly Peace is a place for celebration and public protest. Mao Zedong's memorial hall, where his remains are still on exhibit both as a memorial to his glory or, alternatively, as a reminder of modern China's unprecedented disaster, is also located at Tiananmen Square. There visitors can contemplate China's past and future in whichever manner they feel inclined. See Orville Schell, *Mandate of Heaven* (New York: Simon & Schuster, 1994), Prologue, pp. 15-30.

Army and police were ordered to use force. At this point the reader should be reminded of several facts. First, the officials who called out the troops were Deng Xiaoping and his close colleagues, all Communist Party leaders and successors to Mao, who had died in 1976. They were high enough to force the resignation of Zhao Ziyang, then CCP Secretary General, who counseled moderation. Second, they did so obviously because they thought that only through use of force could they sustain themselves and the CCP in power and ensure their own personal security. Chongnanhai, an enclave of the former Imperial City now residential quarters for top communist cadres, was close to Tiananmen Square and vulnerable to the demonstrators. Third, the demonstrators had fortuitously chosen a most opportune and politically sensitive moment to air their grievances, a moment embarrassing for the Deng government: the world's television reporters were in Beijing to tape the visit of the Soviet leader and reformist, Mikhail Gorbachev, who was in China to patch up relations between China and USSR. Thus for the first time, the regime's brutality was openly visible to the world, without the possibility of artful concealment and dissimulation. To justify to the world its killing of innocent citizens and students, the Party branded the demonstrators as insurgent "counter-revolutionaries." The resultant blood bath, thus justified, then triggered a nationwide wave of repression and hunt for dissidents.

The open defiance of Communist Party leadership by a generation of Chinese born under communist rule marked the nadir of the CCP's reign. Alienation from communism as doctrine had begun much earlier; with the massacre of June 4, 1989 at Tiananmen, alienation turned into open abandonment of communism. If the Chinese communists ever had a heavenly mandate to safeguard, this mandate, ostensibly granted at Tiananmen in 1949, was openly withdrawn at Tiananmen in 1989. The Communist Party's leaders themselves had unwittingly "stage-managed" on global television the overwhelming popular rejection of their rule.

After 1989: Transition to What?

The two events at Tiananmen separated by forty years effectively bracketed what one might regard as the communist half-century of contemporary Chinese history. During nearly two thirds of this period, national policy and governance were either directly under Mao's control or basically shaped by and a response to his doings in the name of an ideological orientation aptly described as Marxist-Leninist-Maoist. During the remaining one-third of the pe-

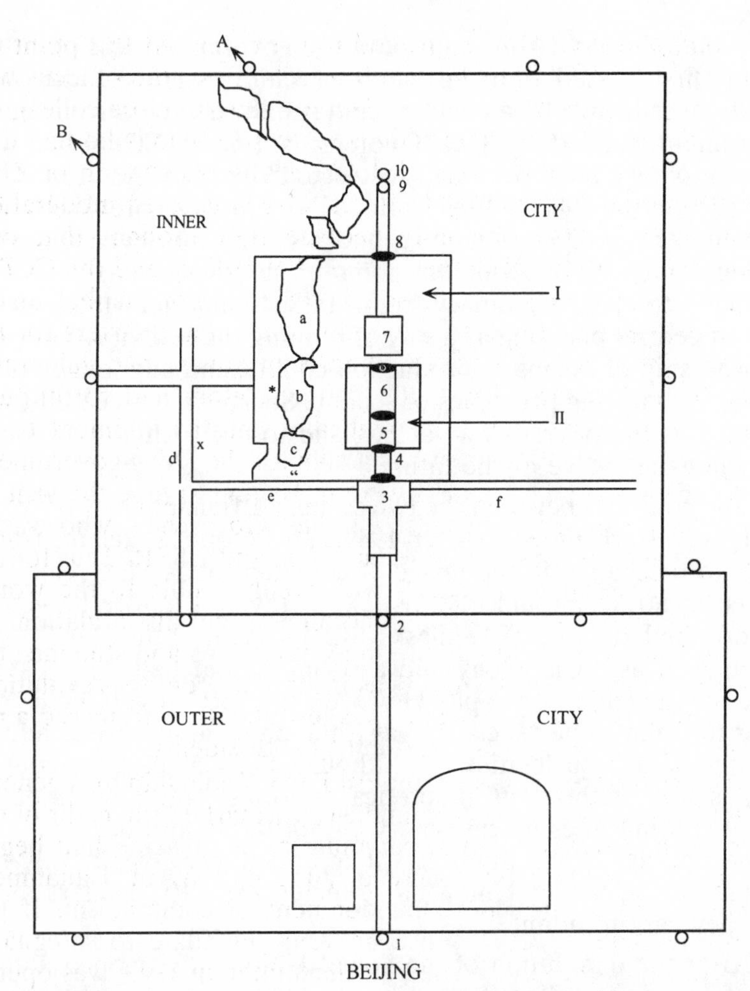

BEIJING

I. Imperial City
II. Forbidden City
A. Road to Ming Tombs
B. Road to Summer Palace
1. *Yongdingmen (Yungtingmen)*
2. *Qianmen (Ch'ienmen)*, front gate of Peking *Zhengyangmen (Chengyangmen)*
3. *Tiananmen (Tienanmen)*, Gate of Heavenly Peace
4. *Wumen*, the Meridian Gate
5. *Taihedian (T'aihotien)*, Hall of Supreme Harmony
6. *Shenwumen*, Gate of Godly Prowess
7. *Jingshan (Chingshan)*, (*Meishan*, Coal Hill)
8. *Dianmen (Tianmen)*
9. *Zhonglou (Chunglou)*, Bell Tower
10. *Gulou (Kulou)*, Drum Tower
a. *Beihai (Peihai)*, North Lake
b. *Zhonghai (Chunghai)*, Middle Lake
c. *Nanhai*, South Lake
d. *Xidan Dajie (Hsitan Tachieh)*
e. *Xichangan Jie (Hsich'angan Chieh)*
f. *Dongchangan Jie (Tungch'angan Chieh)*
x *Xidan Shangchang (Hsitan Shangch'ang)*
* *Huairentang (Huaijent'ang)*
" *Xinhuamen (Hsinhuamen)*
O Other old gates

riod—Mao died in 1976—control of the government and party apparatus first passed into the hands of radical Maoists who were quickly overthrown by a coalition and superseded by a transitional government headed by Hua Guofeng, a typical CCP hack who claimed to have been personally "selected" by Mao. Hua faded out after 1979. From 1982 to 1989, various Party factions prevailed, with the influence of Deng Xiaoping and his followers eventually becoming dominant. But while the communist-led central government continued to claim legitimacy from Marx, Lenin and Mao, neither socialist central planning as a way of running the economy nor public ownership of means of production could claim any longer to be the only organizing principles of society. Socialism has ceased to be accepted as the obvious way of life, and to most Chinese it is certainly not the "wave of the future."

The contrasts between the two scenes at Tiananmen forty years apart were stark indeed. After 1949 and before his death, China began to be shaped in the image of communism as Mao really envisaged it, not as he had told his fellow-travelers before he gradually dropped the pre-1949 masks. In the years after June 1989, communism as an ideology and a social system had long lost its allure for the Chinese people. However, the PRC government continues to claim to be "socialist," as if the name alone would add to its tenuous grip on legitimacy. Although the Chinese Communist Party is now without its theoretical moorings and revolutionary élan, it still mistakes its customary authoritarian and personal rule for the security of the public's willing acceptance. Apparently the collapse of the Soviet Union has affected the PRC leaders more than they care to admit.

After the dissolution of the Soviet Union and its open admission of economic collapse, the Chinese Communists can hardly be expected to make the viability of Stalinist central planning and dictatorship appear convincing even to themselves. The CCP had borrowed thoroughly from the Soviet model in government structure, method and approach to problems, and continued to proceed in the same fashion even after the two countries' total estrangement in the mid-60s. But after some 70 years on a path marked out by Lenin, Stalin and others, the Russians have finally admitted that it really led to nowhere. After the June 4, 1989 public massacre of students and other civilians, the Chinese leaders in Beijing very likely felt a need to prove themselves in the eyes of those whose approval they would have liked to think they had in order to justify their bloody effort to stay in power. For whatever broad mandate was received in 1949 was clearly rescinded in 1989. But whose approval really counts in China in the last several years of this century? How can the mandate be renewed? Or, at a minimum, how can one avoid the PRC's rule being openly challenged again?

When Deng was first touted as "paramount leader" of China after having had a trusted aide, Hu Yaobang, replace Hua Guofeng as Party Chairman in 1978, he had felt the same need for "legitimacy" and sought to demonstrate it through performance. Performance, he thought, could be demonstrated in terms of "modernization," while modernization was to be accomplished through reform. "Reform" was taken for granted to be synonymous with economic reform. In order to avoid undermining his grip on the Chinese Communist Party and his own legitimate dominance over the various factions in it, Deng has stressed the upholding of four cardinal principles in his economic reform and modernization: (1) the doctrines of Marx, Lenin and Mao; (2) the leadership of the Communist Party; (3) the dictatorship of the proletariat; and, (4) the maintenance of a socialist economy. He wisely neglected to mention the degree to which all these terms might be modified.

When Deng finally came into power and installed his own team in Chongnanhai, he apparently believed that the CCP had earned legitimacy after its successful armed revolution in 1949 and the string of military and technical successes thereafter. Therefore, he could best maintain the party's rule of the country by adhering to the same political and doctrinal slogans. However, economically, the CCP, and Mao in particular, was not at all successful. This is why, although Deng could not lightly abandon the names of Marx, Lenin and Mao, he needed a more productive and efficient economy capable of accomplishing two objectives. First, it must be able to offer the population far greater material satisfaction than before. Second, it must be able to provide a stronger military that would remain faithful to the CCP. In short, he wanted more consumer goods, as well as a less costly but more powerful and satisfied military. For these purposes he needed also more investment and, therefore, foreign technology, capital and enterprise. But he was also hamstrung by having to continue to uphold socialism. The real problem Deng faced was to achieve the desired economic reform without seeming to abandon socialism.

With the abandonment of rigid socialism by the Soviet Union's own successor regimes under Yeltsin and others and by former Soviet satellites in Eastern Europe, socialism in the sense generally understood after World War II has become virtually anathema to rational economic performance. The Soviet economic model was led by (1) public demand (primarily for capital goods needed for defense and investment) and (2) supply based on state enterprises. Now that the Soviet model has collapsed, economic reform in former socialist countries implies the replacement of central state planning by a more efficient system, but one without too much private ownership of means of production. This new system the Chinese Communist leadership now accepts. But since the Chinese Communists, like many other groups of humans, cannot openly admit their past mistakes without jeopardizing their legitimacy, they have resorted to calling it "socialism with *Chinese characteristics.*"

"Socialism with Chinese Characteristics"

The reader will perceive the vagueness of "socialism with Chinese characteristics." The cynic may add that the vagueness is deliberate in order to permit continuing adjustment, through trial and error, interspersed with acts born of sheer ignorance, personal whim and desperate improvisation. To put it bluntly, Deng's team had not really thought through with sufficient clarity and specificity what the government ought to do. As we shall see in the course of this book, by Deng's time, the remnant CCP cadres were really not equipped to think through the matter either. It was this reform without careful forethought that led to the 1989 Tiananmen crisis and the subsequent search for a way out and for scapegoats.

Lacking a clear view of final goals in the ongoing societal restructuring and not knowing the *modus operandi* of a changing society amidst increasing political and economic flux, Deng and his party nonetheless continued to demand the Chinese people's acceptance in blind trust of their absolute rule. Could the younger generation in China, who in June 1989 had openly expressed its distrust of the government in power, be persuaded, together with the older members of the society, to give the CCP another chance? Would the huge military and security forces still under CCP command be a help or a hindrance? Obviously, Deng knew that the results of economic reform would not quickly lead to stable institutions and inter-institutional and interpersonal relations and codes of peaceful conduct. The 1989 Tiananmen incident became a crisis because there was as yet no accepted code of peaceful behavior in China to solve a conflict. Might there be other such incidents? Might they be more severe, more insidious and more widespread?

II. CHINA UNDER COMMUNISM IN THE LAST HALF CENTURY: QUESTIONS

Economic Take-Off Aborted in the 1930s: Why?

The preceding paragraphs may bring to mind for persons of long memory a few facts and suggest new questions. First, it is generally known that by the time the remnant Chinese Communists on the Long March reached their base at Yanan in Shaanxi (Yenan, Shensi) in the mid-1930s, they were in no position to resume any large-scale fighting against Chiang Kai-shek's government forces. They were at the end of their tether,[4] having been pursued by government troops in a continuous "extermination campaign." At the same time, the Chinese economy was beginning to "take off" earnestly. By the mid-1930s, it looked as if the "modernization" of China, a long-time dream of Chinese intellectuals and policy-makers of the late Manchu (Ch'ing) dynasty, was truly about to materialize. The continued Communist-Nationalist war and the earlier conflicts among warlords were about to be played out.

Unfortunately, there was not to be a new dawn for the Chinese people as yet. A succession of events of far-reaching consequences occurred at this time: the kidnapping of Chiang by his generals at Xian (the Sian Incident); the ostensible Nationalist-Communist rapprochement which ensued; the heightened pressure for a more vigorous, open anti-Japanese policy; and finally, the accelerated aggression of Japan in China and the outbreak of the long war with Japan in July 1937. This sequence of events, perhaps long-forgotten by some readers, led to the eight-year Sino-Japanese War that ended in a bittersweet victory for non-communist China in the summer of 1945. But all too soon, the curtain fell on non-communist China when hyperinflation brought about the economic collapse of the Republic of China led by Chiang, and the subsequent communist victory was celebrated at Tiananmen in October 1949. What on earth made people think, in China as well as outside, that the Chinese Communists under Mao Zedong would be the salvation of China, we might ask in retrospect. Now in 1996, with hindsight and also more knowledge about the Chinese Communist Party and Mao's real personality and thought processes, we can better re-ex-

---

4. According to one unconfirmed recent report allegedly from the PRC, CCP unpublished archives indicate that the decision to settle down in northern Shaanxi was not carefully pre-planned. Instead it was a decision based on the unexpected news received when the Long Marchers were enroute northwestward, in the hope of moving closer toward the Soviet border, that a local communist base existed there.

amine this immediately pre-Communist, pre-1949 period of Chinese history.

CCP's Ascent in Popularity

Another major question for China scholars raised by the two epochal events at Tiananmen 1949 and Tiananmen 1989, is whether we can produce a plausible, comprehensive interpretation of why the fortunes of communism and the Chinese Communist Party plunged from the towering height they had attained in October 1949 to the depths into which they fell in June 1989. When did the turning points come? How and why?

A closer look at developments in China during this period suggests that the decline of communism as a doctrine and as a coherent (however mistaken) political-economic program of development and governance for China actually happened in a much shorter length of time than the forty years between the two Tiananmen. Although the prestige of Mao and the Communist Party had probably reached its zenith in 1949, consolidation of their control over the entire Chinese mainland was not really completed until 1957, when Mao and his then apparently numerous willing collaborators in the Communist Party were supremely confident of his correct leadership and of their own Party's infallibility. In their eyes, they had by then thoroughly cowed both China's unruly intellectuals and the urban capitalists and mercantile class. Earlier they had already established solid control in the vast agricultural areas through, first, "land reform" and then the formation of collective farms. In external affairs, again in their eyes, they had fought the Americans to a draw in Korea and were allied to the Soviet Union, which was ascending in the international scene as an atomic power and, finally in 1957, as the first nation in space.

Calculating from 1957 onward, Mao's demise in 1976 was nineteen years away. By 1967, in the eyes of ignorant teenage Red Guards, Mao literally was God. Yet the Communist Party apparatus, which had been instrumental in bringing Mao to the height of absolute power, was being literally decimated by his own hands. He was by then held up by a combination of prestige, military power, the terror of the security apparatus and control of information which hid facts and propagated falsehood and Maoist theocracy. The decline of popular acceptance of Maoism and Maoist rule, it would seem, occurred imperceptibly during 1957-68. If this estimate of the time frame is correct, then the political downfall of Mao and

Maoism developed in the course of about one decade, beginning nearly from its zenith.

Events in 1957-68, which sowed the seeds of Mao's downfall and the decline of communism in China, doubtless contributed to the choice of post-1979 policy and attempts at reform under Deng and others, in order to salvage what they could of the overall CCP regime and their own individual vested interests. Many of Mao's victims, when restored to power and privilege, probably became obstacles to a smoother fundamental transition to a competitive, free economy. They would wish to retain as many of the structural parameters of the preceding decades as possible.

There were problems which the PRC had in common with other former socialist countries in Eastern Europe and post-Soviet Russia. But other issues were specific to China. Many were inherited from the previous three decades of communism and Mao's rule. Hence the June 1989 crisis was an outburst of discontent in reaction to the historic Maoist heritage and to the unfavorable consequences of the post-Mao "reform" policies, of their mismanagement and conceptual errors. Some of the institutions which the Dengist reformers had to grapple with, such as the social welfare function performed by the ubiquitous *danwei* (work unit) in the PRC, were Maoist institutions.[5] Others, like the treatment of commercial and service businesses in the socialization of the economy and installation of central planning were part of the ideological baggage imported from Soviet concepts and practice. The much criticized use and misuse of *guanxi*[6] are inherited from pre-communist tradition. (*Guanxi*, meaning connections, or useful human relationships, are of course by no means Chinese alone.) Failure in understanding all these obstacles led to Deng Xiaoping's[7] pragmatic approach of planning reform as it went along. The main problem is to understand how these issues separately and together have re-

---

5. The "*danwei*" is the employer or institution which is responsible for a person's economic and social well-being. It took on substantial welfare functions during the Communist period.

6. *Guanxi*, meaning "special (personal) connections," is really neutral per se. Without appropriate connections to the "right people," some June 4, 1989 victims probably could not have succeeded in fleeing the country.

7. Among Deng Xiaoping's contemporaries were Zhou Enlai and Nie Rongzhen. Marshal Nie was later responsible for the organization of the PRC's nuclear development and weapons production. The three were among the group of Chinese Communists in Europe in 1924. A group photo can be found in Kao Yi-kò, *Mao Tse-tung yü Chou En-lai* [*Mao Zedong and Zhou Enlai*] (Taipei and Hongkong: K'o-ning Publishers, 1993), p. 27.

tarded the Chinese reform effort, communist or not. Ideology, history, haphazardly imported concepts, and the like are all intermingled. They constitute a large body of questions students of contemporary China will have to address.

Alternative Futures for China

The preceding discussion raises questions about the situation in China before the war with Japan and developments leading to the political ascendancy of the CCP during and after World War II. A third group of major questions raised by what happened at Tiananmen in 1989 points to the decades ahead; namely, what are some of the alternative futures open to China?

The fall of communist parties and regimes in Eastern Europe and the Soviet Union since 1989 has taken place quickly. In mainland China, on the other hand, the regime and its central authorities have managed to hang on to the appurtenances and appearances of power in spite of June 4, 1989 and in spite of the alienation of a significant portion of the national elite and the sullen opposition and patient waiting of the common people, all disgruntled to varying degrees. The explanation lies partly in the different paths by which the Chinese and the European communists had respectively won their political control and then lost their grip on power.

Although the outside world is also waiting for the PRC to change, many Western and former communist countries are still preoccupied with the former Soviet Union and Eastern Europe and will continue to be for quite some time. Elsewhere, in the United States in particular, private business has been primarily concerned with economic adjustment as a result of reduced defense spending and the inevitable redistribution of the economic pie. These economic and social issues are disguised in the form of changes in domestic legislation, social welfare, crime and health care. Moreover, the West continues to deal with the PRC gingerly because of the appurtenances of power which the Chinese communists hold—notably the PRC's nuclear arsenals, the country's seat on the United Nations Security Council and in other economically important international institutions (like the International Monetary Fund, the World Bank, and the Asian Development Bank), the size of the country and its market potential in the eyes of individual Western and other non-PRC business interests. Finally, some China observers seem to believe that the PRC is already changing by itself—which is true—and that it is in fact changing in the direction they desire—which, however, is not necessarily true and is most probably untrue. Nor are China's changes inexorably in the same direction or are proceeding fast enough politically and economically, for either the world or China's people. We refer in this respect to the demographic growth and resource decline of the PRC and the new inequalities of wealth distribution and their impact on the world. The impact on the entire Chinese population and its different geographical, ethnic and economic sectors may contain germs of global and regional conflicts in the future that we cannot ignore now.

Misplaced Trust: Can It Happen Again?

As we shall discuss further in the next chapter, many Chinese intellectuals who were dissatisfied with economic conditions in China after World War II and were opposed to the then Nationalist government probably agreed with some of the ideas Mao advanced in his 1940 statement in the *New Democracy*. Some of these intellectuals were no doubt in the Tiananmen crowd on October 1, 1949, and were to be painfully disappointed in 1956-57. During the 1980s, not a few observers of, as well as participants in, Deng's economic reform thought that the then on-going process would be irreversible. Western economists, encouraged by the socialist countries' turn toward a market economy and their praise of democracy—albeit for some no more than lip service—have often without qualification identified transition to a market economy with political democratization as a simultaneous and automatically inseparable process. Implicitly they also seem to assume that "privatization" of state property and public enterprises would automatically imply their substitution by a large enough number of independent businesses each free to join or leave an industry without any social or economic obstacle and each too small to affect the product price. The latter economic scenario in turn would lead to the broad distribution of economic and therefore political power.

In the PRC case, after June 1989, members of the Communist Party, government and military elite very naturally continue to favor the concentration of political and economic power in their own hands. They therefore try to influence the outcome of the economic reform program. Hence the relatively peaceful reform that one assumes is inexorably moving ahead is not being left alone. Nor is the military sector being left out in "modernization." The military and the plutocrats, who were erstwhile communists, or their progeny, have gone into business—including international trade for profit—on a vast scale. Hence for them there is just one future for

China. To have more than one possible future, the competing choices and the outcomes must be influenced from multiple directions. Therefore, the final set of large questions is one of choice for the Chinese people as a whole and for policy-makers in major concerned nations. The alternatives are for future historians to evaluate and comment. They are for those now living to analyze and choose. As we shall see in this book, the choices still open to China are such that one cannot really refrain from making a choice, hoping thereby to escape the quandary. For to refuse to choose will be a choice itself and not one of the best available. For it might foreclose many other choices for a long time.

III. CHINA AFTER COMMUNISM

China in a Global Setting

China must be understood in a global setting. The questions raised in the preceding section have delineated the scope of this volume. Briefly, we wish to know why communism, the Chinese Communist Party and Mao in particular managed to dominate China so completely after 1949; why opposition to Communist rule nevertheless became open defiance in less than forty years; finally, what alternative futures China will face when the present flux slows and/or some other critical condition occurs to remove the CCP as a dominant influence in China. Human mortality will in the end claim all the first-generation revolutionary leaders who celebrated their victory at Tiananmen in 1949. Deng Xiaoping at ninety-one in 1995 may well be the last of the group. But will successors of the same ilk replace them?

The Chinese scene cannot be separated from its global context. The rise of the Chinese Communist Party and of the Mao regime was made possible by developments elsewhere on the globe before, during, and after World War II. From the 1940s to the 1990s, the foreign policies of Japan, the United States, and the Soviet Union towards one another treated China either as a pawn or as one of the bones of contention. The Chinese Communists, as well as the Chinese Nationalists, have both had to take this external general situation and some specific events into account. Neither has been consistently successful, or has consistently failed. By the same token, the foreign powers have not always read the Chinese scene accurately, and the Chinese Communists have equally failed to understand the West. In the post-1991 period, that is, with the breakup of the USSR, the PRC's role deserves special attention, especially if nuclear arms reduction is to be earnestly pursued. The entire world will be affected by what future course a post-Deng and eventually a post-communist China will deliberately choose to follow, or even unwittingly drift into.

Since the population of mainland China already exceeded 1.3 billion (one-fifth of the world) toward the end of the 1990s, its very size makes it a major influence either for good or for evil. A single dollar squeezed out of each of one billion plus Chinese would total an enormous sum, which could be spent either on new military equipment or on a larger literacy campaign. A fascist China governed by a military junta with access to millions of willing conscripts, or a collapsing, chaotic China can both affect the world in a vital manner. So can an economically developing China that is politically well-structured and able to help preserve both peace and freedom for all. Hence the effect of other nations' policies towards a China in flux will have to be realistically and carefully weighed by the outside world. If the outside world helps shape China's post-communist future, it too must also know what it will be doing. For some time already certain Western nations may have indulged too much in wishful thinking about China both before and after the second Tiananmen of 1989.

In this connection, not least important are the thoughts of scholars currently dealing with the future of the Commonwealth of Independent States (CIS), notably of Russia, the Ukraine, and the Central Asian republics adjacent to China. We need to understand much more about the way in which these nations will introduce the market economy in a non-totalitarian society and how they might use their previously accumulated modern weapons and weapons technology as a peaceful means of financing external aid and paying for development. The geographic proximity of China to Kazakhstan and the existence of their respective nuclear arsenal stockpiles urgently invite constructive and innovative thinking about tying arms control to economic development.[8] A constructive China policy has to be thought through as a part of the post-Cold War new world order—for the United States, the European Union, Japan, the successors of the former Soviet Union and the nations in Pacific Asia.

---

8. After the collapse of the Soviet Union, one scheme discussed between Americans and Ukrainians who were interested in both economic development and nuclear arms control was to use diluted weapons-grade uranium suitable for power generation as mortgage to secure bank loans for infrastructure investment at low interest. This conversion process would simultaneously reduce nuclear weapons already in existence and provide financing for projects that would not otherwise be capable of obtaining capital from purely commercial sources.

Burden of History

At this point, let us digress briefly. Let us return to the Chinese scene, but to a contemplation of the communist episode of the last decades as part of a much longer Chinese history. Students of modern China of the last 100 years will recall the series of skirmishes and wars beginning in the middle of the 19th century between the imperial Manchu dynasty and the modern fleet and armies of the then expanding Western powers, with Japan following closely on their heels. Invariably China was defeated during these conflicts, ceding territories and making reparations and concessions as a result. To mention but three of these territorial cessions, one can easily see their historical impact on the world and on China today in its post-Tiananmen future.

Hongkong, which was ceded to the British by China in 1842 under the Treaty of Nanking, is supposed to return to China in 1997. But to what kind of China and within what kind of world and regional order?

Taiwan, ceded to Japan in 1895 at the end of the Sino-Japanese War. Its return to the Republic of China at the end of World War II was agreed to by the Allies at the Cairo Conference (1942). After Mao's proclamation of victory at Tiananmen in 1949 and the retreat of the Chinese Nationalists from the mainland to Taiwan, Taiwan has become the base of a continuing challenge to the PRC by virtue of its remarkable success in economic development and political liberalization, in contrast to the economic floundering and political repression of Mao's People's Republic.

Manchuria, a bone of contention between Imperial Russia (later the Soviet Union) and Japan before and through World War II, recovery of which by China became a political imperative to the KMT and Chiang Kai-shek in 1945-47, which then became a contributing factor to the Communist success in the Civil War. The reconstruction of Manchuria later played a pivotal role in the Sino-Soviet alliance of the early 1950s.

No country, of course, can escape the burden of its own history or the experience of its leaders. But several developments in the Communist phase of contemporary China so closely resembled earlier events in Chinese history that one has good reason to wonder whether there are third factors that act as common causes and not just whether history accidentally is "repeating" itself. When, for instance, in 1966-67, Maoist Red Guards chanted from the Red Book of Mao's sayings, one is reminded of the Boxers (Yihetuan) of 1900 who thought that martial arts and superstitious rites could effectively counter gunfire and substitute for science and knowledge. At a different level, Deng Xiaoping's policy to modernize China under the proviso of upholding the CCP's four cardinal principles and "socialism with Chinese characteristics" reminds one of earlier Chinese reformers of the mid-19th century who tried to introduce Western technology while maintaining the Chinese "Confucianist" sociopolitical system. In short, the modernization of China barely got started under 19th century reformers Chang Chih-tung and Li Hung-chang; the idea of their contemporaries K'ang Yu-wei and Liang Ch'i-ch'ao to develop the country under a constitutional monarchy was cut short by internal political repression in the hands of the Empress Dowager. The Nationalists' pre-take-off decade (1927-36) was interrupted by the Japanese militarists as well as by the Communists themselves. In a historical perspective, would it be entirely inappropriate, two decades from now, to think of the 1989 massacre at Tiananmen, as the end of another cycle of futile attempt at the modernization of China? Would Mao's ignorance and megalomania be comparable to those of the Empress Dowager? An Italian film-maker produced "The Last Emperor" in 1990 as a story of Henry Pu Yi, the boy emperor who abdicated in 1911, became the first puppet emperor of Manchoukuo under Japanese tutelage, but only to die as a gardener in Mao's reign. Might Mao be more aptly described as China's "last emperor" and Pu Yi the "last but one"? Has the history of China's one billion-plus people finally reached a point of inflection and broken out of a circular path?

To speculate on this point requires that we look into some of China's cultural and philosophical roots and raise questions about intangible forces in Chinese society. The May Fourth movement of 1919 tried to replace Chinese roots with Western imports but did not succeed in the effort to modernize China. Mao set back what one normally regards as cultural accomplishments through the rampage of his destructive teenagers and his own willful destructiveness. What needs to happen in the post-Deng era to the Chinese as human beings so that a civil society can again develop as a continuation of China's "interrupted" history? Will the half-century rule of communism in China prove to be no more than a cruel interruption?[9] Whatever the case, how could a single person, Mao, bend more than one billion of his compatriots to his will for so long? Is there something wrong with the Chinese people?

---

9. The well-known scholar-educator Wang Gung-wu of Australia reportedly once said at a conference that he could not imagine how one person could bring a billion people under his control without their being willing in some sense to submit.

IV. THE STRUCTURE OF THE BOOK

The sequence of chapters below follows logically from the issues raised in the previous sections. They deal first with China's national goals and the Chinese Communist Party's political objectives. Next is an analysis of the CCP's seizure, consolidation and unrestrained use of power. Mao's role in defeating the government forces in 1947-49 gave him indisputable leadership in the new regime. However, Mao's often erratic and untested ideas, his machiavellian style of governance, his blind faith in mass movement and class struggle, and his obsession with China's military strength vis-à-vis the superpowers left an indelible, lasting imprint on the Chinese economy and society. The next Chapter discusses how and why the CCP managed to build upon the economic and intellectual background of the interwar period in mainland China and took advantage of the Sino-Japanese War and its aftermath to seize power. Chapter III then provides a chronological account of Mao's reign during which his concern was a two-fold one: (1) to be sure that his present and potential opposition would be suppressed; and, (2) that his bold and often novel policies would be carried out. The striking part of Mao's rule was the total transformation of the Chinese society he aimed at and the ruthlessness of the measures he employed.

Chronologically, China's modernization began before World War I and was meant to be accelerated after World War II. The war with Japan produced a prolonged interruption and ended in cataclysmic hyperinflation.[10] The post-World War II CCP victory in the Civil War then transformed what would have been the resumption of economic development "within the capitalist system" into a restructuring of the economic system. As a result, the economic restructuring attempted under Mao began essentially with orthodox Stalinist central planning but was followed by grandiose Maoist experimentation, *ad hoc* state socialism, and willful intervention from the mid-1960s to the mid-70s.

After first discussing these radical policy meanderings and shocks under Mao in Chapter III, Chapters IV and V then focus, in succession, first, on the social transformation of China by the eradication of the principal pre-Communist institutions of property ownership and economic operation, and then, in Chapter V, on the

---

10. For a discussion of Chinese hyperinflation in the post-WWII period, see *An Economic Survey of Communist China* (New York: Bookman Associates, 1956), by the present author, reprinted by Octagon Books of New York in 1977, Chapters 2 and 3. See also Chapter II below.

acceleration of investment in heavy industry. However, as we shall see in these two chapters, the PRC was not able to pursue economic development in the orthodox Stalinist mode. The central planning approach of the Soviet model was radically modified by Mao's own "big push." The Maoist intervention took place, first in 1958-60 during the "Great Leap" and, again, beginning around 1964 in the "Third Line" defense investment program that continued into the early 70s.

Mao's Great Leap adventure led to his partial eclipse by Liu Shaoqi in 1961-62, followed by his political counter-attack in 1966-69 in the form of the Cultural Revolution. His second radical intervention during the Cultural Revolution then ended with Mao's demise in 1976. This last political phase of the Mao Zedong saga, discussed earlier in Chapter III, is resumed in Chapters VI and VII, which deal with the circuitous transition to the post-Mao period and the Hua Guofeng interlude. Chapter VII describes how Hua tried his own version of a "modernized Great Leap" and failed. Chapter VIII brings us to an account of Deng Xiaoping's accession to power and the nature of Deng's success and failure. Dengist economic reform by trial and error finally began after the replacement of Hua Guofeng by Deng Xiaoping. However, while Hua Guofeng was short of new ideas, the economic reform started under Deng also did not have a complete blue-print.

When the second Tiananmen student gathering of 1989 occurred, a decade of reform had already passed. But the reform agenda and the socio-economic process of change was only partially developed and even less partially understood by the CCP leaders themselves. There are several reasons why, as late as the student protests of summer 1989, two factors underpinning China's economic reform were far from being clearly appreciated. First, how must political and institutional reform be developed to provide mutual support for economic reform? The call for democratization or "the fifth modernization" issue raised by Wei Jingsheng in 1979[11] was a foretaste of the need for institutional building going beyond the reversal of the nationalization process haphazardly carried out in the 1950s. One is reminded of the failure to understand the interconnection between institutional reform and improvements in technology, on the one hand, and between management and interpersonal social conduct on the other hand, both in Chang Chih-tung's time a century earlier and even more so today.

---

11. See Chapter VI, note 25, *infra*.

Chapters V-VIII deal with the gradual emergence of an as yet incomplete reform agenda. They point to the fact that political and economic changes were unavoidably intermingled, both in the emergence or sudden eruption of urgent issues and in the search for solutions. In addition, some of the issues were matters of urgent foreign policy, of national security and of military threat. It is clear that domestic policy for national economic modernization must be consonant with foreign policy and change in domestic institutions. The principal foreign policy issues addressed by Zhou Enlai under Mao's general direction are analyzed in Chapters IX through XII. Chapter XII deals specifically with some economic aspects of external policy. This involves examining the interaction of political and economic developments within the global and regional context, including how China is perceived in other nations' policies. In Chapter XIII, we turn to a quick look at the question whether the PRC's inner doubts and misfortunes were in some sense peculiarly Chinese. That is to say, was Chinese culture at fault—wholly or only in part?

A Final Note

This book as outlined is a personal interpretation of contemporary Chinese history. It is based upon the observations, studies and personal experience of the author, starting in the decade before the Korean War and continuing through this day. One purpose in writing this volume is to raise questions for future scholars so that when new facts come to light they may review and reinterpret the issues discussed by the author. Already the former Soviet Communist Party is opening up some of its files, throwing light on some of the murky aspects of Soviet-Chinese relations. Similar disclosures will no doubt take place in China. Since the 1980s some significant new facts have already come to light. Subjects for research may be found by many scholars from among the problems raised or implied in the author's discussions. There may even be lessons for some of the world's strategists and statesmen, whose decisions will affect those who come after us, just as their past decisions have already affected us, often portentously.

CHAPTER II

SEIZURE OF POWER

I. WAR WITH JAPAN: THE HISTORICAL SETTING

Idée Fixe

For readers unfamiliar with the historical setting of China before the roughly half-century "Communist episode" beginning in 1949, we shall precede our discussion with a brief mention of several major strands of thought and development in order to show that the 1949-89 period represented an interlude in Chinese history that was both a continuation of the past and, very soon after Mao had firmly ensconced himself in Beijing, a radical break with it. Together these interrelated developments provide an explanation of the fortuitous rise of the Chinese Communist Party to political power. Once in power, given Mao Zedong's political acumen, perseverance, resourcefulness and ruthlessness, he was able to dominate the Chinese Communist Party from 1949 through 1957 and then again to regain dominance after a brief interruption.[1] Chapter III will then show how Mao and his reign were to leave a deep imprint on the Chinese nation beyond 1976, when he died. In many ways, China today is still suffering from his long tenure.

During the century and a half of modern Chinese history since the Opium War (1842), two ideas have become widely accepted as China's "national" objectives: territorial integrity and modernization. In their territorial expansion and search for markets during the second half of the 19th century and before World War I in the 20th, many countries from Western Europe, followed by Tsarist Russia and Japan, easily won from a self-centered and self-satisfied, but technologically backward and surprised China many large territorial and political concessions and economic privileges. All the diplomatic exchanges involved in this period are usually lumped together in Chinese school books under "unequal treaties." As a result of the first Sino-Japanese War, Taiwan, where the govern-

1. Mao lost his supreme position in the CCP as a result of his disastrous grain and steel production programs of 1958-60. He did not regain his position until about 1966-67 as a result of the Cultural Revolution. See Chapter III below.

ment of the Republic of China took refuge in 1949, was ceded to Japan in 1895.

During World War I and the inter-war years, Japan continued the Western expansionist approach with a vengeance, especially during the 1930s, first in Northeast China (Manchuria) and along the coast and up the Yangtze, then in North China inside Shanhaiguan, the gateway to China proper from Manchuria. The string of defeats suffered by successive Chinese governments and cessions and concessions was usually attributed to the country's lack of modern industry and its technological and scientific backwardness as an immediate cause and, until the 1911 overthrow of the Manchu dynasty, to an ignorant and corrupt Imperial Court. For well over a decade and a half after 1911, political fragmentation in China under "warlords" and the absence of a centralized national government made it impossible for any single party or group to govern the country. The nation's total intellectual and material resources could not be devoted single-mindedly to making China both "wealthy and strong," a slogan coined in the Manchu era. Hence to do so and to regain national pride became a widely accepted *idée fixe* among Chinese intellectuals and a common theme taught at school. Thus nationalism became the single, most potent influence and rallying call in policy making. It ranked first among Sun Yat-sen's Three People's Principles (the other two being democracy and economic development), which the Nationalist (Kuomintang or KMT) Government, established in Nanking in 1927 under Chiang Kai-shek, adopted as its platform.

But how do you "modernize" and make China both "wealthy and strong"? On this point the pre-1911 reformers had an easy formula: let us graft the technology of the West onto the cultural values and body politic of China. Since they saw nothing fundamentally wrong with the latter—though they were not necessarily satisfied with the status quo—this solution seemed logical enough.

Skipping over nearly one full century to 1982, more than a decade before work began on this writing and six years after a post-Mao interregnum, we find Deng Xiaoping beginning to introduce an increasingly "marketized" economy while inviting the inflow of external capital and technology under generally privileged conditions. Deng, however, insisted on the maintenance of the contemporary political status quo, which included various undefined cultural and social institutions and values, together with four "cardinal principles," or "absolutes." To date they still are: 1) socialism; 2) Marxism, Leninism and Mao Zedong thought; 3) dictatorship of the proletariat; and, 4) leadership of the Communist Party. In bald terms and shorn of excessive verbiage, the CCP still wants modernization while maintaining the existing political structure. In this sense, therefore, the Dengist formula of the 1980s was a repetition of the pre-1911 reformist approach with, however, one fundamental difference, the substitution of the Communist system for the traditional Chinese society.

The similarity of the two approaches, albeit separated by nearly a century in time, is their unquestioned assumption that the methods and efficiency of organizing resource use (including labor) in a country can be independent of the social institutions (including property ownership and the rule of law) and social values (such as the individual's freedom of choice, ethical standards and motivation). The pre-1911 reformists thought that traditional Chinese values in their then largely Confucian garb could continue to provide the substance, while Western science and technology would give the Chinese spirit greater freedom to expand and more capability to sustain itself. But the then reformists did not have time enough to experiment, so that we never knew how far the Chinese traditional system might have adjusted itself to the demands of change. For, not long after 1911, the educators and students and intellectuals were quick to push outward the bounds of initial modernization. Nor did these changes stop at the literary, academic and social institutions and practices.[2]

The Chinese economy was being rapidly reorganized during the late 1920s, and especially in the decade of 1927-37.[3] A private-enterprise market system was being rapidly developed, although a state sector for wartime mobilization was almost simultaneously being energetically set up in the face of the mounting military threat

---

2. The May 4 Movement of 1919 was closely related to the Chinese student protests of the post-World War I period and the contemporaneous drive to replace traditional culture with a Westernized new culture. Although a great deal has been published on this subject, two new books written from different perspectives may be of interest. See Peng Ming, *Wusi Yundong Shi* [*A History of The May Fourth Movement*] (Beijing: People's Publishers, 1984) and Li Shuang-ching, *Wu-sse Yun-tung Cheng-shih* [*Verified Facts about The May Fourth Movement*] (Taipei: Hsien-tai Tsa-chih-she, 1968).

3. See Paul K.T. Sih (ed.), *The Strenuous Decade: China's Nation-Building Efforts, 1927-1937* (New York: St. John's University Press, Center for Asian Studies, 1970).

Long before the Sian incident China's economic and political problems were almost invariably connected with Japan's incursion into China. For a comprehensive analysis of Japan's step-by-step incursion into Manchuria going back to Russo-Japanese competitive efforts in both Korea and China, see Shuhsi Hsü, *Essays on the Manchurian Problem*, China Council, Institute of Pacific Relations (Shanghai: Kelly & Walsh, 1932).

from Japan. There were conflicting trends of institutional and policy development which were soon to merge into a wartime economy. The financial pressures generated by the war with Japan and the post-1945 civil war between the government and the Chinese Communists finally led to post-World War II hyperinflation. The Dengist slogans ushered in during the 1980s is not only still groping for a proven formula to make China both "wealthy and strong" but, as the 1979-89 years of initial reforms and the post-June 4, 1989 "Democracy Movement" have shown, Dengist reform appeared to be also spawning a far freer society than the four "cardinal principles" of both Mao and Deng would permit.

How do you make China "wealthy, strong, and free"? This is the modified new question in China. It is the same question Sun Yat-sen had raised. The pre-Communist mainland did not offer a full-fledged model to return to; it had no opportunity or time to develop one. Deng's prescriptions for an open market economy under the four cardinal principles are, unfortunately for him, already tainted by corruption, license, and an "uneven playing field." In both Eastern Europe and Russia, socialism proved unequal to the task of making the two areas *both* "wealthy and strong," not to mention free. To bypass this apparent difficulty, present-day Dengists have substituted "Chinese socialism" for "socialism" but for obvious reasons have chosen not to define the new term more precisely.

Suppose we could leave freedom aside for the moment, can we hope to make the China that Mao and his Communist Party left behind in 1976 both "wealthy and strong?" Will pride alone be able to sustain the Communist regime indefinitely? To the thoughtful person, nationalism implies both pride, obtained from fear by others, and self-respect. Self-respect may be harder to earn than fear by others. Might the feeling of being strong and feared by other nations conceivably sustain the present PRC regime if these boastful sentiments were accompanied by some people in China becoming better off earlier than others while all may do so gradually, even if only at a snail's pace? Can all those who will climb up the ladder of rising material well-being do so faster than their own numbers will increase? Is there a time limit to this ascent to a materialistic Promised Land, which the Communist Party failed to deliver after Mao had led it to political power? If the PRC's population grows faster than production, will this unending ladder snap so that the devil will take the hindmost? Is it not imperative that we add equality in the sense of equality of opportunity to "wealth, strength, and liberty" as the updated national goals?

A last point should be added since the PRC cannot retreat into isolation. How "strong" does a modernizing China wish to become? How strong does the CCP think it must be—that is, in relation to other nations in the region and in the world? Officially PRC foreign affairs spokesmen have always disclaimed the attainment of military hegemony as a national objective. But the PRC is far from consistent. It claims to fear other nations' possible intention to split up China. If this was a realistic concern at the end of the 19th century, does it still make sense 100 years later?

If all these questions suggest a gloomy and uninteresting future, how then did Mao manage to seize power against what must have appeared to many then as impossible odds? Besides, why was freedom left out of consideration? Why were the ordinary people who had to bear the cost of Mao's ill-conceived vainglory never "consulted"? Were they free to complain? Some might say that Mao rose with the peasants' support. Did he actually rise on the back of a portion of the peasantry, those who were very poor and landless and those who thought that Mao's agrarian redistributive schemes could solve China's overall economic problems? Those who in the end suffered and even died did not have an opportunity to start over again themselves. More than one generation had been lost in this way.

II. THE CCP'S SOVIET TIES: CONSEQUENCES

The Chinese body politic and society on which Dengist reformers at the end of the 1970's hoped to graft modern science and technology were vastly different from those of traditional China at the end of the 19th century. The intervening 100 years of warlordism, Nationalist rule and Communist rule, including Mao's long, turbulent reign, had created a different country. The 40-year Communist episode from 1949 to 1989 was especially a break with the past. But first let us consider the basic nature of the Chinese Communist Party and, to begin with, some aspects of its Soviet ties during its long (1921-49) ascent to power.

Soviet Model

The Chinese Communist Party was first established in 1921, only four years after the October revolution in Russia. The Bolsheviks were then interested in finding political allies and "fraternal" nations of the same ideology. At the same time, China's political and intellectual activists were very naturally looking for guidance and support from forerunners in the international communist community. Not too surprisingly perhaps, the Chinese Communist Party's first official charter (program and bylaws) drew inspiration from Moscow while today its only surviving Chinese language text, one included in the CCP's official *Party Handbook* is a translation from the Russian language version.[4] Although Communist Russia was the first non-Chinese nation to renounce the privileges it had acquired in China under what the Chinese called "unequal treaties," it did not, however, return to China the territorial concessions at the same time.

Under the July 1921 charter adopted by its first CCP National Congress, the Chinese Communist Party (the CCP, total membership then only 53) called upon the "army of the revolution" to join hands with the country's proletariat to overthrow the political authority of the capitalist class, to offer aid to the working class and to continue to do so until class differences in the society had disappeared. Until then the Party would regard the "dictatorship of the proletariat" as the appropriate form of government. As if this language might still not suffice, to show where the new party stood the same Article 2 stipulated that the party would abolish private property and confiscate all privately-owned factories, machines, land and intermediate products and raw materials.

Armed Class Struggle, Advisers and Students

The militant revolutionary language of armed class struggle underlining the above approach was reinforced by the advisers who were sent to China by the Communist International.[5] Chinese nationals were recruited, trained by Moscow and later returned as representatives and/or operatives. Young Chinese work-study groups, centered in France and, to a lesser degree, in Germany, became both recruits and recruiters during the years after World War I.[6] Among the notables were some who, like Zhou Enlai and Deng

---

4. See *Zhonggong Dangshi Cankao Ziliao* [*Reference Material on CCP Party History*] (Beijing: People's Publishers, 1980), p. 279. The charter was adopted in July 1921.

5. Laszlo Ladany, *The Communist Party of China and Marxism, 1921-1985, A Self-Portrait* (Stanford: Hoover Institution Press, 1988). See references to "Comintern."

6. Many senior CCP leaders were in the work-study group in France. Mao was an exception. Zhou Enlai was at one time recipient of a study grant from the Alexander von Humboldt Foundation. The Ye Jianying interview was published in 1993 by Yun Xiang (ed.): *Ye Jianying Yuanshuai Jiaowang Shilu Xulie* [*Interviews of Marshal Ye Jianying*] (Chengdu: Sichuan People's Publishers, 1993).

Xiaoping, later became CCP leaders of "the first generation." Others, younger and less well-known, played key military and diplomatic roles in the Party's rise to power. For example, Wu Xiuquan who worked with Ye Jianying in the Marshal Mission negotiations in the 40s was the CCP representative who first spoke at Lake Success (UN) during the Korean War. Marshal Liu Bocheng, who in 1949 took part in the final battles against Nationalist government forces, was responsible for translating Soviet training manuals from Russian into Chinese, having been sent to Russia for special training himself.

Some of the Third International advisers recommended the strategy of urban uprising which, also advocated by Li Lisan as its spokesman, turned out to be a disastrous failure. Adoption of the strategy had the effect of drawing the attention of potential anti-communist forces to the military threat posed by their communist opponents. The abortive Nanchang uprising, the attacks on Changsha, and the planned attack on Wuhan (1927-30)[7] were good examples of what could be expected. On the other hand, Soviet missteps and failures in China on the issue of urban uprising gave some homegrown communists in China both the need and the impetus to develop their own alternative policies, involving an organized peasant revolution and guerrilla warfare as the first phase of what proved to be a winning strategy. Mao Zedong turned out to be the Chinese communist leader who most successfully filled the role of a homegrown strategist. Setbacks suffered by the rebels following a Soviet adviser's faulty military instructions during the fifth "extermination campaign" of the Nationalists paved the way for Mao's eventual rise to party leadership at the Tsunyi Conference, held during the rebel forces' hurried retreat in Western China.[8]

The Soviet Role in 1936 and 1945-49

The Soviet Union contributed greatly to the Chinese Communist takeover of China. It did so at two significant junctions in recent Chinese history: first in 1936 and then in 1945.

The Soviet role in 1936 remains to be fully confirmed in detail by official Soviet records. The following facts are, however, clear. First, by the time most of the retreating Chinese Communist forces had finally gathered in Shaanxi, with their capital at Yanan, they

---

7. See note 5 *supra*.

8. As only recently reported by a participant of the Long March. If true, this would be of interest to students of early CCP history.

were faced with nominally government-controlled forces under Chang Hsueh-liang. Popularly known as the "Young Marshal," he was the son of the former warlord of Manchuria, Chang Tso-lin. Chang Tso-lin had been assassinated in a bomb plot by Japanese army agents in 1931. After the loss of Manchuria to Japanese occupation following the assassination, the young Chang and troops loyal to him were shifted to Northwestern China on the then relatively quiescent front facing the Communists, now at the end of their Long March. The Communists, however, managed to develop personal contacts with Chang's command, persuading some of his officers and troops that the central government under Chiang Kai-shek's Nationalist Party had its priorities all wrong.

The Communist argument was that top priority should be given to fighting the Japanese militarists who were occupying progressively larger chunks of China, and that not to form a united front against Japan at that time was downright treason. This line of reasoning proved persuasive enough to willing ears and some of Chang's troops staged a mutiny at Xian (Sian) during an inspection tour by Chiang in early December 1936; the mutineers hoped to induce or command Chiang to stop moving militarily against the Communists, who were again showing signs of becoming restive by moving from Shaanxi into Shanxi, a neighboring province. The mutinous troops held Chiang in hostage and demanded a change in national policy. Chiang was finally released by his captors on Christmas Eve, 1936.

The Communists claimed to have been an intermediary in the negotiations between the Nationalists and the mutineers, and rumors have persisted that the Soviet Union urged a similar settlement to release Chiang, out of its own interest in supporting the Nationalist Chinese as the more effective Chinese counterweight against Japan. While the CCP desired a long-awaited respite, the Soviets probably thought that, given the then "Berlin-Tokyo axis" and a potential Euro-Asian two-front threat to itself, a China not fully under Chiang Kai-shek's control, not to mention a united front against Japan in which the CCP would be either a partner or in a position to expand its influence at a later date, would be better for Soviet national interests than a China without Chiang under Japanese influence in spite of the fraternal solidarity among international communists.

Just about a decade later, after Japan's surrender in World War II in the summer of 1945, Soviet troops entered Manchuria, then still known as Manchoukuo (the Kingdom of Manchu, established through Japanese machinations in 1931), to accept the surrender of Japanese forces there. As a matter of fact, the Soviet Union had barely managed to declare war on Japan in time to qualify for a seat at the victors' table in 1945.[9] These arrangements regarding Manchuria were made by Roosevelt and Churchill with Stalin at the Yalta conference during the war so that, after victory over Nazi Germany, Soviet troops could be used in the war against Japan. However, there was no real fighting in Manchuria before the Japanese surrender, which came immediately after the dropping of the two atomic bombs on Hiroshima and Nagasaki. Japanese arms collected in Manchuria by Soviet troops were then used to arm the Chinese Communists, who had rushed into Manchuria ahead of the Nationalist Chinese forces. Former Manchoukuo troops were also absorbed into the Communist Chinese command.[10]

Strengthening the People's Liberation Army

During the war with Japan, the Communist forces in China had already grown in strength. According to the study of military historians of this period,[11] the Sian Incident earned for the Chinese Communists a much needed respite from Chiang's forces, the communist armed strength in the Shaanxi area of Northwest China measured at no more than 32,000 men, including local troops originally in Northern Shaanxi and "young volunteer troops." After the outbreak of full-scale war with Japan on July 7, 1937 and the CCP's public announcement a week later of joining the Nationalist government forces in a united fighting front, the Communist forces were officially incorporated into the Eighth Route Army, but under its own command.[12] Under the command of Zhu De and Peng

---

9. The Soviet Union was aware of Japan's deliberation about surrendering to the Allies. However, the timing of the two atomic bombs dropped on Hiroshima and Nagasaki, followed by Hirohito's order to the Imperial Army to surrender, could not have been fully anticipated by Stalin sufficiently ahead of time.

10. See Lionel Max Chassin, *The Communist Conquest of China: A History of the Chinese Civil War, 1945-49* (Cambridge: Harvard University Press, 1965). See also Liu Feng-han, *K'ang-chan Shih-ch'i Chung-kung Chün-shih ti Fa-chan, July 1937 - August 1945* [*Chinese Communist Military Expansion during the War with Japan*], Reprints of the National History Archives, Taipei, December 1991.

11. *Ibid.*

12. For a view of the future consequences of this command structure, a concise evaluative history of the 1945-49 post-World War II Chinese Civil War, focusing on the military aspects, can be found in Lionel Max Chassin, *supra* note 10. During the final phase of the conflict, the surrender of the Beijing-Tianjin area by Fu Tso-yi and the battle for the defense of Xuzhou-Bangpu (otherwise known in PRC literature as the

Dehuai, the official strength of this Communist force was raised to 40,000, with the implied corresponding logistic and budgetary support of Chiang's Nationalist (KMT) Government.

The extent to which the Communist forces actually engaged the Japanese army as against the pursuit of hostilities between themselves and Chiang's government forces varied in time and place. Different sources of information tended to offer conflicting reports. There is general agreement on only two relatively large-scale engagements between Japanese and Communist-commanded forces. One of these was billed in public releases as involving 100 communist regiments[13] but was actually on a substantially smaller scale. At any rate, it was during the war years that the remnant rebel forces of 1936 grew to a real strength of 570,000 at the end of World War II, nominally alleged to be more than twice in size or 1,270,000 men, made up primarily by the 18th Army Group and the New Fourth Army in Eastern China.

The Soviet entry into the war in its final hours and the Japanese arms turned over to the Chinese Communist forces, plus the delay caused by the negotiations between the Soviet army and the Chinese Nationalists in the latter's attempt to reoccupy the industrial centers in southern Manchuria, contributed eventually to the defeat of the Nationalist forces in Manchuria. During the period (1945-46) of Soviet occupation of the ports and railway centers, Soviet policy contributed directly to the growth in numbers and effective strength of the Chinese Communist forces in Manchuria. Soviet

---

Huaihai campaign) were especially illustrative of the problems Chiang's ROC government had to contend with. Fu Tso-yi's defense strategy prior to his open declaration of surrender was, according to Chassin, more readily understandable if one bore in mind his reported contacts with the Communists. (Chassin, *id.*, p. 210). Fu's later defection may have had something to do with the unusual transfer to his staff at about this time of Chi Ch'ao-ting, an economist and director of the then Central Bank of China's Economic Research Department from Shanghai. Chi wrote on Chinese regional economics and was reportedly a member of the U.S. Communist party. This report from a former Bank staff member, if correct, is illustrative of the weakness of counterintelligence on the ROC side.

The same problem engendered by communist subversion of high-ranking officers apparently was also the case with Wei Li-huang as reported in the *Chuan-chi Wen-hsüeh* [*Biographical Literature Magazine*]. The "defense of Suchow" (Hsü-chou spelled as Suchow in some Western language reports) failed, according to Chassin, partly because of the defection of key elements of some Nationalist units in spite of the gallant efforts of others. But these critical defections might not have occurred had the loyalty of the troops and their officers not been weakened by years of rampant inflation and inadequate pay in real terms.

13. See Liu Feng-han, *supra* note 10.

forces also removed and/or rendered unusable industrial equipment and infrastructure investments in the area developed during Japanese occupation. These measures, demonstrated amply by a U.S. Presidential Commission headed by Edwin Pauley, denied to the Chinese government a primary industrial base the latter had hoped to employ for postwar economic rehabilitation.[14] The Soviet intention probably was to increase the dependence of both the Nationalists and the Communists on Soviet goodwill in the future, however the Chinese Civil War should end.

Nationalistic at the Wrong Time

If Stalin played a rather duplicitous role in dealing with both sides of China's internal political struggle, even though one side was a fellow communist party, Japan's impact on the CCP's rise to power was politically somewhat simpler. By appealing to the widespread nationalistic sentiments in China and the intense personal feelings of those troops of Manchurian origin under Chang Hsueh-Liang with the reminder that the 1931 Japanese occupation of his Manchurian homeland and the murder of Chang's father were perpetrated by Japan and its infamous Kwantung Army, the Chinese Communists succeeded in deflecting the Nationalists' attention and efforts away from themselves. By forcing the government to take a more open stand against Japan in the face of anti-Japanese public opinion, they made it politically impossible for Chiang Kai-shek's government not to take up arms in the summer of 1937 against Japan's unceasing encroachment in North China. Indeed, the Nationalists would have preferred to postpone the inevitable clash with Tokyo to a later date.[15]

As a matter of fact, a protracted debate had been going on in China in the early 1920s and 1930s on the relative priorities of two competing objectives facing the government since 1927, when Chiang Kai-shek's government was established in Nanking and the KMT and the Communists parted company. While Chiang attempted to "exterminate" the armed rebels in a series of abortive

---

14. Edwin Pauley, *The Commission Report on Japanese Assets in Manchuria*, (Washington, D.C.: Commission's own printing, 1946).

15. An unofficial Chinese economic mission of bankers and industrialists headed by Wu Ting-ch'ang (D.C. Wu) went to Japan on behalf of the Nationalist government in an effort to develop internal Japanese opposition to the militarists' designs to engage in new military operations in China. Shortly after the return of this Chinese mission, the Japanese military became even more dominant in domestic politics. Following the Sian Incident in 1936, the die was cast for the July 1937 full-scale Japanese invasion of China.

campaigns that finally succeeded in driving the main body of Communist forces to Northern Shaanxi, his government was actually making considerable headway in building up economic institutions necessary for modernization and an economic "take-off", including the standardization of weights and measures, the establishment of modern central banking, the development of urban retail commercial and savings banks, promotion of selected commodity exports, development of an accurate crop reporting system and of modern agricultural research, completion of several strategic railway trunk lines joining the eastern seaboard to south-central China, and the setting up under the defense command (the Supreme Military Council headed by Chiang himself) of a National Resources Commission for the production of minerals and fabrication of materials needed in the anticipated show-down with Japan.

Unfortunately, the Sian Incident foreclosed the issue. It was no longer possible, given the domestic political climate, to push the fateful date of military encounter away. But the economic base in southwestern China was too underdeveloped to support a protracted war, the impact of the loss of existing industry and sources of revenue in the coastal areas was too grievous, and the withdrawal of Chinese forces from the better developed regions was too fast, so that monetary inflation to finance the war became not only inevitable during wartime, but quickly accelerated after the defeat of Japan. When civil war between Communists and Nationalists resumed on a large scale in 1947, hyperinflation became virtually inevitable. The soon galloping inflation in turn undermined social stability and created widespread inequality of real income, discontent and public corruption, all feeding upon one another.

As large-scale civil war expanded southward from Manchuria and hyperinflation galloped along in intensity, U.S. advisers attached to the Chinese government reportedly recommended the abandonment of Manchuria. Later on, even the abandonment of large portions of the country north of the Yangtze was suggested. However, although giving up Manchuria might have been a viable military option at one time, to be compelled to do so was politically inconceivable to any politician or political party. To most politicians and the public, nationalism demanded territorial integrity and therefore the recovery of territories lost through "unequal treaties." How could China be a victor and one of the postwar Big Five and yet be unable to hold on to Manchuria? The cost of misplaced nationalism turned out to be very high indeed. By concentrating his best forces in the campaign to hold Manchuria, Chiang lost the civil war when he lost the north, including Manchuria and the Peking-Tientsin (Beijing-Tianjin) area.

III. GAINING THE UPPER HAND

Faceted, Protracted Struggle

Let us summarize more systematically the principal factors contributing to the CCP's final successful push toward power after World War II. We shall recount how the Communists gained the upper hand in the protracted struggle.

First, to the Communist Party under Mao the struggle for power is not a theoretical debate in a drawing room seminar. It is an all-out political struggle in which acts of urban terror, peasant uprising, deliberately engineered strikes and student demonstrations, and guerrilla and mobile warfare involving thousands of men and women are all pursued. It is a protracted, long drawn-out warfare with no holds barred and without the constraint of moral, religious or human scruples. A class struggle in Chinese Communist terms means that what is expedient and might serve the objective of the party is by definition a usable means. The end result of the power struggle won is a dictatorship of the proletariat, and further down the road, the fulfillment of the Party's ultimate objective, the realization of socialism. The intermediate and final ends justify whatever means are employed.

Inasmuch as "democratic centralism" rules within the CCP, giving the elected Party Chairman absolute authority, the possibility of an absolute personal dictatorship is a real threat. The astuteness of the Party Chairman and the loyalty of the military may become the key.

Second, winning the upper hand is essentially relative. It involves the reduction of the enemy's power no less than the enhancement of one's own. In the CCP's struggle with the KMT, nationalism both before and after the war with Japan was a theme skillfully exploited by the Communists to induce the Nationalists to make the wrong strategic decisions, both during World War II and in 1947-49.

Third, there were crucial actors in the international environment which could not be controlled but might occasionally be influenced by the CCP. During and after World War II the actions of Japan were probably least susceptible to the CCP's influence. On the contrary, the Chinese Communists could only try to take advantage of opportunities offered them by Japan. The United States, on the other hand, was more susceptible to the influence of ideas propagated to denigrate the Nationalists.

Isolating the KMT: Deflecting Focus

The KMT itself provided ample opportunities for the CCP to exploit. The Communists leveled their attacks on "bureaucratic capitalism" by mostly singling out four families whose members at various times held high positions in the KMT government or party, just as the post-1982 Dengists tried to heap all the sins of the Cultural Revolution period on the "Gang of Four."

Worming from Within

Since 1980, a number of personal memoirs have appeared authored by CCP members who deliberately and allegedly with success engineered either the "conversion" or the betrayal of Nationalist officials[16] to the Communist cause. Former Nationalist generals Wei Li-huang and Fu Tso-yi were well-known examples.

Winning the Intelligentsia

However, in the final analysis, the Communists had to be able to convince the population and especially the educated elite that the CCP represented China's future, that their policies would be the best for China, and that they were sincere, trustworthy and incorruptible people who at least could not do worse than the Nationalists and most likely would do much better.

How did Mao—and his chief of staff in this work, Zhou Enlai—gather together their fellow travelers from among opponents of the KMT? How were these targeted?

On this point, Qian Jiaju (Chien Chia-chü), an economist and prolific writer from pre-World War II days specializing in Chinese agrarian issues, has given us a rather detailed account.[17] Qian had gone to Hongkong in 1948 from Nationalist-controlled China

---

16. General Wei Li-huang, a high-ranking officer under Chiang Kai-shek, for instance, was suborned by the Communists over a long period. See various issues in the journal *Biographical Literature, supra* note 12. Also Chao Jung-sheng, *Wei Li-huang Yao Tsan-chia Kung-chan-tang* [*Wei Li-huang Wishes to Join the CCP*], *Biographical Literature*, Taipei, Vol. 59, No. 3, September 1991, pp. 73-79. Wei's contribution to the military successes of the PLA was partly affirmed by the CCP at his death. He was buried at Babaoshan, the resting place for CCP heroes.

17. Qian Jiaju, *Quguo Yousi Lu* [*Sorrowful Thoughts in Exile*] (Hongkong: Cosmos Books, 1991), pp. 226-302, esp. p. 265. See also Qian, *Qishinian di Jingli* [*Through Seven Decades*] (Hongkong: The Mirror Post Cultural Enterprises, 1986).

before joining the Communist regime as Deputy Director of its Bureau of Private Enterprise a year later. He wrote from Hongkong about an unexpected visit in 1948 from Ma Yin-ch'u, another outspoken economist and educator known for his advocacy of a rational population policy for China. Ma had written to Qian earlier, declining the latter's suggestion to visit Hongkong. He then turned up in Hongkong shortly afterwards in the latter part of 1948. He explained that he had made surreptitious travel arrangements in order to throw off those who he suspected might be reading his mail in Shanghai. He wanted to go to Beijing, where he used to teach, to join the incoming Communist administration after Communist victory, which he obviously expected.

Nationalist troops lost the control of Manchuria toward the end of 1947. General Fu Tso-yi, supreme commander of the North China Command of the Nationalist forces, surrendered to the Communists shortly afterwards. In an earlier public announcement dated May 1, 1948, the Central Committee of the Communist Party had officially asked all "*democratic* parties and organizations," as well as individuals, to convene a National Political Consultative Conference for the specific purpose of establishing a democratic coalition government.[18] (Qian was at the June 1949 preparatory meeting of this particular conference.)

Among those democratic political organizations (key members of which were then in Hongkong awaiting either summons or passage to North China), according to Qian, were the Democratic League of China, of which he himself was a member, and at least four other splinter parties, including the KMT Revolutionary Committee. Qian said that many of the individuals, however, held memberships in more than one such party; others were known Communist Party members; still others were suspected of being secret members of the CCP.

Finally, on September 21, 1949 Mao Zedong addressed the first general meeting of the National Political Consultative Conference (NPCC), which was attended by 600 invited guests. Mao spoke briefly on the CCP's victory over the KMT, which he described as the "pawn of imperialism," namely, of the United States. He also called upon the conference to elect its own National Committee and a People's Government Council and to adopt a Common Program. In effect, he wanted the conference to act as an informal, hand-picked constitutional convention; the Common Program was

---

18. Qian, *Through Seven Decades*, *id.*, 1986, p. 167.

to be its product and to serve as a provisional constitution. Through its customary united-front mechanism and the cloak of nationalism, the CCP and Mao would form a coalition government, as it were, and claim the popular mandate to govern the nation. Mao was to make the same pronouncement at Tiananmen ten days later to the general public. His target on September 21 was a selected group of CCP supporters and opponents to the Nationalist government (not excluding some political opportunists). The larger target on October 1, 1949 was the nation and the world. It is hard to say how many non-communists who were present on these two occasions (leaving aside those in Western chancelleries) had followed Mao's writings on coalition government and foreign policy.

The nationalistic theme used in defeating the Chiang Kai-shek government was easy to understand. There was no doubt that Manchuria, long occupied by the Japanese, had already reverted to the control of the new government. The Russians seemed to be on the Communists' side and in the minds of many Chinese could not by definition be "imperialists."[19] Few outside Nationalist circles or the innermost Communist leadership itself knew then about the degree of the Soviet Union's devastation of the Manchurian economy or could have anticipated its consequences. But what about the concept of a "coalition government"? Did the audience present at the September 21, 1949 conference have any inner doubt?

Mao's Talk of a Communist-Led Coalition, 1940-45

What happened immediately after 1949 is the subject matter of the next chapter. Here we shall focus on what Mao said before the CCP became the party in power. In fact, Mao wrote quite plainly about a Communist-led coalition on at least two occasions before 1949.

In 1940, when the Communist Party was in theory still a member of the united front in the war with Japan and enjoyed unusual opportunities to propagate its ideas, Mao made the point that because China was a victim of imperialist aggression and in a "colonial/semi-colonial" stage, its "national capitalist class" possessed to a degree, and would continue to possess for a time, a "revolutionary" character. Hence, under these conditions, the proletariat had

19. Stalin did not show his hand until October 2, 1949, the day after Mao's Tiananmen announcement. By then he must have convinced himself that he would not be facing U.S. military opposition if he came out on the PRC side forsaking the Nationalists.

the duty to form a united front with the national capitalists against the imperialists and the "bureaucratic-capitalist-warlord"-KMT (Nationalist) government. As for the Chinese state in the future, it could only assume the last of three possible forms. It could not become a republic ruled by the capitalist class. Old-fashioned political democracies of this nature were, in Mao's opinion, already disappearing since the onset of World War II, becoming themselves military dictatorships. (Mao seemed to have regarded the wartime controls in many countries as permanent changes.) Besides, China could not yet become a republic under the dictatorship of the proletariat. Only the Soviet Union was in this category; the other capitalist countries were still evolving toward this form.

Mao's idea was that states still in the colonial/semi-colonial status would take on the third possible form of sovereign states—a transitional form in which several anti-imperialist classes would share power. He then expounded on a "political structure" theme which he defined as the manner in which the governing classes would organize power in order to protect themselves against the "counter-revolutionaries" who were their "class enemies."

Five years later, in April 1945, when Mao, like many others, was still unaware of the development of the atomic bomb and expected a protracted war with Japan, he repeated the same ideas on the "new democracy" he had tried to popularize since 1940. He tried to link it with Sun Yat-sen's Three Principles,[20] but suggested that China would have to go through a phase of development with the aid of "national capitalists" and that such a period would last a minimum of several decades. Socialism was therefore far, far away, so he meant to reassure the "national capitalists" and intellectuals.

If there was a hint that the future could be a little less rosy, it was his statement that "counter-revolutionaries" were not part of the "people" but were "non-persons" and that political democracy would not apply to "non-persons." He failed to mention how numerous such non-persons could be. Perhaps he himself could not know. He was equally vague on the meaning of "democratic centralism," which he claimed was the way in which the government had to be organized if political power for the protection of the gov-

20. For Mao's political ideas about China in the *immediate* post-WWII years, see Mao Zedong, "On Coalition Government," April 24, 1945, in *Mao Zedong Xuanji* [*Selected Works of Mao Zedong*] (Beijing: People's Publishers, 1966), Vol. III, pp. 978-1048, and an earlier piece, "Xin Min-zhu Zhu-i Lun" [On the New Democracy], in *Mao Zedong Zhuzo Xuandu* [*Selected Readings from Mao Zedong's Works*] (Beijing: People's Publishers, 1986), Vol. 1, pp. 348-400.

erning classes was to be effectively exercised.[21] But, as mentioned above, he was explicit and emphatic in denouncing the use of such terms as "citizens" or "nationals" so that "counter-revolutionaries" would be included, and in using the term "political democracy."

Several members of the 1949 Political Consultative Conference received appointments in the new government. No serious misgivings were recorded. Would anyone have dared? Would anyone who might have declined to cooperate have been asked to attend? Some who were there in 1949 were probably political opportunists or "careerists." Still others, like Qian, later regretted and had a change of heart, finding they had been duped by the CCP and its leadership. In 1949, many non-communist Chinese really had no chance to leave China or else could not imagine how bad life under communism would be.

Intellectual Seedbed for Soviet-Style Planning

There were additional circumstances which made the Communist promises of a coalition government and "new democracy" sound plausible or even attractive to some people. The principal reasons can be enumerated here:

First, few pre-World War II Chinese intellectuals could read Russian or had access to objective accounts of Soviet conditions and how economic planning and management in reality worked in the USSR. What has become widely known and acknowledged by Russians and objective scholars about the Soviet economy in the decades under Stalin and in the post-Stalin years leading to the collapse of the Soviet empire in 1989 and dissolution of the USSR in 1991 were nowhere projected in the mid-40s. At the end of World War II, any concern about the Soviet economy was not focused on how inefficient it could be, but on how dangerous its war machine could become. Such fears would have to be founded on the implicit assumption that the economy would be efficient enough to sustain the war machine and the communist dictatorship. Even theoretical analysis questioning the feasibility of centralist planning in the 1920s, 1930s and during World War II were often dismissed as having been penned with a rightist political bias.[22]

---

21. See Mao's "On People's Democratic Dictatorship," dated June 30, 1948, in *Selected Readings from Mao Zedong's Works*, *id.*, Vol. 2, pp. 674-688.

22. As late as 1944 when Frederick Hayek's *Road to Serfdom* first appeared, it was quite often maligned by critics as politically biased.

Chinese scholars trying to learn more about Soviet planning and its applicability to China at that time had to fall back on second-hand information. Wu Ching-ch'ao, a sociologist, had to start his short post-World War II visit to the Soviet Union with the much earlier publications of the British Fabians.[23] Leading CCP cadres who studied Soviet economic practice and theory unfortunately were unfamiliar with Western academic economic theory and objective discussions on economic planning. Younger scholars later dispatched to the Soviet Union for economic studies had the misfortune of being fed biased theories and analyses. At any rate, all that came much later than the 1940s.

A second factor contributing to an intellectual seedbed favorable to the acceptance of central planning and a political control system associated with it is the implied advantage of a plan, as opposed to the absence of a plan, in the sense of a coherent strategy to achieve a given objective, such as the national objective ("rich and strong") discussed in Chapter I. H.D. Fong (Fang Hsien-t'ing) of Nankai University's pre-World War II Institute of Economic Research, well-known internationally for his work on Chinese industrial development and rural industry, wrote in the early years of the war with Japan on Chinese industrial development as he envisaged it at the war's end.[24] As one would expect from an academic economist with wide practical experience, he wrote in this popular tract about the financing of a development program, the priorities of projects and forms of ownership (state, joint state-private and private).

On a policy level, Franklin L. Ho, former director of the Nankai Institute, where H. D. Fong and he collaborated for many years, was professionally in charge of the Nationalists' Economic Planning Council in Chungking in the 1940s during the war. Ho, who later retired from the East Asian Institute of Columbia University, New York, had been one of the small number of economists in and out of the Nationalist government and academic circles who would have contributed to the planning of post-World War II Chi-

23. See Wu Ching-ch'ao, *Youjihua Anbiliti Fazhan Guomin Jingji* [*Planned and Proportional Development of the National Economy*] (Beijing: Chinese Youth Publishers, 1955), and an earlier version, *Chung-kuo Kung-yeh-hua ti T'u-ching* [*Road to China's Industrialization*] (Changsha: The Commercial Press, 1938). In the 1938 book, the author noted that China should not slavishly copy the Soviet Union. His views were substantially altered in the later book during the Mao period.

24. See Fang Hsien-t'ing (H. D. Fong), *Chung-kuo Kung-yeh Tze-pen Wen-t'i* [*The Problem of China's Industrial Capital*] (Changsha: The Commercial Press, 1939).

nese economic development without centralist state planning in the CCP fashion.[25]

While such senior economists like Ho and Fong left China before the CCP completed its seizure of power, their former students and others who stayed behind later worked in a principally technical capacity while the Communist bosses at higher levels were steeped in Soviet methodology and "called the shots."

Finally, it is worth mentioning again that the National Resources Commission (NRC), established belatedly to develop a domestic arms industry and the supply of fuels, metals, and machine manufacturing primarily for the war effort, drew to itself many engineering talents. Universities and technological institutes in China which over the years had attracted talented Chinese youths were also resuming their supply of graduate students to foreign (primarily American) institutions for advanced studies as World War II came to an end. In general, these younger Chinese were imbued with nationalistic sentiments and more than usually dedicated to building a strong China. All these factors contributed to an intellectual environment in which building a free society could easily take second place to developing national power as a paramount goal. This was a state of mind which the capable CCP machine knew well how to exploit.

Hyperinflation

Let us once more review a few figures on hyperinflation. Neither the intellectual atmosphere nor the ferment of frustrated nationalism necessarily would have driven the population under the Nationalists to the CCP's embrace if stable prices and tolerable economic conditions had prevailed and guaranteed the people a living. We shall not try to explain in detail how hyperinflation began. The subject already has been mentioned several times in this volume and a full account of this economic disaster can be found in several places.[26] A few figures will suffice at this point to show how the

25. Franklin L. Ho and H. D. Fong were jointly responsible for the growth of the Nankai Institute of Economic Research before the war with Japan. In the mid-30s, Ho, like T'ing-fu Tsiang, entered government service under Chiang Kai-shek. During the war he was among the economists who tried to plan for postwar development. Later, he returned to academic life at Columbia University in New York.

26. For a thorough understanding of inflation in China in two consecutive periods, the following two volumes written by men who were very close to its development should be consulted with care: Shun-hsin Chou, *The Chinese Inflation, 1937-1949* (New York: Columbia University Press, 1963) and Chang Kia-ngau, *The Inflationary Spiral:*

public's support of the ROC government could evaporate so quickly when faced with the economic conditions.

First, if we take the wholesale price index in Shanghai in September 1945 as 100, the index rose to 256.6 in December of the same year. In December 1946, it was 1,655.5. In December 1947, it had risen to 4,941. In February 1948, at about the time Tianjin and Beijing fell to the PLA, the same price index had risen to 52,900! The demonetization of the Nationalist currency (*fapi*) and its replacement in August 1948 by a short-lived new currency euphemistically named the "gold yuan" was accompanied by the compulsory government purchase of privately-held foreign currency and specie (primarily gold and silver). But there was no way to restore stability or halt the civil war and the PLA's advance, which if halted could have decelerated the monetary expansion process.

The PLA's advance across the Yangtze and southward to western and southern China was accomplished through a combination of defeat and defection on the Nationalist side. Communist agents in key places were later known to have played vital roles in engineering these events.

In the end, the CCP took over what the Nationalists could no longer hold. The anti-communist forces in China simply disintegrated.

The Experience in China, 1939-1950 (New York: The Technology Press of MIT and John Wiley & Sons, 1958).

CHAPTER III

CONSOLIDATION OF POWER: AN UNENDING QUEST

I. CONSOLIDATION NEVER REALLY ENDED

For future students of Chinese history of the second half of the 20th century, the forty years spanning the 1949 and 1989 mammoth mass meetings at Tiananmen can be divided into stages in several ways. In one respect, this period first saw the establishment of an apparently unprecedented, well-organized political dictatorship in China and the transformation of a war torn, over-populated agricultural society into a centralized Soviet-type economic system moving in a frenzy towards industrialization. This phase (1949-57) was succeeded by internal power struggles within the Communist Party that ended with dramatic assaults launched by Mao and his radical followers—especially numerous youthful pawns—against the Communist Party apparatus, with the support of the People's Liberation Army. In 1956-57 before the first phase ended, the Communist Party was at its peak of political dominance and self-satisfaction.

The second period began to gather growing anti-Mao strength in 1959, when Mao's economic and social policies brought widespread disaster to the country and ended with what he called a "Cultural Revolution," the largest nation-wide purge in CCP history. The "Cultural Revolution" wound down in a most messy manner, leading to the post-Mao period. The final phase of the Cultural Revolution was protracted, lasting from 1971 to 1976. A benchmark of the final phase was the reported death of Lin Biao when a Trident airplane allegedly carrying Lin and members of his family crashed and burned in Mongolia on September 13, 1971. Lin, who was then Mao's anointed successor as Party leader, had allegedly died in an unsuccessful flight to the Soviet Union. Coincidentally, just about that time, U.S. Secretary of State Henry Kissinger was reportedly in Beijing in connection with President Nixon's scheduled first visit to the PRC the following year. The timing of the two events alone may make them of particular interest to students of diplomatic relations between the United States and China. Then, in 1976, Zhou Enlai, Prime Minister since 1949, and Mao both died.

Only a month later, a palace coup removed the radical successors of Mao (the "Gang of Four") from power, bringing this phase to an end.

An interim government headed by Hua Guofeng was itself toppled in a bloodless revolution engineered by a coalition of old Party members, former colleagues of Deng Xiaoping, who was brought back from his second exile. The Hua regime too was a transitional one. For the real post-Mao period started only when the Communist Party itself began to experiment with policies that could eventually lead to either a bloodless evolution away from communism or some other convoluted and less peaceful and promising future for China. The last phase focused on Deng Xiaoping, whose reformist aides policies dominated 1982-88, and ended at the Tiananmen crisis of June 1989. During the first half of the 90s China was again entering another transitional period.

An alternative view of looking at the same forty years from 1949 to 1989 is to consider their periodization by focusing on the consolidation of Mao's personal dictatorship in 1949-57, followed by the attack on Mao's personal rule and his tactical retreat and temporization in 1958-65. Mao's counterattack against the Party apparatus took place with the help of the Army in 1966-69. There was an intense struggle in 1971-76 by members of Mao's court to succeed Mao, who by then was already the dying emperor. The gradual ouster of Hua Guofeng, a key co-conspirator in the 1976 coup, was finally accomplished in 1982. The 1976 palace coup toppling the Gang of Four was a continuation of the succession struggle. However, the post-1982 period has very quickly assumed the nature of an internal political struggle revolving around another senescent autocrat, Deng Xiaoping, whose turn it was to face the inevitability of mortality and the uncertainties of succession.

By comparing these two modes of periodization one can clearly see that in the beginning both the Chinese Communists collectively as a revolutionary party and Mao Zedong at its command post shared the same need to consolidate their respective hold on power. Mao, in the first instance, had to maintain control of the Party itself and through the Party control his conquests. As long as Mao's control of the Party was not in doubt, there was little conflict or even divergence of interests between Mao and the rest of the party leadership, who acquiesced to Mao's lead if not enthusiastically followed it. Hence the approach toward the task of consolidating power and the specific measures chosen can be regarded as not only a result of Mao's preferences alone but in effect the outcome of a consensus of the Communist Party leadership. This should be kept in mind as we proceed in our discussion.

In 1958-59 the adverse results of some of Mao's policies became self-evident even to some of his ardent supporters. Questions about policy raised issues for intra-Party debate. But many cadres were still unsure of their own thinking and no one dared to speak openly because nobody apparently dared to doubt Mao. A historical meeting at the mountain summer resort of Lushan in 1959 finally lifted the secrecy that had shrouded the growing opposition to Mao. The intra-Party struggle then developed into a decade of volatile ups and downs in political debate that grew progressively more vicious. The decline of Mao's power in the early 1960s led to a period which in contemporary Chinese history acquired the tragic misnomer of the "Great Proletarian Cultural Revolution." A more apt description of the same events might be Mao's futile battle to build an alternative personal party while destroying the original CCP apparatus he and others had so assiduously created and brought to unprecedented dominion over the millions of Chinese.

How could such a sequence of events have occurred? How could the Chinese Communist Party lose its control to Mao? What did all this mean to the Chinese people? The way in which power was consolidated through 1957 needs to be understood especially by those who today, a generation later, have little personal knowledge, or even awareness, of those events.

Suppression of Resistance, Potential Opposition

The armed forces of the Chinese Communist Party, known officially as the People's Liberation Army (the PLA), are in reality more the armed instrument of the Chinese Communist Party than the armed forces of China. It serves the Party's interests, whatever they might be. Having won the battle in Manchuria, accepting the surrender of Fu Tso-yi in the Peking-Tientsin (Beijing-Tianjin) theater, it was reconstituted into several field armies.[1] While a major decisive battle was fought in the Hsuchou area north of Nanking by the bulk of the Communist forces, the rest fanned out south of the

1. For a relatively detailed account of the reorganization of PLA forces in November 1948 and their disposition "inside the Great Wall," which led to the surrender of Tianjin and Beijing by Fu Tso-yi, who was the Nationalist commander for the North China theater at the time, see Zhang Zanwu, Jiang Jiannong (chief editors), *A Major Glossary of Mao Zedong's Selected Works* [*Mao Zedong Xuanji Dacidian*], new edition (Taiyuan: Shanxi People's Publishers, 1991), pp. 283-286. For more on Fu Tso-yi's defection, see Chapter II.

Yangtze and managed to take over all mainland China in a relatively short time, often through surrenders and defections by Nationalist troops.

It follows therefore that the conquering armies could not disregard the potential risk they faced if the tides of battle were ever reversed. Thus, as new populated areas came under Communist military control, the suppression of all real and potential enemies, whether armed or not, was always the first order of the day. Large-scale public executions took place all over the country and there was no open real official accounting of the numbers.[2]

Even during the war with Japan and before the large-scale resumption of the Civil War in 1947-50, Chinese Communist military control of rural areas was often accompanied by the redistribution of farm land. During 1950 the Communist Party carried out its land redistribution with a vengeance. But the way such "land reform" was implemented little resembled the textbook case of land redistribution with compensation for the original owner. Suppression of the Party's idealized "class enemies" meant outright execution, confiscation, and physical and mental torture with the planned participation of masses of people egged on by agents and agitators, a technique made famous by Mao himself. In essence the approach was to strike terror in a relatively small group of persons (5 to 10 percent by Mao's count) and by involving numerous informants and others who would benefit from the suffering of the victims. Thus the method created a vested interest group that would henceforth bar any return to the original status quo.

At the same time, some of the victims would be so prostrate with terror that they would lose all will to resist. The same technique was then applied to a succession of new target groups, in each case focusing on a different group of victims whose elimination would constitute a further step in strengthening Communist Party control and in transforming the pre-Communist Chinese society.

The PRC's entry into the Korean War (1950) and the need to combat "waste, corruption and profiteering" offered an excuse to purge the new government offices and public institutions of former non-CCP elements, followed by the transformation of the urban mercantile class and "national capitalists" into employees of partially or fully nationalized enterprises. The last measure was also one way of raising revenue to stem inflationary pressure. Thus by

---

2. See Chapter I, *supra* note 10, at Chapters 4, 6, and 9. See also Yuan-li Wu (ed.), *Human Rights in the People's Republic of China* (Boulder, Co.: Westview Press, 1988).

the end of 1956, after only seven years from 1949, the Chinese urban economy had become socialized and the agricultural sector, which had briefly seen "land reform" and the appearance of some owner-cultivators, became agricultural collectives.

True Meaning of Mao's Dictatorship of the Proletariat

Mao's own approach to the consolidation of power was well thought out and amply demonstrated in practice. At any time he was always ready to draw upon his past personal experience. His tireless reading of Chinese history and of the exploits of outstanding characters in historical episodes of radical change—whether monarchs or rebel leaders—was no doubt a major source of inspiration.[3] One may even question whether Stalin and Lenin had very much new to tell him beyond the dogmatic framework of Marxist thought and Lenin's ideas on revolution and techniques of mass control. Under Mao the "dictatorship of the proletariat" is a greatly expanded system of social control through successive drives in the name of "mass movements." The choice of targets and their sequencing was in general carefully planned.

Mao certainly was not shy in expressing himself on statecraft and his own practices. On April 25, 1956, he addressed an expanded session of the CCP's Politburo on what at the time seemed to be the rule of an iron hand under Stalin, comparing his own policy with that of the Soviet Union.[4] According to Mao, the Chinese Communists consciously permitted the continued existence of the remnant democratic parties from the pre-1949 days. Their existence corresponded to the continued existence of classes and the class struggle against them in China at the time. While paying lip service to the eventual possibility that *both* the democratic parties and the Chinese Communist Party were destined to disappear because "what happens in history will also disappear in history," he nevertheless stressed the absolute need to have a party of the proletariat and to maintain the dictatorship. In the latter's absence, it

3. Mao's interest in Chinese history and classical literature, court intrigues, statecraft, novels and peasant uprisings were intensively cultivated in his youth and in the period when he began to work on the Chinese peasantry's problems during the 1920s and 1930s. See Xiao San, *Mao Zedong Tongzhi de Qingshaonian Shidai* [*Mao Zedong's Youth*] (Shanghai: People's Publishers, 1949 and 1950).

4. Mao Zedong, "Lun Shida Guanxi" ["On Ten Major Relationships"], in *Mao Zedong Xuanji* [*Selected Works of Mao Zedong*] (Beijing: People's Publishers, 1983), Vol. 5, pp. 267-88. The sentences quoted, "what happens in history. . ." etc., appear on pages 279-80. See also note 5 *infra*.

would not be possible "to suppress the counter revolutionaries, to resist imperialists, to build a socialist country, [and] to make that country a strong one."

Mao strongly affirmed the "correctness" of the campaign to suppress counter-revolutionaries in 1951-52. Needless to say, counter-revolutionaries were, and should be, dealt with by "killing" them, by "imprisonment," and by requiring them to live under conditions of security control. Some of course would be "released from arrest" although their records would be kept on file, as virtually all residents in China had their *dossiers*. He claimed to be against killing too many people because the wrong persons might be killed , and because live prisoners could be made to work and contribute more than their keep.

These were a source of the PRC's "forced labor" supply. He asserted that those who were killed in 1951-52 were the targets of popular hatred—this claim could in his mind obviously be based on mob participation encouraged in mass meetings and at public executions. The victims therefore "deserved to die." He made no reference to legal procedure or law. There was as a matter of fact no criminal code in the country until 1973, seventeen years later. In 1956 Mao mentioned some persons in public life whose names, like Pan Hannian, Rao Shushi and Hu Feng, were well known to his Politburo audience. They were among those who were not executed but who were on the borderline of deserving to die.[5] Of special significance for the discussion below and for post-1956 developments in China was his assertion that many counter-revolutionaries were still in hiding in government agencies, schools and the military, and that they should be identified and purged.[6] He refused to establish precise rules and criteria to determine the varying degrees of sentencing—from the death sentence down—claiming that the final authority was the Party's own business.

Those Beyond "Redemption"

Mao might have felt confident enough in the spring of 1956 that he already had the country entirely under control. But barely a year later, his tone in public had changed to one demanding greater

---

5. In the same April 25, 1956 speech before the CCP Politburo, Mao expounded in detail the criteria he would employ in assessing the net political advantage of whether or not to execute a "counter-revolutionary." The names he mentioned of those he would not have executed included Hu Feng, Pan Hannian, Rao Shushi (Gao Gang's alleged co-conspirator) and Henry Pu Yi, the last Manchu emperor.

6. Mao Zedong, "On Ten Major Relationships," *supra* note 4.

vigilance and stricter control of counter-revolutionaries still in hiding, even in the Party's own ranks. He was particularly fearful of intellectuals. The Hungarian uprising in 1956 apparently had shaken the complacency of many Chinese Communist leaders, not excluding Mao. Thus, they demanded a re-examination of the Chinese Party's own situation. Conditions in the Chinese agricultural economy were apparently calling for a reconsideration of plans to proceed rapidly in further collectivization; the formation of cooperative (i.e., collective) farms at a faster pace was meeting with resistance.[7] These events, piling upon the short-lived, publicly asserted right to freedom of expression granted to academics and writers, backfired when some daring souls took their new-found right of free speech for real. At this point Mao unleashed his "Anti-Rightist" program, aimed primarily at the intellectuals.

Anti-Rightist Campaign against Intellectuals

On February 27, 1957, several months before the outbreak of this Anti-Rightist storm, Mao Zedong resumed his discourse to the faithful of the previous summer. This time he chose to speak before an audience attending a "State Council meeting at the highest level."[8] From disclosures in subsequent publications, members of non-Communist parties which had lined up against the Nationalist government in 1949 were among those for whom the lecture was also intended, although the text was not published in the official Party organ *People's Daily* until four months later, on June 27, 1957, on the eve of the clamp-down on the brief relaxation towards intellectual dissent.

As a continuation of his 1956 defense of the methods of suppression of "counter-revolutionary" enemies, Mao now spoke of dealing with opponents and critics who were not, *prima facie*, overt enemies. The latter included, however, those hidden in the Party's own ranks. He reminded the audience of an earlier experience the CCP had at Yanan; namely, the 1942 purge under the euphemistic slogan of "rectification of [party] style" in arts and literature, designed to remove infiltrators, miscreants and those who were too hopelessly misguided to be "salvaged." His slogan in 1957 was, as before (i.e., in 1942), "not a single person will be killed. Criticisms will be tolerated; arguments will be met by counter-arguments."

7. See, for instance, Li Xiannian, *Li Xiannian Wenxuan 1939-1988* [*Selected Works of Li Xiannian*] (Beijing: People's Publishers, 1989), pp. 91-99, 121-23, and 257-64.
8. *Selected Works of Mao Zedong*, *supra* note 4, Vol. 5, p. 383.

Wrong arguments that would not be tolerated were those (1) designed to be divisive, (2) inimical to socialist reform and social transformation and (3) destructive of and pernicious to the "people's democratic dictatorship," to "democratic centralism," and to the "leadership of the Communist Party" and/or "international socialist unity."[9] Mao did not state who would actually be applying these criteria in specific cases or what punishments would be imposed.

Mao introduced the above political criteria in February 1957; they were sufficient to put numerous political innocents[10] into years of forced labor. The same criteria were applied in closing down the brief "Hundred Flowers" episode of political relaxation. A violent attack on two non-Communist newspapers, the *Guangming Daily* and the *Wen Wei Pao*,[11] was launched by the *People's Daily* which mentioned the names of errant publishers and editorial writers as responsible for launching attacks on the Communist Party like mad men, meaning apparently like real "counter-revolutionaries."

The "rectification of Party style," i.e., literary and life style in a superficial sense, in 1942, actually a coded reference to the Yanan purge, offers an interesting clue to the many arcane expressions employed by CCP cadres. On that earlier occasion, Kang Sheng, who had worked on security and counter-intelligence for the CCP, was called in by Mao to help with the purge in a thorough manner. Kang's work was clearly satisfactory to Mao both in 1942 and again in 1957 when his service was needed a second time by his master. A decade after 1957, during the Cultural Revolution, Kang was again to aid Mao in extracting confessions from the former's suspected opponents and in sealing their final fate.[12]

---

9. *Ibid.*, p. 393.

10. Harry Wu, human rights activist well known in the West, for instance, was imprisoned for nineteen years in a succession of forced labor camps. He was just a student when he was labeled a counter-revolutionary for a remark on Soviet aggression during the 1956 Hungarian uprising.

11. Chu Anping, editor of the *Guangming Daily*, previously editor of the magazine, *The New Observer*, was a sharp critic of the KMT government, and later fell victim to the CCP's Anti-Rightist campaign. He was presumably killed; no one has heard from him since sometime during the Anti-Rightist campaign.

12. For an earlier pioneer account of the persecution of Chinese intellectuals during the 1957 Anti-Rightist campaign, see Roderick MacFarquhar, *The Hundred Flowers Campaign and the Chinese Intellectuals* (New York: Praeger Publishers, 1960).

Reaching for the Stars

Chinese history commonly refers to the first emperor of Ch'in (Ch'in Shih-huang), as the worst tyrant in Chinese history. The grave of this autocrat who buried many dissenting scholars alive has yielded in recent years numerous life-like terra-cotta figures for exhibition in Western countries. He was the unifier in 221 B.C. of the "Warring Kingdoms." In historian Chien Mu's words, the emperor was basically enraged by the existence of numerous schools of thought that disagreed with the official line.[13] In a poem written possibly in 1936, Mao compared himself to Chinese emperors who founded new dynasties over the centuries and brought glory to the country but said that these past emperors' deeds could well be exceeded by his own.[14]

Mao reportedly gave a copy of his verse to a noted writer in 1945 when they met in Chungking. In this widely known literary work which was first published in the *Takung Pao*, Mao enumerated the first emperors of Ch'in (246-210 B.C.) and Eastern Han (140-87 B.C.), whom he dismissed as barely literate, although the former completed both China's unification and the Great Wall while the latter repelled the Hun invaders from the north. There was also Emperor T'ai Tsung (627-649 A.D.) of the T'ang Dynasty and T'ai Tsu (960-970 A.D.) of the Sung Dynasty; both were "pikers" in his eyes. Even Genghis Khan (1206-1227 A.D.) knew nothing but shooting eagles from the sky. Already then, Mao wrote in his verse: "For the real giants in China's long history, one would have to wait for the coming epoch."

---

13. See Chien Mu, *Ch'in-Han Shih* [*A History of the Ch'in and Han Dynasties*] (Hongkong: New Chinese Publisher, 1957), pp. 22-23.

14. The verse was supposed to have been penned in February 1936. There are several English translations available. Apart from the official Foreign Language Press version, Peking, 1976, pp. 23-24, a translation by Wong Man was published by the Eastern Horizontal Press. Two U.S. translations are known to this author, one by Willis Barnstone (in collaboration with Ko Ching-po), in *The Poems of Mao Tse-tung* (New York: Harper & Row), pp. 72-74, English translation copyright 1972 by Bantam Books, the other by Hua-ling Nieh Engle and Paul Engle in *Poems of Mao Tse-tung* (New York: Simon and Schuster, 1972), pp. 77-78. The Barnstone version also gave August 1945 as an alternative date of writing, making it closer to 1949, the year of Mao's triumph. The Ch'in emperor buried alive around 460 writers (see *supra* note 13). Mao's barbarism terrorized millions more.

An Over-Confident Mao Zedong

The series of successes he had scored during the decade of 1945-57 seemed to have given Mao unbounded confidence. It was at this juncture that he looked upon himself as the one person in Chinese history who could alter the face of China and its future for all time by implementing a set of daring economic and social policies on an unprecedented scale.[15] Always clever in turning a phrase, he raised the slogan of the "Three Red Banners"[16] in order to trumpet his forced march toward socialism. Unfortunately for the Chinese people, Mao's ideas turned out to be based on wrong assumptions about economics, technology and human nature, while his political position and indisputable hold on the Communist Party and the country at the time was such that all questioning voices had been fully silenced.[17] Since no voice of opposition could be raised from outsiders without the offenders being immediately branded as counter-revolutionary criminals, dissent would have to come from within the Party among the proven loyal followers. Peng Dehuai, an able PLA general during the 1947-49 war against the Nationalist forces who later led the "Chinese volunteers" against U.S. troops and other UN forces in South Korea, was eventually to play this dissenting role in 1959. But the 1959 effort of the critics was intended to salvage the dire economic effect on the PRC of Mao's mistakes; it came too late to prevent them. Thus the seeds of more than ten years of political violence within the CCP were sown.

In proceeding down the path heralded by his "Three Red Banners," Mao Zedong was a man in a hurry. Why? A rapidly successful economic development program would open up new horizons. Internally a way might be found to reverse the frustrated effort of the early 1950s to unify China by conquering Taiwan.[18] Within the Communist camp his position could be advanced to one of world leadership, especially since Stalin was no longer alive. The United States still barred the way, but Mao was not one to be stopped by seemingly daunting obstacles. After all, he had taken refuge in Northern Shaanxi with a few thousand followers and had reached Tiananmen barely fifteen years later as virtually China's new em-

---

15. See Chapter V below.

16. The "Three Red Banners" were the "Overall Socialist Line," the "People's Commune," and "Great Leap Forward."

17. See the concluding chapter in this volume.

18. See Chapters IX to XII on foreign relations in this volume. Note especially Mao's frustrations during the Korean War and U.S. and Soviet attitudes toward Taiwan.

peror. We shall return to these and other speculative ideas more fully in Chapter V.

In the meantime, suffice it to point out at this juncture why Mao's political success in 1949-57 brought him to the brink of a disaster that was really his own making. Mao chose to focus his big economic push—a "Great Leap Forward"—on increasing the production of steel and food grains, which were to him symbols of industrial and agricultural production. He chose to do so by mobilizing the *entire* population, whether already employed or not, to form work teams of varying sizes in urban areas as well as villages to produce "steel" by traditional methods of making pig iron. At the same time, he reorganized China's new collective farms into even larger units or communes. Entire peasant families were placed in a labor pool of *work brigades* and *teams* under the command of the commune's communist cadres. The traditional family farms as production units were replaced and the units made up by farm workers who would devote full time to farming and whatever other activity the commune cadres saw fit to assign to them. Payments for the workers were almost entirely in the form of food and living support.

The commune thus became a new social unit of organizing life and work. The resultant intensive labor input was meant to increase food production whereas the new form of communal distribution was regarded as a step toward the communist model of distribution, "to each according to need." As was to be expected, the system destroyed incentive, wasted materials, produced sub-standard products, and in food production actually brought about a sharp decline because the cadres directing production were not experienced farmers, and the production targets were continually decreed from above.

What made the outcome even worse was a total failure on the part of the yes-men under Mao and his lieutenants at successively lower levels to supply the autocrat with correct and timely information. News of failure in crop yield and metal production were withheld. High yield reports were fabricated. By the time the principal fall crop of 1958 and the early crop of 1959 were harvested, the die had been cast. Food reserves were exhausted and hungry people went about the country looking for food. Since people were afraid to tell Mao the truth, and he fell victim to lack of timely and accurate information on the devastating effects of his own policy.

Challenges to Mao from the Mountain Resort (Lushan)

Peng Dehuai sent his findings on the accelerated socialization program to Mao in a personal memorandum of ten thousand words. His became the first salvo of open criticism of Mao's nation-wide policy from among many senior CCP members. An earlier challenge to Mao, branded by the latter as an anti-Party conspiracy, had been brought up in February 1955 in discussions on socialization[19] before the Central Committee when Mao's prestige was still very much on the rise. This earlier hushed-up affair centered around Gao Gang and Rao Shushi (Jao Shu-shih) who were accused of indulging in factionalism in an attempt to split the Party and to take its leadership away from Mao. The accusation was made during the fourth session of the Communist Party's Central Committee in February 1954. A decision of the Central Committee, presumably first adopted by the Politburo, resolved to expel both Gao and Rao from the Party. But it was not until more than a year later that a National Conference of Party Representatives was able to listen to Deng Xiaoping's report on the matter. Deng also informed his 1955 audience that even after being confronted with the accusations and evidence arrayed against him, Gao refused to confess and bow to the Party's dictum. The delayed report of 1955 then stated that Gao had the audacity to commit suicide *as a gesture of defiance*.[20] The Gao-Rao challenge, or, more precisely, Mao's perception of it, is instructive in interpreting subsequent events in China and the CCP's intra-Party politics.

Gao was in Shaanxi when Mao's remnant troops arrived at the end of the Long March. Upon the surrender of Japan, Gao was sent to Manchuria along with Lin Biao, Peng Zhen, Chen Yun, and others to secure the territory for the Communists. Later Gao was made head of the Regional (Northeast) Party Committee as well as Regional Administration. He was on familiar terms with Soviet representatives in Manchuria, then the focal point of Soviet-PRC relations, and with Soviet aid to China. In 1953 he was recalled to Beijing as head of the new Economic Planning Commission. He was then accused of trying to line up co-conspirators and of succeeding in securing the cooperation of Rao Shushi, who held a com-

---

19. See the CCP Congress resolution of March 31, 1955 on the anti-Party alliance of Gao Gang and Rao Shushi. *Zhonggong Dangshi Cankao Ziliao* [*Reference Materials on CCP Party History*] (Beijing: People's Publishers, 1979), Vol. 8.

20. Presumably to kill himself without confessing was to deny the Party the satisfaction of being always in the right. In practice the chance was that Gao was killed in the same way as many others had been killed, namely, by Kang Sheng's agents.

parable position in Shanghai, the Party and administrative center of East China. Gao and Jao, together with others of lesser importance, were then subjected to the above-mentioned kangaroo trial in 1954.

Nikita Khrushchev reported in his memoir[21] that Stalin talked to Mao about Gao, noting especially that from what Gao had told Soviet representatives, relations between the two countries were not as harmonious as Mao had made it out to be. Khrushchev claimed further that Stalin in fact betrayed Gao and this was why Mao recalled him to Beijing and why later Gao was liquidated. In our view, Mao's reasons for being suspicious of Gao were probably a great deal more complex. Fear of a regional alliance between Gao from Manchuria and Rao from Shanghai, the two principal economic bases of China, might have conjured up memories of historical instances of over-ambitious, strong regional satraps turning against the emperor. Suspicions against Gao as a potential Soviet sympathizer may have added to the decision to eliminate him in so drastic a manner. Going through the charade of expelling Gao from the Communist Party was done in a sense to supply a post-facto justification for dealing with Gao as a "counter-revolutionary" deserving the severest sentence.

With the Gao-Rao affair in mind, one can detect points of resemblance when Marshal Peng presented Mao with his findings on the Three Red Banners. Peng had also just returned from a tour abroad, and had visited with Tito, who subsequently served as the object of Mao's invectives that were really meant for Khrushchev. Mao was suspicious of Peng's relations with other CP leaders. When Mao called the Lushan conference together, he could even have been thinking of a repeat performance of the 1954-55 meetings that made short shrift of Gao Gang and Rao Shushi. Zhou Enlai had obviously sensed what Mao was planning and absented himself from the meetings until the initial storm had passed and Peng's fate had been decided.[22]

Events in 1958-59 occurred in such close succession that it would have been hard to separate the interwoven strands leading from contrary sources to their respective opposite and even unexpected outcomes. When the Communist Party leaders of the Central Committee, which was elected by the Eighth Party Congress (chaired by Mao), met at an "expanded meeting" of the Politburo

21. Khrushchev suggested that Stalin deliberately betrayed Gao Gang to Mao. See *Khrushchev Remembers* (New York: Little, Brown & Co., 1976), p. 244.

22. See the introductory essay by Ting Wang in his 1970 volume cited in note 25 *infra*. See also Yan and Gao, *infra* note 29.

at the summer resort Beidaihe in August 1958, they apparently did adopt a resolution to establish communes that were ideologically and organizationally one step ahead of the "advanced" form of the farm cooperative. However, as Peng Dehuai later claimed,[23] the intent was only to set up the framework of the commune, not to push it forward as Mao did. Apparently, strenuous intra-Party opposition necessitated continual debate at two follow-up conferences at Zhengzhou and Wuchang respectively.

It was at the latter session (the Sixth Plenum of the Central Committee) at the end of November 1958 that certain issues on the people's commune were outwardly resolved. But the drift of the discussion fell far short of Mao's objectives and there was in consequence a slowdown of the program. At the same meeting, Mao also offered to resign as Head of State while retaining his positions and prerogatives in the Party. But it was not until the Seventh Plenum of the same Central Committee that Liu Shaoqi was made officially Head of State. Thus if Mao had originally called the Lushan conference (the Eighth Plenum) to deal with Peng's "rebellion," the outcome was far from being one-sided.

On the one hand, Peng was soon replaced by Lin Biao as head of the armed forces. On the other hand, Liu's position in the administrative apparatus seemed to be confirmed. The latter development enabled Liu and his followers to institute a slower socialization pace and even a partial reversal of Mao's more extreme policies. Mao's ability, however, to retain his authority within the Party—perhaps especially as head of its Military Commission, which controlled high military appointments—enabled him to plot the subsequent attacks on the internal structure of the Communist Party itself.

Therefore, it is no exaggeration to say that the 1959 Lushan meeting was a landmark which made the post-1959 political dictatorship in China intrinsically a dualistic system: (1) the orthodox dictatorship of the Communist Party which temporarily faded as the Cultural Revolution gradually unfolded in 1965-71, ending with the "flight of Lin Biao" in 1971 and the short-lived ascendance of the radical Gang of Four; and, (2) the political dictatorship of Mao Zedong himself which more and more resembled that of a personal struggle by an emperor who saw himself being pushed aside by powerful court officials. Both dictatorships came face-to-face with a dilemma in 1976—Mao's death. Mao's personal dictatorship finally

---

23. See Ting Wang, *infra* note 25.

came to an end when his widow, the dowager Jiang Qing (Chiang Ch'ing), was overthrown in a typical palace coup involving the "betrayal" of her praetorian guards led by Wang Dongxing, a co-conspirator.

The Party's dictatorship which Mao had so strenuously shattered could not be automatically passed on to a single successor or a well-balanced group because no single person then alive and in a position of authority to take over had enough prestige, power and legitimacy. Zhou Enlai had died half a year earlier than Mao. Lin Biao had died mysteriously. Liu Shaoqi had met his end in a "secret prison" eight years before Mao. Deng Xiaoping had just been banished "for the last time." Hua Guofeng's claim to be Mao's successor was based on an informal scrap of paper seeming to register Mao's ease of mind if Hua were in charge. Hence, given the history of the Communist Party's factional struggles, its authority in the people's eyes after Mao's death had to be built up anew, through performance in handling the nation's affairs. Appealing to the Party's performance before 1957, sometimes even referring obliquely to Sun Yat-sen, founder of the KMT, probably in the light of the one-time KMT-CCP "cooperation," in order to have a minimal claim to historical continuity, also has been deemed necessary.

II. THE CULTURAL REVOLUTION

Prelude

Mao's push to accelerate his program of communization and "socialist industrial development" went into high gear in the latter part of 1958 apparently at a time that disrupted the principal fall food crop of 1958 and sowing for the following crop year. Although Mao ceased to be head of State toward the end of 1958 following even more undeniable evidence of failure of his policy, Liu Shaoqi did not formally take over that administrative post until August 1959. Even if Liu had been able to act effectively and immediately, it would not have been possible to reverse the consequences of the previous disastrous harvests and the damages done to the farm land, its fertility and the agricultural system. The lasting economic effects will be discussed in a later chapter. We wish to point to the time lag at this juncture in order to draw the reader's attention to the impact of delayed and inaccurate information on the real conditions in a country where correct information, even if available, is too often concealed, deliberately distorted and delayed.

Mao was forced into a tactical political retreat after late 1959. A new farm policy was more or less instituted and a partial return to the pre-commune state of affairs took place as a result of the political compromise. However, emergency regulations to undo the damage caused by Mao's communes were issued in November 1960 only and then again in May 1961. Correspondingly, parallel efforts to slow down overzealousness in the non-agricultural sector followed the revised policy in agriculture. But by the time of the Tenth Plenum of the CCP Central Committee in September 1962, the Liuist journey of backpedaling in effect came to a halt.

Mao's Short-Term Fall from Absolute Power

Although Mao was titular head of the Chinese Communist Party, Liu Shaoqi was not far behind. Liu was the Party's Deputy Chairman and Deng Xiaoping was its Secretary-General. The "Liu-Deng team" was able to put some of its own men in the critical areas of influence, namely, in (1) information and propaganda, (2) security and the military, and (3) party administration and organization. Mao at first kept a low profile and may have deliberately feigned disinterest. He did so partly by staying out of Beijing, the capital , traveling around the country in his special armored train, stopping wherever he chose to renew contact and influence. His means of transportation and erratic train schedule apparently had the side-benefit of making assassination attempts, even by the military, inordinately difficult.[24]

As we can tell from the support Liu and Deng gave to Mao until the "Great Leap" and communization policies proved to be undeniable failures, there was no deliberate attempt on their part to reestablish capitalism in China at that time. Deng's staunch effort twenty years later (in the 1980s) to hold on to (1) "socialist thought," (2) the Party's "proletarian dictatorship" and (3) Maoist "legitimacy" was, therefore, a further confirmation of his real personal belief. This may well explain why they had not gone further toward "revisionism" or capitalism's restoration as Mao had publicly asserted.

But why did Liu, Deng and others keep Mao as Party Chairman? His past glory and prestige probably saved him because his outright removal might have weakened the Party's claim to invaria-

---

24. See Li Zhisui, *Mao Zedong Siren Yisheng Huiyilu* [*The Private Life of Chairman Mao*] (Taipei: China Times Publishing Co., 1994), Part III, pp. 417-598 and Part II, pp. 183-416.

ble "correctness" in policy and 100% foresight. If some non-Maoists thought that being made "Chairman" was in effect "retirement," Mao obviously did not think so and a dramatic turn of events was soon to unfold.

The Tenth Central Committee Plenum in September 1962 was an occasion for Mao to return to the subject of class struggle and to use the appearance of income differences among farmers as a sign of the re-emergence of capitalism and class differences. Mao in effect identified income differences as class differences. To some of Mao's opponents in economic policy, warning against "revisionism" might seem to be no more than an ideological foible the Chairman liked to indulge in and could therefore be tolerated, as it were, just to humor the old man. To Mao, who was far more cunning than they, this was a theme he could exploit with great political effect. By staking out a logically extreme position of requiring any increase, statistically, in *per capita* income to be a real equal increase, he could in a sense maintain his ideological purity, perhaps even founding a new orthodoxy of Utopian Communism. For the idea of "continuing revolution" would follow logically from treating every growth of income inequality as a justification of renewed revolutionary struggle against "exploitation." At the same time, Mao's growing quarrels with Khrushchev and the Soviet Union probably helped him politically at home if he could tie the stigma of "revisionism," an epithet he used to describe Khrushchev, to Liu Shaoqi at home.

Soviet advisors on aid projects in China were recalled by Khrushchev in mid-1959 when the PRC was in the throes of its economic crisis as a result of the Great Leap aftermath. Soviet aid withdrawal was decidedly a part of Khrushchev's pressure tactics at that time. The sparring between the two countries is discussed in greater detail in Chapters IX-XI. While the departure of Soviet advisors was visible to many Chinese, the ordinary Chinese in China probably did not know that the Central Committee of the Soviet Communist Party actually wrote in May 1960 to invite Mao to visit the Soviet Union "for a rest,"[25] picking up on Mao's pretense that he had to give up work because of ill health.

---

25. In a letter dated May 12, 1962, the Central Committee of the Soviet Communist Party invited Mao Zedong to visit the Soviet Union for a "rest," apparently in view of his alleged health condition. This specific invitation was mentioned in the March 30, 1963 communication of the CPSU Central Committee to its counterpart in the CCP. See Ting Wang in his monumental volume *Chungkung Wenko Yuntung ti Tsuchih yu*

The invitation to Mao was clearly intended as a test to see how Mao was doing in the Chinese power struggle and simultaneously to put pressure on Mao, and on the Chinese Party leadership, to toe the Soviet line. Subsequently, the PRC was required to repay Soviet loans through the 1960s during the worst years of the Chinese economy. In Mao's eyes, Soviet actions were not only hostile to the PRC; the Soviet Union could also be giving Mao's opponents in the CCP additional ammunition to aim at Mao. In view of the role the Soviet Union and Stalin played in trying to manipulate the Chinese Communist leadership, might Mao not see a genuine conspiracy involving Liu Shaoqi and others whose policies were truly "revisionist" to a degree and who were obviously against him?

The real full story behind Mao's launching a "revolution" against some of the Party leaders as well as the regular Party apparatus may become known some day when both the relevant Soviet and Chinese archives are finally opened. (The Soviet files might actually become available sooner than many scholars dare to hope.) But it is certainly plausible to hypothesize a genuine belief on Mao's part that there was a revisionist conspiracy against him. There was not too much Mao could do to discredit his opponents in the Chinese Party immediately after 1958-60 when the misfortunes China suffered were indisputably more his own doing than theirs. But by 1965 when Zhou Enlai could again report on the completion of the economic "adjustments" after the three years of "natural misfortunes," Mao was ready to mount his preemptive strike in counterattack.

Not the least formidable problem anyone in Mao's position had now to face was how to devise an avenue of attack aimed at bringing down the leadership of a stupendous organization such as the Chinese Communist Party. A second question was why did Mao choose to launch the attack when he did?

Key Ingredients of Mao's Success against Liu

While Mao eventually succeeded in bringing down the PRC's head of State and many key members of the latter's government and party apparatus, he did so by acting as if he were "cleansing" the Party of usurpers. He approached this task by acting as the duly elected head of the Communist Party. Yet at the same time, he ac-

Jenshih Wen-t'i [*Organization and Personnel in the Cultural Revolution Movement of Communist China*] (Hongkong: Contemporary Research Institute, 1970), p. 21, note 6.

ted as if he had been an outsider. How did he accomplish such an extraordinary task?

In an expanded meeting of the Central Committee on May 18, 1966, Marshal Lin Biao who had taken over the Defense portfolio from Peng Dehuai after the latter's confrontation with Mao in 1959, asked to address the group on the alleged "revisionist" (read anti-Mao) tendencies of major figures in the then still Liuist government.[26] The marshal spoke expansively on how even a ruling Communist Party could lose power, normally an unmentionable subject. He mentioned two possibilities: an open counter-revolutionary challenge and an internal coup within the party. In this connection, Lin spoke of Chairman Mao's concerns about the corrosive influence of individuals holding key positions in the military, in the propaganda, information and communications apparatus, and in the judicial and political branches. Lin Biao mentioned names, including persons who had been under attack from the very beginning of the Cultural Revolution.[27]

The Great Proletarian Cultural Revolution acquired the epithet "cultural" because it began with an attack on a review of a historical play dealing with the dismissal of a high official who dared to criticize an emperor. Furthermore, this political purge was in a sense also aimed at human behavior and the party leaders' value system which interacted with contemporary culture. The playwright, Wu Han, allegedly enjoyed the support of Peng Zhen, then mayor of Beijing. Criticisms and counter-attacks led to an ever-expanding debate. Critics of the play thought that the playwright alluded to Mao as the "emperor" in the play and Peng Dehuai as the dismissed premier. Lin Biao used the Peng case to make several points: that in Marxist theory cultural expressions like plays are part of the superstructure of the social system while the cultural superstructure in turn constitutes a link to the exercise of political power by Party functionaries closely instrumental in exercising State power. In particular, these were the military and persons responsible for security and judicial affairs, including without saying the Party's secret service. Luo Ruiqing (Lo Jui-ch'ing) had been in

26. Both the text of Lin's speech and the Central Committee's written comment, dated four months later on September 22, 1966, can be found in *Chung-kung Yen-chiu* [*Studies on Communist China*] (Taipei: Institute of Communist Chinese Studies, 1970), Vol. IV, No. 5, Documents Section, pp. 123-31.

27. Luo Ruiqin, Lu Dingyi, Yang Shangkun and Peng Zhen were among the names mentioned in the published speech. See *infra* note 29, pp. 124-25.

charge of public security and had been involved with both military intelligence and secret service operations for many years.[28]

By inference, Mao's tactic should be first to appoint his own people in these key positions within the central government, replacing Liu's appointees and others suspected of being "revisionists." To be "revisionist" was to be suspected of being anti-Mao openly, i.e., being only one step away from treason! How was one to know who was a "revisionist" or had been one? Through confession and accusation and denunciation in public meetings and kangaroo courts called together ostensibly by youngsters from schools and colleges on their own who were only out to defend the Chairman and to support him in his fight for communism. This approach was Mao's well practiced and historically successful public agitation and "mass movement" technique. In the past, this tactic was usually used against non-communist authorities by the communists. Mao merely inverted the process by calling upon youngsters, who could be more easily induced to follow him blindly to the point of personal worship, to turn against "usurpers" within the party.

The "innocent" students and others—Mao's Red Guards whom he received periodically during the Cultural Revolution[29] in audiences at Tiananmen—thus became pawns in a widely trumpeted (by the controlled media) series of attacks against Party bureaucrats who, having allegedly drifted away from the true faith, should be brought back to the truth pronounced by him *ex cathedra*. The Red Guards were directed against specific targets—individuals and government offices—by experienced agitators and Maoist functionaries in "Cultural Revolution" groups which very soon became semi-official institutions themselves, virtually a second Party Central and government. They were able to defy the regular police and other government authorities because Maoist members in many institutions had seized control earlier.

The military under Lin Biao and the security apparatus, apparently under Kang Sheng's men, were both openly and covertly providing direction and support. The interminable accusations and self-criticism meetings were carried on at all levels of government and the attacks became both physical and verbal, literally day and night.

---

28. According to the memoir of Mao's personal physician, Li Zhisui, Mao's roaming armored train turned out to be "bugged" by agents working for his opponents, which could have implicated Luo.

29. Red Guard groups often engaged in armed fights with one another. For details see Yan Jiaqi and Gao Gao, *Chung-kuo Wen-ko Shih-nien Shih* [*A Decade of Cultural Revolution*] (Taipei: Institute of Communist Chinese Studies, 1988).

From time to time, Mao, Lin, Jiang Qing (Mao's wife) and others assumed an openly leadership role. Some of Mao's reviews of Red Guards took place at Tiananmen with pomp and circumstance, deliberately to enhance the Chairman's personality cult. Regional and provincial governments became affected all over China in the same way. There were open armed fights.[30]

Liu's Fall: Effects on the PRC Government

What might seem at that time to outside observers as an orderless, haphazard, mad assault on the Communist Party and governmental establishment nevertheless accomplished some of its original purposes. There were, of course, unintended results which were a great deal more than mere side effects. Furthermore, the principal purpose of the Cultural Revolution turmoil was the defeat, in Mao's eyes, of Liu Shaoqi's challenge to Mao's political authority and Party leadership. But others, like Lin Biao and Jiang Qing, as well as other members of the "Gang of Four," who were intended to be Mao's political tools, also had their own agendas to pursue and scores to settle. When the effects of the latter's actions were added to the Great Proletarian Cultural Revolution's core purposes that motivated Mao, they gave rise to consequences more far-reaching than Mao and his followers—one might add, and their opponents—could have ever imagined. But first let us consider some of the original more narrowly focused purposes.

Liu Shaoqi, the arch-"revisionist," or "China's Khrushchev" in Maoist jargon, was brought down by Mao through sheer persecution without the restraint of either law or human decency. Step-by-step, Liu's aides were eliminated from positions of power and influence; Liu himself was harassed, tormented and subjected to increasing indignities, as were his wife and children under conditions that were not conducive to carefully calculated and patient responses, although Liu demonstrated great ability in both respects. Liu was progressively isolated from those potentially able to help him. By casting the net of the purge so wide, and making the consequences so dire in terms of life, employment and personal relations, the attackers effectively discouraged Liu's sympathizers from coming forward. Liu died a prisoner at Kaifeng (K'ai-feng) to which city he had been removed— when the Sino-Soviet border dispute reached a peak in 1969—on the pretext of keeping Liu out of the reach of

30. Probably the most notorious case of armed conflict in which some faction heads were held hostage by others occurred in Wuhan. See Yan Jiaqi, *id.*

potential seizure by unfriendly interests. Before his removal from Beijing, he had been expelled from the Party at the end of 1968. The act of expulsion, like that of Gao Gang and Rao Shushi, was tantamount to making Liu a "counterrevolutionary," a pariah and non-person to be treated as an enemy deserving no pity.[31]

Liu's aides in charge of communications, the media and the security machine, Lu Ding-yi and Lu's wife, together with Luo Ruiqing, were among the first of those targeted for self-accusation, confession, dismissal, imprisonment and exile. On the other hand, not all the principal political enemies of Mao and those of his chief minions met with death. Peng Dehuai, who triggered the post-1959 criticisms of Mao, and thus was responsible for the Chairman's venom, was a rival of Lin Biao. Peng, however, survived demotion and ill treatment at and outside Red Guard sessions. He did not die until 1974 when Lin Biao himself was already dead and Lin's name was in disgrace. Or, take the case of Luo Ruiqing, who lost a leg from improper surgical treatment, reportedly at the direction of his tormentors, and lived through the decade of purge and purgatory.

On the other hand, He Long, one of Mao's generals, fell victim, it seems, to Lin Biao's wrath. Wang Guangmei (Wang Kuangmei), the PRC's one-time First Lady, was a primary target not only because she was Liu Shaoqi's wife, but possibly even more, as rumors had it, because public acclaim and news photographs of her when she accompanied her husband on a state visit to Southeast Asia made her a target of Jiang Qing's wrath. The active role of Lin Biao's wife in the persecution of Liu supplied another source of this convoluted conflict of personal animosity and political venom.

III. AFTER LIU SHAOQI

The Post-Liu Cultural Revolution

The downfall of Liu Shaoqi did not immediately bring the Cultural Revolution to an end. Mao, in fact, found himself in a no less disagreeable position than before. Ten years had passed since 1959 when Mao saddled the Liuists who were his partial replacements with the aftermath of a bankrupt and irrational economic policy. Liu, his deputy in the Party, had openly disagreed with him and pressed him hard to retreat. In 1969, Liu was no more, but Mao now had a deputy in the person of Lin Biao, the victorious general in Manchuria who had also played a major role in taking over the

---

31. See Yan and Gao, *supra* note 29.

Beijing-Tianjin coastal triangle in North China, thus opening the heartland of the Nationalists to the PLA. Lin was also the commander of a then newly-formed 151st division of the famous Communist Eighth Route Army in the days of the war with Japan (1937-45). He became Mao's Deputy in the Party at the end of 1968 during the Twelfth Plenum of the Eighth Central Committee.

Lin was then not only in support of Mao but he had been the promoter of "Mao Zedong thought," purporting to make Mao a glorious, omniscient leader both of China and of Marxism-Leninism in the world. In short, Lin was the one person who did most in making Mao the prophet of a new Maoist fundamentalist cult. Unfortunately, Lin happened also to be the leader of China's armed forces and he had helped Mao in eliminating all old-line leaders who might contest his second-highest ranking status. Lin's troops and officers were now stationed in most government offices, regionally and in Beijing. Lin was simultaneously handling affairs at the Party's nerve center, the Military Affairs Commission. Lin Biao had become too much of a threat in Mao's eyes. Unfortunately, unlike Zhou En-lai, Lin Biao did not seem to know how not to be second to Mao.

When Mao tried to remove Liu Shaoqi, he had both Lin and Jiang Qing's Cultural Revolution Group at his command as helpers. The Red Guards were directed by both and were physically supported and later controlled by Lin's military. For Mao to rid himself of Lin would be more difficult.

Information is still scanty today nearly one quarter century later. But a few chronological facts are indisputable. First, in April 1969, a new Ninth Party Congress was at last called—it was the first since 1956—and Lin Biao became the Deputy Chairman of the CCP. Lin's status as heir-apparent to Mao was also written into the CCP constitution. Second, at the Second Plenum of the new CCP Central Committee a year later, Lin Biao and Chen Boda (Ch'en Po-ta), one of Mao's original Cultural Revolution Group members, proposed the restoration of the head of State's post as a governmental position. The post had stood vacant since Liu Shaoqi's removal. This proposal was struck down by Mao who might have suspected it as the first step to ease him out of power. The 1969 Second Plenum met at Lushan and virtually marked the end of a decade since Peng Dehuai's confrontation with Mao.

The Lin Biao Mystery

Thoroughly convincing details on events at the "Mao court" during the short period between August 1970 and September 13, 1971, are still wanting. Journalists and historians probably will have to wait patiently for the opening of relevant undoctored files in Beijing (if they exist) and elsewhere. But one confirmed fact was the crash of a PRC Trident plane on the night of September 13, 1971, in Mongolia, and the bodies were said to include Lin Biao's wife and son and, according to the Chinese side, also that of Lin Biao himself. As of this writing (1996), there exist several variants of the Lin Biao story[32]. One claims that Lin planned a military coup against Mao and then attempted to flee when the plot was discovered. The British Trident carrying him and his family crashed in Mongolia either because it had run out of fuel or because it was shot down. A variant of this version had Mao deliberately ordering Zhou Enlai not to have Lin's plane shot down but the plane nevertheless crashed when it tried to land. A second version suggested that Lin was killed in China while his family was in the fatal flight attempting to escape. But this version cannot explain why Lin's body was found at the crash site if the body was correctly identified. Ambiguity remains. There is no plausible and clear explanation of the role of the Jiang Qing group, if any, in the mystery. Mao's role is even more ambiguous. Zhou Enlai, on the other hand, was clearly implicated because he supposedly was monitoring Lin's plot and subsequent flight. Another vignette indirectly linking the Russians to Lin can be found in Chapter XI.

A Vacant Throne and a Failed New Orthodoxy

Mao Zedong died barely five years after Lin. But he was unable to plan a personal succession that would uphold his own dictatorship a few years longer, through the Hua Guofeng period until Deng Xiaoping could take over. But Mao's idea of a perpetual class

32. Part II of Yan and Gao, *id.*, contains a full account of Lin Biao's alleged plot against Mao. It follows essentially the description circulated from presumably unconfirmed official sources code-named "A summary of the 571 engineering plan." One somewhat fictionalized account was provided by Yao Ming-le, which suggested that Lin was killed on the ground. Other versions, including one published by *Newsweek*, all repeated the official version of Lin's death in the plane crash. Apparently no one has explained what led to the plane crash. But according to Dr. Li Zhisui, Mao's private physician, Lin's Trident plane ran out of fuel because the party did not have time to take on enough fuel before the flight. In this version the entire family died in the plane crash. Li Zhisui, *supra* note 24, Part III, pp. 514-20.

struggle and of continuing revolution could not be accepted by enough Chinese Communists to last beyond mid-1977, the date of Deng's return from exile. What may yet happen to the Communist dictatorship, after Deng, remains again to be seen. Human mortality precludes an immortal dictator, yet a dictator can never plan a smooth succession after his own passing. Herein lies a hopeless dilemma for dictatorships.

Unintended Effects on PRC Polity

There were other serious unintended effects of the Cultural Revolution beyond the Lin Biao mystery which few of those involved in the intra-Party struggle Mao unleashed realized at the time.

The succession of Party leaders and of lower echelon cadres falling victim to the purge meant a numerical loss to the natural succession of persons of experience and ability who could move up the normal career and generational ladder in Chinese politics. There were inevitably fewer qualified persons to take over when the Mao dictatorship ended who might have made an easier run of succession, even from the very narrow Communist Party perspective of maintaining its own dictatorship. Not the least of the effects was the gap created from 1965 to the mid-1970s in the supply of technical and other trained personnel and of reliable information needed for a more orderly resumption of the country's development and advance planning for it.

The inevitably increasing role played by Lin Biao and his military followers and troops led to a virtual take-over of governmental machinery in most aspects of the country's life. Given Lin Biao's final elimination, this particular phase of the Cultural Revolution offered us a foretaste of what could well have become a military dictatorship. For a time at least, the Communist Party was barely in command of the gun; the gun came very close to controlling the Party. At the time of this writing (summer 1996) is there a lesson to be learned in the perhaps not too distant future when the present PRC government faces the possibility of a more radical change? Will the latest brush with military dictatorship be sufficient to warn the Chinese people off another ordeal at the end of which they could be even less lucky?

Did Zhou Enlai Save China from Mao or Was It Patriotism Truly Misplaced?

Next, one should give thought to the kind of people who helped Mao's dictatorship by keeping the country afloat even as the Chairman of the Communist Party struggled to regain supreme power by removing his real and potential rivals. There is no doubt that Zhou Enlai should receive a great share of the credit, or blame, for keeping the country together, but under Mao's leadership. Or does the last sentence contain an irreconcilable contradiction?

Zhou died in early 1976. He had engineered the return of Deng Xiaoping to government service in January 1975. Upon Zhou's death, Deng was again ordered out by Mao on the advice of the Jiang Qing group, who now held sway after the Tenth Party Congress in 1973, although Mao was ostensibly still Party Chairman. Had Zhou lived longer, the post-Mao period of Communist China could have been quite different.

However, Zhou certainly helped keep Mao's dictatorship in China longer than many thought it had any call to be. He was extremely successful by avoiding the position of ever becoming Mao's deputy or, in any other way becoming a threat to Mao in the latter's eyes. Yet he was to the last able to serve as Mao's faithful adjutant, making himself very useful and reliable to Mao, that is, as far as a suspicious person like Mao would ever make himself dependent upon any other person. As a man of many parts, Zhou was able to give the People's Republic a world image in its early years, and to steer Mao to a rapprochement with the United States in 1971-72, which probably saved the regime from an even more perilous future. Yet one needs to bear in mind that allegedly all final orders of execution or ultimate disposal of a major opponent (like Liu Shaoqi) had to be passed on to Mao for approval through Zhou. As a conduit of such orders, Zhou therefore made himself a guardian of many secrets, which could be safe only as long as he was always a really indispensable aide. But this also made Zhou an "accomplice" of Mao's worst deeds. One wonders what was the real story between Mao and Zhou ever since their Tsun-yi tête-à-tête on the Long March.

Mao was an avid reader of Chinese history. The historical examples cited by Lin Biao in 1966 were unquestionably familiar to Mao. Was the killing of Han Xin (Han Hsin), one of the first Han Emperor's great generals, by Empress Lü a parallel to the fate of Lin Biao? Was Zhou Enlai a near-parallel to Chang Liang (Zhang Liang), the self-effacing advisor of the same emperor? Zhang Liang retired from public life and preserved personal integrity. Zhou's historical appraisal must still await at least the opening of many official files and other records. Will such an event ever take place? In January 1975, Zhou managed to bring Deng Xiaoping back to the Central Committee as vice-chairman. Inasmuch as Deng was next only to Liu Shaoqi as the earlier chief "revisionist" targets of Mao's wrath, it would be interesting to know how Zhou accomplished this maneuver in view of the mutual dislike the Jiang Qing group and Deng had for each other and what role, if any, Mao at this stage of his physical decline still could consciously play. However, as fate would have it, Zhou died in February 1976, and only one month later, Deng was again forced out, this time not to return until one year later, in July 1977. Had Zhou lived longer, one wonders whether Hua Guofeng would have been able to take over upon Mao's death in mid-1976, albeit only for a few years.

In two respects, the Mao dictatorship in China exceeded that of other Chinese historical periods in harshness. First, it was all-embracing and virtually succeeded in encompassing all aspects of public and private life and human activity. This is fully illustrated in a 1988 historical and analytical account of the human rights environment in the PRC through the 1940s to the 1980s.[33] Second, unlike military dictatorships that hold people down by coercion and are satisfied with their obedience, Mao was not satisfied until he thought he had made converts and fanatic believers of all who obeyed him. The dictatorship he built was not only totalitarian in the physical sense, it was also intellectual.

As peasant revolutionaries, the early rebel leaders and troops were often unlettered. Some prided themselves as fighters and many distrusted the underground urban contingents who lived for long periods in government-controlled areas, often finding shelter under foreign jurisdiction—in foreign concessions in the 1920s and 1930s and in Hongkong before December 1941 and after World War II. The fact that many leading cadres like Liu Shaoqi, Bo Ibo and Peng Zhen worked for long periods under such conditions[34] was used against them by the radicals during the Cultural Revolution. During different periods of the Communist Party's development, the Soviet Union was a source of ideological and political training and technical preparation (in intelligence work, for exam-

33. See *supra* note 2.
34. These individuals were released from prison in 1936 by the KMT government.

ple)[35] for many Chinese Party members. This background was often reflected in intra-Party struggles for power, which sometimes took place in terms of the Stalin-Trotskyist division. There was thus a division between the foreign-returnees group and the homegrown Chinese communists.

One frequently overlooked fact is that PRC leaders like Zhou Enlai, Deng Xiaoping and Nie Rongzhen all spent time in Europe in work-study programs and supplied the core of post-World War II Communist Party leaders able to handle foreign activities. Many of the recent publications bear witness to their earlier wanderings. Mao was an exception. He was not a foreign-trained Marxist and apparently read communist literature only in translation. But he came "through field work" in guerrilla warfare; he was an avid reader and prolific writer, unquestionably a self-taught master of Chinese political history. A psychoanalyst might say that he probably was looked down upon by some academics in Peiping (later renamed Peking, still later Beijing) when he spent a great deal of time reading in university libraries there. Without a university degree or diploma and not being a "returned student," he could easily have developed a complex that could have evolved into a contempt for many "intellectuals" which, when combined with the unlettered party cadres in positions of power, could lead to a deadly policy for China's intellectuals.

On the other hand, the CCP could not do without intellectuals—a loose term which in Chinese includes all literate, relatively educated people, not just academics and scholars—and some should have been knowledgeable enough to think for themselves. When in opposition, the CCP needed them to expand their party's influence and popular appeal. Immediately after 1949, intellectuals provided support from non-communists. The more educated had to be recruited for modernization and technological and educational development in the widest sense. But they were also the most critical minded, being used to thinking for themselves, and they were the hardest to convert.

The contradictory attitudes Communist Party members have had, even in the post-Mao period, explain why the Party's policy toward Chinese intellectuals was inconsistent, volatile and basically unfriendly in practice. Under Mao, there were several occasions when intellectuals were singled out as targets of thought control,

---

35. The Chinese CCP leaders who participated in these activities included Kang Sheng and Chen Yun.

investigation, "rectification" and suppression.[36] Starting from the 1942 "rectification" at Yanan, which helped eliminate opponents to Mao within the Party, to the mammoth intra-Party purge during 1966-69 aimed again at Mao's real and imagined "revisionist" opponents, with the 1957 Anti-Rightists drive in between, it was always Mao who tried to eliminate every hint of deviation from his own line of thought.

In capsule form, Mao's basic assumptions were as follows. First, a person's world view was determined by class status and could not be altered except through living as a member of another class. Second, intellectuals were generally of bourgeois origin and born to be slaves of the capitalist class. Third, they could not be absorbed into the working class and had to learn from peasants, farmers and soldiers, who were the core of the revolutionary alliance. Hence, intellectuals periodically had to live like peasants and laborers. This accounted for the idea of sending academics and even Party cadres to tend pigs and cows or plant rice, or to work at hard labor as a part of reeducation and soul-cleansing. A common method of soul-cleansing was to write out one's self-criticism and confessions until one could almost believe the lies that one thought might be acceptable to the group instructed to supervise this continual effort.

The reader may wonder how such mental and physical discipline could be enforced and who would be the enforcers? The answer, as one searches for it, seems always to be the secret police, the protectors of the Party chairman's personal security. In 1942, Kang Sheng was Mao's trusted lieutenant.[37] During the Cultural Revolution, Kang again played a major role.[38] Wang Dongxing, who commanded Mao's praetorian guard and took part in the palace coup overthrowing the Gang of Four, also played a role. In the final analysis, Mao possessed all the dogmatic and repressive traits which he accused the traditional and "feudalistic" Chinese intellectual of possessing. One can well imagine, except in the case of blind faith on the part of some mindless and ignorant teenage Red Guards, who

36. For a full account of Mao's treatment of intellectuals, see Tang Buo, *Chung-kung yü Chih-shih Fen-tze* [*The Chinese Communists and the Intellectuals*] (Taipei: Young Lion Cultural Publishers, 1988), especially pp. 129-307 and 419-72.

37. Kuo Hua-lun, *Chung-kung Shih Lun* [*On CCP History*] (Taipei: East Asia Research Institute Publication, 1971), especially Vol. VI, Chapter 41, pp. 249-92.

38. See John Byron and Robert Pack, *The Claws of the Dragon* (New York: Simon & Schuster, 1992), which contains a full description of Kang Sheng's activities in CCP intelligence.

waved Mao's Red Book during the 1960s or like Boxers who tried to stop bullets with magic, outward obedience could not be dependable. Except when megalomania had the better of him, Mao must have suspected that much of the reverence people had for him might not be real. This may be another reason why the task of consolidating power was for Mao an unending one. The suppression of intellectuals was always the severest when he suspected premeditated organized efforts to topple him. One self-defeating outcome eventually was to blind the Party leadership, including himself, from the effects of their own folly. The Great Leap and the "Third Line" investment program that accompanied the Cultural Revolution, to be discussed in Chapter V, became examples of disasters to which the Party could never fully admit.

CHAPTER IV

PRIORITIES IN ECONOMIC POLICY (1949-1956)

I. ECONOMIC STABILIZATION, GROWTH AND TRANSITION TO SOCIALISM

The Trojan Horse: Coalition and Social Democracy

The CCP professed to be dedicated to the improvement of China's economic well-being under its socialist government. How did it propose to do so? Immediately after the establishment of the new regime, the problem was how to extricate the economy from the morass of the Civil War and the war with Japan. But in the long run, how did Mao's new administration expect to "modernize" China where others had failed?

During the early 1940s, when Mao Zedong was still only the leader of the armed opposition to the Nationalists and when the CCP was making every effort in both Yanan and Chungking to win over the Nationalists' foreign supporters and the young Chinese students as well as the older disillusioned and tired intellectuals, its widely publicized economic program often sounded like that of European social democrats. Even though socialism and the eventual abolition of private property ownership were advocated, these ideas were usually soft-pedaled as ultimate goals that were essentially academic and many years away from realization. Besides, the CCP wanted to make the people it tried to persuade believe that their goals would be attained under a democratic political system with multi-party participation. As a matter of fact, Mao often talked about a coalition government while negotiating with the Nationalists in Chungking. This was precisely what many Allied leaders were considering for postwar Eastern Europe. Hence no one outside China had reason to be alarmed.

Even as late as the mid-1940s when the war in Europe was coming to an end, there was no compelling reason to think seriously of the transformation of China into a society with Mao Zedong in charge. Neither the Chinese population nor the budding political parties thought of a communist regime in postwar China as a practical proposition. Even the intellectuals who cried out for economic and political change instinctively thought in reformist terms. Never did they imagine what was to come in the following decade.

Monetary hyperinflation, which the Nationalist government desperately tried to arrest, became the primary factor that contributed to the disintegration of the Chinese society. But even as the economy disintegrated, long-existing internal political differences, submerged during the Japanese onslaught, were resurfacing. As military defeats aggravated the economic chaos and political disaffection, the power of the central government declined. By mid-1949, the mutually reinforcing adverse factors which had brought down the Nationalists became the economic issues which the Communist Party now had to face itself. They were more imminent than anyone in the CCP could have anticipated. In short, the immediate goals were still monetary stabilization and the rapid restoration of stalled production. Without these preconditions, Mao the new "emperor" and his regime could not hope to consolidate control or even maintain themselves.

But how about the transformation of the Chinese economy to socialism? Was not this the real goal? Would this process really take as many years as Mao and Zhou Enlai in Chungking had led their sympathizers to believe? How about the even longer-term tasks of economic development that might really make China "stand up" in the world as Mao had proclaimed at Tiananmen? Were the new leaders themselves prepared? Could they use advice from the non-communist intellectuals? Was the Soviet Union ready and willing to help? Might the CCP not in time even forget what it had ostensibly fought for? There were no simple answers to these questions.

Extraordinary Success Followed by Monumental Disaster

Broadly speaking, the new regime succeeded within a few years in suppressing hyperinflation and in replacing the Chinese market economy with a chaotic Maoist transition. Almost in the same breath it also proceeded to introduce a far stricter dictatorship in the place of China's prewar loosely authoritarian society. Monetary disinflation was accomplished with revolutionary terror and by fiat. The Korean War provided a background for extraordinary measures under the pretense of nationalism. The First Five-Year Plan (1953-57) was then carried out after the Korean armistice in 1953.

These events were usually chalked up on the positive side of the Chinese Communist Party's scoreboard of success during the first ten years of its rule. Yet during the same first decade and barely eight years after the first Tiananmen celebration in October 1949, Mao's unrealistic and untutored economic policy was to lead China to an unprecedented economic disaster that nearly toppled him. Then, by 1962, after the Communist Party's political fortune had spun around another semi-circle, the resilient Chinese agricultural economy, aided by the less damaged more modern industrial sector, was seemingly again able to resume recovery. The economy also survived the onslaught of the ideological break with the Soviet Union in the early 1960s, highlighted by Khrushehev's peremptory withdrawal of Soviet technical assistance. Chinese technicians were even able to stage their own successful nuclear test in 1964. Once again, however, the Chinese economy was not able to settle down to steady growth.

Incomplete Information and Disinformation

Full details about China's economic development from 1965 to the end of the Cultural Revolution after Mao's death and the overthrow of his radical successors in 1976 have to this day been shrouded in mystery, locked in unopened official files in China, assuming that honest and accurate records of this period existed. How much damage was done in the economy during 1960-76 through turmoil within the Communist Party, the government and the productive enterprises has not yet been fully assessed. A major cause of the information gap was the dismissal of government workers in many state planning, statistical and other economic agencies at all levels, and disruptions of the country's routine operations. Many untrained Party ideologues and military men were employed in central and local government agencies toward the end of the 1960s and in the early 1970s to fill vacancies when regular employees were required to do political penance or were imprisoned outright. Even if knowledgeable bureaucrats stayed in place, they were probably far too frightened to do anything other than repeat existing routines or follow orders whether they made sense or not.

The Party stalwart, Chen Yun, played a most vital and pragmatic role in helping the Chinese Communists seize and consolidate power. Though far less known to the outside world than either Deng Xiaoping or Zhou Enlai, Chen deserves to be compared to both. Before his death in 1994, Chen published a three-volume memoir which contained many excerpts of varying completeness from straight-talking statements he made while addressing bureaucrats and high Party cadres on both political and economic matters covering the entire thirty-year period 1956-85. But Chen was completely silent during 1963-76.[1] One surmises that he probably was too vigorous in opposing Mao's break with Khrushchev and feared the serious economic consequences of over acceleration of defense construction. For a loquacious person of wide experience and unquestionable loyalty to the CCP, Chen's silence in these perilous years undoubtedly was at least in part by choice.[2]

But there were perhaps times when even Chen might not have known enough about what actually went on. The arrest during the Cultural Revolution purge of Bo Ibo, a long-time collaborator of Chen and head of the National Economic Commission in charge of the implementation of the annual economic plans, was another example of the disruption of economic administration by the radical Maoists and by Lin Biao's military cohort. As we shall see below and in the next chapter, there was disinformation on top of misinformation, not only for foreign consumption, but even for the leadership.

The Soviet Union's Mixed Roles

Unlike the Soviet economic system, which fell into disarray with the dissolution of the USSR in 1991, Beijing's initial communist government succeeded in maintaining some control in spite of its weakened central government after June 1989. Thus while some of the unbelievably poor conditions of the Soviet civilian economy have become known in the West during the 1990s, the same cannot be said of the degree of information disclosure on the PRC economy in its entirety outside the Special Economic Zones and some urban coastal areas.

The PRC economy and the Chinese Communist Party's control of the country both benefited and suffered from the Soviet experience. Learning from Lenin's NEP (New Economic Policy) decidedly helped Beijing in its initial economic stabilization. The Soviet

---

1. See *Chen Yun Wen Xuan (1956-1985)* [*Chen Yun's Selected Writings*] (Beijing: People's Publishers, 1986), edited by the CCP Central Documentation Editorial Board (*Zhonggong Zhongyang Wenxian Bianji Weiyuanhui*). There was a gap between March 7, 1962 and March 13, 1977, five months after the toppling of the Gang of Four, Mao's radical successors.

2. Chen's experiences in the Chinese Communist Party included service in the "underground party," personnel and organizational work, training in Moscow, and close collaboration with Moscow during the early postwar period in Manchuria as one of Mao's advance men. He is of course better known as the PRC's "economic czar" until he fell silent in the early 1960s.

impact on the subsequent collectivization of farm land and nationalization of private business during the First Five-Year Plan period was far less obvious. It is hard to say how much Stalinist central planning techniques contributed positively to the Chinese planners' success, despite Mao's idiosyncrasies, in avoiding total economic collapse during the years of Mao's irrational economic experimentation (1958-61) and Maoist-inspired purges and political power grabs in 1965-76.

What might have happened to the Chinese economy if Liu Shaoqi had retained political control after 1963 when Chen Yun fell silent, or if Liu had been skillful (or ruthless) enough to outwit Mao in 1966-67 is an intriguing question. Would the inherent shortcomings of the centralist planning system based on Marxist economic policies have eventually caught up with the PRC economy? Once consumer demand and the use of resources in production had reached a certain level of complexity, would the PRC economy have sustained an increasing military demand for defense needs, as happened to the Soviet economy? Was the investment drive dictated by Mao's domestic and foreign policies, which he tried to push through regardless of their disruptions of the rest of the economy, at the heart of the PRC's economic failures? These points will have to be addressed later in this and the next chapters.

II. MODERNIZATION: A GOAL SHARED WITH THE NON-COMMUNIST PAST

Two Missed Opportunities: the Viceroy of Kuangtung and Kuanghsi; the 1911 Revolution

Those Chinese born after the resurfacing of Deng Xiaoping at the end of the 1970s[3] may well think of Deng as the originator of the slogan of "modernization" as a national goal. Deng called for the modernization of industry, agriculture, technology and the military in the 1982 PRC constitution as it replaced the Mao/Lin Biao image of China in 1969. To put these goals differently in today's language, one can speak of economic and technological improvements as means of enhancing economic well-being and national security. Such a formulation might be more in accord with the

---

3. Deng was dismissed for the second time from Mao's court in 1976 following Zhou Enlai's death but before that of Mao. For details, see the end of Chapter VI below. Deng's movements were interwoven with those of his colleagues like Chen Yun, his aides like Hu Yaobang and Zhao Ziyang, and his competitors and opponents like Hua Guofeng.

thinking of Western readers. However, both Deng's goal and the proposed means to achieve them are not new to China.

Nearly 150 years ago, Viceroy Chang Chih-tung of Kuangtung and Kuanghsi (Guangdong and Guangxi),[4] petitioned the Manchu court to establish a new educational system focusing on Western technology as a replacement of the system of Imperial civil service examinations. Chang was motivated by the growing popular sentiment of nationalism, having seen first hand, as a high official trusted by the ruling Empress Dowager, how China had been humiliated in a string of military defeats and territorial losses at the hands of Western colonial powers and even of Japan. The immediate objective in Chang's time was to speed up the country's economic development and to construct new industrial plants (including, symbolically, the establishment of the Hanyehping iron and steel works, to be financed jointly by both public and private funds; it was a distant cousin of today's Wuhan steel mills). These were the initial means Chang envisaged.

In the jargon of our time, the first step Chang proposed was investment in heavy industry and technical training. Nor did Chang wish to stop at a recommendation of importing Western technology alone. In his exposition of the proposed new system of national education based on Western science and engineering—which drew initially on the successful experience of Japan,[5] he stressed the importance of going beyond learning by rote. In Chang's words, students should be encouraged to ask "why"—not merely "what" and "how"—and to develop an inquisitive mind.[6] Pursuing this line of reasoning, one would come to the conclusion that radical institu-

---

4. For a comprehensive discussion of Chang Chih-tung's ideas on modernization and reform of China's traditional system of education, see Chang Ping-to, *Chang Chih-tung P'ing-chuan* [*A Critical Biography of Chang Chih-tung*] (Taipei: Chung Hwa Book Company, 1972), especially Chapters 2 and 7, pp. 15-47 and 221-37. Details on the original works of Chang Chih-tung may be found in these chapters.

5. Chang Chih-tung persevered in his reform proposals and as a pragmatic and effective advocate did so successfully "within the system." The external stimulus to the Manchu Court and the Chinese people in general to embark on reform was probably felt most acutely when China was finally defeated by Japan, which not too many years earlier had been barely a pupil of the Western powers herself.

6. Conventionally, Chang Chih-tung's reform proposals are regarded as merely adding a superficial Western veneer to an unaltered Chinese substance. A careful examination of Chang's many other ideas and practices in altering the educational and examination system suggests that to Chang the Chinese "substance" or ethos was the body of ethics and moral values in Chinese tradition (equivalent in his mind to Western religious teachings) that should be a fertile receiving ground of Western ideas and institutions over and above Western science and technology. To Chang new learning should

tional change would follow logically from the initial importation of Western knowledge.

Chang Chih-tung was not alone. He and others hoped to effect economic, technical and military-political change "within the imperial system," that is, without removing the Empress Dowager herself from power, thus preserving national integrity in the face of external pressures from all sides. Chang did not seek to overthrow the regime. Advocacy of more radical political change at the time might have cut short his career, if not his life, under the autocracy of the Dowager. Others, like K'ang Yu-wei and Liang Ch'i-ch'ao, who were less patient and less hopeful about reforming "within the system,"[7] sought to establish a constitutional monarchy under Emperor Kuang-hsu (Guangxu) through the withdrawal of the Empress Dowager from power. They failed to change the system, and some of K'ang's companions even paid with their lives. (Readers of this phase of Chinese history will not fail to recognize its resemblance to the June 1989 incident when Deng Xiaoping, Zhao Ziyang and student radicals re-enacted the scenes of a century earlier.)

At first glance, the opportunity to initiate simultaneously both systemic political reform and a viable strategy of economic development came again in 1911 when the Manchu monarchy was overthrown by the Nationalist Party (KMT) led by Sun Yat-sen. Unfortunately, this opportunity turned out to be more illusory than real. Sixteen years of civil and external wars were to pass before another opportunity reappeared. These wars were fought mostly among warlords, between the central government and warlords, and against Japanese aggression. Military conflicts were interspersed sporadically with short periods of economic development in parts of the country. But there was no steady economic growth along with greater equity in income distribution in the country as a whole. The immediate reasons for the lost opportunity after the 1911 revolution were three historical factors: the role played by the military elements in the initial phase of the revolution overthrowing the Manchus and the subsequent emergence of regional warlords; the continued efforts of foreign powers (primarily Japan) to main-

---

come from all sources, foreign or domestic. See Chang Ping-to, *supra* note 4, who seems to share this interpretation.

7. Whether K'ang Yu-wei meant originally to alter the hopelessly incompetent Manchu court at the cost of overthrowing the imperial system, as did Sun Yat-sen, is a matter of debate according to Huang Chang-chien, *Wu-hsü Pien-fa Yen-chiu* [*The Constitutional Reform Movement*] (Taipei: Academia Sinica, 1970), p. 660.

tain or expand their vested economic interests and political influence in China; and, the absence of a consensus even among the intellectuals, not to mention the larger public, on the most appropriate political system and approach to economic development in the then international climate.

Post-Manchu China simply had an ineffectual central government, too many regional warlords pursuing personal gain and power, numerous bureaucrats of varying degrees of competence and, in relation to the size of the population, too limited savings and too small an intellectual elite and pool of entrepreneurial talent to initiate a truly national development over a vast territory. It was not until 1927, a year marked by the establishment of a new KMT central government under Chiang Kai-shek (Sun Yat-sen's successor who had succeeded in reaching Nanking after a military campaign that started in Canton) that national development began in earnest. But the KMT's break with an armed Communist Party was soon to develop into a continuing civil war that never completely stopped even during the war with Japan. In the meantime, Japan's designs on China accelerated in 1931 with the occupation of Manchuria by the Japanese Kwantung Army, which set up the puppet Manchoukuo under the former boy-emperor of the Ch'ing Dynasty, Henry Pu Yi.

Two Competing Ideas: Development or Defense?

The lessons learned from these circumstances produced two strands of intellectual development and concrete events; both were favorable to the subsequent establishment of the Communist Party's economic system and the step-by-step administrative controls that led to it.

The first principal development was an increasingly wider conviction among policy makers and economists that the defense industry and a domestic heavy industrial base should enjoy unconditional priority in China's post-World War II economic development. For all intents and purposes, the procurement of arms from abroad, the effective inward transfer of foreign technology and the assured supply of all necessary inputs for domestic arms R&D and production would be quite impossible for a country of China's size. While in the very long run a highly developed economy would enable any country to mount a strong national defense and build the necessary R&D base required, the path from the development of the civilian sector of the economy to national military power can be far too circuitous and time-consuming. Moreover, the focus of prewar economic development pursued before July 1937 was concentrated in areas surrounding the treaty ports and foreign concessions, too distant from the interior provinces of China, where defense in depth would have to be built up. H.D. Fong of Nankai University,[8] as mentioned in Chapter II, and other academics generally agreed on this point. Japan's attacks on coastal China in 1937-38 and its occupation of all of China's more developed industrial and commercial centers along the lower section of the Yangtze and the major rail line on the eastern side of China proper (south of Manchuria) deprived the Chinese government of centers of industrial production and tax revenue. The economic development of interior China had to be pursued; this was also an approach in the mind of Wong Wen-hao, a geologist and wartime Minister of Economic Affairs in Chiang's government in Chungking.[9]

It was in anticipation of this arms supply quandary that Chiang Kai-shek had set up a National Resources Commission (NRC) to plan, build and operate various plants for a rudimentary heavy industry complex to support the production of arms and for metals export (especially tin, antimony and tungsten)[10] to help pay for imports. The NRC was later transferred from the Supreme Military Command to the Economic Affairs Ministry of the government. Wong Wen-hao as a geologist by profession was naturally inclined to think in terms of the input requirements of defense production beyond the purely financial considerations of economists. The

---

8. Fong's ideas about industrial location and development in prewar China appeared in many places. A summary of wartime and post-World War II approaches can be found in H. D. Fong (Fang Hsien-t'ing), *K'ang-chan Ch'i-chien Chung-kuo Kung-yeh chih Mo-luo chi ch'i Fu-hsing chih T'u-ching* [*The Wartime Decline of China's Industry and the Way to Recovery*] (Ch'ang-sha: The Commercial Press, 1941). For a recent analysis of the ideas enunciated in Fong's prolific writings see Chuang K'un-ming, "Fang Hsien-t'ing Kung-yeh-hua Li-nien Hsi-lun" [An Analysis of H. D. Fong's Concepts of Industrialization in China] in *Chin-tai Chung-kuo* [*Contemporary China*], Taipei, No. 87, February 1, 1992. The impact of China's prewar industrial location is also discussed by the present author in his *An Economic Survey of Communist China*, original edition, Bookman Associates, New York; reprinted in Octagon Books, New York, 1977.

9. See Wong Wen-hao (Weng Wen-hao), *Chung-kuo Kung-yeh Cheng-ts'e* [*China's Industrial Policy*] (Shanghai: Chih-hui Book Company, 1948).

10. Toward the end of World War II, the National Resources Commission began to think of postwar economic development in terms of GNP growth and its allocation; Simon Kuznets, then at the University of Pennsylvania and subsequently a Nobel laureate, was involved as an adviser on this pioneering project. This was the first large organized national income study after World War II although even earlier studies, both before and during the war, had been conducted by Ou Pao-san and Ta-chung Liu. The latter's national income study with K. C. Yeh at Rand Corporation in Santa Monica became widely known in the late 1950s and later years.

NRC's constellation of plants, plus other government-owned heavy industry facilities, many built by Japanese in the Manchoukuo period, plus a large number of Japanese firms producing consumer goods (heavily concentrated in textiles) provided a substantial state sector of the economy[11] to be taken over by the post-1949 PRC victors of the Civil War. Some senior bureaucrats of the NRC even stayed behind to serve the new government. Among the latter were officials who had at one time been quite close to Chiang.

Intellectually, many Chinese academics who were anxious to contribute to China's postwar development were also quite impressed with economic planning in both the Soviet Union and Hitler's Germany and their successful mobilization of resources for national defense. The sociologist Wu Ching-ch'ao[12] of Tsinghua University, for instance, who visited both Germany and the Soviet Union a year before the outbreak of the Sino-Japanese war, wrote favorably about the German and Soviet modes of rapidly mobilizing resources in anticipation of war. Wu Ching-Ch'ao's European visit followed closely upon the Webbs' publication[13] on the Soviet Union; his impression could well have been inspired by theirs. The intellectual environment and the seemingly shared objective of building a self-supporting industrial base for defense could make the Communist Party's takeover at the time acceptable to many Chinese technically trained in the West.[14]

That the CCP's draconian measures went far beyond what many were ready to accept seemed clear on the basis of what we have later learned about the Anti-Rightist purges of 1957. But the situation before 1949 was different to academic Chinese Marxists, who genuinely believed that the Chinese Communist Party possessed a real key to the cure of the country's long-term malaise. To the Chinese nation's great misfortune, too many acted as if the strongly Marxist-oriented critics of the KMT, who later became disillusioned with Mao and his party, had the following to say in the 1930s.

---

11. See the Supplement to Wong Wen-hao's book, *supra* note 9, by Wu Ching-ch'ao, then a consultant to the ROC Ministry of Economic Affairs, who stayed behind in mainland China in 1949.

12. Wu Ching-ch'ao, *ibid.*

13. See Sidney and Beatrice Webb, *Soviet Communism: A New Civilization?* 2 volumes, (New York: Charles Scribner Books, 1936).

14. There was apparently a large group of intellectuals who had grown impatient with the gradual process of national improvement and thought a strong dose of statism was necessary for rapid change. This national mood was characteristic in the 1930s in China.

Qian Jiaju's Thesis

According to adherents of this view,[15] the agricultural sector in China, which had been depressed for a long time, was close to total collapse in the mid-1930s. A combination of factors was responsible for the farmers' dire straits, including natural calamities and unsettled social conditions caused by banditry and marauding soldiers. However, the basic economic reason was the small size of the average farm holding and the tenant or part-tenant farmer's obligation to pay high ground rent. When the crop was too small for the rent, lack of normal borrowing facilities would drive the tenant or part-tenant into debt at a usurious rate of interest. A better-off farmer, possibly a landowner, who not infrequently was the borrower's landlord, might be the only lender to whom the borrower had access. The chance existed that such a borrower might end up by losing some or all of the land he owned. Thus, an increasing proportion of farm land could fall into the hands of an ever smaller group of landowners. To put the story somewhat differently, one could represent this course of events as a diversion of the landowner's savings away from potentially productive nonagricultural investment or investment in improvements in agricultural production into acquisition of more farmland by a small number of landowners, thus resulting in a more unequal distribution of land ownership.

However, this course of development implicitly assumed several conditions, namely, that farm output could not be improved through R&D; that farm income could not be augmented with nonagricultural activities on the spot through what in China was then generally known as side-line activities and cottage industries, or in the recent Deng Xiaoping period as "village industry"; and, that financial wherewithal would not be made more readily available from outside the agricultural sector as non-usurious agricultural loans or as capital investment for the development of a progressively improving modern cottage industry. The cottage industry in the writings of H.D. Fong and Franklin Ho predated by over one-half century the "township and village industry" proposed by modern-day authors. Industrial cooperatives promoted by some Western enthusiasts at the time pointed in the same direction.

15. See the many essays collected in Qian Jiaju [Ch'ien Chia-chü] (ed.), *Chung-kuo Nung-ts'un Ching-chi Lun-wen-chi* [*Collected Essays on the Chinese Farm Economy*] (Shanghai: Chung Hwa Book Co., 1936).

In the mid-30s some of those who were genuinely concerned about the depressed state of Chinese agriculture thought of the combination of high ground rent (sometimes exaggerated by disregarding services and/or equipment supplied by the landowner), usurious loans and lack of alternative borrowing facilities as the deliberate, malicious "exploitation" of one class by another in Marxist terms. The landowners were invariably called "feudalistic exploiters," and ownership transfers resulting from defaulted loans viewed as coercive exploitation by those who served the interest of their capitalist masters.[16]

Still another alternative that might offer the landless peasant a way out would be employment in the nonagricultural sector, such as urban industry, that is, looking forward to industrial development as a means of absorbing rural labor, starting with the rural unemployed.

Those who shared the first view on Chinese agriculture as described above often argued that the second way out was also closed. They maintained that imperialist foreign manufacturers and importers had effectively dominated, if not monopolized, the market of goods that Chinese manufacturers knew how to produce. The former were able to enjoy an advantage in competing with Chinese products, as a result of China's loss of tariff autonomy after the successive defeats in foreign wars beginning with the Opium War of the 1840s. Putting these views together, domestic capitalists and foreign imperialists became the principal villains of China's delayed modernization. In the popular mind, any Chinese government worth its salt should be anti-imperialist and anti-capitalist (or at least protectionist). In contrast, any government refusing to be such should be replaced, by armed rebellion if necessary. This was of course the simplistic populist argument the Chinese Communist Party advanced in the 1930s, at the time of the Sian Incident and during the war with Japan. Foreign capitalists from the West and Japan were therefore lumped together with domestic landowners as a combined class of "exploiters," to be combated by nationalism and domestic revolution.

The Economists' Approach Derailed by Japan's Invasion

If the war with Japan had not broken out when it did in 1937, the economic development of China conceivably might have followed a pattern containing a large dose of state capitalism—some

16. *Ibid.*

might say, of socialism. The beliefs of the body of intellectual elites as a whole were perhaps not as markedly so inclined as the preceding discussion may have indicated. Some Chinese economists trained in Japan, like Chang Kia-ngau and Wu Ting-ch'ang, both prominent bankers,[17] were also familiar with British and other Western liberal ideas and were inclined toward market capitalism, regarding state intervention primarily either as a corrective measure against private excesses or as a guiding and encouraging hand to move the economy forward at a faster pace. They would use public capital and other assistance to accelerate economic development, perhaps now and then nudging private business in a particular direction. Nascent private capitalists, including both former local agents and allies of foreign businesses and entrepreneurs who had emerged after World War I and in the 1920s and early 1930s independently and outside what one might in today's language call "special economic zones," had begun to exert an increasing economic importance on government policy. But the Nationalist government in power before 1937 and headed by Chiang Kai-shek was following a course dictated by defense needs, moving along according to his personal time-table, strategy and ideological beliefs. Unfortunately for the Chinese people, this was also the case with Mao Zedong, who in 1945-47 had become so successful politically and militarily that there was no one left to dispute his beliefs or to curb his untrammeled ambitions.

To repeat a point made before, the military collapse of the Nationalist government in the post-World War II Civil War combined with its financial mismanagement, resulted in hyperinflation, leading to the rapid demonetization of the national currency (*fapi*) as legal tender in 1947-49. Neither the money supply nor commodity prices stopped rising after the fall of Shanghai, the country's financial capital, in May 1949. An unceasing rise of both in 1949-50 as the Communist forces swept across the Yangtze to the west and south of the country continued to fuel the hyperinflation in the areas newly occupied by the Communists in terms of the latter's

---

17. Some Chinese bankers in the late 1920s and 1930s before the war with Japan, contrary to the populist brand of Maoist Marxism, were not the "feudalistic" exploiters they were portrayed to be after 1949. The Bank of China, under the long stewardship of K. N. Chang (Chang Kia-ngau), and other banks, notably the "four Northern banks," were among the institutions that tried to bring credit to the rural market in order to expand agricultural credit for farmers. For a discussion of various aspects of economic development up to 1937, when war broke out with Japan, see Paul Sih, Chapter II, *supra* note 3.

renminbi or "people's currency." The most draconian measures, some of which could not have been taken by any government observing legal constraints, were employed in the face of an impending collapse of the new Communist government. A few statistics, which continued to be available during the first year of Communist rule in Shanghai, will serve to remind readers of both the financial chaos during the last days of Nationalist rule and the precarious hold the Communists faced at first.

Postwar Hyperinflation

If we take September 1945 as the base period (=100), the index for the money supply as represented by the volume of *fapi* notes rose more than tenfold to 1,023.6 in April 1947, at about the time of the resumption of the Civil War. Shanghai's wholesale price index rose during the same period from 100 to 4,130, i.e., about 41 fold, registering a simple average increase of 212 percent a month. The much higher increase in prices reflected the acceleration of the rate at which *fapi* was being spent by its users, including both government agencies and the private sector. Another sixteen months later, in August 1948, the same note issue and wholesale price indices had risen respectively to 296,648 and 1,368,048.9—September 1945=100, that is, averaging respectively 18,476.5 percent or 184.76 times a month for money supply and 85,244.9 percent or 852 times a month for prices. The precipitate drop of *fapi* as a viable currency took place in the first half of 1949 when the Nationalist army suffered the decisive defeat in Shantung in defense of the capital Nanking. The *fapi* was then replaced by a new currency, the "gold yuan,"[18] which went the same disastrous route as the *fapi* in less than a year's time.[19]

Continued Inflation after Communist Takeover

In Shanghai and other cities the same inflationary forces that had fanned the price and wage increases before May 1949 continued through 1950. Fighting continued sporadically here and there in the country until the PLA occupation of Canton and Hainan, where the Nationalist central government briefly stopped while the territory coming under PLA control rose by leaps and bounds, thereby increasing the demand for the new currencies issued by the Com-

18. See Yuan-li Wu, *An Economic Survey of Communist China* (New York: Bookman Associates, 1956), pp. 49-55.
19. *Ibid.*

munist note scrip issuing agencies, for increasing the money supply was still the only principal means of financing military activities other than direct requisition. In the large urban centers, former government employees were being retained by their new masters. The latter dreaded a sudden explosion of unemployment and the chaos that might ensue.[20] Similarly, private and former government factories which were being taken over were instructed to continue operation at a reduced rate. As a result, credit operations by banks were implicitly allowed to continue working, losses being borne partly by the Communist government (and therefore continued inflation) or through sale of assets, dishoarding and other deflationary measures.

On the basis of the same Shanghai wholesale price index employed during the Nationalist period, a 69 percent increase was recorded for the first eleven months of the new regime, between May 28, 1949 and February 28, 1950.

Economic Stabilization under Chen Yun

A series of economic stabilization measures was finally promulgated in mid-March 1950.[21] Chen Yun, then head of the Economic and Financial Commission in the Communist cabinet, was particularly concerned about the pernicious demoralizing effect of inflation, which he well understood. He now repeatedly addressed his staff on the need to reduce spending, increase production and carefully manage the supply of food for the population and of raw materials for Shanghai's cotton mills and other factories.[22]

---

20. Bo Ibo wrote in 1991 that following the surrender of Fu in 1949, 18,000 of the latter's officers were each paid 30,000 RMB as severance pay and that their dissatisfaction with the amount became a "source of obstruction to the subsequent pacification of Suiyuan." The amount paid was said to be equivalent to three months' salary, which is highly questionable in view of the hyperinflation then. Bo Ibo, *Ruogan Zhongda Juece yu Shijan di Huigu* [*Many Major Decisions and Events in Retrospect*] (Beijing: CCP Central Party School Publishers, 1991), Vol. I, p.15.

21. The March 1950 date should be regarded as a benchmark of Chen's monetary stabilization policy, later to be upset again by Mao's entry into the Korean War.

22. Yuan-li Wu, *supra* note 18, p. 88. See also the sources cited in notes 1-3 in this chapter. Chen was quite explicit in stressing the importance of holding adequate stocks of grain and cotton for price stabilization. (These were also the principal components of the price indices used for bond issue in commodity terms.) The present author still recalls clearly that the commodity price indexed bond was first proposed by Professor Sho-chieh Tsiang to the Nationalists before the Communist takeover. Tsiang, a prizewinner from the London School of Economics during World War II, and a fellow L.S.E. student in World War II, later became an advisor on monetary policy to the ROC authorities in Taiwan and played a very constructive role in Taiwan's price stabilization in

Conceivably some of the disgruntled economists and other intellectuals who joined the first Political Consultative Conference under the new regime in 1949 may have suggested the encouragement of savings and the addition of other harsh monetary retrenchment ideas to Chen Yun's stabilization program. Two specific measures smacked very much of ideas worthy of a monetary theorist. One was the introduction of an indexed treasury bond tied to the market prices of specific quantities in a commodity basket used in the everyday consumption of ordinary citizens.[23] The market value of the bond at the time of subscription and redemption was fixed at the local market values of the items in question. This was known as the "victory bond."

A second measure was the deliberately sudden forced contraction of liquidity in the private sector, at the time when the compulsory and virtually instantaneous collection of new taxes was introduced. The new taxes assumed the form of unpaid "back taxes" of earlier years, ostensibly on the ground that previous tax payments had fallen short of tax liabilities in real terms when prices were rising rapidly during hyperinflation. But the amount due was arbitrarily assessed and collection was instantaneous and on demand. (Forcible collection of such funds from suspected delinquent taxpayers with the aid of police "persuasion" was frequently reported at the time.) Since businessmen to whom this method was applied, in order to raise money, sought to liquidate commodity stocks which they had previously hoarded to beat inflation, the authorities' objective of contracting the money supply could be attained even more effectively by dumping officially held commodity stocks (grain, flour, cotton yarn and cloth, coal, etc.) at the same time. These stocks had come into the new authorities' hands from

---

the 1950s and 1960s. He was the founding director of Taipei's Chung Hwa Institution of Economic Research.

23. See, for instance, Chen Yun's reports to the CCP Central Committee on January 22, and February 1, 1950, which he jointly submitted with Bo Ibo. See *Chen Yun Wen Xuan (1949-1956)* [*Chen Yun's Selected Writings*] (Beijing: People's Publishers, 1984), pp. 53-59. In a speech on May 16, 1951, Chen spoke of the benefit of having a grain stock of 10 billion catties (5 million metric tons) on hand. He assumes the need in a famine to feed 50 million peasants at one-half chin or catty (one-quarter kilogram) a day or 7.5 kilograms a month, for six months, plus 15 million urban residents at 12½ kilograms a month for twelve months. These rations would total 4.5 billion chin each for the two groups, making 9 billion chin in all. To this amount he threw in another billion chin, thus making 10 billion chin or 5 million tons, the minimum reserve against a famine from either drought or flood. Chen said that he would prefer to see such a reserve in the farmers' own granary plus one of equal size in the hands of the government. Cf. also Yuan-li Wu, *supra* note 18, pp. 108-10.

warehouses confiscated by the incoming Communists from Nationalist agencies, former state enterprises and many private enterprises owned by persons now conveniently labeled as "bureaucratic capitalists" or even "war criminals." Thus a portion of the private sector's assets was seized, confiscated and dumped on the market along with a sudden increase in old and new taxes and their collection. These turned out to have the desired deflationary effect.

In their speeches during the early 1950s, and in snatches of dispatches and briefings opened to the public since the late 1980s, both Chen Yun and Bo Ibo have demonstrated their concern about the pernicious effects of inflation[24] and the need to secure full control over the supply of resources (finished agricultural and industrial goods and their sources of production) and the sources of demand for them, including the selective exclusion of uses not meeting the Communist Party's approval.

These CCP leaders themselves, of course, did not mention that the Civil War was the root cause of the postwar inflation and that the CCP too was no less a party to the conflict. The CCP's policy objectives at first focused on economic stabilization, which began with the post-occupation period, but soon extended to the entire Korean War years. The conversion of the economy to a socialist system, largely modeled after the Soviet Union, then became the next step. Originally construed as a gradual transformation lasting up to one-and-a-half decades, it was subsequently accelerated during 1954-55 so that the entire process of socialist transformation virtually ended in 1956 before the close of the First Five-Year Plan. How these interwoven developments came to pass deserves a closer look because of their ruthlessness as well as their far-reaching consequences, unexpected by the instigators.

---

24. Four episodes of rampant hyperinflation between April 1949 and February 1950 were reported by Chen Yun as follows:

"Index of National Average Prices"		*Base Period = 100*
April 1949	280	(March 1950=100)
July 1949	280	(June 1949=100)
November 1949	450	(September 1949=100)
February 1950	190	(January 1-10, 1950=100)

Source: Chen Yun, *Selected Writings*, *supra* note 23, Chen's Note 74, p. 348.

Centralization of Resources Through Monetary Control

A breakthrough in imposing centralized control over the private sector of the post-1949 inflated Chinese economy came in March-April 1950 with the promulgation of a series of measures that concentrated all government receipts in a central depository and established stringent control over cash disbursements. Government funds were pulled out of all deposits with commercial banks which, like other private businesses, were ordered to raise their own capitalization in order to increase the banking industry's need for liquidity under government control. Commodity stocks were centralized in government warehouses so that supplies could be either liquidated or allocated as required in the interest of price stabilization.[25] As a result, the worst of the previously rampant inflation was reduced to a more moderate pace.

But these severe controls were only indicative of more fundamental changes to be imposed on China's "national capitalists" in urban areas many of whom Mao's followers were still "courting" with an iron hand in velvet gloves. The true colors of the Communists' subjugation of private business were not revealed until a year later in 1951. As will be seen later in Chapter IX, this was the first year of intense fighting in Korea in which PRC troops were involved. The process of socialization in China, however, was just beginning. But at this point, we must first consider what took place in rural China when the Communist Party gained military control.

III. STEPS TO RURAL AND URBAN ECONOMIC CONTROL

The Redistribution of Land in Establishing Rural Control

+80%

More than eighty percent of mainland China's population consisted of farmers. The peasantry supplied the bulk of the rebel troops that overcame the Nationalist army which obtained its own recruits from the same population pool. Hence, the peasants were needed by the Communist Party for political support; in consequence, from the CCP's point of view, the incentive offered to its own supporters should not be available to supporters of its KMT opponents unless the latter's troops were to change sides. Although the private modern business sector in China was then numerically small, its non-resistance, if not collaboration, was needed by the

---

25. See Chen Yun, *id.*, pp. 76-83, on the supply of food in 1950, especially in urban areas.

new regime to keep the population and the Party cadres, troops and bureaucrats both old and new, supplied at least on a minimal level of subsistence. Hence one can readily see how the economic task of establishing control must have appeared to Mao and his advisers in 1947-49: how to win over the bulk of the peasantry and the urban population and private businessmen? What should be the proper combination of (1) instilling fear, (2) encouraging wishful thinking, and (3) splitting potential opponents? In dealing with both farmers and urban businessmen under Mao's "new democracy," it would have been necessary at an early stage of CCP rule to reconcile its new policy of faster socialization with past public promises and popular perceptions of what the Communist Party apparently stood for, with national economic revival and multi-party participation in nation-building given top priority over a significant length of time. The developments in reality were quite different.

The Redistribution of Land and Rural Wealth

When one looks back at this early phase of the Communist take-over, the redistribution of land and other tangible possessions from the "rich" to the poor among the agricultural population probably was seen by the victors as the only sure and logical step to consolidate power. The redistribution of farmland in favor of tenant farmers and the landless would serve to redeem the CCP's reputation as a land-reform party. Such an undertaking was its political promise to Chinese peasants and taken for granted worldwide by foreign sympathizers. It was, however, the scope of the wealth redistribution and the intensive and widespread terror with which this policy was deliberately conducted as a mass movement that made the CCP's political cynicism and inhumanity stand out.

In the short run, when numerous armed non-Communist opposition forces were still at large, and fighting had not yet stopped, some poor peasants probably saw the redistribution sponsored by the new masters as an extraordinary opportunity to enrich themselves. The Communists on their part might be Machiavellian enough to think that by involving more individuals in acts of violence against established authority they would enlist more desperate supporters just in case the tables were turned against them given the fluctuating fortunes of the Civil War. Thus the severity with which the expropriated property owners were dealt with varied from place to place. The wide discretion lower-level Party cadres in charge enjoyed in carrying out "land reform" was also a cause for reports of regional variations in land-reform practices, as were considerations about the harvest and the need to assure supply for urban consumers.[26] In the long run, several outstanding characteristics of this land-reform movement not only radically altered China's economic and political landscape, they also left an indelible mark on the behavior of the Chinese rural poor, a topic which future students of Chinese history and socio-anthropology may well investigate at some length.

Characteristics and Effects of Rural Wealth Redistribution

First, the redistribution of rural wealth dictated by Mao's Communist Party was carried out without compensation. The transferors who would have to bear the loss had to be singled out first, and the transfer process had to be justified and enforceable. The manner in which this was done was not a simple division of the farm population into rich and poor but the complete classification of the farm population based on the individual households and their respective sources of income. The four principal household groups or Mao's "classes" were (1) "landlords," i.e., rent collectors, (2) "rich peasants," i.e., recipients of interest income or money-lenders, (3) "middle peasants," i.e., owner-cultivators, and (4) "poor peasants," i.e., landless tenants and hired hands. Many individuals would fall into more than one category, thus giving rise to cross-category overlaps, necessitating an arbitrary choice determined by the Party chiefs in charge of such "class identification," which served as the basis of the land transfer, as well as that of tools, farm animals and other assets, including household and personal property.

Second, the assignment of the individual peasants to specific "classes" was carried out under Party supervision during public meetings when "democratic appraisals" were carried out by experienced agitators and informants. The latter individuals led the way in working up mass hysteria. In addition to bringing about the desired asset redistribution, an equally important goal was to criminalize the losing side of the compulsory transfer by labeling the victims as "local despots," oppressors in a "feudalist" economic system now being wiped out by class struggle. The "proletariat," represented by the tenant farmers, the hired hands and the unemployed, in theory spearheaded this process while the Communist Party ostensibly merely supplied the necessary political and moral leadership. Those who lost their property not only suffered physical and personal losses including their homes, farm implements and animals, if not

26. See Bo Ibo, *supra* note 20, p. 5.

their lives, but did so under the double jeopardy of being labeled "criminals."

Third, the deliberate destruction of the social standing of China's traditional rural gentry also had the effect of removing the CCP's rural competitors in social standing. Another long-term effect of the process was retention of the same class label by the family members of the victims. For instance, the children of a "landlord" or a "rich peasant" would forever retain this label and as such be subject to discrimination, e.g., in access to education and employment as members of a new "underclass." What originally was described as a reform of the land tenure system led in this way to the creation of several sub-classes in society.

Although "landlords" were the principal target of the compulsory redistribution of 1949-51, if the land made available for redistribution to the poor peasants proved insufficient for the CCP's political needs, "rich peasants" would become the next victim group through local readjustment.

For readers unfamiliar with the literature on Communist land reform in the PRC, the method of class differentiation employed in 1949 and afterwards was the handiwork of Mao Zedong when he was still a "guerrilla field worker" at Jinggangshan (Ching-kang-shan) in 1933. No details on this topic were publicized when he wrote on the "New Democracy" in 1940. But the same 1933 text was reissued by the CCP in 1948 and again by the new PRC government on August 4, 1950, following the promulgation of the Land Reform Law at the end of June in the same year. To be fair, it would be untrue to say that the CCP's and Mao's personal victims had not been forewarned at all. Some chose not to believe the announcements; others never listened; still others might not have known about such a document or bothered to find out!

IV. TIGHTENING CONTROL ON THE URBAN ECONOMY

Although the Communist Party was unschooled as administrators of urban centers, they knew their own lack of experience and tried hard to prepare for the new task. In November 1948, Peng Zhen and Ye Jianying were appointed by Mao Zedong as his top officials in all party, military and government affairs in Beijing (then still known as Peiping). Huang Kecheng (Huang k'e-ch'eng) headed both the military and the party in Tianjin; Huang Jing (Huang Ching) was named mayor of Tianjin. Mao also sent Bo Ibo, recently appointed head of the Northern Bureau of the CCP, which had an overall supervisory function in the entire newly conquered region, to lead an advance party.

According to Bo's account,[27] Mao instructed him to bear in mind that the principal physical targets of the impending take-over in the cities were the economic interests of "bureaucratic capitalists"; the industrial and commercial interests of "national capitalists" were on the contrary to be protected. Possessions of the former group were to be seized "lock, stock, and barrel, sealed and undisturbed."[28] The phraseology in quotes was the translation of Mao's own words, and was also cited by others carrying out the same task elsewhere. Again, according to Bo Ibo, Mao added that China was then just entering a phase of "people's democratic dictatorship," not yet the period of "dictatorship of the proletariat." This fine distinction was based on Mao's assertion that the success of the Communist Party in urban China depended on the working class as well as the "class of national capitalists." To put these dicta more bluntly, Mao's thought reflected a recognition that both the country and the security of Communist Party control required the rapid restoration of order, production and stability, and that the Communist cadres themselves did not then possess the technical and administrative know-how to meet the necessary demands of a national administration.

When he interviewed Bo for the taking-over of the country's first two large cities, including the peaceful surrender of the ancient capital, Beijing, Mao mentioned an article by Guo Moruo (Kuo Mo-juo) on the tragic experience of Li Zicheng (Li Tzu-ch'eng) and the sack of Peking at the end of the Ming Dynasty prior to the Manchu conquest of China. The rebel army's sack of the imperial capital was followed by feasting, rampage and excesses which Guo, who was subsequently appointed to head the PRC's Academy of Sciences, appealed to Mao not to repeat.[29]

Mao enjoined Communist occupation forces to follow two principal rules which had both an economic and a political purpose. The first was to avoid any serious and prolonged unemployment, disruption of production and rapid price inflation. The second was to maintain the appearance of a disciplined, revolutionary people's

---

27. *Ibid.*

28. See Chen Yun's speech of July 20, 1951, on the need to pay attention to private businessmen through the Party-led Association of Industry and Trade, in Chen Yun, *supra* note 23, pp. 155-56.

29. See Bo, *supra* note 20, pp. 5-7 and 9-10.

army that had been ready to die for a much loftier goal than material gains and comforts of the flesh.

The great care with which the initial Communist occupation of Peiping, Tientsin and Shanghai was handled, in conformity with Mao's general ruling as outlined by Bo Ibo, probably had much to do with reports of poor PLA discipline from Manchuria and by Zeng Shan in Chinan, Shandong province. Negative reports also came on the occupation of such North China mining towns as Jingxing (Ching-hsing) and Yangquan and the industrial center of Shijiazhuang.

Bo Ibo and Guo Moruo deplored the arrogance that overcame the rebel Li Zicheng and his army after their unexpected conquest of the imperial foe at the end of an arduous campaign. They feared that Mao and his followers might commit the same fatal error. Their worry turned out to be premature—by several decades!

Was There to Be a Coalition Government?

A great deal of the political work preparatory to Mao Zedong's appearance at Tiananmen on October 1, 1949 took place at the Li Village at Pingshan, some 100 kilometers from Shijiazhuang. The Central Committee of the Chinese Communist Party had moved there after leaving Yanan. According to Qian Jiaju, the contingent of the Democratic League and other personages (of similar political orientation) who had left KMT controlled areas (Shanghai in many cases) for Hongkong were brought to this Communist controlled territory by sea via Yantai before moving to Peiping. It was the latter city in February 1949 where these literally-speaking "fellow travelers" were met by another like-minded group that had reached the city via the port of Yinkou in Manchuria. These were many of the same individuals who were to constitute a new Political Consultative Conference and put their signatures to the Common Program for the new People's Republic yet to be established on October 1, 1949.

The arrival of many non-communist supporters of Mao and the CCP in China's ancient capital was greeted by a massive welcome party. A similar celebration planned earlier for the official entry of the Chinese Communist Central Committee, presumably on an even grander scale, was canceled on Mao's orders so as deliberately to keep a low political profile of the CCP, thus giving the noncommunist opponents of the KMT greater prominence. This was a public-relations ploy for the benefit of the outside world. It also inflated the same individuals' feelings of self-importance, hence their readiness to do their best for the party that had defeated the KMT and made their personal good fortunes possible.[30]

The Common Program which the new Political Consultative Conference adopted did not even mention the word "socialism" as a goal of the new People's Republic. This omission was deliberate because, as Zhou Enlai, the new Prime Minister, stated on September 22, 1949, the Common Program had on purpose left out the pursuit of socialism and communism as long-term goals because their desirability would be proven to the people in good time and therefore become self-evident. Besides, the term "common" indirectly implied a "shared" program of a "coalition" without making an open assertion of such an entente of political parties. A day earlier, Liu Shaoqi, who addressed the opening session of the new PCC as the Communist Party's official representative, spoke of the Common Program as the minimal agenda of a policy of national construction by stages, insofar as the Communist Party was concerned. Thus Liu's statements reflected the same view expressed by Mao personally when he spoke before the PCC's preparatory meeting a month before, on August 26. For them to talk about the distant future at this stage would be to indulge in "empty talk."[31]

As we shall see, the CCP left itself a degree of freedom of action the nature of which none of the assembled intellectuals and "national capitalists" could ever have anticipated. Did they lull the unsuspecting into unjustified complacency? Did they mean to do what they led others think they would? Or did they honestly change their minds later because, after all, circumstances had changed?

Since the Common Program of 1949 was nominally a joint product of the Communists together with other "democratic parties", it reflected the common political understanding of several social groups. The political groupings used in the document were nevertheless couched entirely in the Chinese Communists' special terms of (1) "workers," (2) "peasants," (3) "small individual businessmen and handicraft workers," (4) "national (private) capitalists," (5) "capitalists" in "mixed enterprises (i.e., businesses containing state capital), and (6) members of "semi-socialistic cooperatives." Corresponding to these classes, their representatives were to take their place in the new government. Zhou Enlai, acting

---

30. Qian Jiaju, *Quguo Yousi Lu* [*Sorrowful Thoughts in Exile*] (Hongkong: Cosmos Books, 1991), pp. 61-63.

31. Bo, *supra* note 20, p. 31.

on Mao's instruction, according to Bo Ibo's account,[32] allotted to "non-communists" 3 of the 6 vice-chairmen of the People's Government, 27 of the 56 members of the Central Government Council, 2 of the 4 vice-chairmen of the Government Administrative Council (GAC, later renamed the State Council), 9 of the 15 GAC members and 15 of the ministerial portfolios. In reality, however, since a number of these "non-communist" appointees subsequently either openly revealed themselves to be in fact Communists all along or "resumed" their Communist Party memberships, there was a rather pronounced farcical aspect to the entire performance. Qian Jiaju stated candidly[33] that many of the intellectuals in the "democratic group" who went to North China to join the Communists and entered the new government in the first PCC and were really CCP members and identified several as Communist "moles."[34]

Threat of Inflation during the Korean War

Three months after the monetary and fiscal measures for currency stabilization had been put in place in March 1950, the mainland Chinese economy began to look more or less under control. Coincidentally, it was at this time that the invasion of South Korea by the Communist North occurred. Looking back, it would seem that President Truman's decision to go decisively to the South's aid took both Kim Il Sung and Stalin by surprise. Why Communist China then intervened in less than six months' time remains to be discussed later. Given this fateful decision by Mao on October 8, 1950, a number of developments ensued.[35]

Three scenarios of the Korean War's possible effects on the PRC economy were first postulated by Chen Yun at the Second National Financial Conference on November 15, 1950: (1) fighting near the border, China's territory inside the border not affected; (2) fighting near the Sino-Korean border, bombing inside the PRC border; and, (3) enemy landing at PRC ports, fighting to expand.[36] In

32. Bo Ibo, *Ruogan Zhongda Juece yu Shijan di Huigu* [*Many Major Decisions and Events in Retrospect*] (Beijing: CCP Central Party School Publishers, 1993), Vol. II, pp. 32-33.

33. Qian Jiaju, *Qishinian di Jingli* [*Through Seven Decades*] (Hongkong: The Mirror Post Cultural Enterprise Co., 2nd edition, 1988), pp. 166-67.

34. Qian Jiaju, *supra* note 30, pp. 157-87. Many of the "democrats" brought along by Mao as described by Bo in note 32 were discarded as "rightists" in the Anti-Rightist drive, according to Qian.

35. Bo, *supra* note 20, p. 44.

36. Chen Yun, *supra* note 23, pp. 112-20 and 140.

the published portion of his speech, Chen claimed that China could easily deal with the first situation, but he was seriously concerned about the scope of U.S. military intervention inside China, considering it an incalculable factor because of the effect on price stability.

To promote all-out support in China of the war effort, Chen suggested reducing industrial capital investment in 1951 and an even greater cutback of government spending on education and other economic items. The slogan, "increase production and reduce cost," was introduced to complement the political call to "resist America and aid Korea" in an appeal to nationalism. In the inevitable war, Chinese peasants would carry a heavier tax burden.

Chen seemed to envisage the allocation of a larger share of an increased national output to the war effort. In his view, neither the sale of more bonds nor even heavier taxation within the only recently regularized tax system offered encouraging prospects for the time being. His recent experience in currency stabilization taught him the importance of increasing the supply of industrial goods—in his mind, essentially textiles— to the peasants in exchange for more farm produce, which he thought possible. As a result, he expected greater tax revenue from both industrial and agricultural sectors. This meant for Chen the acquisition of large grain and cotton stocks for market management and keeping the budget deficit to be financed by new note issue to a minimum.

In practical terms, monopolization by the state of the distribution of raw cotton and cotton textiles introduced at the end of 1950 would serve the purpose of financing the war. In terms of other taxes, little was said of the need for any extraordinary sources of revenue. However, such extraordinary sources might in fact have been a paramount issue for discussion in the PRC's inner circles. This might very well have been the case, as we shall soon see.

Prices, of course, did not remain unaffected by the outbreak of the Korean War even before China's active participation in it. Two oft-quoted sharp price increases were those of sugar in Beijing and Tianjin in August 1950 and of caustic soda in Beijing in 1951.[37] However, market prices had ceased to be regularly published and available to outsiders, except for some controlled prices. In order to reduce unemployment, government purchases of agricultural by-products and manufactures had been used as an economic stimulus

37. Bo, *supra* note 20, p. 164.

in the latter half of 1950, and some of the increased purchases were probably related to preparation for war.

During 1991, Bo Ibo wrote in his memoir in strong military expressions, describing the resultant further cost increase in government spending starting at the 1951-52 year-end as a "madman's assault" on the national economy by capitalists that had to be met by an all-out counter-offensive spearheaded by the Communist Party on a nationwide basis. The first part of the counter-offensive was directed at the government's own workers, ostensibly to rid the increasingly interventionist bureaucracy of its corrupt, bribe-taking and overweening members.[38] The mass movement in question started October 1951 and worked down to February 1952. Presumably some of the victims were hold-overs from 1949. The second part of a longer and more far-reaching drive was aimed at businessmen in industry and trade. As we shall see, capitalist members of the "Democratic League" and other fellow-travelers in the intelligentsia who had survived the first two years of the Communist regime would soon lose their presumed immunity from the wrath of their "coalition" partner.

Capital Levy in Disguise

According to reports covering all southwestern China and 67 cities in the other five Administrative Regions, just under one million cases (999,707 exactly, according to Bo Ibo's account)[39] were involved in the "Five Antis" campaign up to that time. A total of 1509 persons received sentences of varying severity. Of those given definite sentences, 1.26 percent received the death sentence (including cases with execution suspended). These numbers were not really national totals, nor did they include persons prosecuted as "enemies of the people" whose cases had not yet been dealt with at the time of the reports. Some of the victims committed suicide as a result of the relentless persecution and psychological and physical torture. Some businessmen who went back to the Chinese mainland

38. This was the "Three Antis" movement which had several different facets. From the narrow Communist Party's point of view, it was a "rectification" campaign. It was also a process to rid the bureaucracy of elements taken over from the previous regime. Finally, it was a prelude to the transformation of the "national capitalists" into "candidate-members" of the working class under socialism. After all, these capitalists were supposed to be in cahoots with the corrupt bureaucrats, targets of the rectification drive.

39. Bo, *supra* note 20, p. 178.

after having successfully fled to Hongkong in 1949-50 were victims in this category. They had grossly misjudged China's new masters.

The government workers who were charged with colluding with capitalists were accused of crimes that included "corruption," "taking bribes," and irregular "bureaucratic practices." Their counterpart, the capitalists, supposedly committed crimes ranging from "offering bribes to government or party cadres," "failing to pay taxes and other dues or not making such payments in full," "nonfulfillment of all stipulations in government contracts," and "theft of government intelligence [which would include incomplete disclosure of prices they charged the government] for private enrichment." All these categories of offenses were based on excess profits earned by businessmen beyond what was thought their due. However, since most businesses were accused of keeping inadequate books, what constituted "legal" and permissible profit was determined entirely at the accusers' discretion.

The accused were arraigned during by-now-the-customary mass trials in five categories varying from fully in compliance with the "law" to fully in contravention of the "law." But there were no codified law or legal rules of procedure, or of defense. Political expediency served to determine the ratio of persons among the accused to be sentenced, both in individual urban groups and in a particular locale. Bo Ibo, who was responsible for dealing with the special case of major Shanghai businessmen, discussed the deliberations in which Zhou Enlai also participated, and reported on such a decision in favor of Rong Yiren, a kin of Shanghai's pre-1949 textile and flour magnate Jung Tsong-ching (Rong Zongjing) and currently the PRC's noted capitalist frontman in the National People's Congress and founder of the International Trade and Investment Trust under Deng Xiaoping three decades later.

Since all the penalties meted out to the accused in both the "Three Antis" and the "Five Antis" campaigns entailed financial outlays in the form of fines and restitution to the government, the total sum reached phenomenal figures. For Shanghai alone, the total levy reached ten trillion yuan[40] in the pre-1955 currency, which Bo estimated at 20 percent of all private capital. Following upon tax payments and other contributions to the "Resist American-Aid Korea Fund" of 1951, this new capital levy was clearly beyond the capacity of the business community. Bo's final solution was to set the payments at 20 percent of a lower amount (7 trillion) to be paid in

---

40. *Id.*, p. 174.

cash, plus another 20 percent in stock, and 60 percent by installment later. This payment method not only resulted in a new revenue of 1.4 trillion yuan (old RMB)[41] from the larger businesses and individuals in Shanghai alone, it turned out that the same capital levy also resulted in the emergence of many new enterprises of joint state-private ownership. Thus about four years before the final nationalization of all private capital, a major step was taken already in 1952 toward the full control of the urban sector of the economy.

Accelerating the Nationalization of Private Business

In 1949, Mao appeared to think that immediate nationalization would constitute wrong timing. He held back the radical CCP members who wanted to take more stringent measures against China's capitalists.[42] As he told his inner circle, the Party still needed the businessmen's collaboration; it needed their managerial and technical know-how. They were also politically useful because Taiwan under Chiang's leadership was still continuing its military activities against the Communists. However, by 1952, the situation had changed sufficiently. The Communist Party was in a much stronger position to dominate the business sector. First, government orders to sustain government and, later, military expenditures during the Korean War and increased demand for domestic production (with imports under the UN embargo), had given private manufacturers a large increase in government business.[43] The other side of government orders was the dependence they created which could be doubly risky—a more appropriate adjective is "deadly"—to the independence of private businessmen because the latter's source of financing was now under the same controlling state sector. The nationalization of the government banks and the priority given to financial deflation through capital levy and taxes (including fines) in consequence of the "Five Antis" and "Three Antis" campaigns had reduced private liquidity further.[44] The private business sector of "national capitalists" by then was demoralized enough to accept the next step of socialist transformation the Communist Party had prepared for them. As a matter of fact, the alacrity with which they lined up like lambs for slaughter may have even surprised some Communist leaders. Statistics in the memoirs of PRC officials have

---

41. See Chen Yun, *supra* note 23, p. 116.

42. Bo, *supra* note 20, pp. 165-167.

43. It is not clear how much businessmen knew at the time how land reform was conducted nationally and how such knowledge affected their own transformation.

44. See Yuan-li Wu, *supra* note 18, Chapter II, pp. 395-423.

cast new light on this process although they have left some questions unanswered.[45]

A conference convened by the Economic and Financial Commission, which Chen Yun headed, in January 1954 reached the conclusion that the rate of forming joint state-private enterprises had to be accelerated if the potential output capacity of private industry was to be fully utilized. An Extraordinary Review of how private capital might be best utilized and how worker "supervision" of management should proceed was convened at this critical time. The Korean armistice had been signed and the First Five-Year Plan of economic development was to be implemented. On the other hand, the attacks on businessmen in the 1952-53 nationwide campaign had so crippled the private sector that from its self-serving perspective the government was now compelled to play a more active role to promote productivity. To do so, the proposed approach coming out of the conference and approved by higher authorities was to form more joint (state-private) enterprises faster. In concrete terms the proposal was to convert private industrial enterprises, each employing more than ten persons, according to a definite time-table—651 firms accounting for 23 percent of the aggregate gross value of production of the state and joint state-private industrial enterprises in 1954. But the actual number of firms converted into joint enterprises turned out to be 800 in that year.[46]

At 1954 year-end, including the 800 newly formed joint enterprises, 1,764 such firms were established, accounting for 33 percent of the aggregate gross industrial production of the sectors of private and joint enterprises combined, and 23 percent of their total employment.[47] The speed of socialization continued to accelerate, however. In the following year (1955), after another conference on speeding up the formation of joint enterprises, a procedural innovation was introduced. Separate small firms in the same industry began to be absorbed into a single joint state-private enterprise. The argument again was to increase efficiency and expand production. Since large private firms were generally targeted for socialization first, the smaller and less efficient ones were being left behind. They would find it even harder to compete. Besides, the government as well as state and joint state-private firms would discriminate against them. Therefore, to the enthusiasts in the movement, it would make

---

45. Bo, *supra* note 20, p. 410.
46. *Id.*, at p. 416.
47. *Ibid.*

sense to socialize *en gros*, i.e., by an entire industry at a time. The official proposal to do so for both industry and commerce was approved by the Central Committee on October 15, 1955.[48] No opposition from the other political parties was reported in the press.

V. AMALGAMATION AND SOCIALIZATION IN ALL NON-AGRICULTURAL SECTORS

The PRC's First Five-Year Plan, which was nominally scheduled for 1953-57,[49] had a twofold purpose: to lay the foundation for industrialization and to transform the economic system from that outlined in Mao's "New Democracy" under a "coalition government" to one of socialism as understood by the CCP. Both the dominant form of property ownership and the development of the method or "mode of production" were to be fundamentally altered from those of traditional China and the KMT period. Given such an ideological notion of the Communist Party and the latter's conceptualization of its economic mission, although Mao and his close associates were more practical politicians and strategists than theoreticians, one could detect the economic logic underlying the successive measures they adopted through 1951-56. The ideas were enunciated in varying degrees of candor and clarity in the writings and speeches of Chen Yun, Bo Ibo, Zhou Enlai and Mao himself.

A Theory for Controlling All Distribution

The Communist leaders, especially Mao, rejected giving precedence to developing consumer goods production, although some intellectual supporters of Mao may have advocated a less Spartan approach than was actually adopted. Mao opposed such an approach because it would not enhance China's national military power fast enough and would do so too indirectly. They dismissed reliance on importing the capital required, dismissing it as impractical, which of course was true, given Mao's decision on a totally pro-Soviet foreign policy stance and his vigorous prosecution of the Korean War as a Soviet surrogate. Mao thus left but one option for his own country, that is, if it were to pursue industrial development, prosecute the war and increase national military power simultaneously, it would have to proceed self-sufficiently. It would then have to keep capital investment at a maximum and personal consump-

---

48. The proposal was submitted by Li Wei-han, in charge of dealing with the non-Communist groups. See Bo, *supra* note 20, p. 424.

49. The underlying reason for the time-table is rather complex. See the next section.

tion and nonmilitary public spending as low as possible. These conditions would unavoidably promise a very hard life for that country's citizens. Mao's lieutenants, particularly Chen Yun, were largely responsible for devising practical measures to turn this vision into reality. With the passing of time, they increasingly had to try to prevent Mao himself from upsetting their efforts through his impatience and interference with their more pragmatic plans by going over their heads with his half-baked ideas. But Mao knew only too well how to organize and incite extraordinarily powerful social movements that could manipulate and bend people to his will.

Chen Yun, who in economic exposition easily understood by his audiences, usually wanted to make sure that the surplus of production over consumption (including the quantities used as input for production) of both "grain" and "cotton" (here representing agricultural and industrial products in general) would be available at their maximum levels. He wanted to see this surplus available for export in exchange for imported goods and technology. To do so, he wanted to minimize any unnecessary accumulation of stock at the points of production and use, or "in the pipeline" of distribution. "Idle" inventory in the hands of traders would represent waste. Such "unnecessary" accumulation would in his mind constitute hoarding. The possibility of hoarding in turn would imply that speculation resulting in price variation could take place. On the basis of his personal experience in both inciting monetary instability and price volatility during the KMT period and his subsequent experiences in suppressing both, Chen was from the very beginning of the battle against renewed hyperinflation an advocate of making the purchase and sale of grain and cotton government monopolies. With the introduction of comprehensive economic planning in view, the monopolization of all channels of distribution by the state therefore became the next urgent item on the government's agenda in 1954-55.

Socialization of the Network of Trade and Handicraft Workshops

Accordingly, apart from the collectivization of agriculture—to be discussed in the next section—which the Chinese Communists had long announced they would copy from the Soviet Union, there were two other sectors to be "collectivized" or "nationalized," the wholesale and retail trade and the individual "handicraft" workshops (China's small manufacturer), including independent service establishments. While drafting a Directive for the Party's Central Committee on strengthening market control in July 1954, Chen used seven to eight million as the number of stores and retail-stall keepers in China at the time.[50] If we round the mainland Chinese population at the time to 600 million, this figure would give up to 1.3 store- or stall-keepers to 100 persons in China, an apparently gross underestimate. A pertinent question is how a task of such a gigantic scale could be accomplished within a time-period of any practical significance.

The task of organizing independent craftsmen into cooperatives or absorbing them into the ranks of wage-earners in larger firms (through nationalization or formation of joint state-private enterprises) was a no less daunting project. Bo Ibo, who had been delegated to oversee this undertaking, reported that Liu Shoaqi was always the cautious one. Liu thought that the target of forming cooperatives should be set at 70-80 percent of all craftsmen.[51]

Apparently, the leading cadres who directed the new all-out cooperativization drive must have been satisfied with their own achievement. For when Mao was briefed on the successful outcome on March 4, 1956, barely three months after Liu spoke, the Chairman remarked on the stupendous result of organizing three million craftsmen in cooperative units within the first two months of 1956. Whereas only two million persons had been put under the co-op umbrella through the end of 1955, by the end of 1956, 99,100 cooperatives of handicraftsmen of all categories had been organized in the country as a whole. These craft cooperatives boasted 5,091,000 members out of a national total of 5.53 million craftsmen. Each such cooperative averaged 51.4 members.

There were doubtless many regional variations in what actually happened in the merger of retail and wholesale merchants and the formation of cooperatives by individual craftsmen, and the absorption of some of the individual businessmen and self-employed persons by state and semi-state firms. At the time of the initial drive to amalgamate traders and craftsmen, like the formation of cooperative farms, the individual member was free either to join or not to do so. Some perhaps did not, while others were probably left out by the organizers on purpose so as to make their own task simpler.

Haphazard Restructuring of the Handicraft Industry

At any rate, accelerated collectivization in such haste would not have been possible, even if only on paper, without some radical

50. Chen Yun, *supra* note 23, pp. 232-40, especially p. 234.
51. Bo, *supra* note 20, p. 449.

procedural shortcuts. This was apparently done by grouping individuals together "by industry" at any given locality, forming a cooperative by treating such a group as a single unit while units at different places were joined in a single cooperative. Theoretically such a larger amalgamated cooperative expected to be more efficient through the practice of "rational economic accounting," making sure that cost would be at least below benefit! The real outcome turned out usually to be different. Several examples given by Bo Ibo in 1991, thirty-years later, are illuminating.

According to Bo, 88 craftsmen's cooperatives in Shijiazhuang were merged into 31; of the new co-ops the largest had 1400 members. Some amalgamated general co-ops actually were made up by members in 14 different occupations. A new metal craftsmen's co-op in Meishan County was formed by including makers of space-heaters and scales, bicycle repairmen, watchmakers, and others geographically scattered in 13 rural *xiang* (districts). A single visit to all of the members' places to make wage payments took seven days. In northern Shenyang, Liaoning Province, 103 tailoring shops were organized into a single cooperative with ten store-fronts for serving customers.[52] Combining many separate businesses and individuals into a single production unit in a totally haphazard manner would *prima facie* have little conceivable economic advantage if the products and services bore no relationship to one another. In fact, production should decline sharply as would buyer satisfaction.

A Final Solution

If there was any benefit to be derived from wholesale collectivization, it could accrue to the Communist authorities through the accelerated formation of joint state-private enterprises by a group of firms in one industry, all at one time, and so forth, industry by industry, in the entire modern sector. The end of this process consisted of a pitiful appeal of all remaining private businessmen in the sector to Mao to take over what was left of their equity. This virtual plea for mercy and relief began in 1955 and was completed in 1956. According to official statistics, 860,000 private businessmen[53] formed such industry-wide joint enterprises with the state in 1956, counting in those who had earlier done the same by themselves as individual firms. No detailed statistics are available, but we can safely assume that this was not a count of stockholders but of heads

52. *Id.*, at p. 450.
53. *Id.*, at p. 437.

of the firms. Of course, this figure left out those businessmen who had been killed, forced to suicide,[54] or otherwise deprived of their enterprises and properties during the Five Antis and other campaigns.

Mao personally administered the coup de grâce in talks on December 5, 7 and 10, 1956 with leaders of the Association of Industry and Commerce, which had been formed in October 1953 to speak for the businessmen.[55] His arrangement with those businessmen consisted of a promise to pay annual installment payments for the purchase of their assets. These payments, later fixed at 57 percent of the remaining value, net of taxes, fines and other dues owed to the government, were to be made over a number of years.[56] The details subsequently revealed by Bo turned out to be 5 percent for 6 years, or 30 percent in total. How the original total value was arrived at was, however, never revealed. To some the total seemed to be much less. To those whose annual payments were not large (apparently substantially under 10,000 yuan) the recipients were allowed to refuse the state's offer of compensation. As a reward they in turn would have their "capitalist" label removed from their respective personal files. In the Communists' vernacular, they could "doff their capitalist hats"—and join the officially sponsored labor union as new members of the working class. Unfortunately, even this last promise was never redeemed in Mao's lifetime. Accordingly, for some 700,000 persons who were affected, the pejorative label "capitalist," which their family members also carried, was not removed until 1979, about a quarter-century later, thus condemning several million persons to an "underclass" until three years after Mao's death.

VI. COLLECTIVIZATION OF AGRICULTURE

The collectivization of agriculture was a major policy issue discussed during the all-important Sixth Plenum of the Seventh Communist Party Central Committee in October 1955. In conjunction with the transformation of the nonagricultural sectors of the economy to socialism, Mao Zedong revealed at the meeting his private thoughts about the socialization of industry and commerce five years earlier. He said that it would not have been wise politically to

---

54. Including a number of well-known businessmen with whom the author was acquainted.

55. A Preparatory Committee was formed in July 1952.

56. Bo, *supra* note 20, p. 437.

mount an attack on the then-existing economic system in all directions at once. Without the prior redistribution of land under the land reform campaign (described above), the peasants would not have come over to "our side." It was only after "land reform" that the capitalist class had begun to sense its own isolation in the country. Now that the urban economy was coming under the state's control, the collectivization of agriculture was the next step that would make the entire proletariat come to "our side" in a real "peasant-worker alliance of the proletariat."[57]

The Chinese Communists viewed collectivization as the agricultural counterpart of the eventual substitution of state enterprises for private firms. Peasants would become workers employed by the state in farm enterprises. But unlike workers employed by private factories who do not live in the factories, the peasants lived with their families on the farms and many were actually owners of their own farms. Hence to collectivize agriculture resembled more the amalgamation of private businesses owned and run by craftsmen working at home with members of their own families. To collectivize such individual owner-operated farms was to amalgamate them into a single enterprise and to replace the many owner-operators with a single manager.

Obviously a natural question is, why should such a restructuring of agriculture be necessary? While the logical answer should be based on economic advantage, with Mao the underlying reasoning became rather obscure. Several ideas were simply accepted by Mao as revealed truths:

(1) The larger the farm unit, the more productive it is.
(2) The less the private means of production (such as land, farm animals and equipment contributed by peasant members of the farm), used as a way of accounting for the individual farmers' shares of the result of the farm operation, the more "advanced" is the stage of development of the farm on the mythical ladder of socialist evolution. Therefore, collectivization should be carried out in three stages: (i) Individual farmers would only work together on specific projects or during special times (such as sowing, harvesting and irrigation); and, (ii) Individual members of a cooperative farm, run as a single unit, would choose their manager and distribute the farm income according to their respective contributions in terms of (a) labor and (b) private property contributed. The latter contribution presumed the use

57. *Id*, at p. 407.

of some agreed formula in evaluating the relative worth of the different assets and the existence of book-keeping and honest and knowledgeable personnel.

(3) In the most "advanced" cooperative farm, output would be distributed solely according to the labor input contributed, the share of property having been abolished entirely.

Since the original land reform was welcomed by the landless peasant and some tenant farmers who became owner-operators by taking over other persons' land during the 1949-51 political take-over, collectivization at the second and third levels started a process in the opposite direction. In theory, peasants were free to join or to leave a cooperative farm. In practice the history was one of compulsory collectivization. That distributing income and assigning work by illiterate individuals would create chaotic results can be readily expected. However, official statistics seemed to suggest a numerical record of incredibly fast accomplishments, as follows:

NUMBERS OF COOPERATIVE FARMS OF THE 1ST STAGE IN MAINLAND CHINA

December 1951	300
June 1952	3,000
December 1953	14,000
September 1954	100,000
(Before Fall Harvest) 1954	120,000
Spring 1955	670,000
End 1955	60% of all peasant households
End April 1956	1,000,000
(Bo Ibo, 1991, pp. 326-29.)	

Bo Ibo in his 1991 memoir graphically presented the unbelievable acceleration of reported cases of successful collectivization in 1954-56 and the development of serious debate on the desirability of pushing through the program. A central figure opposing Mao's seemingly dogmatic political decision to do so was Deng Zihui, in charge of agricultural affairs in the Party bureaucracy.[58] In the end, Mao won the debate; one would not expect otherwise.

58. *Id.*, at pp. 326-401.

Conclusion

Several conclusions are warranted at this stage: First, the success shown by the statistics on cooperative farms and, earlier in this chapter, on craft cooperatives was very much a report of success on paper. The new institutional units formed did not at all function as they were supposed to do, and probably not at all. In the case of the craft cooperatives and merged retail and wholesale units (perhaps even some manufacturing firms), those enterprises that were not made a part of the new units were no longer allowed to exist.[59] This loss of production and economic activity and the eradication of established business connections are often overlooked by observers. Second, the surge of success reported, especially in 1955, illustrated the mutually stimulative effect between the Party leaders, especially Mao, and the lower-level operators whose enthusiasm for more numerical movements often carried themselves too far. Third, Mao, perhaps like Deng Xiaoping more than three decades later, would make inspection tours in order to ascertain facts for himself. But the leader—in any country—can be fooled and many in history were. In the final analysis, it was Mao's impotence to achieve complete control of a vast country like China and his confidence in his own ability to the contrary that drove his persistent push toward the goal of rapid socialization.

59. Some "underground factories" reportedly managed to operate nevertheless.

CHAPTER V

ECONOMIC DEVELOPMENT AFTER SOCIALIZATION—BUT FOR WHAT?

I. WHAT AFTER SOCIALIZATION?

After concluding the socialization drives in 1950-56, which essentially consisted of "land reform" (followed by collectivization) and the nationalization of privately owned nonagricultural businesses of all sizes in both rural and urban areas, the Eighth CCP Congress met in September 1956. It was at this Congress that the principal guidelines were announced for the country's economic development during the Second Five-Year Plan (*1958-62*). We italicize the time period deliberately because it was quite early during this second five-year span that the original plan was first modified and then totally side-tracked. More precisely, the plan was overwhelmed at Mao Zedong's personal initiative. Mao was consumed in 1957-58 by a desire to speed up industrialization, relying primarily on his own special brand of mass movements.

The "Great Leap" was an expression used throughout China to describe Mao's spectacular effort to push the country toward industrialization, which he hoped would enable the PRC to catch up with the United Kingdom in steel production in 15 years and eventually to become a grain exporting country, as well. However, the "leap" turned out to be an unprecedented disaster that lasted approximately five years, beginning from 1958 through part of 1961, which could be regarded as the upper turning point of a "growth path," followed by a trough, or lower turning point, in 1961-62. Economists might even call this period in China an arch-example of a politically-induced depression. This period of precipitate economic decline, which became especially noticeable to the world at large in agriculture, has since been obliquely admitted even by official PRC sources as the "three years of natural disaster," although there was little that was purely the fault of nature, and the famine lasted more than three years, producing deaths of 20-40 million.[1]

---

1. At a CCP Central Committee "work session" on May 31, 1961, Liu Shaoqi stated unequivocally that the decline in agricultural and industrial production in China

A whole series of questions can and should be raised at this point. The first is what made Mao think that accelerated economic development was both possible and imperative in China at that time. With new information coming to light in the 1980s and 90s—especially since 1989—as a result of revelations on the process of decision-making practised by leading officials surrounding Mao, and of recent studies on Mao's relations with Stalin and post-Stalin Soviet leaders, partly based on disclosure from the Soviet side, the extraordinary phenomenon of the "Great Leap" can now be better explained. A very complex set of circumstances and their particular timing were responsible for this bizarre development, the effect of which on the PRC lasted well beyond the reign of Mao.

But let us pause for a moment to examine the process of economic development in the abstract from the perspective of a socialist planner. Logically the task would seem to be relatively straightforward and the proper approach to it, as advocated by Chen Yun, would be to plot some kind of a planned growth path in which the demand for resources could be matched with their supply both sectorally and in terms of the aggregate monetary flow of goods in value terms that are supplied and the corresponding flow of expenditures on them. Now that the nation's resources had in theory come under absolute control by the Communist Party at the center as described in Chapter IV—demand and use of resources in unplanned directions having been reduced to a minimum after the total socialist transformation of 1956—why should Mao and the CCP try to accelerate growth to such an excess as virtually to lose control?

The Drive to Excel

A partial explanation may be found in Mao's frenetic drive to excel. While in Moscow attending the celebration of the 40th anniversary of the November Revolution on November 18, 1957, Mao asked Pollitt, the representative of the British Communist Party in attendance, how much the steel production of Britain was and what level it could reach by 1972, that is, at the end of three Chinese five-

---

was "90 percent a result of human [i.e., policy] error" and only "10 percent caused by bad luck." The proportional figures were the reverse of those Maoists had used. Liu said that he had consulted Party leaders in a number of provinces, citing Hebei, Henan, Shandong and Shanxi. Liu further rated the policy error as one just short of being a wrong "Party line," his words being a coded CCP expression of one demanding a new Party leadership. See *Liu Shaoqi Xuanji* [*Liu Shaoqi's Selected Works*] (Beijing: People's Publishers, 1985), Vol. II, pp. 335-341, especially p. 338. *Infra* note 31.

year plans. Pollitt, according to Mao, gave an approximate figure of 20 million tons for 1957 and thought that British steel production could be as high as 30 million tons by 1972.[2] This conversation could well have impelled Mao to announce that the PRC could surpass the United Kingdom in industrial production in 15 years. Throughout the following year (1958), whenever Mao had occasion to urge the PRC planners and administrators including Wang Heshou, then his Minister for Metallurgy, to raise their plan targets, he always spoke of surpassing the U.K. in steel output in 15 years, as if such a feat alone would be tantamount to making China an industrial nation. No doubt steel was a symbol of power in his mind, and Mao was obsessed with such symbolism. Perhaps this state-of-mind had to do with his memory of the Opium War and the whole sorry record of China's foreign encounters in the 19th century. The United Kingdom was to fit the role of becoming in Mao's mind—and that of many other Chinese—the first Western power to be bested by China since 1842.[3]

In the same connection, Mao often looked at the economic growth rate of the Soviet Union in its earlier years and that of Soviet steel production then when instructing PRC planners not to treat past Soviet records as the upper bounds in their own target-setting.[4] This was also Mao's practice in later years. In 1957, he had begun to compare in his mind the imagined dash to catch up with the U.K. even as Khrushchev boasted of catching up with the United States. It was in 1957, we should remember, that the Soviet Union became the first nation to send a satellite into space.

However, the drive eventually to be Number One could not have been the only motivating force of the vastly accelerated push toward industrialization. A second consideration was Mao's greatly exaggerated self-confidence based on his string of political successes since 1945. Still another factor was probably Mao's fear that the Soviet Union, especially the post-Stalin USSR, could not be re-

---

2. Bo Ibo, *Ruogan Zhongda Juece yu Shijan di Huigu* [*Many Major Decisions and Events in Retrospect*] (Beijing: CCP Central Party School Publishers, 1993), Vol. II, pp. 691-92.

3. During his reign Mao used the United States and the Soviet Union as the two powers always anxious to dominate the world, while he pretended to be the spokesman of the "third world" of developing countries and, therefore, ipso facto, placing China on the same footing with them.

4. Bo Ibo, *Ruogan Zhongda Juece yu Shijan di Huigu* [*Many Major Decisions and Events in Retrospect*] (Beijing: CCP Central Party School Publishers, 1991), Vol. I, p. 528. The average annual rates of earlier Soviet industrial production growth cited by Bo were: 1928-32, 19.2%; 1933-37, 17.1%; 1938-40, 13.2%.

lied upon for unstinting support. As matters developed, Mao's "Great Leap" and the accompanying commune movement to reorganize agriculture, not overlooking his dealings with Khrushchev in connection with his ambition to conquer Taiwan, may have served as a trigger to the CCP's later break with the Kremlin in the 1960s. Mao simply overreached himself in his attempt to ensnare Khrushchev. But let us return to mid-1956 when the Communist Party proclaimed its second major success after the establishment of the new "People's Republic" on October 1, 1949.

Sources of Self-Confidence

The conversion of the pre-Communist market economy of China to a progressively more centrally administrated system in the name of socialism took far less time than the Chinese Communist Party had led China's naive businessmen and intellectuals to expect. Businessmen, large and small, who were praying for an end to hyperinflation saw their goal realized in less than two years after the founding of the new regime.[5] However, within another five years, i.e., by 1956, ownership of private property in producer goods for sale had by and large disappeared. During the same period, Chinese peasants who desired above all to become owner-farmers had seen their private holdings collectivized into "farm cooperatives" and themselves reduced to poorly paid workers in these state-owned, controlled, and cadre-managed agricultural units although nominally cooperative farms. Intellectuals who in 1949 wished to become fellow builders of a "new democracy" soon found themselves in the status of automatons rubber-stamping and applauding the CCP's decisions and not allowed either to desist or to remain silent.

From one point of view, many Chinese could not but blame themselves for having been hoodwinked. However, from the opposite perspective, the Chinese Communist leaders were virtually at the height of their success in 1956, and Mao Zedong in particular had reason to consider himself a superb practitioner of ruthless statecraft unprecedented in Chinese history. He had joined the ranks of successful manipulators of human beings in history, but on an unsurpassed scale. It should surprise no one if he then became confident of his own unfailing ability to accomplish the seemingly impossible.

---

5. See Yuan-li Wu, *Human Rights in the People's Republic of China* (Boulder, CO: Westview Press, 1988), especially Parts I and III for the costs to the many victim groups.

Doubt Cast by External Events

But was the inner Mao truly so confident that he felt he could lead the country to industrialization at full speed? How much opposition did he expect to encounter? The answer in his own mind seemed quite simple in April 1956 when he wrote and spoke for the CCP cadres on the "ten critical issues" yet to be resolved.[6] He also spoke of Khrushchev's denunciation of Stalin at the Twentieth Soviet Party Congress as being overdone. To him "internal contradictions among the people" should not be treated in the same manner as "struggles" against class enemies. The opponents did not have to be put to death "at one stroke." From these colorful statements so typical of Mao one could conclude that he was almost ready to permit some open airing of public dissatisfaction because he probably thought that the discontents were not serious. But the uprisings in Poland and Hungary during the second half of 1956 led to more than a mere passing interest in Mao's own headquarters. Events thereafter in Eastern Europe produced far-reaching results in China.

Bo Ibo was one of several CCP elders when he wrote in his 1993 book that because of the events in Eastern Europe the Politburo of the CCP Central Committee's Standing Committee met some 14 times between October 21 and November 19, 1956.[7] Discussions centered around the significance of the Polish and Hungarian uprisings, their possible impact on the PRC, and the best counter measures to be taken.[8] Afternoon, evening and Mao's habitual nocturnal discussions were held on successive days involving top officials like Liu Shaoqi, Zhou Enlai, Deng Xiaoping, Wang Jiaxiang, Chen Yun and, on occasion, the resident Soviet and Polish ambassadors. A special mission composed of Liu, Deng and Wang was then dispatched to Moscow, for a briefing by the Russians, and for policy coordination.

According to Bo's account, the PRC authorities judged the Poznan strike of June 28, 1956 as having been initially brought about by mishandling on the part of incompetent and ignorant officials and that the strike was successfully settled later by adroit political measures. To the same Chinese officials, however, the Hungarian affair was an entirely different matter. It was not just a result of the Hungarian Communists' ineptitude in handling recent

6. See Bo Ibo, *supra* note 2, Vol. II, p. 569.
7. *Id.*, pp. 574-77.
8. *Ibid.* Bo added that he was in attendance at a number of these meetings.

grievances. Rather the root cause was the Hungarian CP's earlier failure to suppress political opposition more thoroughly "through class struggle," both during the Hungarian land reform and in the elimination of urban capitalists in Hungary. In Mao's judgment, the class enemies there were simply removed from positions of influence; they were not liquidated outright. Therefore, the Hungarian uprising lasted nearly a whole month. It was suppressed only by the use of Soviet force. Such an event of course would fall under the Maoist conceptual category of a "counter-revolutionary" assault on the Communist party and government, to which Mao was extraordinarily sensitive. (If the reader would take a quantum leap to June 1989, he could not fail to notice the analogy of Deng's evaluation of the students' occupation of Tiananmen Square to Mao's assessment of the Hungarian uprising 33 years earlier.)

From March 1956 to September 1957, an increasing volume of news poured into Beijing from the country, reporting on student and worker strikes, public protests and demonstrations, and withdrawals by farm households from newly organized cooperative farms. Bo also gave some numbers: up to 200 workers per strike, up to 1,000 persons in each student strike or public protest, more than 1,100 "collective farm incidents in Zhejiang province," and withdrawals of 12,000 households from collective farms in Guangdong.[9] In the course of these "disturbances," apparently the cry in public "let's have ourselves a Hungary" was heard by some CCP leaders and led to Liu Shaoqi's laconic remark that a "contradiction among the people" (i.e., not among the "non-people") could be brewing. More bluntly, a "counter-revolution" could be about to erupt.

These events in China were a gathering storm caused by the acceleration of agricultural collectivization and socialization of small businesses on top of modern manufacturing, and their mishandling in 1955-56. Political developments in the Soviet Union and Eastern Europe now made Mao and his close lieutenants even more apprehensive and more sensitive to signs of domestic resistance to their own rule.[10] In consequence, we saw the reversal of a policy which was first made public by Zhou Enlai only in early 1957 to encourage Chinese intellectuals to engage themselves more actively in economic development and education for the country's modernization under CCP centralist planning during the Second Five-Year Plan. The reversal of this very short-lived official policy

9. Bo, *supra* note 2, Vol. II, p. 570.
10. Reported openly by Bo after 37 years, *ibid.*

toward intellectuals at this point was marked by the initiation of Mao's "Anti-Rightist" drive. The brief "thaw," known to China scholars as the "One Hundred Flowers" movement, was very deliberately and repeatedly encouraged by Mao Zedong personally and then equally deliberately cut off at Mao's command in the spring of 1957.

As mentioned in Chapter III, the political effect was to shut off all open objection by knowledgeable persons to Mao's bull-headed and ignorant policies over a long time, even when their disastrous impact on the country had become imminent and irrefutable. The long-term impact on China, including the Chinese Communists themselves, was incalculable. A second and even more torturous path of development that followed the reversed policy toward intellectuals seemed to be a more favorable treatment of engineers and scientists, whose work in the weapons and technical field was recognized by the PRC military leadership, and a small group of dedicated technocrats. Unfortunately for the Chinese people, this favorable treatment of a small group in "hard science" and weapons-related engineering was carried out in complete isolation from any tempering humanistic influence that might have come from social scientists, philosophers and other humanists, had they not been killed, imprisoned, or at best, exiled to perform hard labor so that they might absorb "politically correct" doctrines. The net effect was to manifest itself in the long-term diversion of resources to weapons development and the over-emphasis of capital goods production in isolated unsuitable geographical areas. We shall return to this point later.

How Much Time Did Mao Think He Had to Prepare for the Next War?

There were perhaps two related political and foreign policy questions in Mao's mind. First, might the PRC become involved in an external war? After all, before the 1953 Korean armistice Chen Yun's principal fears were Allied bombing of Chinese industry, transport facilities, and the like, and the economy's ability to sustain the war effort. Following the Korean armistice Chen volunteered on one occasion the thought that three years might be available for the PRC to concentrate on developing the economy. At the time of the Eighth CCP Party Congress (September 1956), Mao apparently was thinking in terms of 12 to 15 years of peace during which the PRC could try to "catch up" industrially with the developed world.

In short, his planning horizon would take him through a period of two and a half to three five-year plans. In this connection one should recall that his memory of the Korean War and his thought of security and of China's ability to fight a sustained war on its own could never be very far from his mind. Therefore, to be ready economically would be a prerequisite to any military build-up. Mao was a man in a big hurry and behaved accordingly. Whatever might be Mao's worries about the imminence of another military conflict, however, his economic advisers, among whom were Chen Yun and Bo Ibo, were clearly always concerned about the constraint of productivity and the inadequate supply of immediately available specific resources. Hence a constantly gnawing question was how to increase production without large new domestic investment. Common sense demanded an answer.[11]

At the time, the likelihood of augmenting resources through foreign aid and the effectiveness of Soviet economic assistance and its timeliness had already come into question. As early as April 1951, Chen Yun told the first national conference on organizing economic work during the Korean war that neither the CCP nor the Soviet Union was really prepared to embark immediately upon putting Soviet aid to China in high gear. For one thing, even the necessary geological data were not there. Soviet advisers sent to China were ignorant of Chinese conditions. An example cited by Chen had to do with one of the first aid projects to design an automobile manufacturing plant for the PRC by Soviet experts. The contract for the project was signed during the Mao-Zhou visit to Moscow in 1950. When the experts arrived in Beijing, the location of the plant was a subject of heated discussion: some suggested Beijing; others named Shijiazhuang; Taiyuan was another option. Chen himself suggested that a location farther inland like Xian (Sian) might be better. Upon examination, it was discovered that all these ideas were impractical.[12] For instance, according to Chen, a 30,000-car annual capacity auto-plant would require an electric power plant of 24,000 kw. At that time, Xian boasted of only one 9,000 kw power plant. Furthermore, the auto plant would demand over 200,000 tons

11. See *Chen Yun Wen Xuan (1949-1956)* [*Chen Yun's Selected Writings*] (Beijing: People's Publishers, 1984), pp. 234-44 and *Chen Yun Wen Xuan (1956-1985)* [*Chen Yun's Selected Writings*] (Beijing: People's Publishers, 1986), pp. 1-14 and pp. 40-49, dealing respectively with the first and second five-year plans. Also Bo Ibo, *supra* note 2, Chapter 36, pp. 1047-1069 and Chapter 43, pp. 1278-1287.

12. Chen Yun, *Chen Yun Wen Xuan (1949-1956)* [*Chen Yun's Selected Writings*] (Beijing: People's Publishers, 1984), pp. 132-33.

of steel and other ferrous products. But the Shijiazhuang plant was not expected to start production until five to six years later. Transportation and coke supply presented additional bottlenecks. After wasting two months in Beijing in fruitless discussion, the bi-national planners ultimately settled on Changchun in Manchuria because the complementary demand for related inputs could be met there more easily.

Again, in connection with the more modern equipment the Soviet Union had agreed to supply under the 1950 agreement for the First Five-Year Plan, as Chen Yun explained in January 1957, the truth was that installation in most cases took place only during the fourth year (1956) of the PRC plan, in some cases even as late as 1957.[13] Hence, little either of the increase in production or of the new expansion of industrial capacity during 1953-57 should be ascribed to new investment from Soviet aid in the years usually described as Mao's best. If Soviet aid was responsible at all, it was more technical than equipment assistance and from equipment previously installed by Japan and not taken away from the northern parts of Manchuria during the occupation by Soviet troops as was done in some Southern Manchurian industrial centers that Soviet troops stripped. This is a historical point yet to be ascertained by future economic historians, perhaps from former Soviet files.

As for imports from the Soviet Union for some 109 new investment projects under the Second Five-Year Plan communicated to his Soviet counterpart by Li Fuchun, who was in the state planning apparatus in charge of the PRC's Soviet purchases, Soviet supplies under these PRC orders could not start until 1961, i.e., the final year but one of the second Chinese Five-Year Plan, if not even later.[14] Hence a protracted delay in plan implementation seemed unavoidable inasmuch as the Soviet Union was to withdraw all its advisers from China in mid-1960 and had begun to do so a year earlier, as described in Chapter XI below. (Both PRC planners and the CCP political leadership had feared such a development.)[15] This half-anticipated suspension of Soviet advisers prompted PRC planners to accelerate the development process and orient it toward self-reliance with a high degree of autarky.

---

13. Chen Yun, *Chen Yun Wen Xuan (1956-1985)* [*Chen Yun's Selected Writings*] (Beijing: People's Publishers, 1986), p. 47.

14. The delay implies an unavailable supply and some necessary revision of the Second Five-Year Plan.

15. See Chapters IX and XI on Sino-Soviet relations in this volume.

The development of a close Soviet-PRC relationship began under Stalin with a one-sided dependence on Mao's part but netted Mao considerable military support in his war with the Chinese Nationalists. But this support was not without a substantial long-term cost. Even the eventual CCP success in securing a dependable domestic source of weapons-grade uranium 235 through some "unintentional" Soviet aid was not an unmixed blessing. It led to a long-term problem for China by creating a "nuclear power's burden" for a poor developing country.

The change in Kremlin leadership from Stalin finally to Khrushchev and Brezhnev made the PRC-Soviet relationship quite different from the Stalin-Mao entente. Suffice it to say at this juncture that "milking the uncertain-tempered Soviet cow" as long and as hard as it was safe clearly was an imperative from Mao's point of view. This would also seem to be a strategy on which many of Mao's domestic political doubters and opponents might have agreed with Mao.[16] They were not really totally without responsibility for what happened after 1957, as some of them claimed in the 1980s.

II. RATIONALE OF MAO'S IRRATIONAL ECONOMIC PLANNING

If there were good reasons for Mao to engage in an all-out effort to speed up the industrialization of the PRC, why did he adopt methods that brought on an unprecedented calamity? The immediate answer was ignorance; he did not know that he was on the wrong path. How such a grievous error could be made deserves analysis and thought.

Back in the summer of 1955 on the Beidaihe beach,[17] when Mao was given a situation briefing, which the various government agencies had put together, the three principal annual production goals for 1967 publicly disclosed by Bo Ibo in his memoirs about 37

---

16. A source quoted in a 1993 study by Guncharov, Lewis, and Xue, *Uncertain Partners: Stalin, Mao and the Korean War* (Stanford: Stanford University Press, 1993) states that between 1950 and 1955, Soviet military deliveries to China totalled 1.2 billion rubles which, at the then Soviet official ruble-dollar exchange rate of $1 to 4 rubles, would exactly amount to $300 million, which happened to equal the entire amount of the 1950 Soviet loan to the PRC. This does not necessarily mean that the "economic" loan was really a military loan or that funds were diverted. But a partial use for military purchases may have received Stalin's consent. This is another subject on which Beijing's many unopened files might shed some light.

17. Bo Ibo, *supra* note 4, Vol. I, pp. 531-35.

years later were: food grain, 300 million metric tons; raw cotton, 2.8 million metric tons; and, ingot (crude) steel, 18 million metric tons. These figures were apparently taken from the initial draft of the Second Five-Year Plan (1958-62) and regarded by Mao as too low, probably for the reasons advanced above. In each case the target was revised upward as a result. Inasmuch as Mao firmly believed (1) that the human will could move mountains and (2) that a mass movement on a national scale in which he was a recognized expert could achieve unbelievable results, he was ready to mobilize labor resources to fight this economic battle.

In this respect he was drawing upon his experience in numerous mass campaigns and human-sea attacks from the time of the final stages of the Civil War and during the Korean War, as well as through the socialization drives of the early and mid-50s. Within the Party the more passive elements and doubters about such a national effort were egged on by the activists, the higher authorities by the lower ranks, and then, vice versa, in a reverse cycle. Thus the movements went on in one region and province after another. The dynamic effect was to produce a continuous escalation of "Plan" targets during 1958-59, and in some areas, well into early 1960, when the bubble had already burst.[18]

One can well imagine how the multiple plan targets and their successive upward revisions would prove confusing to the planners themselves, especially when continuously changing instructions from a high level had to be transmitted to producing units.

In an attempt to cut through this confusion, Bo Ibo, then head of the National Economic Commission in charge of the annual production plans, originated a reporting method by maintaining two sets of plans, or, in his own terms, two "sets of books." Thus, at the central government level (C) the first set of books (AC) would register the minimum levels of production (or investment) targets that had to be achieved while another set of targets (BC) would consist of a list of higher figures which the central authority would like to accomplish and would therefore do its best to strive for but half feared that it could not succeed.[19] The center would hold AC close to its chest while instructing the level of authority immediately below it to accomplish BC. Depending upon the subject in question, the number of layers of authority would vary. In the case of only

18. For a blow-by-blow account, see Bo, *supra* note 2, Vol. II, especially Chapter 26, pp. 679-727.

19. *Id.*, p. 682.

two levels of local authority below the Center, the authority at the first lower level (level L) would treat the instructions (BC) it received from C as its first set of books (AL), and produce on that basis its own B L, which it would then issue to the tier of authority below.

In agricultural production, given the existence of a succession of tiers of authority (provincial, county, commune (*xiang*), production brigade, and production team), at each lower tier, there would very likely be an upward adjustment of the targets received. In the then political atmosphere of inflated ego and competition for the favor of one's superior, exaggerated and untruthful reports would very naturally occur. If authorities at higher levels were affected by the enthusiasm of lower levels, supported by false evidence, target setters at the top level might themselves revise the original minimum plan AC. Thus the entire process would continue as if in a never-never land. This seems to be how the targets set by the CCP leadership under Mao both for the Second Five-Year Plan and for the prospective plan of 1958-67 were raised time and again during the Great Leap.

Several factors aggravated the situation even further.

Half-Baked Ideas

Mao Zedong obviously fancied himself an agronomist. In any case, he enjoyed so much authority that his innovations were never seriously reviewed by Party members who might have expert knowledge and experience. Few high level political leaders dared to raise their voices until nearly three years later when the Lushan conference (1959) was called into session by Mao to discuss Peng Dehuai's irreverent criticism of the Great Leap but ended in condemning the marshal as an "anti-Party" (read anti-Mao) conspirator.

Mao's own handiwork, an outline of the Draft Plan of National Agricultural Development, was first published on January 25, 1956 after its adoption at a Supreme State Council meeting. A revised version was released at the end of the Third Central Committee Plenum (of the Eighth CCP Congress) that took place in September-October 1957. According to Bo Ibo, the revision pushed the long-term target date of plan fulfillment to 12 years from Mao's original 5 to 7 years, but left Mao's original target of grain production the same as before, thus not really more realistic than before. Mao wanted to see annual production at a per capita level of 2000 chin (jin, according to Pinyin; 1 metric ton) in five years' time.[20] His basic assumption was that productivity could rise to a point when per mou yield could be as high as one metric ton,[21] i.e. 6 tons an acre. During the months of October-November 1957, Mao seemed prepared to try to reach this ambitious goal in his own way. Meetings of CP representatives at the provincial and autonomous region levels were convened and peasants in unprecedented numbers were ordered to work on water irrigation and the collection of natural fertilizers in preparation for the Great Leap. Reminiscent of but surpassing the "human wave" assaults the PLA had mounted on the battlefield of Korea, the present labor force mobilization attained an order of magnitude of 20 to 30 million men in October 1957 in the country as a whole, according to Bo. It reached an order of magnitude of 80 million in December. A peak of 100 million men was reportedly mobilized by January 1958.[22]

The Third Plenum of the Eighth Central Committee met at Nanning (Guangxi) ostensibly to discuss economic planning and the national budget and to listen to briefings from the provincial and municipal party levels. After the Plenum, Party chiefs from several rice-producing provinces like Zhejiang, Jiangxi, Anhui and Guangdong began again to propose shortening the 12-year (1956-67) Agricultural Development Plan to 5 years. Henan, a wheat producing province, likewise proposed to cover the province with irrigation facilities before the harvest and to eliminate simultaneously what were commonly known as the "four pests," viz., rats, flies, mosquitoes and sparrows, the last subsequently replaced by bed bugs, sparrows being belatedly considered useful. Still another target to be attained during the same year was the eradication of all illiteracy in the province. These "plan targets" were apparently taken very seriously by the CCP cadres whose enthusiasm in pushing ahead a social movement initiated and supported by the all-powerful and all-knowing Party Chairman was not tempered by either skepticism or knowledge. Common sense had deserted them.

Assigning huge quantities of labor input to a single task was Mao's typical style. Mao had also learned from a commune in Shandong how turning over the top soil before planting succeeded in doubling the commune's crop yield. He saw the possibility of applying the same labor-intensive method to "deep plowing," assum-

---

20. *Id.*, p. 680.

21. Mao's idea was to make the per mou grain yield one ton in 50 years' time.

22. Bo, *supra* note 2, Vol. II, p. 681.

ing that yield per mou would vary proportionately with the depth of soil cultivation. The party chief of one Zhang county stated at the Nanning meeting that the soil surface of the entire county was to be dug up to a depth of 1.5 chi by April 1958.[23] Mao then instructed the farmers to do the same nationally, in an area totalling 1.2 million mou. Similarly, Mao also issued instructions on planting rice seedlings very closely. In effect, Mao was engaged in micromanaging Chinese farming on the basis of little more than hearsay. After all, was not Mao Zedong the CCP prophet? His command of the party machinery enabled him to extract blind obedience from the local level cadres.[24] Mao was indeed highly imaginative. However, to quote Confucius in *Hsueh Er* (*Analects*, Book II, Chapter 15), "thought without learning is perilous."

The same approach was adopted by Mao in dealing with steel. As mentioned earlier in connection with his 1957 conversation in Moscow, Mao took steel as the hallmark of general industrial development. When modern steel mills in China did not have enough capacity for his planned goal, he ordered the construction of "small modern steel mills" and "small native furnaces" to augment steel output, little realizing that too much sulfur and other impurities would make the products useless. Furthermore, the aimless destruction of trees and ore outcroppings in search of fuel and ore made the cost of attaining steel inordinately high whether all costs were recognized in monetary terms or not.[25]

One of Mao's schemes to aid Chinese agriculture by introducing a new type of steel plow turned out to be another fiasco. Mao's original idea was to produce 5 million 2-wheel, double-blade steel plows.[26] Eventually 1.7 million units were produced up to October 1956. Of these, 800,000 were reportedly sold. But 150,000 were returned by their buyers. The bulk of the rest hung on the walls of the state stores and cooperatives unsold. A principal reason was that the plows were designed for wheat growing but were also produced for paddy fields and distributed in rice-producing areas.

---

23. *Id.*, pp. 683-89.

24. *Id.*, pp. 683-85.

25. One should bear in mind that during this period, goods and labor were often taken by command and assigned to one task and then shifted to another without monetary payment and the "transactions" were not priced. Nor was there any kind of "shadow pricing." Hence the concept of "cost" and, therefore, of any cost-benefit calculus was absent. See Yuan-li Wu, *et al.*, *The Economic Potential of Communist China* (Menlo Park, CA: Stanford Research Institute, 1962), Vols. I and II.

26. Bo, *supra* note 4, Vol. I, p. 538.

Fantasy and Reality

More than enough has been said of the mechanism of goal escalation in production that led to the fantastic Great Leap claims. Only a few figures will suffice to show today's reader at least a generation after the event how the CCP leadership and enthusiastic cadres following the utopia painted by Mao succeeded through wishful thinking, ignorance and total callousness in dreaming up a plethora of unrealistic plan-goals and target dates.

In 1957, nominally the last year of the First Five-Year Plan, mainland China's food grain production, as mentioned in Bo Ibo's 1993 book, was 390.1 billion jin (195 million metric tons). The plan, as drafted in 1957, aimed at producing an annual output of 230 million tons in 1962. Two years earlier, as we have said before, when the CCP leaders met at Beidaihe, a prospective plan for 1967, the end year of the original third Five-Year plan, had drawn sharp criticism from Mao for suggesting a grain production target of 300 million tons only for 1967. The planners then presented an "alternative goal" of the same amount, viz., 300 million tons, but this time for the year 1962![27] (Readers are to be reminded that the original plan period for the third Five-Year plan which was discussed at Beidaihe, as mentioned above in the text, was later revised after the failure of the Great Leap to 1966-1970. The gap years were the "years of natural calamity" officially recognized after the failure of the Leap.)

The actual national production of grain turned out to be totally different. The 1958-61 grain production figures appeared to be as follows: 1958, 199.8; 1959, 169.8; 1960, 143.4; and, 1961, 147.5 (all in million metric tons).[28] At its lowest, grain production in 1960 and 1961 was below that of 1952, the year before the First Five-Year Plan, when grain production was 160.6 million tons.

In the case of crude steel, Mao's symbol of industrialization, the course of events was similar. Actual production was said to be 5.35 million metric tons in 1957. The optimistic, "high goal," however, went up from 10.7 million tons for 1958 to 30 million tons for 1959, and 80-100 million tons for 1962.[29] Ke Jingsi, one time mayor

---

27. *Id.*, p. 542.

28. See Bo, *supra* note 2, Vol. II, p. 884. These figures are estimated from compulsory purchases.

29. A "prospective plan" figure for 1962, set in 1957, was to be 11 million metric tons. Later in 1957, the figure was changed to 12 million metric tons. Bo, *supra* note 4, Vol. I, pp. 530-31.

of Shanghai, and Wang Heshou, Mao's Minister of Metallurgy, were among the most enthusiastic seconders of the Chairman's fantasies. But as late as 1967, steel production remained at only 10.3 million metric tons.

In reality, the lower quality "steel " produced with high-sulfur pig iron and other impurities turned out to be useless.[30] The machinery industry was unable to supply the required steel-making furnaces. Farm equipment, which was of a wrong design for the market as mentioned earlier, wasted steel. The simultaneous increase in demand for labor in different industries served only to create problems of supply for the producers and confusion and frustration for planners.

It is hard to say which was the worst aspect of the failed Great Leap. But one of the worst certainly was the transformation of the collective farms into communes, which resulted in making huge numbers of mobile laborers subject to the haphazard and reckless direction of communist cadres who sent these virtual slaves from one assignment to another at the whim of higher echelons in the party bureaucracy, all the way up to Mao himself. For varying periods during 1958-59, it was the practice within the communes in most places to feed everyone in public canteens without charge. This practice contributed to an increase in food consumption on the farm. (The practice was supposed to constitute "distribution according to need" under communism.) The rise of rural consumption plus increased urban demand for food drew down the country's grain stock, causing compulsory grain purchase to be increased from declining production. Grain production fell partly due to the practice in the commune to pay production units equally regardless of differences in productivity, partly because of the nonsensical Great Leap farm practices mentioned above. The net result was famine in many areas of the country, although this dire situation was not known to the outside world until nearly a quarter of a century later.[31]

---

30. *Id.*, p. 538.

31. This situation came to the open through demographic statistics on birth and mortality by age and sex in the age distributed population data which made the Great Leap period stand out, in comparison with the years before and after, in the 1982 census. See Ansley J. Coale, *Rapid Population Changes in China, 1952-1982* (Washington, DC : National Academy Press, 1984). A separate figure for victims who died of famine in 1959-62 given by Cung Jin (pseudo?), *Quche Fazhan di Suiyue* [*The Zigzag Years of Development*] (Henan: People's Publishers, 1989), p. 272. I am grateful to Professor Jurgen Domes for the above 1989 reference. A subsequent report listing other estimates, including an Academy of Social Sciences Study, may be found in the Washington

III. MAO'S NEAR FALL AND POLITICAL COUNTERATTACK

In order to understand the full impact of the failure of the Great Leap on the Chinese economy, one must begin with an overview of the original CCP development scheme as envisaged in the Second Five-Year Plan (1958-62). This scheme was presented to the Chinese Communist Party and the entire Chinese population at the Eighth Party Congress in September 1956. Since the world's other communist parties were also present at the conference, the CCP had a great deal at stake. Unfortunately for both the Chinese Communist Party and Mao—but even more so for the Chinese nation—the ensuing events were more than a severe economic decline that might occur in the business cycle of any market economy. An economic downturn in a market system would normally be followed by recovery even if a new business cycle were again to start.

The PRC case was quite different, however; in Mao's eyes, economic recovery would be accompanied by a radical change in direction away from Maoist policies. Hence, this about-face was followed by a Maoist political counterattack that lasted nearly a whole decade during which Mao's opponents—the orthodox but, to Mao, "revisionist" CCP leaders headed by Liu Shaoqi —were overthrown. What would have been the latter part of an upswing in pure economic terms was cut short around 1965. Replacing it was a public spectacle of a ferocious and extraordinary political struggle for the whole world to see.

This political phenomenon, known to the world at large as Mao's Great Proletarian Cultural Revolution (GPCR), resulted in placing much of the state-run industrial sector and the operation of many government agencies more or less under the mixed supervision of the military and of Maoist party radicals, in the form of "revolutionary committees," toward the middle of the 1970s. What happened during the GPCR through the death of Lin Biao in September 1971 until the overthrow of Mao's radical successors in 1976 has remained to this day murky. Parts of this missing gap will be discussed in the next section. This section will focus on the slump induced by the Great Leap and the uncertain recovery up to the eve of the Cultural Revolution.

Post National Weekly Edition, entitled "The Horrors of Mao" by Daniel Southerland, August 1-7, 1994.

Depths of the "Mao Slump": Delayed Recovery and Policy Response

Mao's intended Great Leap became in reality a great slump for which his ideology and policies in their totality were responsible. The contrary effects of these policies were unexpected by their leading proponent, Mao, and his followers, including those Mao converted who were at first doubters. As the literature that has become available after 35 years (1958-94) shows, many leading CCP cadres were more than just involuntary followers. For example, there was Bo Ibo's suggestion to "keep two sets of books," encouraging cadres at every level to aim at higher targets than those handed down to them from the immediately higher echelon. This process of policy-making and its internal dynamic contributed to a progressively higher set of targets and an expanding gap between the desired and the possible. The slump was not the result of insufficient demand but the outcome of shortages and bottlenecks of supply which kept on expanding and multiplying. Mao's employment of his well-tried social movement method, using the Communist Party organization as a means of mass mobilization, had the effect of widening the scope of the economic sectors affected by an egregiously mistaken policy. For instance, if an input needed for steel-making became unavailable to one steel maker, it might be obtained at the expense of a non-steel maker or even another steel maker politically less agile in scrounging from a supply source located elsewhere. Or priority in transportation might be obtained by the first steel-maker at the expense of another unrelated project. Thus failure in one economic sector or one producer could generate a rippling effect.

Furthermore, the "Great Leap" fervor itself was infectious. The fact was that the reward and punishment that party cadres received depended upon performance in accomplishing the immediately assigned task in obeying orders originating from Mao. Thus a narrowly defined task was accomplished even if it was ultimately irrational. (One would melt down a steel object to fill the shortfall of steel ingot production even if the object itself was what the ingot conceivably could be used ultimately to manufacture.) Furthermore, the fulfillment or non-fulfillment of an assigned task was often determined without real inspection and verification. "Quality control" was nonexistent. Hence faulty and falsified reports (including statistics) became common. The absence of an independent system of checks (such as the market price system that could flash warnings of a serious crisis), aggravated by self-interest on every level beneath, or even including the summit of power, namely, Mao, both delayed the adoption of counter-measures and widened the ripple effects of the crisis.

The following table contrasts the goals of grain and steel production set by PRC authorities for 1962 and 1967, respectively the last years of the Second and Third Five-Year Plans, if the disaster of the Mao slump had not occurred. The actual production figures are disclosed in a scattered manner by Bo Ibo in his memoirs.

The reader will recall that grain and steel were used by Communist Chinese leaders—not Mao Zedong alone—as indices of economic development, not just as a measure of success in Mao's Great Leap. Steel production in particular was also the popular symbol of modernization in Chinese eyes, by no means just in the eyes of Mao's faithful followers. It was considered by many Chinese as a symbol of the PRC's international standing in terms of national power.[32] At Beidaihe, in the summer of 1955, when Mao and his top lieutenants reviewed the prospects of the Chinese economy in 1967 (end of the Third Five-year Plan), they thought that Chinese agriculture might be able to produce 300 million metric tons of food grain a year.[33] The optimistic Mao later raised this goal to 475 million tons. For the year 1962, Mao's lieutenants aimed in 1955 at a respectable target of 230 million tons, which, as a result of Mao's urging, was later raised to 300 million tons, i.e., the original goal for 1967, five whole years later.[34]

In reality, mainland China's grain production fell by about 26 percent to 143 million tons during 1960 and stayed at 147.5 and 155 million tons in 1961 and 1962, respectively.[35]

In terms of steel production, the second major index during the Great Leap, the original goal for 1967 was set by Mao's officials at 18 million tons, which was subsequently raised to 24 million tons. The corresponding targets set for 1962 were 11 and 12 million tons, respectively.[36] Comparison of the actual production figures with the

32. National power was paramount in the PRC leaders' minds when they spoke of surpassing the United Kingdom in 15 years.

33. All the grain figures should exclude soybeans, which occasionally used to be counted in PRC grain statistics.

34. As pointed out earlier in the text, some Maoist aides seemed to have simply moved the original target date by five years.

35. The 1963 grain figure is taken from U.S. Department of Agriculture, *Agricultural Statistics of the People's Republic of China 1949-1990* (Washington, DC: U.S.D.A., Economic Research Service, 1990), p. 40.

36. See Bo Ibo, *supra* note 2, Vol. II, Chapter 31, especially pp. 885-97.

ILLUSTRATIONS OF PRC PLANNING AND PERFORMANCE 1957-1967 GRAIN AND CRUDE STEEL

I. Goals
(Million metric tons)

	Grain Production	Crude Steel Production (Ingots)
A. Goal for 1967, at Beidaihe briefing in the summer of 1955	300 (6 billion jin) 600	18.0
A'. Goal for 1967 reported to the CCP Central Committee by the State Planning Commission on January 14, 1956	475 (9.5 billion jin) 950	24.0
B. Goal set for 1962	230 (4.6 billion jin) 460	11.0
B'. Revised* goal set for 1962 after Mao Zedong's instructions	300 (6 billion jin) 600	12.0

II. Actual Production
(Million metric tons)

	Grain	Steel
1957	195.1	5.6
1958	191.2	7.9
1959	162.5	13.9
1960	143.0	19.0
1961	147.5	8.7
1962	155	6.0

* The revised target was set after remonstrations by Mao following the 1955 Beidaihe briefing. Source: Bo Ibo, *Ruogan Zhongda Juece yu Shijan di Huigu* [*Many Major Decisions and Events in Retrospect*] (Beijing: CCP Central Party School Publishers), Vol. I (1991), Chapter 21, pp. 521-61; Vol. II (1993), pp. 698-703, 883-89 and 1062.

1957 base shows that at the lowest level reported during the economic collapse, 8.7 million tons of crude steel were produced in 1961 and only 6 million tons were finally produced in 1962. Peak production was reached at 19 million tons in 1960. Thus the paths traced by the collapsing economy were not entirely parallel between the agricultural and industrial sectors of the economy. Food shortage was somewhat less severe in the urban areas because of the increased requisitions of grain from the communes due to the arbitrarily raised compulsory deliveries demanded by local CCP cadres. The requisitions reached nearly 40 percent of production in 1960, probably in part as a result of faulty information on the real crop yield. This is hard to believe but not inconceivable given the nature of Mao's reign at the time.

The steel production series from 1957 to 1962 based on the disclosures of Bo Ibo and others mentioned above conceals a far more complex story than was usually understood during and immediately after the Great Leap years. The varying extent to which production from sub-standard "steel furnaces" (both "small modern" and "native" furnaces) was included in the output reports presented a serious problem to the PRC. However, although imported equipment from the Soviet Union for the First Five-Year Plan began to arrive for installation only in the last two years of the Plan (as described earlier in this volume) some of it could well have begun to enter production in 1959-60. Second, because of the extraordinary priority accorded by Mao (and such persons as Wang Heshou under him) to steel making and related heavy industry plants and new plant construction, indiscriminate withdrawals from materials in stock and diversions at the expense of other uses could well result in an unsustainable, temporary increase in steel produced.

A few disclosures on capital construction and the completion of new investment projects lend support to the view that PRC economic planning in the modern sector at the time was grievously dislocated and that this led to a downward spiral. Capital construction expenditure in 1960 was reported at 38.4 billion yuan, 11% higher than in 1959, but 180% above the pre-Leap year of 1957. The original plan had put capital investment in 1960 at 50 billion yuan. There were 982 separate on-going construction projects of large and medium scale within the Plan in 1957. This number went up to 1,815 or 83 percent higher than the corresponding figure of 1957. In contrast, during 1957, 26.4 percent of the then on-going capital construction projects were completed while the corresponding project completion rate fell to 9.8% in 1960. A sharp curtailment of investment was decided upon only during a Beidaihe meeting on July 5 - August 16, 1960, when Li Fuchun briefed the conferees on the official announcement of Soviet withdrawal of technical advisers and the disruption of aid shipments. This was the coup-de-grâce administered by Khrushchev to Mao's dreams for the PRC industrial sector which Mao had himself undermined with his Great Leap policy.

However, the nightmare of the Great Leap was Mao's own way of making the PRC less vulnerable to Soviet pressure. But he had promoted his ideas in terms of a vision of "walking on two legs," a dualistic shortcut to industrialization by employing both modern and his own "revolutionized Chinese traditional technologies." In doing so, he was seconded by his followers in the party who did not know better, while those who did dared not oppose him. Adjustments following the severe economic sanctions applied by the Soviet Union required a reexamination of the country's priorities, especially because the economy had to be rescued from the failure of Maoist economics. However, before we proceed further on the economic crisis and recovery from it, it is necessary to take a step back to look at the original Second Five-Year Plan and to acknowledge how badly it was shaken by still another development on the side of defense and national security from the CCP's perspective. This is too often ignored by students of the period.

Original Second Five-Year Plan

It is important at this juncture to bear in mind the nature of the original economic plan for 1958-62 which was to be carried out with Soviet technical and material assistance and as a continuation of the First Five-Year Plan. During 1953-57, 36.2% of capital construction was in heavy industry in contrast to 6.4% in light industry and 7.1% in agriculture, making up a total of 49.7%.[37] The remaining 50.3% was accounted for by (1) defense, (2) transportation, (3) communication, (4) trade, (5) undertakings in culture, (6) health, (7) education, (8) science, (9) urban construction, (10) acquisition of vehicles and ships, and (11) the expansion and alteration of existing plants. Although no details are available on military investments, item (1) and a portion of items (2), (3), (8), (10) and (11) should also be included under defense, as should a part of the first 49.7% of investment in heavy industry.

Of the 921 projects "above norm" in size which were scheduled for 1953-57, 156 projects were to receive Soviet aid.[38] Of the 156, construction work had begun probably during 1955-57 on 146 and an additional ten were not started. Bo Ibo grouped the 156 projects as follows:

37. Bo, *supra* note 4, Vol. I, p. 263. For more details see Chapter 13, pp. 284-307.
38. *Id.*, pp. 296-97.

1. Defense Industry		44
Aeronautics	12	
Electronics	10	
Weapons	16	
Space	2	
Shipbuilding	4	
2. Metallurgy		20
Steel	7	
Nonferrous Metals	13	
3. Chemical Industries		13
4. Machine Fabrication		24
5. Energy		52
Coal	25	
Electric power	25	
Petroleum	2	
6. Light Industry and Pharmaceuticals		3
Total		156

Thirty-five of the 44 primarily defense projects were located in Central and Western China, including 21 in Sichuan and Shaanxi. Of the remaining projects, many were defense related: 50 were in the Northeast and 32 were in Central China. As far as possible, these new investments had avoided locations in the eastern coastal areas. In this respect the PRC planners had learned from the bitter experience of the Nationalist government in the 1937-45 war with Japan.

A second major consideration was the obvious need to restore the many Japanese-built plants in southern Manchuria.[39] Unfortunately, in this respect, the planners had no choice but to make the most of the Manchurian industrial complex Japan had left behind in spite of its proximity to the coast. The strong defense emphasis of the first development plan reflected the PRC leaders' consensus on increasing the country's military power. Heavy PRC casualties in the Korean fighting and a constant fear of bombing by UN planes had much to do with the location of new industries, as distinct from the utilization of restored pre-1949 Japanese plants. The locational shifts of new investments during 1953-57 succeeded in reducing investments in the coastal areas to 41.6% of total investments in 1957

39. *Id.*, p. 298.

from 43.4% in 1952; the share of the interior provinces in the contrary rose to 49.7% in 1957 from 39.3% in 1952.[40]

Liu Shaoqi presented the principal report on the Second Five-Year Plan to the Eighth CCP National Congress. He stressed as its principal characteristics the Second Plan's continued emphasis on heavy industry and on greater "self-reliance" in the sense of learning to acquire the capacity to produce domestically as many categories of industrial products requiring more advanced technology as possible without forswearing external assistance. Furthermore, Liu's statement on the Plan revealed the intention to undertake a number of major construction projects in Gansu, Qinghai, Xinjiang and the Sanmenxia section of the Yellow River.[41] This seemingly innocuous remark, however, does not merely indicate a simple confirmation of the desire to shift industrial development away from the coastal areas, which the First Five-Year Plan had stated, but the specific locations mentioned included the by-now-well-known test sites and related R&D and nuclear-material production locations of major concentrations of the PRC's nuclear, missile, and other advanced weapons programs. It was at these places that the PRC in the 1950s started preparing for (1) its first nuclear explosion in 1964, (2) its nuclear warhead-cum-missile test two years later and (3) its first hydrogen bomb test in June 1967.[42] Pursuit of this long-range program was apparently decided upon in the mid-1950s toward the end of the First Five-Year Plan. The decision to manufacture "the bomb," even without a Soviet "educational prototype," to put it mildly, was not unrelated to the final open estrangement between Mao's PRC and Khrushchev's Soviet Union. Once Soviet assistance to the Chinese nuclear weapons program was reduced and finally halted, the economic cost of the development effort, to be continued on a primarily self-sufficient basis, also mounted. A successful Great Leap would have helped advance both Mao's domestic program of accelerated industrialization and his breakthrough defense effort. His version of communism and world leadership might have appeared to be at hand, at least in his own eyes. But all this was not to be.

---

40. *Id.*, p. 299.

41. Speech by Liu Shaoqi in *Zhongguo Gongchandang Quanguo Daibiao Dahui* [*Documents of the 8th CCP National Congress*] (Beijing: People's Publishers, February 1957), pp. 11-72.

42. See John Wilson Lewis and Xue Litai, *China Builds the Bomb* (Stanford: Stanford University Press, 1988), and *Nie Rongzhen Huiyi Lu* [*Nie Rongzhen's Memoirs*] (Beijing: PLA Press, 1986), especially Chapter 24, pp. 767-845.

Two Parallel Paths: Nuclear Weapons and the Economic Disaster and Recovery

Students of Chinese history, economics, or politics during the Mao period can easily and understandably overlook certain aspects of specific military matters that were usually shrouded in secrecy. But in a developing economy of technical backwardness and limited readily accessible nonagricultural resources for the prior fabrication of intermediate products, any large-scale diversion of resource use for defense that would require sophisticated industrial and technical support would certainly impact on the economy and society by creating specific bottlenecks not easily bypassed.

The kind of economic system Mao had created made full, but at the same time wasteful, use of resources. The diversion of additional scarce resource to defense use made such an adverse effect all the more serious. Mao started as a guerrilla fighter who was well versed in Chinese strategic thinking and history. He had succeeded in besting a militarily vastly superior foe, the U.S.-aided Nationalist Chinese army. The PRC leadership could not but be constantly alert to changes in relative power between itself and other nations, especially the United States, a foe in the Korean War, and the Soviet Union, a difficult ally growing increasingly demanding and unreliable. Mao himself was doubtless especially worried, however unconcerned he might have pretended to be by publicly ridiculing the atomic bomb as a paper tiger. During the Korean War, U.S. nuclear power was not used on the battlefield, yet it was constantly a factor in Chinese strategic calculation.

The PRC's awareness of the Soviet Union's fear lest it become a target of U.S. nuclear weaponry was in Chinese eyes forever restraining the Soviet Union in any open aid to China. After the Korean armistice the PRC sought to test time and again how far both the Soviet Union and the United States would go, each in support of its particular ally—respectively the Chinese Communists and Taiwan—without running too high a risk of nuclear war.

Such a test was made by Mao in 1958 when he initiated the bombardment of Quemoy. Mao asked for Soviet assistance without avail when U.S. ships supported Nationalist Chinese vessels reprovisioning the garrisons on Quemoy. At the same time U.S. warships did not come close enough to mainland shores to become unavoidably engaged in hostile action. On the one hand, Mao was probably sufficiently assured that the immediate risk of a deliberate U.S. attack on the PRC was small. On the other hand, he probably also concluded that the Soviet nuclear umbrella was also not reliable enough to be tested seriously. If these inferences were indeed those of Mao, to try to acquire an independent nuclear capability would seem to be a logical conclusion, setting the cost issue aside.

As a matter of fact, the PRC's effort to gather together a group of outstanding Western trained scientists and technical personnel for R&D in the interest of economic modernization in general, but with a strong applied and especially defense emphasis, began early under the Communist regime in 1950-51 (such was also a Nationalist policy before World War II); Soviet aid to the Chinese Communists in the military and industrial areas contributed naturally to this emphasis. Mergers and regroupings of research and educational institutions, together with their attached scientists and technical personnel, and sending large numbers of students and trainees abroad, especially to the Soviet Union and Soviet satellite countries in Europe, contributed to a rapid growth of such skilled manpower. But it is hard to imagine how the PRC could have developed its own nuclear capability, as well as an appropriate industrial support system, without a great deal of Soviet hands-on guidance.

During 1955-56, the Soviet Union and the PRC began their initial cooperation in nuclear research and geological survey of uranium and rare metal reserves and mining potential. By the time of the Eighth CCP Congress in September 1956, it was already possible, as mentioned above, for the Second Five-Year Plan to include the provision of future test sites and missile and atomic research facilities among the planned constructions.

The earlier part of the year was spent in drawing up a comprehensive assessment of the PRC's science assets. Filling some of the identified gaps became the object of a twelve-year development outline for science and technology. By October 1956 Nie Rongzhen was appointed to take over from Chen Yi the latter's work within the party on science matters, even as Nie continued his responsibility for the defense industry and weapons procurement for the PLA.[43]

An agreement with the Soviet Union dated October 1957 began a period of about two years when Soviet aid to China in nuclear and other weapons research, as well as in defense industry planning and management, was on the broadest scale. This was an opportunity which the PRC used well. It was only in 1959 that the two countries began to dispute over naval cooperation, in the course of which the PRC claimed that the Soviet Union wished to establish a

43. *Nie Rongzhen, id.*, Chapter 24.

communications facility in China for radio communication with its submarine fleet in the Pacific and to build a joint Sino-Soviet naval force under Soviet command.

All these developments pointed clearly to a "gestation period"—1956 to 1958—in the PRC's nuclear research and development effort, to be followed by a second period of manpower expansion and institution-building with Soviet aid, accompanied by the necessary design and planning of the command and manufacturing structures within the PRC's own defense establishment. These years happened to overlap with Mao's preparations for the Great Leap and its launching.

When the Soviet Union refused to deliver a prototype of an atomic bomb to China and then stopped its advisory and aid program in succession in 1959-60, the PRC economy was just getting deeper and deeper into the mire of the "steel-making" frenzy. The Maoist communist party cadres tried to attain ever-rising goals of steel and to meet the insatiable demand for heavy industry products merely by taking materials and services (e.g., rail transport) in short supply away from investment and current production in light industry and consumer goods manufacture. At the same time, the immediate construction and other investment needs of the developing nuclear armament industry had the same effect of diverting more scarce specific resources away from consumer goods as well as capital goods that could be producing for the civilian economy. Marshal Nie Rongzhen in his memoirs spoke of the employment of "top priority delivery and purchase orders" "printed in red" of the Central Military Commission to command the speedy delivery of needed supplies, cutting through interference from all other demands. In addition, under the "greater cooperative area" (*daxiezuo qu*) arrangement of the economic planners, resources and skilled technical manpower were virtually drafted for these top defense construction tasks. One can well imagine the devastating effects on the limited supplies of skilled manpower and capital goods industry—not to mention what the Soviet Union might be demanding of promised PRC exports of consumer goods and rare metals in return for previously delivered aid. The reduction of certain resources available to the PRC's civilian economy beginning in 1961 as a result of the decision to produce "the bomb" at all cost followed closely upon the heels of the economic retrenchment due to the failure of the Great Leap. Hence the retrenchment had to be more stringent and it also lasted longer.

Chinese demographic statistics of this period, as may be seen in the following data, bear silent witness to the tragedy. The fact that many of the defense constructions were in remote, totally undeveloped areas like Xinjiang, Qinghai, Gansu and Ningxia added to the capital investment in the infrastructure required and the cost of accelerated construction by forced draft in human terms.

CHANGES IN BIRTH AND DEATH RATES IN THE PRC'S TOTAL POPULATION IN 1959-61 COMPARED WITH 1953-57, AND 1958-1962

	Birth Rates	Death Rates
	Number per thousands	
Average for 1953-57	34.7	12.33
1958	29.22	11.98
1959	24.78	14.59
1960	20.86	25.43
1961	18.02	14.24
1962	37.01	10.02

Zhonghua Renmin Gongheguo Ziliao Shouce, 1949-85 [*PRC Data Book*], Beijing, p. 90.

A comparison of the crude death rates between 1951-57 and 1958 with those of 1959-62 offers an indication of extra deaths as against "normal death." These extra deaths were probably due to famine-related conditions. A similar comparison of the birth rates between 1958 and 1959-61 shows the decline in live births during the famine. More graphic descriptions from a study of the Chinese Academy of Social Sciences and others suggest a famine mortality of possibly 43 million. But officialdom in the PRC still tries to maintain a conspiracy of silence.

IV. AN INTERIM SUM UP

Scrambled Planning Structure

The loquacious Bo Ibo served for many years as Mao's trouble-shooter and head of the Economic Commission responsible for the annual economic plan. The latter in theory should make all necessary adjustments in annual production in the light of current and anticipated performance of the economy so that it would be consistent with the long-term objectives of the State Planning Commission. Alternatively, the State Planning Commission should when necessary adjust its long-term plan. The need to modify the two sets of plans was apparently often discussed at Beidaihe in the summer. Both Bo and Chen Yun often spoke of the need to adhere to macro indicators to regulate the economy, watching closely "rates and proportions" dealing with such variables as national income, accumulation, basic or capital investment, and the revenue and expenditure stipulated in the state budget.

According to the planning method imported from the Soviet Union when the First Five-Year Plan was formulated, it would be considered a mistake to have too much going on in the economy outside the Plan's purview. From the planners' point of view, the socialization process nominally completed in the PRC in 1956 was a welcome development. But in practice, the planned use of all of a country's available resources in development through large-scale investment in a multi-sector economy is always a difficult problem. The difficulties are greatly enhanced if the economy is changing rapidly and growing in complexity in both the kinds and specifications of products, services and inputs. For plan implementation would require information and knowledge in growing detail and speed that no planner could expect to possess. To assume otherwise is a fundamental fallacy into which utopian socialists, communists and statists in general have fallen time and again, at great cost to a populace credulous enough to follow their lead precisely when the ordinary person's gripe should be the poor performance of the society and the planning bureaucracy. Members of the general public suffer from the lack of fairness in the distribution of physical output and economic opportunity which the people wish to be free to exploit on their own.

A planned system may appear simple enough to operate to an engineer or mathematician used to dealing with inanimate machines possessing no free will. One could even manage a simple economy with limited production choices for subsistence and succeed in surviving in the wilderness of northern Shaanxi as did Mao's army in the 1930s and 1940s, but that experience would not be particularly helpful when complexities stepped in. We abstract here from "inconveniences" to the implementation of any plan presented by illiteracy and unfamiliarity with computing and coordination at different levels of the bureaucracy.

Both in the PRC and in its mentor socialist state, the Soviet Union, the size of the country is a factor that time and again calls for decentralization in organizing economic activities. Mao Zedong in 1958 was himself in favor of delegating certain powers to lower levels of administration. Unfortunately, this became a negative factor by increasing the number of separate bureaucratic authorities arbitrarily dictating to individuals under their respective jurisdictions without increasing the freedom of action of individual enterprises at the workshop or farm level. Nor did the lower level authorities which now could dictate to the individual workshop or farm possess any more knowledge or information on the spot than party cadres in Beijing. Economic decentralization during this period apparently added to the investments outside the national plan. Thus, Mao's haphazard economic dictates, the defense construction projects run on the writ of the Central Military Commission and the projects of authorities below the national level outside the official Second Five-Year Plan added to the aggregate demand for resources. Quoting the State Bureau of Statistics, Liu Shaoqi reported on January 27, 1962, that more than 20 percent of the aggregate "basic investment" of 1958-60 was "outside the plan" and amounted to 21.7 billion yuan.[44] Chen Yun, Liu Shaoqi and, one might add, Deng Xiaoping, then in charge of the Party Secretariat, were in favor of cutting back the unrealizable investment plans inasmuch as the Great Leap had obviously already foundered and should have served as a lesson.

Increasing Incentive and Improving Enterprise Management

As one looks back to the time when Mao's reckless application of his personal experience to industrialization policy had to be reversed,[45] there were really very few options left. Of course, ideology ruled out from the outset a return to the market economy. Chen Yun, Liu Shaoqi and Li Fuchun probably saw a partial reversal of collectivization and a reduction of the grain tax and compulsory purchase, together with restoration of private plots, as a way to increase incentive for the peasants. The peasant's pay depended upon the value assigned to various kinds of work he performed. By putting this job of fixing the "wage unit" in the hands of the individual production team rather than the larger production brigade, the more productive person in the smaller distribution unit would have less objection to having his own yield averaged downward with that of the less productive members of the same team. The underlying assumption was that in the larger production brigade which could contain many teams, the discrepancy in yield between the most and

44. *Liu Shaoqi Xuanji,* Vol. II, *supra* note 1, p. 379.
45. See Bo, *supra* note 2, Vol. II, Chapters 32 and 33, pp. 900-78.

the least productive individuals, and/or teams, would tend to be greater.

By the same token, in industrial and other non-agricultural enterprises the Soviet practice of putting a technocrat rather than a party cadre at the top was another obvious and preferred solution that might lead to greater efficiency. These methods of factory and farm management of income distribution were in fact eventually methods of economic reform adopted in 1961 and 1962.[46] But such an enterprise management reform alone did not really lessen the totality of rules enterprise managers had to follow. The technical manager was still overwhelmed by regulations the state planning system continued to interpose. "Red or expert" was a problem that had already permeated the PRC's economic life for a decade at least.

A Startling Report in 1964 —More Preparation for War

In a report to Mao on April 24, 1964 the PLA's General Staff raised several critical issues on the PRC's economic vulnerability. Some, but not all, of the issues were well-known. They included the over-concentration of the country's industrial capacity in a few large cities, the location of major intersections of principal rail and non-rail transportation routes close to the same cities and other population centers, the country's lack of air defense both for civilians and for critical junctions in the national transportation network (bridges, docks, ship and rail yards), and the limited ability large water reservoirs had for emptying their water content in an emergency. Whether this report was that which triggered Mao's alarm or not it is hard to say. There might have been other warnings too.

But the international situation was certainly by no means tranquil from the PRC's standpoint. The political break between the Soviet Union and Beijing had become an open and loud quarrel. Mao had been disappointed by the very obvious Soviet reluctance to become involved in disputes China might pick with the United States. Moscow, from Mao's perspective, seemed to have favored India in the Sino-Indian border conflict. The post-Gulf of Tonkin U.S. position in Vietnam signaled to Mao a more aggressive American policy toward the Chinese communists. After the first Chinese nuclear test in October 1964, the PRC's military might well worry about a surprise surgical strike from abroad. Would the two super-

46. *Id.*, p. 1194. Deng Xiaoping was then on Liu's side in charge of the Party Secretariat.

powers conspire against Beijing, focusing on China's nascent nuclear bases? These were all reasonable concepts of the PLA's operations department that briefed Mao in April 1964 and thereafter.

Why the "Third Line"—Planning Defense in Depth?

Although "the Third Line" is sometimes translated as "the Third Front," the word "line" expresses more accurately the generic meaning of the term as the third of a series of defense lines in depth against invaders who in their advance would have to pierce, or bypass, the first and second lines of defense before reaching the innermost third line.

It was no doubt this meaning that Lin Biao as Minister of Defense had in mind when he in 1962 spoke of the indefensibility of Shanghai in the event of an attack from the sea and the need to fall back to Suzhou, which lay on a second defense line.[47] However, some authors have used the third "front" which is more descriptive of a region and of the intent of the PRC's strategy of defense in depth and the corresponding plans to set up new industrial bases beginning in the mid-1960s. Such a strategy might seem conducive to carrying on a protracted area defense warfare in potentially disconnected geographical enclaves or even larger areas. Mao's idea of first drawing enemy troops on to Chinese soil and of then engaging them in a protracted "people's war," that is, in a kind of modernized guerrilla warfare with technically more advanced tools of war, appeared to be the underlying thinking of his defense plan.[48] The idea was to confront the incoming enemy or enemies with not just one war zone but a series of war zones and lines if the PRC were attacked.

One might ask how a scenario of warfare like this that might be envisaged by Mao in the mid-1960s would be compatible with the nuclear weapons program which was being pushed by him at the same time. According to Bo Ibo, Mao did express the belief in June 1964 that the atomic bomb was not going to determine how ultimate victory would be won in a final showdown between the capitalist and communist camps.[49] It is likely that he had not yet

---

47. Lin Biao's speech before the conference in January 1962 attended by 7,000 cadres and often referred to by that attendance number. See also Barry Naughton's very informative paper in the *China Quarterly* (Abingdon: Burgess and Son for the London School of Oriental and African Studies, September 1988), p. 352.

48. Bo, *supra* note 2, Vol. II, Chapter 41, especially pp. 1199-203.

49. *Id.*, pp. 1199-200

thought through a viable strategy for the nuclear age. The more plausible explanation was that it was Mao who wanted to pursue more than one option at a given time. If this approach was in his mind, he again grossly miscalculated the scale of the necessary undertaking.

Looking at mainland China as a whole, Mao apparently thought of the coastal regions as the "first line," the area of Central China as the "second line," and "interior China" as the "third line." All or major portions of the provinces of Sichuan, Yunnan and Guizhou, plus the western parts of Hunan and Hubei were to enclose an entire area of the "three lines of the Southwest." All or most of Shaanxi, Gansu, Ningxia and Qinghai, as well as Western Henan and Western Shanxi, would constitute the "three lines of the Northwest."[50] Both the Northwest and the Southwest had their respective "principal three-line defenses" while in the coastal area and in the Central China provinces the respective interior areas in these two regions would serve as another set of minor "three line" defenses. It is not clear whether detailed plans were ever fully developed. But a crash program apparently was developed and very serious efforts were made to implement it.

In August 1964, Bo Ibo, Li Fuchun and Luo Ruiqing jointly produced a contingency plan for the national economy in the event of a sudden enemy attack. They proposed that a 14-member task force be established under the State Council, and a proposal was adopted by the central authority of the party, which also made the following decisions: (1) construction of new factories and of branch factories in Third-Line regions; (2) moving factories supplying items demanded by Third Line factories, as well as important factories of which only one of a kind existed in the PRC, to the Third Line (presumably in either the Northwest or the Southwest; (3) organization of the entire country's industrial production and equipment to support the Third-Line program.[51]

These specific tasks were respectively assigned to the State Planning Commission, the State Construction Commission and the State Economic Commission. Additionally, a contingency plan proposed to resuscitate the Civil Air Defense Commission, to evacuate parts of the principal research and higher education institutions to Third-Line regions, to speed up the construction of the Beijing underground, to prepare for subway construction in Shanghai and

50. See *supra* note 48.
51. Bo, *supra* note 2, Vol. II, p. 1201.

Shenyang, and to stop building "large" and "medium-sized" water reservoirs.[52] The work assignment and many of the rational contingency measures obviously chosen to reduce war-time vulnerability suggest that these plans enjoyed the support of many PRC leaders and that they were not the products of a feverish brain, of a mad man or a single person like Mao.

As a result, by 1965, sectoral emphasis adopted in the original Third Five-Year Plan for 1966-70, which listed the consumer-goods industry first and defense last in priority, was completely reversed. Furthermore, while Deng Xiaoping in his role as chief of the CCP's Central Secretariat had put capital investment for the Third Five-Year Plan period at a maximum desirable level of 100 billion yuan, Mao lightheartedly suggested that another one-and-a-half billion would provide easily for the provincial governments' concomitant construction plans under the new defense program. For example, he said that he had been most favorably impressed by proposals from the Guangdong authorities on this subject.[53]

Inasmuch as many of the Third Line construction projects were to be located in areas remote from the more developed centers, new roads and rail lines, including some previously scheduled projects the construction of which had to be delayed for lack of funds, had now to be rushed through although costs were a great deal higher. The cost of constructing the new Chengdu-Kunming and Chongqing-Xiangfan rail lines connecting Sichuan with the rest of China was quoted in one report to be two to three times per kilometer costlier in spite of the low labor cost by calling upon the aid of PLA engineers and conscript labor.[54]

Haste, poor design, inadequate transportation and the frequent deliberate choice of work sites more with an eye on concealment in wartime than for future cost minimization all served to inflate cost and delay the completion date. Thus, until the period of frenetic construction apparently ended in 1972, when diplomatic contact between the PRC and the United States was "fully" resumed by President Nixon's visit, the Third Line investment program had an economic effect on the Chinese civilian economy, through over-investment and the concurrent pursuit of multiple projects, comparable to the nuclear weapons program, with which the Third Line plan overlapped. The official and often unintended tendency was to

52. *Ibid.*
53. Bo, *ibid.*, and Naughton, *supra* note 47.
54. Naughton, *supra* note 47, p. 376.

depress consumption, while incurring waste in investment, and diminishing the accumulation of new capital equipment to a later date for a faster increase in domestic production, thus postponing any increase in consumer goods to later years than originally planned.

On the other hand, construction projects such as the new metallurgical complex at Panzihua on the Sichuan-Yunnan border, another auto plant (possibly in Hubei), and the railway network finally linking southwest China with the rest of the country may well have laid their groundwork for future development during this period. This we have yet to see. Was the cost excessive? How should such costs be measured and charged? Over how long a time horizon? Less certain is whether without the perception of an imminent threat of war such a construction program would have been carried through. Both the value and cost of the Third Line have yet to be fully and objectively assessed even at this writing (1996).

Still another observation on the Third Line is that it adds a different dimension to our evaluation of the period of the Cultural Revolution and of events in the last ten years of Mao's life. Surely any disruption of the Chinese economy as a whole should not be entirely attributed to the mindlessness of rampaging Red Guards and party radicals or to the ignorance and mistakes of military overseers in the civilian economy under Lin Biao. All these undertakings were largely a result of Mao's domestic policy, his all-consuming desire to keep personal power, and his mistaken world view. The Third Line, a frantic response to a perceived threat for which Mao's foreign policy was itself in part responsible, was at least a major factor during Mao's final decade.

According to Bo Ibo,[55] the available per capita supplies of certain basic consumer goods in the country in 1962 compared with the corresponding values in 1957 were respectively:

	Per Capita Output Index in 1962 (1957=100)
food grain	81
edible vegetable oil	45
pork	43
cotton cloth	54

55. Bo, *supra* note 2, Vol. II, p. 1193.

In 1972, the PRC population was estimated at 871.8 million, 29.6 percent greater than in 1962 (672.9 million) and 34.8 percent greater than in 1957 (646.5 million). These population growth rates will give us a basis to look at some of the per capita economic effects of Mao's economic and defense policies. Through the years of the Great Leap, the initial period of the PRC's nuclear weapons program and the defense preparations of the Third Line, the economic situation in China did not improve very much. By 1972, Lin Biao had died. Twenty more years later, even the Soviet Union had ceased to exist, not to mention Mao and Zhou. But what of the PRC, whose population now numbers more than 1.2 billion, and how are we to judge the Third Line and its relation to the other fantastic and disastrous policies of the Mao decades?

CHAPTER VI

ONCE MORE IN TRANSITION AFTER MAO: FROM HUA TO DENG

I. CIRCUITOUS ROUTE TO SUCCESSION

From Mao to the Radicals and Hua

As we have explained, even at the peak of his success in the 1950s, Mao Zedong never seemed to feel entirely secure. He was always fending off real and imagined enemies. Having been somewhat shunted aside after the self-inflicted Great Leap disaster, Mao spent most of the second half of the 1960s trying to triumph over Liu Shaoqi, whom he regarded as his nemesis. He finally succeeded in October 1968 to have Liu expelled from the CCP and stripped of all official positions in the government and party.[1]

In 1969, Lin Biao, who had helped make all this possible, became the titular heir-apparent to Mao in the new Constitution of the Chinese Communist Party at the Ninth CCP Congress. Lin was now for all intents and purposes in a position to take over the Chairman's mantle eventually.

At this point, an outside observer of the Chinese scene might well have concluded that Mao was perhaps really beginning to consider the succession issue. Was he planning a smooth transition of power to the next leader? Could this be possible inasmuch as the next person on the ladder to supreme power was often the one exposed to the most risk and, therefore, could never be groomed properly. To do so there would have to be complete trust. Was not Liu Shaoqi a close enough example? Was Liu also an example to Lin? Did both Mao and Lin regard Liu Shaoqi as an example, each

---

1. The expulsion of Liu took place at the second session of the Eighth Central Committee of the CCP in October 1968. For details see *Major Events in the History of the Chinese Communist* Party (*Explanatory Notes*) [*Zhonggong Dangshi Dashi Nianbiao Shuoming*] (Anshan, Liaoning: Xinhua Bookstore, 1983), edited by the CCP's Party School, especially pp. 193-253. The Chronicle in question contains explanations supplied during the Deng Xiaoping period following the passage of the "Resolution of the CCP on Certain Issues in the Party's History" at the Plenum of the Eleventh Central Committee which was held in June 1981.

not wishing to see the case repeated, this time with himself as the victim?

The official chronicles of the Chinese Communist Party's history assign the entire decade of 1966-76 to the Cultural Revolution, starting from the time the Cultural Revolution Task Force (or Group) was formed at Mao's command in May 1966 and ending with the arrest of the Gang of Four as a result of the October 1976 coup, smoothly executed by the Group's opponents a month after Mao's death.[2]

Chinese history of the post-Mao period would have been simplified greatly for future students if one could say that the end of the Cultural Revolution in 1976 was immediately followed by a national policy under a different leadership. The real course of events surrounding the succession to Mao was, however, far more complex or, to use the phraseology of contemporary political writers from the PRC, far more "circuitous" (*quzhe*). Other contemporary writers have chosen to describe the path leading to the Deng Xiaoping period as "uneven," which is less appropriate. "*Quzhe*" means changes in direction, not just bumps on the road.

In the first place, Lin Biao's ascension to the number two position in the CCP hierarchy was accompanied by the naming of a young Shanghai worker, Wang Hongwen, previously a successful Cultural Revolution activist, to the extraordinarily exalted position of Deputy Chairman of the Party. Wang, together with Jiang Qing (Mao's wife), Zhang Chunqiao and Yao Wenyuan, thus came to comprise the infamous "Gang of Four" to whom all misdeeds were credited subsequent to their arrest in 1976.

Their names were then also linked to that of Lin Biao, who as Minister of Defense not only was nominally in complete control of the military, but whose support and tolerance of the rampant Red Guards were essential to the latter's destructive activities. In September 1971, Lin was suddenly reported killed, together with members of his family, in a plane crash in Mongolian territory while trying to flee the country. Lin was subsequently declared a traitor, turncoat and conspirator who had tried to assassinate Mao, allegedly fleeing when the plot was discovered. Lin's chief aides in the top echelon of the armed forces were put on trial, together with the Gang of Four.

2. *See id.*

Lin Biao's Death and Détente with the United States

The death of Lin Biao was followed by the return of Zhou Enlai to center stage in the last phase of Mao's rule in mainland China. Without Zhou, aided by Chen Yi, it would have been unimaginable for Mao to pull off the seating of Beijing in the United Nations in 1971, however favorable to the PRC the external circumstances had become.[3] The visit of U.S. Secretary of State Henry Kissinger to Beijing, which happened to coincide with the UN vote on the China representation issue, was a telling sign of how the U.S. position had shifted since the Korean War.

The change in Chinese representation led logically in time to rapprochement between the PRC and the United States, symbolized by Mr. Nixon's visit in 1972 to see Mao and the proclamation of the Shanghai Communiqué.[4] If Lin Biao had not died, would there have been a different course of development in China and its relations with the United States? According to President Nixon, early in 1971 Zhou Enlai had mentioned in a message via the Romanians that the PRC was prepared to receive a special U.S. envoy in Beijing. Zhou especially noted that both Mao and Lin Biao were privy to his message.

What was Lin Biao's view on the Mao-Zhou message to the U.S.? This was not disclosed but by implication Zhou had given the impression that Lin had agreed with the message. Mao's subsequent decision to meet with the U.S. president and Lin's death remain a historical question to be examined when PRC files become available, but are so far not fully explained. For Lin met his death not too many days after Zhou's message to Washington.[5] Did either Mao or Lin (or even Zhou) first decide that one of the first two had to go before the rapprochement could smoothly take place?

Competing Heirs Surface

When the body of the "heir to the throne" and a prominent marshal of the powerful PLA was found after an alleged attempt to flee the country and to defect to the enemy camp, the news was too dramatic and electrifying not to arouse wild speculation. Several

---

3. For an across-the-board analysis of the impressions other nations had of the 1971-72 U.S.-PRC rapprochement, see Yuan-li Wu, *U.S. Policy and Strategic Interest in the Western Pacific* (New York: Crane & Russak, 1975).

4. *Ibid.*

5. Richard Nixon, *The Memoirs of Richard Nixon* (New York: Grosset and Dunlop, 1975), p. 547.

versions of the story are available. An officially inspired explanation was the first to find its way outside China. It assumed the form of a code-named plot, the "571 Engineering Project."[6] This consisted of a conspiracy to assassinate Mao Zedong and was supposedly concocted by Lin Liguo, Lin Biao's airforce son, together with Ye Qun, Lin's politically ambitious wife, as well as high-ranking members of the several armed services and the joint staff and logistics departments. The plotters were said to have been betrayed by Lin Liguo's sister (Lin Lihen), out of loyalty to Party, country, and of course, the Chairman. In the nick of time, the information went to the ever watchful Zhou Enlai, whose intervention then brought about Lin Biao's botched flight, crash and death in the Mongolian wilderness, and widespread arrests thereafter.

An interesting telephone conversation between Mao and Zhou Enlai seemed to be intentionally attached by anonymous editors to the account of the "571 Engineering Project." Zhou allegedly asked Mao for instructions on what should be done about the Trident plane containing Lin's party during its flight. The conversation contained a question implying whether the plane should be brought down. In colorful language customary to Mao, he allegedly replied with a rhetorical question: that if heaven wishes to rain or if a son finds his widowed mother eager to remarry, what is anyone to do? The implied answer was to let things be!

We mention the "571 Engineering Project" for several reasons. First, it gained currency in mainland China in circumstances suggesting that it was an informally circulated cover story of official origin put abroad without giving it official status. As a matter of fact, it might have been deliberately planted and circulated as a red herring to draw attention away from speculations as to why Lin Biao and his immediate family with the exception of the daughter (nicknamed Doudou) were killed and, therefore, how they were killed and by whose orders.

Second, this particular story deliberately absolved both Mao and Zhou from ordering the shooting down of Lin's Trident. Yet, if Lin did not die in the plane crash, which could be explained as being no one's fault, his execution must have been ordered with Zhou's knowledge and at a minimum with Mao's consent. Both might have had explanations to make. In any case, would Mao have left such a critical matter to chance? From Zhou's point of view,

---

6. The code word "571" supposedly corresponded in sound to the three Chinese characters meaning "armed uprising or to arms."

this version also had the advantage of affirming that the truly loyal government headed by Zhou was still holding the reins when the security of the supreme Chairman was at stake, however strange the latter's public conduct had been in creating the chaos of the Cultural Revolution.

Several other versions of the Lin Biao affair have appeared, all equally semi-fictionalized.[7] A common theme was that Mao either had Lin killed on the ground, or had ordered him to be killed, which was why the survivors of the Lin family—with or without Lin—took sudden flight. The several versions, including that of the 571 Engineering Project, differed from one another on whether Lin's body was found among the remains at the crash site. Although both the Mongolian and the Soviet authorities, as well as PRC officials, allegedly sent their respective investigators to the spot, no final, agreed-upon, authoritative statement seemed to be available as the credible "last word." A gap must remain on this point at least until all related Soviet and Chinese official documents are available for inspection by historians.

Zhou Enlai benefited from the death of Lin as did Jiang Qing's group. Zhou's opposition to the Lin military faction's support of the radicals' sometime open armed conflict with other groups and among themselves seemed almost calculatedly ineffectual. One may well wonder whether Zhou was biding his time, awaiting a misstep by Lin and/or a change of tactics by Mao. Jiang Qing saw in Lin Biao a rival in Mao's Cultural Revolution and an obstacle to her group's ascendancy. The radicals had been building a separate militia through Wang Hongwen. Hence, one outcome of Lin's departure from the Mao succession scene was a sharpening of the infighting between the Gang of Four and Zhou's remnant bureaucrats and other CP cadres.

The Zhou-Deng Team and the First (1976) Tiananmen Incident

From the PRC's perspective, the 1972 U.S.-PRC (or Nixon-Mao) meeting was unquestionably an occasion for self-congratulation on Zhou Enlai's part. We have seen at the beginning of this volume how Ambassador J. Leighton Stuart waited in vain in Nanjing, after the fall of the Nationalist capital to the Communists, for a

7. The account which suggests that Lin Biao was killed on the ground by Wang Dongxing's men is contained in Yao Ming-le, *The Conspiracy and Death of Lin Biao*, with an introduction by Stanley Karnow (New York: Alfred A. Knopf, 1983). See Chapter III, note 32, *supra*.

signal from Mao through Zhou to initiate official contact between Washington and the Communist regime. That waiting turned out to be futile.[8] Zhou could well have pointed to the fact that 23 years later, in 1972, the mighty United States finally chose to meet Mao and Zhou in PRC-controlled territory in the midst of the final phase of the Vietnam war.

Zhou apparently succeeded in convincing Mao that he (Zhou) needed the help of Deng Xiaoping to straighten out the disorderly state of administrative and even military affairs which the "revolutionary committees" and their "power grabbing" had wrought in various government organizations and enterprises. Deng's assistance would leave Zhou time to pursue matters of foreign and overall policy. Thus Deng was recalled from exile[9] in 1973 and immediately threw himself into the job with such gusto that the radical faction concluded that his real objective was grossly in excess of the mission assigned to him by Mao. Both Zhou and Deng were obviously trying to bring back to power many of their former colleagues. Zhou's health was deteriorating rapidly. Yet evidence of Zhou's unceasing activity up to January 1975, a year before his death, can be seen in the collection of remarks and conversations published in September 1992 as *Selected Writings of Zhou Enlai on the Economy*.[10]

One can then easily understand why the radical faction, nominally led by Jiang Qing, in its continuing struggle for power, chose to link this attack on Lin Biao to Confucius—meaning in fact Zhou Enlai, but without actually naming Zhou.[11] The particular political issue singled out in their opposition was the Zhou-Deng attempt to overturn the numerous Party resolutions and extreme disciplinary measures taken against high officials and cadres under the rulings of the Cultural Revolution Task Force, which had in effect supplanted the Politburo and the latter's Standing Committee.

---

8. One story from Chinese exiles had Huang Hua visit Nanjing in Zhou's place, but a U.S. offer was turned down.

9. This was Deng's return to power under Zhou only to be dismissed by Mao in April 1976 after Zhou's death three month earlier.

10. See Zhou's remarks at a meeting of the State Planning Commission on February 26, 1973 in Zhou Enlai, *Jingji Wenxuan* [*Selected Economic Speeches by Zhou Enlai*], edited by the CCP Central Committee Archives (Beijing: Xinhua Publishers, 1992), p. 638.

11. Confucius at his time often referred to the Duke of Zhou as the man of righteousness. Hence the radicals used "Confucius" to refer to the Duke of Zhou when they meant Zhou Enlai in a satiric sense. Linking Zhou to the fallen Lin Biao was to condemn Zhou Enlai as a concealed anti-Mao "revisionist" and bureaucrat.

For the same reason, after Zhou's death in early 1976, the radicals' ceaseless criticism now levelled against Deng was continued with vigor, as was the refusal to overturn the measures taken against many cadres who had generally been castigated as revisionists, crypto-capitalists, spies and moles from the capitalist camp. One can hardly doubt that the radicals' intention was to prevent their own path to power after Mao's death from being blocked by Deng and the latter's cohort of old revolutionaries who had been removed from Mao's court since 1966. The radicals wanted to stop any widespread rehabilitation.

Both Zhou and the radicals were of course always ready to use the Chairman's prestige to further their own ends by magnifying every little expression he let drop that might be interpreted as a nod in a particular direction. Of course, Mao's own personal inclinations and methods in regard to his concept of "perpetual revolution" through class struggle and his advocacy *in the abstract* of anti-authoritarian behavior and bold thinking were well-known.[12] So were his preferences for greater decentralization of power among others and his frequent double-dealing. Hence it was not altogether surprising when Mao openly threw his weight to the side opposing the reversal of the severe sentences meted out to the numerous CCP cadres of standing in the name of the Party itself. This he did on April 7, 1976.[13]

Thus did Deng Xiaoping once again fall into political disgrace when the first Tiananmen Incident occurred on April 25, 1976.[14] For when university students and members of the public demonstrated in April 1976 in Zhou Enlai's memory, the authorities called out the security forces and broke up by force this expression of pub-

---

12. Mao was philosophically a person impatient with accepted conventional ideas. In his youth he was notoriously rebellious and headstrong. In order to oppose the orthodox Party stalwarts who also controlled the governmental apparatus, he exploited the teenage rebellious youth as his Red Guards and appealed to their tendency to defy authority. Hence the "big character posters" that Mao penned himself during the Cultural Revolution were welcome reading to his youthful readers. Yet Mao was quite ready to use the PLA through the intermediation of Lin Biao to suppress over-ambitious and over-militant Red Guards. As a dictator who could never be wrong, Mao wanted his authority never to be questioned. The demand for absolute obedience was what he meant by "democratic centralism" in practice.

13. See Fang Weizhong *et al.* (ed.), *Zhonghua Renmin Gongheguo Jingji Dashi Ji* [*Major Economic Events in the People's Republic of China*] (Beijing: Chinese Social Science Publishers, 1984), p. 564.

14. Gao Xin and Ho Pin, *Gaogan Dangan* [*Files on Leading Cadres*] (Taipei: Hsinhsinwen Publishers, 1993), p. 363.

lic sentiment. The event was subsequently known as "the first Tiananmen Incident" to distinguish it from the 1989 demonstrations at Tiananmen that led to the June 4, 1989 massacre. Deng was blamed by the Party's radicals as the behind-the-scenes instigator of the 1976 demonstrations and was dismissed from all posts *not ever* to be reemployed by the Party again.

Unfortunately, at that stage of his life, only a few months before his own death in September 1976, Mao very likely was not above being manipulated himself by members of the radical section and his entourage, including Jiang Qing and his nephew, Mao Yuanxin, who acted as his constant liaison with high Party and government officials. Deng was efficient, resourceful, patient and more than cunning, but he was probably somewhat less astute than Zhou and occasionally given to impulsiveness.

Whatever might be this slight shortcoming—maybe it was sheer bad luck—Deng's fall in 1976 made the succession to Mao of Hua Guofeng possible. The Hua interlude delayed the onset of the Deng Xiaoping period by several years and made the process of Deng's reemergence more laborious. In our view the subsequent reform program had to pay dearly for this delay. Deng's own position in the CCP from which he had been expelled became dependent upon many Party elders and diehard reactionaries whom he had to help rehabilitate and whom he had then to reward because they were instrumental in helping him finally reach even greater power, becoming the first among more or less equals.

Removal of Gang of Four and the Hua Guofeng Interlude

Hua Guofeng had been a member of the CCP for more than thirty years when he was brought to Beijing from Hunan in 1972. He started as a party secretary of Xiangtan County (Mao's home county in Hunan) and had risen to the top post in charge of all party, political and military affairs of the province before he was transferred to Beijing. He was therefore a follower of the Chairman and a high Party cadre in the center of power during the post-Lin Biao phase of the Cultural Revolution. On the other hand, he was not high enough at the beginning of the Cultural Revolution to be closely identified with the inner circle of the Jiang Qing faction of radicals. But he obviously knew how to rise to increasingly higher rungs of the CCP career ladder because by 1975 he had already been made a Vice Premier of the State Council and Minister of Public Security. The single most important qualification that recommended him was Mao's trust. A piece of paper on which Mao had scribbled how he (Mao) felt secure with Hua in charge was later used by Hua as a testimonial recommending himself to be Mao's successor in the Party, although the wording could easily be Mao's expression of satisfaction with Hua's performance in a specific assignment.[15]

At any rate, Hua was named Deputy Prime Minister on February 2, 1976 after Zhou's death in January. On April 3, he became Prime Minister and, following Deng Xiaoping's dismissal on April 25 as a result of the first Tianamen incident, First Vice Chairman of the CCP Central Committee. Finally, after Mao's death and the overthrow of the Gang of Four, Hua became the first post-Mao head of the CCP and Chairman of the Military Commission.

Perhaps an even more important qualification in Hua's favor was his not possessing any strong convictions of his own other than the views that the Chairman thought all good communists should have. His potential opponents probably thought that Hua could be easily managed. If so, they proved to be wrong.

"Whatever Mao Said; Whatever Might Be the Chairman's Previous Decision"

The sketchy information available to Western observers about Hua the man suggests that he was a political "opportunist" and not necessarily fired with personal ambition. Intellectually he was no match for either Zhou or Deng. There is no way to tell how with Mao gone he might have fared in a no-holds-barred political contest between him and the Jiang Qing group at a time when the Chinese Communist Party itself was still "radicalized" and "infiltrated" by Lin Biao's military men. He had reached the top of the Party hierarchy but succeeded in doing so only with Mao's backing and probably the half-hearted acquiescence of the radicals. The latter's attitude in the longer run could be quite undependable, and this Hua doubtless knew.

Not having a strong personal program for the post-Mao Communist Party or for China, Hua's safest course of action after he had been ensconced at the head of the Party-State was to follow the path Mao had drawn. This attitude is known through the expression

15. According to Chen You-wei in his article on Qiao Guanhua, Hua Guofeng had in his possession three such pieces of communication in Mao's own handwriting. One of these contained the words that could be interpreted as Hua claimed, but could well refer to less weighty matters than "dynastic succession." According to Chen, Mao resorted to such means of communication when his slurred speech became hard to understand. Chen You-wei, *The World Journal*, San Francisco, October 3 and 10, 1993.

in the section heading which gained currency in Hua's time. Given time, conceivably he could have carved out a special niche, as he might have hoped, for himself. But such a sequence of events would have required his being confirmed in the position of supreme power he already nominally occupied on April 7, 1976. A few factors that could have influenced the situation should be pointed out in order to explain why Hua joined the other top conspirators in the coup that overthrew the Gang of Four after Mao's death. The counterpart of Hua's downfall was the rise of Deng. The lack of success of Hua's policy provided one of the essential conditions of Deng's ability to replace him.

A Political Deal?

Future political historians will have a number of questions to answer about the fall from power of the Gang of Four. One of these had to do with the disposition of military forces guarding Beijing and the personal security of the radical leaders and the conspirators, respectively. Wang Dongxing, commander of the special guards responsible for the security of the leaderships' residences in and about Zhongnanhai, was a key person. He too had joined the conspirators, like Hua Guofeng. In order to neutralize Wang Dongxing's guards in an eventuality, it would have been necessary to make sure that those armed forces in and around Beijing consisted of elements supporting the conspirators and that they would be able to block others sympathetic to the radicals. The inexperience and technical ineptitude in military affairs of Wang Hongwen, who was apparently entrusted with building a militia force outside the PLA, were largely responsible for the radicals' failure to establish a creditable force in October 1976 to oppose the coup plotters, including Hua.

In this respect, the respective roles of Li Xiannian and Ye Jianying, military men of long standing, deserve special scrutiny. A 1993 paper published by a former high PRC diplomat in the United States suggested that Li Xiannian was not particularly anxious to see Deng regain a prominent role. Ye Jianying too might have been similarly ambivalent at the time.[16] Of course, other military personnel may have played a more crucial role than has been disclosed so far. Mao Yuanxin, Mao's nephew who was in command in Manchuria not too far away, might be worthy of the historian's attention. General Chen Xilian was another key person. Of all the persons

16. *Ibid.*

involved in the coup only the Gang of Four as victims of the coup were put on trial four years after the event. No detailed official record has been made public thus far.

Why did Hua turn against the radicals? The other side of this question was his value to the plotters and why they needed him. As Chairman of the Party and of the Military Commission, he would have had authority to legitimize the coup, to arrest the radicals in the name of the Party, and to order the relocation and use of troops. Success of the coup would have been more acceptable with a minimal use of force, more narrowly targeted at the unpopular Gang of Four. Deng Xiaoping had always been a soldier-politician and may have played a more direct role than was publicly disclosed even when "in the wilderness." Before his renewed exile after the first Tiananmen affair(1976) he was Vice Chairman of the Military Commission and Chief of the General Staff after his return to power upon Zhou's strong urging in 1973, still during the Cultural Revolution period. What were his activities relevant to the subsequent coup? Surely Deng knew that Mao's health in early 1976 was already failing and that the radicals might have to be forcibly removed? Would he not have made whatever advance preparations were needed if he had the opportunity to make them?

Hua Guofeng also had his weaknesses. His personal roots in the CCP were far less deep than those of Li, Ye and Deng. He had little known military connections. His tenure at the Ministry of Public Security was far too recent to give him enough leverage on high cadres of wide influence. He might have been more than a little unsure about whether the casual testimonial Mao allegedly gave him could really stand up to close scrutiny.[17]

These constituted the background of a possible political "deal" between Hua and the Li-Ye group of conspirators. Wang Dongxing was in a key position as commander of the "praetorian guards" in the Mao court. After the coup Hua Guofeng retained his position at the head of the Party for two more years. For his reward Wang was able to retain his position on the Politburo for three years. Was there really such a deal? Only time will tell, time for more inner party records to spill open and time for more truths to be told about the Gang of Four's latter-day activities.[18]

---

17. The note allegedly stated in Mao's handwriting, "My mind is at ease when you are in charge."

18. There is still very little information on Wang Hongwen's militia that has found its way to the public domain. For instance, if the militia was well armed, what happened to the arms it had?

Radicals' Ineptness and Deng Xiaoping's "Resurrection"

One should not overlook several other crucial circumstances that made Deng Xiaoping's return to Beijing in 1977 and his eventual assumption of power possible. In the first phase, the radicals' relative ineptness was more than matched by the skill and determination of their opponents. With Zhou Enlai gone, Ye, Li and Deng probably looked upon the overthrow of the radicals as their last chance to survive. With Mao also gone, the last, undependable restraining force of the radicals had been removed. Left to their own devices, striking a deal with Hua Guofeng and Wang Dongxing gave the coup a high chance of success. Future historians may regard favorable military deployments as all the conspirators needed to avoid bloodshed in a successful coup. This condition they seemed to possess.

Still another factor underlying Deng's return to power was the step-by-step infiltration of the Party old guards back into the center of power. A most revealing account of this process can be found in reports on some of the Party's important activities during the short period when Hua Guofeng was Chairman right after the successful coup against the radicals in October 1976. Both Ye Jianying and Li Xiannian repeatedly advocated the return of Deng to the power center. Then, in February of the following year, Deng openly spoke up against Hua's policy to continue to uphold Mao's general concept of "continuing class struggle," his big-push developmental effort, and equal pay for workers in disregard of performance.

In March 1977, at a workshop of the Central Committee, Chen Yun and Wang Zhen jointly asked for the reversal of the verdict on Deng in the April 1976 Tiananmen case. Both before and after the Eleventh CCP Congress in August 1977, the group formed by Ye and Li further enlisted two marshals of high popular standing to its side. Xu Xiangqian and Nie Rongzhen, together with Deng himself, campaigned vigorously for a revised interpretation of Mao Zedong thought. This new interpretation stressed the pragmatic aspect of Mao's thinking and his emphasis on securing wide popular support and participation in implementing public policy (the "mass line"). This aspect of "Mao thought" was raised to lend a "doctrinal" air to Deng's subsequent line of establishing a socialist society in the PRC in consonance with the realities of the country.[19]

---

19. See *Zhonggong Dangshi Dashi Nianbiao* [*Chronicles of Major Events in CCP History*], edited by the Party History Research Office, (Anshan: Xinhua Publishers), 1983, pp. 220-221.

Communist Party historians have cited other instances as evidence of the methodical approach of Deng's expanding activities. These included public discussions and articles in the *People's Daily* on the correct Party line and errors committed during the Cultural Revolution, and new foreign policy possibilities opened up by Deng's two visits to Japan and his trip to Washington between October 1978 and January 1979. Only as a result of such long drawn out machinations was Hua Guofeng finally ousted in June 1981 as Chairman of the Chinese Communist Party at its Sixth Central Committee Plenum, two and a half years after the Third Plenum of the Central Committee of the 11th Congress in December 1978, when the final assault on the rearguard action of the Maoist regime under Hua Guofeng was mounted with the combined strength of the old cadres who had survived the Cultural Revolution.

The contest between the Maoist faction under Hua and the Deng-led old revolutionaries-turned-reformists finally came to an end in favor of the latter. But it was really more like a "no contest" decision on the part of the Maoists, who had run out of workable ideas.

But we need to review quickly why the Maoist ideas without Mao also did not work. What were they? Could Deng really make a new start? Did he have to?

II. WHAT SUSTAINED A REFORMED CCP IN POWER: DOGMA OR PERFORMANCE?

Hua Guofeng Tried and Failed

Thanks to the call to the inner sanctuary of the Mao court, Hua Guofeng rose to succeed the Chairman and managed to hold on to some semblance of power up to mid-1981, although he was greatly weakened after the Third Plenum of the Eleventh Central Committee. During the four plus years (1977-mid 1981) when he held on tenuously to power, he very naturally could not and probably did not wish to discard the Maoist heritage. However, without tying himself to specific Maoist concepts that could remind everyone too vividly either of the painful experience of the Cultural Revolution or of the equally disastrous Great Leap, he escaped into ambivalence.

He introduced a pair of precepts: the Chairman's decisions and the road map Mao had drawn for China were invariably correct and should be followed, whatever they might be. This method of sloganeering was a campaign technique by no means limited to politicians in the PRC, although Mao Zedong popularized it most successfully during his reign of a quarter century. Hua's choice was not a happy one. He evidently failed to realize that the dicta he was bandying around carried a sense of rigidity, of lack of imagination and worst of all, in the final analysis, of futility.

In the years so close to Mao's demise after the turbulence of the Cultural Revolution, it was simply impossible to cast Mao so belatedly again as a Communist Moses. The Chairman had long demonstrated his poverty of truly innovative ideas. If he had enjoyed the benefit of a string of successes from 1949 to 1957— "successes" as the then believers could point to without registering their costs—by 1976 he had garnered a string of monumental disasters and an incalculable heap of bewilderment, if not hatred. To promise more of the same could hardly be attractive to anyone except the unregenerate Mao worshipper.

A New Periodization Covering Lin Biao and Hua Guofeng

The Dengist group took pains after its take-over from Hua to review the Party's history and issued in a 1983 volume entitled *On Selected Historically Important Party Resolutions since the Establishment of the People's Republic, with Explanatory Notes.*[20] This 626-page tome was edited by the Research Office of the Party Archives Division of the Central Committee when Hu Yaobang was head of the Party Secretariat. It was released for internal distribution in June 1983. The revised explanations inserted by the editors at this time presumably would reflect the post-Mao, post-Lin Biao and post-Gang of Four perspectives.

A careful reading of the comments on the country's economic straits and other difficulties would be most illuminating to those who are interested in the Hua Guofeng period from 1976 to 1978, and the relatively short Lin Biao period between 1969 and 1971, as well as the longer years of radical politics of the Cultural Revolution from 1966-67 through September 1976 when Mao died. If we attach the Hua period to the Cultural Revolution years when Mao was alive, we have a total of nearly fourteen years (1966-78/79) when Mao's radicalist ideology was the dominant force in shaping PRC policy.

20. This volume, *Guanyu Jianguo Yilai Dangdi Ruogan Lishi Wenti Di Jueyi Zhushiben* [*CCP Resolutions on Certain Issues in Party History Since 1949, Annotated*], was published in 1983 for the CCP Archives Office of Research. See especially the section on the Cultural Revolution period, pp. 366 *et seq.*

During the same decade and a half, for eighteen years if we include the Great Leap period, Mao's perception of the world behind events and especially of U.S. and Soviet intentions were probably the most fundamental factor in his foreign policy calculations and related strategic preparations. Economic policies were in turn greatly affected by the latter non-economic considerations, and too often new economic and political policy adjustments had then to be made to correct errors of preceding periods. The discussion below will attempt to describe the kinds of problems, as enumerated by the editors of the Party archives and by writers associated with the Academy of Social Sciences, for the period of Lin Biao and Hua Guofeng.

A most frequent complaint about the country's economic bottlenecks during this period by its critics was the inability of the rail network to meet demand. There were reports of trains being held up at key junctions stopping traffic in all directions, of lack of rail cars to ship products out and, of course, concomitantly of cars to bring goods in; of failure to control freight train schedules and, therefore, of confusion in rail yards, and other problems.[21]

Such reports were as a rule made by the writers to point to deliberate efforts of either Lin Biao's military control apparatus or of the Gang of Four to sabotage the economic system in order to advance their cause in the political struggle. However, in the course of the "Third Line" construction frenzy that coincided with the height of the Cultural Revolution, freight shipments to support these defense-oriented projects conceivably could be a source of transport disruptions, including the shipping by rail of materials and men for Third Line projects and Red Guard movements. The same applied to the impact of the nuclear development projects on rail transportation.

One should note especially that constructions under these programs were in locations requiring rail shipments to remote terminals, thus lengthening the turnaround time and increasing the number of engines and rolling stock needed. Of course, if workers in railway administrations were too busy at struggle meetings to take over the incumbents' offices—to "seize power" in the communists' arcane terminology—the orderly working of the rail system could very easily fall into disarray. As to who was responsible, both the radicals and Lin Biao entered into the confusing fray but they

---

21. See *supra* note 10.

did so indirectly at Mao's command and bidding to which other cadres at high levels failed to object in time and in unison.

A second common complaint was poor coordination at various levels of development projects. Harbor congestions toward the end of this period when large-scale equipment import took place had to do with poor scheduling of shipments from foreign exporters to inadequate facilities for unloading and shipping. The poor planning of the expansion of the steel industry at Wuhan, which led to delay and low utilization of costly imported equipment, offered a similar example of technical inadequacies at different levels and phases. But these shortcomings were not in any sense new. They no doubt existed in years when numerous Soviet advisers were working in China. They probably were problems not uncommon to the Soviet Union itself. Why had such matters not been attended to earlier? One cannot fail to notice the long-term effect of the neglect of education and training and of lack of free discussion of such technical inadequacies because party cadres were preoccupied with being ideologically correct .

Speaking before the State Planning Commission on February 26, 1973, nearly eighteen months after the Lin Biao plane crash, Zhou Enlai asked about steel rolling, noting that inability to turn the vast amount of crude steel into finished rolled products was a sheer waste of energy resources. He pointed out further that it was the identical problem ten years earlier, i.e., during the Great Leap.

The planning and management failures noted by Zhou Enlai and others during the entire 1969-76 period and in the earlier years of the Cultural Revolution were both characteristic of Maoist economic policy and of the logical consequences of the hastened Third Line program noted in Chapter V. In summary, they were: an excessively high rate of capital accumulation, excessively long lists of separate investment projects, mutually aggravating bottlenecks, sharp increases in the payroll of workers in state-owned industry[22] and continued budget deficits.

Given the controlled PRC economy which was run like a war economy but without a well-coordinated, macro-control planning mechanism, one can imagine how the civilian sector of the economy must have fared. In the circumstances, to offer the basically Maoist

---

22. The effect on the disruption of input-output relations in production between one economic sector and another and on overall production was therefore a characteristic of the entire period. This effect was probably felt most in the civilian sector given the neglect of the CCP on the population's consumption. This development worsened the living conditions, as noted in the preceding chapter.

program as a guide to future policy, even when moderated by omitting Mao's mass movements and "native technology," would hardly have been appealing even to many Communist party cadres. The latter had steadfastly allowed themselves to be led by a "helmsman" (as Mao was known) who obviously could not read a professional navigational chart on any sea. The navigational device Mao was accustomed to was created out of sheer imagination, without the benefit of technical knowledge and reliable data about the economy.

III. AT LAST, DENG AS THE REAL SUCCESSOR TO MAO

Western Great Leap Forward (*Yang Yaojin*)

Yet it was precisely Mao's policy of massive investment in heavy industry that Hua offered at the first session of the Fifth National People's Congress in February 1978. His "plan" of economic development for 1976-85 was to start building in China ten major steel industry centers, nine bases for nonferrous metals, eight major coal mines, eleven oil and gas bases and thirty large power generation stations. This list of grandiose investment projects reminded one of Mao's lists of major constructions that characterized the early phase of the PRC development effort when Soviet aid conjured up the country's optimistic economic prospects in the flush of victory over the war-weary ROC government on the eve of the First Five-Year Plan. This time, however, it was not Soviet technical and financial aid that Hua had in mind. Instead of Mao's Great Leap based on a heavy dose of labor-intensive "native technology," Hua's forward leap was to rest on imported technology embodied in Western machines (hence the term "*Yang Yaojin*," or "Western Great Leap Forward").

Not having an original economic program of his own that was defensible, what Hua had to offer consisted mostly of those he inherited from the Mao period. That some of the "Third Line" constructions might easily have belonged to this category of capital-intensive projects was natural. True to the practice of the Mao period, one would also expect to read about joyous reports on high outputs in quantitative terms, completions of rail connections in remote areas (the rail line through Xiangfan linking Hubei and Sichuan provinces, for example), new highways, increases in plan production targets, and the like. As Mao and his aides often did before, evaluations of either monetary or "opportunity costs" were usually left unmentioned.[23] There were many such news releases in the short period before Hua's final replacement by Deng Xiaoping.

According to one report, 22 contracts for major equipment imports were concluded in 1976 alone, at a total fixed capital investment equal to the government's entire budget revenue of that year. Inevitably, the rate of capital accumulation was raised to a level second only to that of the Great Leap years. One suspects that the "Stalinist/early Mao" approach was probably the handiwork of the State Planning Commission under Yao Yilin's influence. It is possible that the idea was to try to fill the country's production and engineering gaps quickly from a primarily engineering point of view under given assumptions that certain production targets should be attained, together with some very rough ideas about what domestic industry could do. To what extent the rapprochement with the United States in 1972 and the prospect of establishing even better economic relations, leading to vastly improved prospects of foreign capital inflow, may have played a role already in the mid-70s requires further examination. The full impact of the great earthquake of 1976 which destroyed the Tangshan mining center, causing numerous casualties also has yet to be fully investigated.

Political Restructuring at the Top

When the Third Plenum of the Tenth Central Committee met in July 1977, it created temporarily the appearance of a duumvirate by naming Hua Chairman of the Chinese Communist Party and Deng Xiaoping Deputy Chairman. One month later, at the new Eleventh Party Congress, in August 1977, Hua still presided as Party Chairman and was followed in ranking by Ye Jianying, Deng, Li Xiannian and Wang Dongxing. They were the leaders of the 1976 coup, with the Deng faction emerging in dominance.

Three political developments ensued: the gradual ouster of Hua and Wang, the two "temporary partners" of the coup; the rehabilitation and posthumous commemoration of old-guard victims of the Cultural Revolution; and, the naming of Deng Xiaoping's chief aides to serve under Deng, along with a few tentative steps to put the future of the Party in a new direction.

---

23. For details, readers should consult the monthly reports in *Zhonghua Renmin Gongheguo Jingji Dashi Ji* [*Major Economic Events in the People's Republic of China*], edited by Fang Weizhong *et al.*, (Beijing: Social Science Publishers, October 1984) and Office of Research of the CCP Central, *Zhonggong Dangshi Dashi Nianbiao Shuomin* [*Explanation of the Chronicles of Major Events of CCP History*] (Liaoning: Xinhua Bookstore, May 1983).

In December 1978, the Politburo made Hu Yaobang the CCP's Secretary General and let go Wang Dongxing as Office Director of the Central Committee. A month earlier, in November 1978, the first Tiananmen affair of 1976 was officially reinterpreted, thereby clearing Deng of any stigma of anti-Party intent of which he had been accused by Mao and the radical faction. This was a decisive step in Deng's rehabilitation.

Peng Dehuai, who distinguished himself at the Lushan Conference (1959) as the first open critic of Mao, was commemorated during the Third Plenum. The one-time head of State, Liu Shaoqi, and model communist whose overthrow was laboriously plotted by Mao through and during the Cultural Revolution was finally restored to a place of honor in the Party's history in February 1980, eleven years after his death in incarceration in 1969. By February 1980, Hu Yaobang and Zhao Ziyang were both members of the Standing Committee of the Politburo as Deng's principal aides. Peng Zhen, who fell victim to Mao's attacks at the beginning of the Cultural Revolution, and Chen Yun, Mao's chief economic trouble-shooter in the 1950s, were both returned to places of honor. Peng Zhen became a member of the Politburo after the Fourth Plenum of the Eleventh Central Committee and in 1983 became head of the National People's Congress, being thus on a level in ranking comparable to the Head of State, to succeed Ye Jianying. Chen Yun was named to the Party's new Committee of Discipline and Investigation and began to act as the conscience of socialist planning.

The Sixth Plenum of the Eleventh Central Committee meeting in June 1981 at long last elected Hu Yaobang to the CCP's chairmanship, replacing Hua Guofeng who, however, remained on the Politburo's Standing Committee following Hu, Ye, Deng, Zhao, Li and Chen in descending order. Thus, by then, Hua had become the only more or less Maoist successor of Mao, having been ostensibly anointed by the Chairman personally. One of the few publicized acts of vengeance symbolizing justice in the eyes of many Party members was the formal expulsion of Kang Sheng and Xie Fuchi, successively heads of public security during the Cultural Revolution, from the Party in October 1980. A year earlier, in September 1980, Zhao had replaced Hua Guofeng as Premier. Finally, the Gang of Four and several military aides and companions of Lin Biao were tried in public in October 1980 and sentences were announced in January 1981.

The Twelfth CCP Congress was convened in September 1982, at which time the post of the Party Chairman, then held by Hu

Yaobang, was abolished. Hu became the Party's new Secretary-General, leaving the matter of broader policy in the hands of the elders in the Politburo and, more immediately, its Standing Committee. Deng's work of Party reorganization was largely complete in terms of restructuring. But what about policy and performance? Would Deng Xiaoping's new team be able to deliver where Hua Guofeng could not?

An Invisible Time Pressure for Reform

It took Deng Xiaoping a long time to undertake *political restructuring at the top*. Deng returned from exile after Mao's death when Hua Guofeng, a Maoist, was still very much in power. It was not until September 1980 when Zhao Ziyang as a key aide to Deng could take over administratively from Hua. One might say that only then was Deng's overall control of the CCP relatively secure. The abolition of the post of Party Chairman was no doubt intended to reduce the chance of the emergence of a new strong man from seizing excessive power. The replacement of Hua from the peak of CCP power took two steps: his replacement by Hu Yaobang first as Party Chairman (mid-1981), and abolition of the post of the chairmanship and its replacement by a Secretary General (still Hu Yaobang) in mid-1982.

To fill the new Secretary-General's post with Hu Yaobang required consent from key Party elders and non-Maoist, non-radical factions Mao had not had killed and Deng had carefully resuscitated. There were obvious concerns among members in the last group about their own vested interests in terms of political and economic power and personal privileges. Ideological concerns were no less relevant. Already in 1980-81, the party's Propaganda Department had raised the issue of ideological training and its common baseline.[24]

Not the least problem to the changing roster of leading cadres may have been caused by the practice of using "big character posters" to air public grievances and the first soundings of young political critics and dissidents. Deng himself welcomed these public expressions that helped undermine Hua Guofeng's legitimacy. But he could hardly wish himself to become right away the butt of new political attacks. He needed time to demonstrate economic success. Hence it was he who ordered the imprisonment in 1979 of Wei Jing-

24. Li Xiannian, a cautious bureaucrat under Mao, was probably a sometime supporter of Hua and could not have been an early enthusiast of Deng.

sheng,[25] the foremost open critic of communism's one party dictatorship. Thus, Deng demonstrated to the world that he was not a liberal democrat as some had hoped.

Deng and his cohorts, who shared the common misfortune of being victims of the Cultural Revolution, did not overthrow the Maoist radicals only to hand over their hard won power to third parties. While some of the rehabilitated cadres might really begin to question the kind of party that could produce for so long such senseless and brutal intra-party struggles with far-reaching societal and cultural impact as transpired during the Cultural Revolution, many would desire to regain their previous positions of influence and even advance their own interests. This situation generated expectations that the new Deng team had to take into account when new policies were introduced and when political vacancies had to be filled. Job vacancies might even have to be artificially created in order to accommodate returned cadres from exile or prison. Since some older deserving cadres were no longer able to work, often it was their children or close relatives who were given jobs.

In the case of top ranking cadres who had to be either compensated or rewarded, special considerations had to be made, perhaps "negotiated." Accordingly, although economic reform was called for as a matter of urgency, policy-making had to make room for personnel arrangements. In this way the manner in which high-level appointments and other arrangements were made became the raison-d'être of "feudalistic," traditional practices that passed on the privileges enjoyed by one generation of the PRC *nomenklatura* to another. This is one aspect of the Chinese Communist Party's

---

25. Wei Jingsheng was only 16 when the Cultural Revolution began in 1966. As he described himself then, he became a fanatic Maoist and joined a "Joint Action Committee of Red Guards" in Beijing. Personal experience and observations in the poorest farm areas of the country, as well as his readings, led him in a different direction. In late 1978, when Deng was on his way back up again politically, he encouraged the ideas Wei and others were advocating in writings posted on "democracy wall" (a low wall to the west of the Telegraph Building on Xidan, a busy street in Beijing). Wei was arrested on March 29, 1979 and sentenced to 15 years imprisonment on October 16. He was finally released on parole in 1994, but was rearrested in 1995 and sentenced again to 14 more years. His first arrest was a signal of Deng's decision to put an end to the propagation of free political public discussion. The second arrest in 1995 was a sign that Jiang Zemin was determined to impose a stable environment to herald his hoped-for succession to Deng. Wei's autobiography was first translated by Mrs. Mirian London and Professor Ta-ling Lee and published in *New York Times Magazine* under the title, "A Dissenter's Odyssey" on November 16, 1980, p. 134. For other details on Wei Jingsheng at a recent date see "*Supplement to China News Digest,*" Chinese News Digest (ND-CM, No. 72, Nov. 27, 1995.)

succession problem that affected both Party personnel and national policy, to be discussed more fully in the next chapter. At this point, however, we need only note the inevitable delay in initiating reform after Mao and Hua.[26]

Eleven years Mao's junior, Deng was 72 years old when Mao Zedong died. But by the time he could really dominate the CCP and the PRC bureaucracy in 1980-81, Deng was already in his late 70s. Even if he had been able to put into practice a fully developed reform program, he would not have too many years to see through such a program. Unfortunately, there was no blueprint for economic reform. The PRC had no Soviet mentor to follow—the Soviet Union had not yet collapsed. Deng and other non-Maoist Chinese communists had to head the way back from communism by themselves.

In Deng's words, one must try to cross the river by feeling for the stones on the river bed. Reform by trial and error and implementation from localized experimentation to general application on a national scale became the only prudent way, so it seemed, to institute new policies. Such an approach necessarily takes time. Given the need for time to experience the result of reform, there is inevitably a greater chance for those who wish to protect or enhance individual vested interests and privileges either to obstruct reform in its real essence or to exploit loopholes in the new policies. Time is needed to identify effective reform policies. Time is needed to develop a consensus on broad policies as well as detailed rules, regulations and laws. Time is needed to educate and train new bureaucrats for the new tasks.

Yet time precisely was at a premium. By 1989, when the second Tiananmen event took place and when the Berlin Wall fell to signal the collapse of communism as a political ideology and a way of implementing the "dictatorship of the proletariat," Deng Xiaoping was 85. Both Li Xiannian and Ye Jianying had died. Yet the PRC state was still lurching from one economic pothole to another. Communism had lost its allure. But do the PRC central government and the PRC state have a future?

At this writing (1996), the PRC must again face the succession issue. Will Deng's successor(s) have a transition period as lengthy as the one he himself had? Given the passage of time, many param-

---

26. See the detailed discussion on inner CCP factional maneuvers in Chapters XX and XXI of Lazlo Ladany, *The Communist Party of China and Marxism, 1921-1985, A Self-Portrait* (Stanford: The Hoover Institution Press, 1988), pp. 386-431.

eters which are taken for constants during the implementation of reform ideas and approaches may turn out to be themselves variables. This process itself is still continuing. Hence the redoubled uncertainty!

Musical Chairs

In summary, the post-Mao transfer of power did not stop after the overthrow of the Gang of Four. The October 1976 Coup was engineered by a number of temporary allies who shared the same enemies. Hua Guofeng, whose role as CCP chairman after Mao's death was needed by the other co-conspirators, was a common target to Deng Xiaoping and the old guards like Ye Jianying. But removing Hua needed time and Deng needed time to enlist assistance, both by rehabilitating potential allies still incarcerated and by adding new party workers at the center. From the Third Central Committee Plenum (July 16-21, 1977) of the Tenth CCP Congress to the Sixth Central Committee Plenum of the Eleventh Congress (June 15-29, 1981), it took virtually four years before the Dengists managed to remove Hua—and many of their other active or potential opponents—from the center of power and install their own men, headed by Deng's principal aides, Hu Yaobang and Zhao Ziyang. Six years later, in 1987, Hu was himself ousted, at an informal meeting of party elders. Barely two years later, on the occasion of the Tiananmen crisis, Zhao Ziyang, who himself was ousted, was replaced by Jiang Zeming. The first phase of this schedule, distinguished in part by shortening intervals, may be presented in greater detail as follows:[27]

July 16-21, 1977	Third Central Committee (CC) Plenum (of the Tenth CCP Congress)	1. Hua confirmed in his posts as CCP Chairman and Chairman of the Military Commission. (These posts were assumed by him at an expanded session of the Politburo on October 7, 1976, the day after the coup.) 2. Deng Xiaoping restored to • CCP CC • CCP Politburo • CCP CC Politburo Standing Committee • CCP CC Vice Chairman

27. *Chung-kuo Ts'e-huei* [*Chinese Terms*], (Taipei: China Publishing, 1985), edited by China Publishing Company Ltd., pp. 11-21.

		• Vice-Chairman, Military Commission • Vice-Premier, State Council • Chief of Staff, PLA
December 18-22, 1978	Third CC Plenum (of the Eleventh Congress)	1. Chen Yun, Deng Yinchao, Hu Yaobang and Wang Zhen elected to Politburo membership; Chen appointed head of CCP Disciplinary Commission. 2. Affirmed "collective leadership" for the party. 3. Rehabilitation to continue. Peng Dehuai, Tao Zhu, Bo Ibo, Yang Shangkun and others rehabilitated.
September 25-28, 1979	Fourth CC Plenum (of the Eleventh Congress)	1. Yang Shangkun, Lu Dingi, Bo Ibo, Zhou Yang, Peng Zhen and others elected to CCP CC membership. 2. Zhao Ziyang and Peng Zhen also advanced to CC Politburo membership (Zhao became Premier, State Council shortly afterwards.) 3. Hu Yaobang and Zhao Ziyang advanced to CC Politburo Standing Committee membership. 4. CCP Central Secretariat restored and Hu Yaobang appointed General Secretary. (Hua Guofeng's chairmanship in Party untouched.) 5. Liu Shaoqi rehabilitated. 6. Wang Dongxing removed. Ji Dengkui, Wu De and Chen Xilian removed from all party and governmental leadership positions (2 1976 coup co-conspirators included in ouster.) 7. The Four Freedoms halted, including the "Xidan Democracy Wall," leading to the imprisonment of Wei Jingsheng.
June 15-25 and 27-29, 1981	Sixth CC Plenum (of the Eleventh Congress)	1. CCP Chairmanship vacated by Hua Guofeng, replaced by Hu Yaobang. 2. Chairmanship, Military Commission, vacated by Hua Guofeng, filled by Deng Xiaoping. 3. Zhao Ziyang elected to Vice-Chairman, Military Commission.

		4. Hua Guofeng now only listed as sixth (last) ranking CCP Vice-Chairman. 5. Resolution on Party History adopted (de-Maoization)
July 31 - August 6, 1982	Seventh (and last) CC Plenum (of the Eleventh Congress)	Amended CCP Regulations adopted.
September 12, 1982	First CC Plenum (of the Twelfth Congress)	Hu Yaobang elected as Secretary General, in effect reaffirming collective leadership.

CHAPTER VII

TRANSFORMATION FROM COMMUNISM: A DIFFICULT BIRTH

I. LEADERSHIP AND POLICY CHANGES IN THE PRE-1989 PERIOD

Beginning of the Deng Regime

By September 1982, as the gavel passed to the new Central Committee of the Twelfth CCP Congress, the policy-making team in the Standing Committee of the Politburo consisted of Hu Yaobang, Ye Jianyin, Deng Xiaoping, Zhao Ziyang, Li Xiannian and Chen Yun; of the six, three were original 1976 coup conspirators, two were Deng's chief aides, and one was a major spokesman for Soviet-style planning who wanted more efficiency, but limited economic reform. As for political reform, the division leaned toward restrictiveness and ambiguity, as we shall see. Thus, for more than a decade, long before Deng Xiaoping's role was to be weakened by advanced age and declining health, his words were the voice of authority.

However, while Hu and Zhao were both ideologically rather more liberal and moderate, Ye, Li and Chen were more orthodox, distinctly of the stripe and style of communist bureaucrats. Thus, anyone who thought that the onset of the Deng regime signaled the beginning of some kind of gradual and irreversible evolution from Maoist communism to a form of European democratic socialism was bound to be disillusioned. An irrefutable proof came in 1989 when the Communist leadership under Deng was confronted by student demonstrators at Tiananmen. At this juncture, the leadership chose to use tanks to suppress what it took to be an East European type uprising ready to overthrow the regime and the post-Mao/Hua leadership.

Actually it was only during the time before Wei Jingsheng was imprisoned on Deng's orders in 1979 that there were signs of some nascent liberal ideas at large in the PRC. Wei Jingsheng, a self-educated thinker and human rights activist, espoused ideas which in the late 1970s were helpful to Deng's political re-emergence in opposition to Hua Guofeng and were therefore tolerated by Deng. Hu Yaobang's own thoughts were also more tolerant of non-orthodox, unconventional views. But they were too radical for the CCP elders. Already in 1987 the changes in political atmosphere were enough to force Hu to resign his party position on the ground of the imported spirit-polluting effect. As a matter of fact, at that time, economic reform and the inroad of Western economic and social institutions and cultural influence had barely begun.

As we shall see in the next section, when Zhao Ziyang took over the management of CCP policy, and in spite of the offsetting influence of Li Peng's orthodoxy on the State Council, economic reform continued. Discontent too rose rapidly, so that within two years' time student protests against corruption and inflation brought on a political sit-in. A bloody suppression then followed. Yet economic reform outside the agricultural sector was still in its early stages. The flight of reform activists from the country marked June 1989 as the end of the first period of reform. There are obviously a multitude of questions that require explanation.

The first question the Dengists had to answer was a most fundamental one. Why was a new approach to economic reform necessary? Now that Mao, Lin, the Gang of Four and Hua were all gone, the CCP had to admit that their predecessors' respective economic policies were all failures. Mao had run the Chinese economy to the ground by adopting the "big push" approach without modern technology, finding that labor, traditional techniques, mass organization and political exaltation had severe limits. Lin Biao's military organization and management were both disruptive and politically unreliable to the CCP, even the Chairman. The technically poorly trained military officers of the PLA were quite unprepared to manage a progressively more complex economy with or without Lin Biao. The Jiang Qing group had no real understanding of managing any economy beyond Mao's ideas and communist ideology.

If Hua Guofeng had been skillful enough to hold on to power, he might have in due course moved from slavishly following the Stalinist approach of "early Mao," i.e., the Mao of the First Five-Year Plan period, to steer the Chinese economy toward what Chen Yun, the late Liu Shaoqi, and even Deng might have done. Politically Hua's removal might be desirable. In addition, Hua's program of a technologically more modernized version of "Great Leap" proved to be also a failure and he was replaced.[1] Deng was therefore faced with no political rival to blame and no potentially acceptable economic policy to embrace that might also be acceptable to the CCP elders and to the indigent Chinese population.

Deng probably was forced to adopt a pragmatic approach by two factors. First, Hua's new "Big Push" policy during his brief tenure in power (1976-78) had deepened the PRC's economic straits and something drastically different had to be done. Second, in certain regions and especially in the agricultural sector, people had begun to take matters into their own hands. We shall deal with the second factor in the next section.

The deteriorating economic condition of China was apparently kept from the public's view in the controlled media. In a study published in 1988 when Hu Yaobang and Zhao Ziyang were carrying out their reform in earnest, the public was told to compare some of the plan coefficients of the Hua Guofeng years with those of the First Five-Year Plan. From 1976 to 1978, investment in basic construction in "heavy industry" was responsible for 55.7 percent of total industrial investment. Annual farm income (presumably on a national basis) averaged barely 134 yuan ($77.9) per capita in 1978; the urban wage-earner's annual wage averaged 614 yuan ($357), both U.S. dollar figures converted from Chinese yuan (renminbi) at the then exchange rate of 58.2 cents to one yuan.

These and similar data pointed clearly to a living standard for the population as a whole not better than in the 1950s, possibly even worse. Whereas various notable physical accomplishments should be acknowledged, such as railroads, bridges and capital assets that did not exist before the four decades (1949-88) of CCP rule, their economic cost consisted of the stagnated consumption level, which the CCP allegedly claimed they had tried to improve but was too often totally ignored.

The Hua Guofeng years were equally hard for the farmers. Hua's successors pointed out how the decline of food grain production led to grain imports during 1976-78 that the ordinary citizen could not always obtain, in addition to withdrawals from stock. This too was blamed on Hua's inept management.

In short, Deng Xiaoping really had no choice but to turn away from the policies his predecessors had pursued, even though blaming the failure on them alone was hardly fair.

1. Xu Feiqing (ed.), *Zhongguo di Jingji Tizhi Gaige* [*Systemic Reform of the Chinese Economy*] (Beijing: Xinhua Publishers, 1988), Chapter 1, pp. 7-18.

The Taboos: The Four Cardinal Principles Reinterpreted

However, Deng could only change CCP policy within limits. For not all economic measures could be tolerated. There were, in the first place, some "cardinal principles"; they should not be touched.

Deng's policies after the Hua Guofeng period aimed primarily at finding better and more effective ways to modernize the country under socialism. But these policies should not encroach upon the regime's political control of China. The taboos are what has been written into the 1982 Constitution of the PRC as the four "cardinal principles." The 1982 constitution stipulated that the PRC's national goal was the modernization of industry, agriculture, science-and-technology and defense, in short, the modernization of the economy and defense. The taboos are (1) Marxism, Leninism and Mao thought, (2) socialism, (3) the dictatorship of the proletariat, and (4) the leadership of the Communist Party. As we shall see, however, neither the taboos nor the national goal(s) are unambiguously defined.

Marxism and Leninism are cited in the constitution apparently for the sake of doctrinal purity. Marxism is supposed to be "scientific" and serves to guarantee the correctness of the CCP's statement of doctrine. It provides the ideological backstop for Mao. Maoism is tagged on also because of Mao Zedong's lingering charisma to those who never knew the true Mao and how he evolved into an absolute dictator in everything but name. The present generation of communist leaders seems to think, albeit to a slowly diminishing degree, that they still need the image of the Mao who brought the CCP to power and control up to 1957. Thus, the first taboo which delimits the reform proposals is meant to safeguard the regime's political legitimacy. Deng wanted also to reassure the remnant Maoists.

Socialism is included as a basic organizing principle of the country for two reasons. First, unless socialism is preserved as a part of the "brand name," its omission would diminish the raison-d'être of the Communist Party itself. Socialism is meant to imply planning and economic equality in income distribution. It conjures up democratic socialism in the minds of some intellectuals in China, as in many Western circles. Besides, in 1982, the socialist camp had not yet collapsed in Europe. At the time Deng took power, the fall of the Berlin Wall and the collapse of the East European Soviet satellite countries, and ultimately of the USSR itself, were still nearly a decade away. The time had not yet come to junk "socialism" altogether.

However, by the time the Soviet Union itself was dissolved in 1991, socialism as an organizing principle of the economy could no longer be defended, or be held up as a standard. Likewise, too many communist elders and prominent cadres who had suffered in Mao's hands and/or during the Cultural Revolution probably demanded taking Mao himself down a peg or two. Thus, without junking Marxism and undermining the CCP's doctrinal purity, the "scientific correctness" of Marxism was safeguarded by inventing the theory that China was still in a period of "primitive socialism" and that it had mistakenly bypassed this necessary stage of development before it could enter the blissful phase of socialist planning, not to mention pure communism. Likewise, it was reluctantly admitted that Mao erred after 1957.

Of course, if Mao did err in his lifetime,[2] he was not a god, perhaps not even a demi-god. To the thoughtful Chinese and to the many cynics, these were in effect doctrinal concessions on the part certainly of the CCP diehards and of Deng Xiaoping. Thus at least two of the "cardinal principles" turned out not to be real absolutes. The absolutes were then the last two items; the "dictatorship of the proletariat" and the "leadership of the Communist Party." Translated into simple terms for the common people in China, this means that the program of modernization must be carried out without infringing upon the CCP's political dictatorship, which it must enforce on behalf of the proletariat. This implies that the CCP is the agent of the larger Chinese proletariat, which further implies at least a high degree of political and economic equality—at a minimum a relatively low degree of inequality in the long run. It further presumes a strong PLA obedient to the political will of the CCP and, needless to say, more than strong enough to defend the PRC against all external and internal "counterrevolutionaries."

Such being the case, where should the Dengist program of modernizing the economy begin? Moreover, how about modernizing defense? In the final analysis, this is a most fundamental question.

---

2. See CCP Central Document Research Office, *Guanyu Jianguo Yilai Dangdi Ruogan Lishi Wenti di Jueyi Zhushi Ben* [*CCP Resolutions on Certain Issues in Party History Since 1949, Annotated*] (Beijing: People's Publishers), for internal distribution, especially pp. 424-456.

In summary, Deng Xiaoping wanted to modernize the country faster and more efficiently than he thought Hua would have been capable of doing, while keeping the CCP and himself securely in power. But how hard he and his followers would fight just to uphold socialism, meaning state ownership of means of production and centralized economic planning, would be a different matter. In this respect a great deal of ambiguity has crept in during Deng's reign. What was deemed ideologically indispensable, even politically, has changed over time and with respect to different groups of the CCP membership—from old revolutionaries to the lowly party bureaucrats in small townships. The leaders have so far tried to downplay their "genuine" revisionist outlook by introducing undefined terms, such as "socialism with Chinese characteristics" or a "socialist commodity economy," and by avoiding the political nuances and implications of these terms.

II. AN OVERVIEW OF ECONOMIC REFORM POLICY

Agriculture for a Start

The previous section discussed the reason the PRC leaders finally decided to adopt a new economic policy. They simply had to. But limits were set to the reform policy's parameters. Although some of the original fence posts were later made less restrictive, the political taboos became very real in 1989. On the other hand, in the early 1980s, reform took the form of reducing certain controls of the Mao period.

In the absence of a comprehensive economic reform program, the strategy of Hu Yaobang and Zhao Ziyang was to focus on one specific set of interrelated issues after another. The agricultural sector received immediate attention because, as reported by a number of practitioners in the field working under reformist leaders, peasants in several localities had already started such a reform of their own. Inasmuch as their unofficial practice had the desired effect on production, the reformists of the Party merely gave it official sanction *post facto*.[3] The beginning of the 1980s therefore saw the dis-

3. Following the formation of the commune system in 1958, income distribution was for a very brief period based mainly on the individual's food consumption and subsistence. During the early 1960s when Liu Shaoqi's policy moved away from the Maoist rules, the individual worker's wage was calculated from "work points." The value of the work point in real terms was based on the aggregate value of the entire production unit's output after deducting collective items. The production unit for this purpose varied from the "production brigade" to the smaller "production team." The choice of the size of the basic collective unit varied with the degree of deviation toward

mantling of the structure of production management by "brigade" and "commune." (Strictly speaking, this was illegal.)

In essence this reform in agriculture consisted of two elements. First, decision-making on what crops to plant and how to produce them were made the responsibility of the individual farm household leasing land from the local authorities. Second, the lessee of the land undertakes to deliver the agricultural or land tax (assessed in kind at a fixed official price) to the state; he is allowed then to retain the rest of the crop to be freely disposed of as he sees fit.

These new regulations meant a national leasehold system in effect came into being, sub-dividing property rights in agricultural land into two parts: the right to use land to produce income as against the right to dispose of the lands, including the right to transfer it to a third party.

Since the farmer was required to give up only the agricultural tax portion of his output, rather than receiving only the wage portion (equal to the value of his wage units) of his output as calculated for each production brigade or team within the erstwhile collective farm, the household's income became positively linked to the productivity of the farm. His income would not be adversely affected by the poor productivity of other farmers in the same brigade or team. It would depend on his own productivity.

These rules were first tested by farmers themselves in certain localities where the lower level cadres were sympathetic to changes that would enhance incentive, thus raising production without lowering the government's revenue. These bold experiments took place in several counties in Anhui and Sichuan, then governed by liberal CCP members Wan Li and Zhao Ziyang, respectively. The tests took place apparently only after the coup that overthrew the worst ideologues under Jiang Qing and company while Hua Guofeng and his followers were too busy protecting their own flanks. The resultant improvement in agriculture in these two provinces then led to imitation of the same measures elsewhere and their general adoption, as noted by Chen Yizi, Wen Guanzhong, Cheng Xiaonong and others.[4]

"revisionism" of the prevailing party line the cadres at a given time dared to practice. By the time the agricultural reform began, practice in the country as a whole was probably mixed, leaning perhaps more to the smaller "production team."

4. See Chen Yizi, *Zhongguo: Shinian Gaige yu Bajiu Minyun* [*China: A Decade of Reform and the 1989 Democracy Movement*] (Taipei: Lienching Publishers, June 1990), 1st edition, pp. 17-45; and G. Z. Wen (ed.), *Zhongguo Dangdai Tudi Zhidu Lunwenji*

The above measure was later welcomed by the government authorities partly no doubt because prior payment of the land rent was guaranteed by the farmer-lessee at the level stipulated by the authorities before the farmer could claim the remainder of the output as his own. The government was particularly concerned about its ability to supply the urban consumers and consumers in agricultural regions unable to feed themselves. A stable food supply of staples at low prices had always been a primary policy objective the Chinese Communists were proud of accomplishing.

However, if the excess of production over the agricultural taxes, net of additional government purchases, should leave too large or too small an amount for the free market to take off at unchanging prices, price volatility on the market could occur. This would in turn affect the government's hope to maintain food stocks at a certain planned level. When these phenomena became common to many counties in the PRC, they became issues for the urban population and often for the steady improvement in the farmers' well-being, which might threaten to slow down.

Important Longer-Term Economic Ramifications: Private Property, Population and Class Inequality

Once the farm household can make its own crop production plans, subject to the terms of its contract with the government,[5] it will try to keep all available manpower in the household busy all the time. In times of slack in farm work, members of the farm would engage in handicraft and other subsidiary activities. This was exactly how the prewar "cottage industries"[6] had come about and how its survival in the face of the competition of imports was often raised as a political issue of "imperialist exploitation" when tariffs could not be raised. If the farm household under the new system has excess manpower over and above the land and other resources it can muster will require, the surplus manpower beyond its own farming need might choose to migrate in search of employment elsewhere. Such internal migrations are an unavoidable natural out-

---

[*China's Contemporary Land System, a Collection of Essays*] (Changsha: Hunan S & T Publishers, 1994), especially the chapter by Lo Xiaopeng, pp. 174-96.

5. The "contract" signifies an agreement between the government and the producer, in this case, the farm household. It is also known as the "household responsibility system." There is an implied declaration on both sides that the terms of a contract cannot be changed unilaterally. In reality this promise is only as reliable as the degree of ease with which law can be changed.

6. See Chapter V above.

come once the local labor force is no longer tied to the agricultural collective like serfs, be it the farm commune or the smaller collective farm. On the other hand, the subsequent rapid development of enterprises in townships and villages in the PRC in the middle and late 1980s had the effect of diminishing the flow of internal migration to seek seasonal and longer term employment.

Leasing public land to private farm households for cultivation raises other economic and legal issues. A fundamental one is the length of the lease (usually 15 years in the early practice of the system) and its transferability through sale, inheritance and the like. In this respect, economic reform in the PRC very quickly began to impinge on institutional restructuring. As long as the farmer faces insecurity of his right to use the land, investment of either labor or financial resources is bound to be discouraged. Apparently recognition of this problem has led to a progressive lengthening of the lease so that inheritance from father to son, both being farmers, has apparently become in effect possible.

Restoration of Private Ownership of Farm Land?

At this point, one can raise a number of questions concerning the restoration of private ownership of land. Inasmuch as Chinese peasants always aspired to become owner-farmers while the reform measures introduced by the farmers themselves after 1979 greatly encouraged productivity, wouldn't the restoration of private farm land ownership be a logical extension of the reform that has already proved its effectiveness? Abstracting from the objection that such a step would be an ideological and political retrogression that the CCP could not concede, there is a real economic as well as political problem. If private farm land ownership is restored, disparities in farm productivity could very quickly lead to an increasing concentration of ownership of farm land. The reemergence of private land owners versus tenant farmers would appear in the next stage of development. Such a development might look too much like a "revisionist" economic scenario of the pre-1949 era. Perhaps even the radical economic reformers would find such a situation hard to swallow.

How to Increase the Income of Rural Residents from All Sources

Alternatively, one would have to increase the rural residents' income short of introducing private farm land ownership, that is, not until other forms of ownership of wealth-producing assets also became more easily available.

One can also look at the problem from a slightly different perspective. Thus far, the modification in the land tenure system and the manner in which the production and distribution of farm output are carried out have had a one-time positive effect on productivity. For continuing growth of income in the agricultural sector, there would have to be: (1) continuing improvements in technology (including new products); (2) continuing growth of inputs from agriculture as well as non-agriculture; (3) markets for both the agricultural and non-agricultural products originating from the agricultural sector (including export markets); and, (4) rising investments in both agriculture and non-agriculture in the rural areas, including investments in transportation, irrigation, land conservation and reduction of environmental deterioration. In short, the benefit of economic reform in agriculture and the rural areas can be sustained and multiplied only if reform is also carried out elsewhere in the economy.

III. INITIAL ECONOMIC REFORM IN THE CITIES AND IN NON-AGRICULTURE

A Second Step in Economic Reform

When Chen Yizi wrote in 1990 about his personal involvement as Zhao Ziyang's aide in developing the PRC's successive economic reform efforts before 1989, reform of the urban economy became the central focus only after the Third Plenary Session of the Twelfth Central Committee in 1984. Only sporadic experimentation took place at Zhao's initiative in Sichuan beforehand. As readers of this volume well know from the 1989 Tiananmen student demonstrations, urban economic reform, to put it mildly, had had rather mixed results up to that time. The CCP cadres knew much less about what to do with the urban sector than they did about agriculture. Besides, agricultural reform was conceptually simpler and the farmers had taken the initiative themselves.

The PRC imported its economic planning system from the Soviet Union, and the system was then nurtured by Chen Yun until Mao's defense-oriented big-push approach to development greatly upset the inter-industry structure and created serious sectoral bottlenecks, as explained in Chapters V and VI. Efforts by the State Planning Commission, probably under the influence of Yao Yilin and Song Ping, and others during the Hua Guofeng years continued to stress capital-intensive investments but apparently failed to correct the sectoral distortions. Thus, the initial emphasis in urban economic reform merely sought to return to the principles of achieving equilibrium in demand and supply, i.e., "material balance" in the inter-industry structure and equilibrium between aggregate demand and supply.

Accordingly, as subsequent events were to show, two giant steps had yet to be taken. These were, first, to *decentralize* decision-making in production by removing restrictions on managers at the enterprise level and to introduce effective material incentives, such as bonuses for workers. The second major step was to grant limited economic freedom of operation by state firms within the confines of a centrally administered economy (with diminishing command and increasing guidance) and really to introduce, in the prevailing PRC jargon, a "socialist market economy"; that is to say, there would be competition by state-owned firms producing for sale on the market. However, this second major step was not attempted until late 1984, when after much debate the political decision was taken by Deng's team to turn to the price mechanism and profit and cost comparisons as guide posts of economic decision-making.

Believe it or not, what the reformers laboriously rediscovered was what more than fifty years earlier, pre-World War II economists in Great Britain and Germany had described as "competitive socialism" and what Abba Lerner[7] in his work with Hayek at the London School of Economics and Political Science wrote about in Lerner's *Economics of Control.* Unfortunately, once central planning had been installed and operated for decades—even though the PRC system was by no means a full-fledged centrally administered planned economy, it was by no means easy to re-introduce "the market" and competitive behavior to maximize profit. Individual managers of state-owned firms just do not know automatically how to behave in order to maximize profit under perfect competition as if they were true owners with full property rights. Nor would they do so even if they knew what they should do. Very likely they would not even dare.

It was this second major step that provoked reactions from two sides: (1) entrenched vested interests on the part of CCP cadres; and, (2) the general public who suffered from price increases and their social effects. Students and intellectuals deplored the effects of the increasing inequality of income and opportunity that accompanied the onset of a market economy. The effort to reinstate the

7. Abba P. Lerner, who taught at the School of Social Research in New York City in 1946, worked with Hayek at the London School of Economics where he wrote the *Economics of Control,* which the author read in manuscript form.

market mechanism in a society of oligarchic, non-competitive access to resources and market, which the communist Chinese system was, led to the developments in 1984-89—inflation and corruption—ending finally in the political crisis of June 1989. A price increase due to shortage could not lead to an increase in supply. Instead, producers and officials having the power to determine their profitability divided a larger immediate profit among themselves by creating or maintaining conditions of continuing shortage and unequal access without the trouble and uncertainty of expanding supply.[8]

The Pre-1984 Reform—A Foretaste of Complex Economic and Administrative Issues

During the first phase of urban economic reform in 1980-84, which Zhao Ziyang instituted in Sichuan, some forty large and medium-sized firms were given greater autonomy to decide on their own production and sales plans provided the targets specified in the state plan had been reached. For enterprises included in the trial, the usual rigid plan goals were partly replaced by softer stipulations in the nature of government guidance. In addition, wages were raised through bonus payments which were very quickly adopted by 60 percent of Sichuan's state enterprises.[9] However, it should be pointed out that these reform measures were at once both very limited and, in some respects, very extensive. They were very limited because they touched upon small micro-management issues of a very small number of state firms in Sichuan. Yet they were potentially very extensive because Sichuan was a very populous province which in 1988 boasted a population of 105.8 million (excluding military personnel), about 10 percent of the PRC's total population, so that if 60 percent of the province's state firms had been given a wage increase, both the number of workers and the payroll affected must have been sizable even though the magnitudes are unknown.

Zhao's early test measures were significant because they were indicative of certain developments which were scheduled to follow: they were both good and bad from the point of view of reform and its political and social consequences. First, if a reform measure en-

---

8. See the fuller discussion below in this chapter and an earlier monograph coauthored by Richard Y. Yin and the present author, *Can One Unscramble an Omelet? China's Economic Reform in Theory and Practice* (Baltimore, MD: University of Maryland, School of Law, 1993, Occasional Papers/Reprints Series in Contemporary Asian Studies.)

9. Chen Yizi, *supra* note 4, p. 58. See also note 7 *supra*.

tails immediate material benefits, such as bonus payments to workers or enterprises, it would be welcomed by the firms involved. However, the original intent of the reform could be distorted. For instance, bonus payments were sometimes awarded to all workers and thus unintentionally became a general wage increase. Since wages were extremely low, such a general wage increase at the then level of productivity and subsistence might not be out of line from whatever point of view. Further indiscriminate wage increases could pose an economic problem if the payroll could not be trimmed and the unintended cost increase continued.

Second, to allow an individual enterprise to manage its own affairs is always taken as axiomatic by those who favor the market economy as a way of organizing economic activity. The very natural, implicit assumption is that those owners who wish to see the firm earn an acceptable profit, if not to maximize it, would naturally wish to put an efficient manager in charge. That this assumption might not be true even after Mao's death may not sound strange to those familiar with the protracted argument on the appropriate criterion of selecting leading cadres for administrative or even purely technical posts; namely, whether ideological purity or technical competence was more important. Although there was a shift in favor of technical ability and managerial merit during the early phase of economic reform, a more decisive turn came after 1984.[10] Besides, assuming that profit maximization became accepted as a guide to the manager, one must then focus attention on the valuation of the net worth of a state enterprise on which profit should be earned for the firm. An equally nagging question would be what to do if net worth fell to zero or below when in the market economy under capitalism, the next step could lead to the bankruptcy court.

Third, during the pre-1984 phase of urban economic reform, the issue of net asset valuation anticipated in the preceding paragraph was still several years away. But there were instead some other knotty problems immediately ahead. The term "decentralization" of power in economic administration was one. In a country

---

10. The selection of a firms managers on the basis of technical competence rather than ideological purity and political partisanship or familial lineage was related to the issue of separating the CCP from the governmental apparatus. Opposition to such a separation increased when Hu Yaobang headed the CCP. When Hu was ousted in 1987, Zhao Ziyang was nominated by Deng. According to Chen Yizi, Zhao preferred to stay as Premier but was named to the party post by Deng nevertheless. Thus Li Peng became Premier, and the economic reform program came under greater uncertainty. See Chen Yizi, *id.*, Chapter 6, pp. 125-145.

the size of mainland China, a thoroughly centralized all-embracing economic plan would have the State Planning Commission serve as the arbiter of the entire State plan coordinating the plans of individual state enterprises reporting through the central government's "industrial ministries." But under the central authorities, there are provincial, autonomous region, district and county (*xian*) level agencies corresponding to those in Beijing, together with coordinating planning organs at the respective lower levels. When " decentralization" took place, some units at the lowest level (firms), for instance, would be transferred to the control of agencies below the central government level. Not only would there be new administrative adjustments to be made, but the vertical lines of inter-administrative-level and sectoral coordination of economic activities at various horizontal levels could easily result in total confusion.

Below the central government, the provincial authorities had the greatest political power. The authorities at the provincial level in a large province with many, many millions of inhabitants and large aggregate resources could wish to play a larger political and economic role than was assigned to them in the state plan and in the nation's or the CCP's political agenda. A province might wish to invest more within its own borders instead of using what it would regard as rightfully its own revenue, most likely through the intermediary of the central government, to help develop another province or region. In short, protectionist policy on an inter-provincial, or even intra-provincial, basis could arise.

Economically, such developments could work against the interest of economic reform aimed at installing a nation-wide market economy, whatever may be the dominant form of ownership (e.g. public versus private). The lack of a distinct division between government and party in theory at every level of the country's administrative system and the continuing tendency for the first party secretary and his staff at any level to upstage the government bureaucracy at the same level added to still more frictions and inefficiency. Thus, urban economic reform could not be treated entirely as an economic issue of adjusting the structure of decision-making in economic activities. The issue goes beyond the role of the individual firm in relation to the state in economic or political theory.

IV. TWO MORE SLIPPERY STEPPING STONES

Since some four-fifths of the population in mainland China still lived in rural areas in spite of the costly economic restructuring efforts of the Mao regime, and many of the farmers in some areas barely eked out a meager livelihood, economic reform in the agricultural sector had a nation-wide beneficial impact on the country during the 1980s. Similarly, another reform measure that was expected to have a profound effect on the country as a whole was the long hoped for technological progress by opening up the country to the outside world. Hence, as a slogan, the "modernization of technology and science," because it can increase productivity, is equally important in the eyes of many more Chinese than just economic reformers. This section will call the reader's attention to two developments that have had far-reaching and widespread impact: the establishment of "Special Economic Zones" (SEZ) and the emergence of "township and village enterprises" (TVEs) using surplus rural labor. Each of these developments has led to consequences probably far beyond their original intent. The SEZs are inseparable from the non-economic aspect of Western influence, and therefore what orthodox communists, with Maoists at the extreme end, and other conservative Chinese regarded as a source of spiritual pollution. The relatively free-wheeling TVEs potentially pose a threat to state socialism (or state capitalism) made up by the larger state firms. However, they also have their own potentially unwholesome social consequences.

Special Economic Zones

In 1979, at the time economic reform in the agricultural sector started, Deng Xiaoping called for the modernization of science and technology in China by opening up the PRC to the world. Economically, this meant that the coastal provinces of Guangdong and Fujian whence many "overseas Chinese" had emigrated to Southeast Asia and North America over many years could now again try to attract capital from abroad for their own development. The geographical propinquity and the economic success of Hongkong were special advantages. Apart from Hongkong, the economic success of Taiwan, Singapore and South Korea in the years after 1949, followed by that of Malaysia, Indonesia and Thailand, have offered examples of export-oriented development. In particular, one can assume that Taiwan's several export processing zones (EPZ) were looked upon by some mainland observers as potential Chinese examples the PRC should emulate both as enclaves in the PRC to attract foreign capital and promote exports by themselves and for their demonstration effect to the rest of the Chinese mainland.

These factors led to the rapid establishment in 1980-81 of three EPZs at Shenzhen and Zhuhai in Guangdong, adjacent respectively to Hongkong and Macao, and Xiamen in Fujian across the Taiwan Strait, close to the site of a former British concession. In comparison with the PRC itself, taxes for SEZs were lower for foreign investors; bank loans were more liberal; and applications to set up foreign-owned or joint enterprises were easily sanctioned.[11] The SEZ authorities also undertook to develop the necessary preconditions for new fixed investments by foreign investors in terms of infrastructure, work sites, worker housing and duty-free importation of materials for export, in the same fashion as did the EPZs of Taiwan.

In short, the reformers' aim was to induce foreign investors to import capital, technology and materials to the SEZ for the manufacture of exports with cheap Chinese labor supplied locally. The foreign investors are of course in turn permitted to remit profit out of the SEZs.

There were those who opposed the SEZ concept inasmuch as it in effect recreated a capitalist enclave in a society that still claimed to be socialist while restoring private ownership of means of production together with the institution of "exploitation." In time, different life styles and living standards also developed that might be regarded as class differences in the economic superstructure. The latter manifestations quickly became the targets of attack by Deng's political opponents as "spiritual pollution." Chen Yun and Yao Yilin depicted the SEZs as "foreign concessions" of the pre-World War II period in disguise.[12]

A real distinction between the SEZ and the earlier foreign concessions is the absence of non-Chinese troops, police, and "extraterritoriality," especially that of a non-Chinese judicial system on Chinese territory and the presence of foreign nationals not subject to local laws. Perhaps the existence of this real distinction was convincing enough; perhaps Chen, Yao and others were unable and unwilling to oppose Deng and the rising influence of the reformists at this time. At any rate, as a result of Deng Xiaoping's visit to Shenzhen and Zhuhai during the lunar New Year holidays in early 1984, the trend in PRC policy-making circles once again swung in

---

11. For a recent comprehensive discussion of foreign investment and the PRC's economic development see Chen Wenhong, *Zhongguo Jingji Wenti Luncong* [*Essays on China's Economic Problem*] (Shanghai: Sanlian Bookstore, 1991). Also Duan Xiansheng and Lang Guomei, *Waiguo Zhijie Touzi* [*Foreign Direct Investment*], (Shanghai: People's Publishers, 1993), especially pp. 1-5 and 99-154.

12. Chen Yizi, *supra* note 4, pp. 63-64.

favor of the SEZs. The argument Deng, Hu, Zhao and others used was the need for a "revolution in science and technology."[13]

The direct effect of some of the SEZs in introducing advanced manufacturing and other methods may have been somewhat exaggerated because foreign investors at this time were more interested in taking advantage of the large supply of cheap Chinese labor than in investing in capital-intensive machinery embodying sophisticated technology or in purely technology-intensive establishments. The kind of investments Hongkong, Taiwan and Japanese investors were prepared to make tended to be labor-intensive processing facilities (for textiles, shoe-manufacturing, toy-making and the like). One economic effect was to induce the transfer of similar operations from places like Taiwan where the wage level of low-skill labor was rising to the new mainland SEZs. Another was to introduce the new arrivals from Chinese farms to work in factories. Many of the investments offered the owners a short turnover period, thus reducing their exposure to risk that was unavoidably associated with the unstable political environment surrounding economic reform in the PRC. Some SEZ investments might even consist of renovated second-hand equipment which could no longer be profitably employed at their original plants.

Yet for labor-intensive manufacturing, merchandising, service and hotel industries, and the construction of hotels, and office and commercial buildings, the SEZs offered attractive opportunities to investors from outside the PRC. Government agencies in the PRC apart from the central authorities in Beijing also became interested in the coastal SEZs as their own windows to the world. In a sense, therefore, the SEZs had a demonstration effect on the PRC as a whole. According to Chen Yizi, proposals were pressed upon Beijing by many provincial and city authorities so that altogether 14 coastal cities in eight provinces were soon opened up for foreign investment during 1984.[14] In 1987, the island of Hainan (in area smaller than Taiwan), until then an appendage of Guangdong, was elevated to the status of a province, and was also opened up to foreign investment. The successive extension of the territorial scope

---

13. *Ibid.*

14. Chen Yizi, *id.*, pp. 84-85. The opening up of the Liaodong (South Manchuria) and Shandong peninsulas together with Hainan took place during this period. The fourteen coastal economic centers declared as "open cities" are Dalian, Qinhuangdao, Tianjin, Yantai, Qindao, Lianyungang, Nantung, Shanghai, Ningpo, Wenzhou, Fuzhou, Guangzhou, Anjiang and Beihai, located in eight provinces, although several of the cities are administratively municipalities of provincial ranking.

for foreign investors after the mid-1980s meant that the entry points of foreign technology began to multiply. If foreign direct investment is really an effective vehicle of new technology, then the encouragement of foreign investment, especially foreign direct investment, was pointing to the proper direction of development and reform. That is to say, barring other considerations.

Foreign investments in SEZs can lead to greater exports. But exports can expand only if foreign importing countries do not clamp down on PRC exports. If the products manufactured with foreign capital are allowed to sell to the PRC's domestic market, a potential balance of payments problem could arise, leading to demand for reform in the exchange rate and other reforms. These additional problems must in turn be resolved. Of course, if a country is unable or unwilling to make the necessary additional adjustments in policy, it will be in conflict with other countries. This development has resulted in continuous Sino-U.S. trade disputes in the 1980s and 1990s.

Township and Village Enterprises

We turn next to the rise of township and village enterprises (TVEs) as a natural outlet for surplus labor in the countryside that could not find productive employment in farming. Following the agricultural reform of the early 1980s, a farm household desiring to increase its income over and above the outpayments in tax and other fees as land rent to the state has had a strong incentive to increase the household's productivity. Labor not needed during the slack period would be free to seek nonagricultural employment, either in local industry, transportation, construction, or the like, or away from home. Those who travel to distant areas and the more developed port cities (including SEZs) join the throngs of migrant workers that visitors to the PRC have observed at many rail stations. Others finding work closer to home have supplied labor to the TVEs (township and village enterprises), which have begun to rise.

Improvements in the income of farm households due both to the contract responsibility system and to simultaneous increases in crop prices have accounted for some of the reported increases in savings for investment in the TVEs.[15] Since the hitherto rigid con-

15. A very comprehensive economic overview of the PRC in English based largely on official data furnished by the PRC can be found in the World Bank's 1992 study (Country Economic Memorandum), *China Reform and the Role of the Plan in the*

trols of small business in retail and general merchandising became more relaxed at about the same time in different places, the fortunes of the TVEs have varied by location. A very detailed survey in 1989 of TVEs in the Shanghai municipality points out how TVEs in the area benefited from subcontracting from larger firms in Shanghai. This locational advantage also included the availability of technical help in the form of engineers and skilled workers from the metropolis moonlighting as weekend workers.

However, the TVEs are not necessarily identical to purely private-owned business firms although some are. Many are owned by local village, township and county entities. Some may even have obtained a part of their capital from lower level government authorities outside their immediate local jurisdiction. In some areas, collectively owned holding-company type "township industrial corporations" have been established. Elsewhere "township planning and economic commissions" have been set up to govern the local TVEs. The individual TVE or TVCE (i.e., township and village community enterprise) may not be an entirely autonomous enterprise. It conceivably could even function like a miniaturized and bureaucratized public-owned "enterprise."

When TVEs in a coastal "open city" are directly or indirectly financed by foreign investors, they would seem to differ little from firms in an SEZ. While SEZ enterprises were initially designed to promote exports, the TVEs have already made their début by serving the domestic market, or, even more narrowly, the rural market. As the Shanghai study has mentioned, a principal determining factor of the TVE's course of development is their ability to increase profit through new technology, not just to engage in the replication of the same production unit through "extensive expansion." Access to financing then becomes crucial. Will there be an impartial supply of capital, or will capital supply be tilted in favor of or against

---

1990s. However, some more narrowly focused reports may be more informative inasmuch as institutional restrictions may limit the sources of information to be used. According to a 1991 study, *China: Economic Development in Jiangsu Province, IBRD*, it was suggested that about one-half of the province's exports in 1990 came from TVEs. The proportion might be even higher on the national level. The discussion in the preceding text on the growth of TVEs in the satellite towns of Shanghai with respect to the dependence of TVEs on contracts from Shanghai firms and their competition with those located in the metropolis are based partly on the accounts of a returned American economist who spent some time there. The author is grateful to him for some of his observations. For a study on the TVEs and their relation to privatization and marketization by a West European economist, see Willy Kraus, *Private Business in China* (Honolulu: University of Hawaii Press, 1991), translated from the German by Erich Holz.

them? During the phase of economic contraction in the 1980s, state banks doling out credit reportedly often acted in favor of the state-owned firms instead. If TVEs owned by foreign interests can also obtain local bank loans and are established in a coastal open city, they would become in effect private firms in a domestic market. (It can of course also be in the export business.) But enterprises like that may not be subject to as much state control as the authorities would wish and may engage in competition with state-owned firms to the latter's disadvantage.

V. MOUNTAINS OF REFORM BUSINESS AWAITING IMPLEMENTATION

Moganshan Conference

A conference on economic reform was convened by the reform planners under Zhao in July 1984 to review the progress of the reform program and to draw up the forthcoming agenda.[16] This session was the first thorough discussion on urban economic reform, according to Chen Yizi, attended both by academic personnel (including graduate student researchers) and by government-employed field workers. Apparently the discussions and research work related to this conference were instrumental in calling the authorities' attention to the following groups of topics: (1) the issuance of stocks as evidence of ownership, making it possible to pull together capital from diverse sources in order to establish an individual firm; (2) adjustment of existing commodity prices, or outright removal of all price controls; (3) establishment of a central bank in the nature of a genuine central monetary authority instead of the Soviet type People's Bank of China, which was essentially a bookkeeping agent of the State Planning Commission and the cashier/treasurer of the Ministry of Finance, and establishment of investment banks specializing in particular industries; (4) reform of the taxation system; (5) revamping of the foreign trade system; and, (6) reform of the country's economic administration.

Let us recall how Deng Xiaoping had said that economic reform in China was without a well-tested blueprint; it was in the nature of "crossing a stream by feeling for the stones buried under the water." The topics brought out at the Moganshan Conference actually constitute the principal economic features and institutions of a market economy that the PRC would have to establish out of its then still disorderly flux, which had grown haphazardly from a

---

16. Chen Yizi, *supra* note 4, pp. 64-99. Moganshan is a resort area near Hangzhou.

jerry-built controlled system that was no longer "later day Maoist" or early Stalinist. The program identified five issues: a price system for resource allocation; a monetary policy for governing aggregate effective demand and supply; a clear definition of the role of the state in administering economic policy; regulation of the activities of non-state entities and private persons; and, a definition of property rights. Unfortunately, merely listing the contents of such a program does not by itself provide the blueprints and the sequencing of the measures to be followed.

According to another saying frequently attributed to Deng, "whether a cat is black or white does not matter as long as it can catch mice." But like many such pithy remarks, they are incomplete. Whether certain reform measures are good or not must be tested, especially if the choice is made by individuals without the benefit of prior knowledge based on theory and experience. In these unfortunate circumstances, one cannot rule out policy errors or mistaken objections to sound policies. Hence one could not avoid policy reversals that put the blame on the wrong party and for the wrong reasons, leading therefore to new errors.

Should Controlled Prices Be Freed Or Adjusted?

Starting at the Moganshan Conference, a long-lasting debate in PRC economic circles had to do with the method of freeing prices from rigid control. Since in the beginning many consumer goods were in short supply, removing controlled prices was expected to provide the incentive to increase supply. But to the authorities, a price increase might be interpreted as the beginning of additional increases to come and finally of general inflation if and when staple foods and key consumer items were involved. The subsidy prices paid to farmers for staple foods purchased by the government and sold to urban consumers at lower prices is a drain on the government's coffers, but a sharp food price increase could result in social unrest.

Low energy prices have been a factor causing the excessive use of coal in industrial production. Low rent discouraged new housing construction, but once private building was allowed, raising the rent ceiling could increase the housing supply. Conflicting arguments between advocates in favor of a general removal of price control and those who advised caution led to a policy in the mid-1980s of making only limited adjustments of the prices of selected commodities in short supply. Some items could continue to be bought at low controlled prices but only up to a point, beyond which the prices would be freely determined at significantly higher levels on the free market.

Combining rationing (at a fixed price) with the free market in this manner produced a dual price system. The reformers may have thought that additional supply would be encouraged by the possibility of its being sold at the higher market price. Furthermore, new producers interested in competing with the existing producers should and would be encouraged to enter the market, thus bringing about even more supply.

Zhao Ziyang may actually have thought that this train of reasoning was how the lower priced portion of national supply would gradually become smaller and eventually quantitative restrictions would disappear as fewer commodities would be controlled in this way. Reportedly this was how Zhao described his outlook on reform to a visiting American free-market advocate.

Barring the total abolition of controlled prices altogether, the dual price system was in effect not a one-time price adjustment, but the beginning of a process of price adjustments, each time trying to guess at the price at which demand and supply would be equal, i.e., trying to reach the equilibrium price.

Of course the equilibrium price may be below the existing controlled price, and the supply should then be cut. (Excess supply or the piling-up of inventory may also reflect substandard products and poor quality control.) Such a situation implies that some existing state enterprises probably should be eliminated. For this contingency, a bankruptcy law was published in the mid-1980s. But the idea was soft-pedaled, the main reason being the CCP leaders' unwillingness to close down large state-owned firms. As late as 1992, Li Peng made it very clear at the Fifth Session of the Seventh National People's Congress that failing firms should be eliminated in some other way than through closure. The other ways included merger, shifting to different lines of production, and even sale to others, including non-state owners. Conceivably, sale to foreign investors could be considered. However, as both PRC residents and visitors would agree, too many inefficient enterprises have been producing goods no one wishes to buy and have done so for too long. This condition remains true to this writing (1996). But let us return to conditions before June 1989.

Collusion, Corruption and Obstruction of Free Price Competition and Market Entry[17]

If the supply of a commodity for which potential buyers are prepared to pay a much higher price than the officially prescribed price ceiling but production cannot be increased for a variety of reasons, what might then happen? First, those who can buy at the official price could divert their purchase to the free market and resell at a higher price. This would be the usual case of wartime illegal sale of rationed goods on the black market. Alternatively, the original supplier and the official price setter and administrator could work together and divert all or a part of the output directly to the free market, sell it at above the ceiling price, and share the extra profit. Such a practice would imply collusion between the producer and the controlling official agency for the purpose of stealthily raising the controlled price. Or there would be a case of outright corruption, and exchange of "favors." However, the higher market price can prevail only as long as supply is not increased through the appearance of new suppliers on the market.

A special case in the latter half of the 1980s in the PRC was the possible credit discrimination against certain TVEs in favor of larger or politically influential state firms. Control of indispensable inputs or of physical access to the market or to indispensable raw materials or transport through imposition of tolls can play the same role. In short, restriction of supply—in the extreme case, monopoly—can artificially enhance profit.

By sharing the monopolist's extra return with those who control the inputs or whose permissions are required to operate, corruption can actually become an impediment that slows down the expansion of supply and simultaneously keep potentially more efficient producers out of the market. Corruption can slow down the desired effect of economic reform.

However, if there is a general contraction of spending, it would be difficult to keep up artificially maintained high prices and to shut out eager competitors for long. On the other hand, if general or aggregate spending is on the increase, the high price scenario described above is more likely. Hence we must consider why increase in both investment and consumption spending occurred in the mid-1980s.

---

17. See *supra* note 8.

Inflation and the Dual-Price Practice

Several of the issues demanding the reformers' attention listed by the aides of Zhao Ziyang in 1984 were all related to monetary and fiscal matters. In his 1992 account of the active reform period before June 1989, Chen Yizi noted the endemic and systemic tendency toward inflation in conjunction with the economic development of a developing country. Chen mentioned that inflation in the PRC in 1984-85 was not "cost-push" by which he probably meant the practice in the West by producers themselves because of increases in their own cost. This was essentially true because during that period producers in industry simply did not yet enjoy the authority to set their own prices. At the same time, he claimed that prices were not pulled up by voluntary increases of aggregate demand. Yet Chen did note both increases in the consumer and investment demand feeding the inflation.

It seems that there was a deliberate increase in investment as well as consumption expenditure during this period, interspersed by efforts of the government to regain control. Several factors may have been responsible for this development:

First, public investment on construction projects was often approved in a most haphazard manner. For projects ostensibly in the state plan, last minute horse-trading (like dividing the pork barrel) was more an exercise of relative political power than rational economic decision-making. Such a political process is not likely to be accompanied by the careful calculation of funding needs and resource availability.

Second, major investment projects were probably tied to foreign project loans and promising feasibility studies such as those by the U.S. State Department's very useful Technical Development Program (TDP) and by international agencies like the World Bank. However beneficial such external inflows of material and technical resources might be, complementary domestic spending could very well be just so much more spending at the wrong time and place.

Third, decentralization of economic decision-making from the central government to lower authorities gave rise to investment expenditures at provincial and even lower levels of government and public agencies. Some expenditures may be outside the budget and/or the plan. They may be financed by bank credit. Credit extension may be made by both banks and non-banks. Public enterprises owned by local governments or agencies can be the recipients of credit from local branches of banks or other lenders subject to the pressure, if not jurisdiction, of local politicians. This factor becomes part and parcel of the fiscal as well as political relationship between the central/local CCP and government agencies and individual officials. These party/government relations have remained unresolved to this day.

Fourth, the desire to modernize the economy and to speed up the process also contributed to spending. Many reformers probably were themselves convinced that some degree of inflation was inevitable during economic development and did not matter, just as some of their colleagues in the West may believe that inflation actually would accelerate economic development without substantial lasting ill effect.

Fifth, one aspect of the problem of pricing discussed at Moganshan was wages. The specific question was, should wages be raised? One school of thought was that if wages were raised, food sold by the government to urban consumers can be sold at higher prices, thus reducing the central government's subsidy payments. Others questioned whose wages should be raised first. In the end, wage increases were ordered, favoring CCP cadres, and the dual-pricing system was adopted.

Finally, a common practice noted by visitors and in news reports was the relatively large expenditures on public receptions, travel, and entertainment, literally converting personal consumption into public expenditure, or vice versa. Conspicuous consumption, exhibitionism, display of new-found wealth in the midst of poverty began to become part of the life style in the PRC in the 1980s.

Toward the 1989 Crisis

The step-by-step expansion of economic reform finally draws our attention unavoidably to the state enterprise sector of the PRC economy which still overwhelmingly dominates the country's industrial economy. Actually, some of the state-owned firms also have ownership and control interests in TVEs and other collectively-owned firms. In 1989, the distribution of industrial production by ownership was as follows: state, 56.6%; individual-owned, 4.8% (of which rural, 4.4%; urban, 0.4%); and, collective-owned, 35.7%. Of the last group, 10.0 percent and 9.6 percent were respectively from township and village enterprises, with 2.3 percent being "joint urban-rural enterprises".[18] Thus, state-owned enterprises accounted for a total real ownership interest doubtless in excess of 56%. In the same year, firms in this sector reported 100 billion renminbi of profit as against 23.4 billion yuan of reported loss. These figures imply that the size of real profit or loss in the state sector could have a decisive impact on the PRC economy. (An NCNA [New China News Agency] report from Harbin on July 21, 1996 stated that losses suffered by State sector firms in the first quarter of 1996 for the first time in history exceeded the reported profit by firms in the same sector.)

Since the group of industrial workers totaled 95.7 million in 1989 and the employees of state-owned firms were generally better paid, closures of such firms would impact on major vested interests and spark large outcries. Important members of the CCP leadership would resist reforms leading to such an outcome. On the other hand, subsidy payments to loss-making state firms in all sectors in 1989 amounted to 3.8% of the country's estimated GNP (1,013 billion yuan at 1980 prices). If the loss-making state-sector continues to be kept alive by subsidy, if financing of the subsidy is by inflationary means, and if the continued existence of these inefficient state firms bar the entry of more efficient competitors (for the two phenomena are really two sides of the same coin), one cannot but expect the patience of radical reformers to be exhausted.

Not to be overlooked is the expansion of PRC exports stimulated by the inflow of foreign investments that began to increase during the 1980s. Suffice it to point out here that favorable exchange rates are an indirect subsidy; thus allowing exporters to convert foreign currencies into renminbi at free market rates can be a form of indirect subsidy.

---

18. These data are taken from *China Statistical Yearbook*, 1991, pp. 353 ff. *and Zhongguo Jingji Tongji Nianjian* [*Chinese Economic Statistical Yearbook, 1990*], pp. 74 ff.

CHAPTER VIII

THE 1989 TIANANMEN CRISIS AND AN UNFINISHED REFORM AGENDA

I. A GATHERING STORM

Interruption of Economic Reform

Chapter VII covered the first phase of the post-Mao and post-Hua Guofeng period of "economic reform." At the end of this first phase, a new Deng Xiaoping sought to modernize China through "socialism with Chinese characteristics." Since neither Deng nor his principal lieutenants, Hu Yaobang and Zhao Ziyang, knew ahead of time what the Chinese characteristics were supposed to be, their attempts were inevitably a process of trial and error. Consequently, the net positive results were slow to emerge. The growth observed in the economic sector was accompanied by inflation, corruption and uneven distribution. The relaxation and feeling of liberalization common to all nouveaux riches became "spiritual pollution" to those who wondered whether such changes were worthwhile and whether corrections might be called for. As a result, opposing political forces came against each other, leading to open conflict.

But conflicts did not have to occur in the form of a bloody massacre then and there. Some optimists apparently thought that economic reform had already made the orthodox communist leaders sufficiently open-minded as to be tolerant enough to carry on a peaceful dialogue with those who demanded even faster reform. In reality, the real power-holders had become alarmed by the speed of change and were frightened enough to think that their own lives and vital interests were imminently threatened. In terror and confusion, they took to arms. How such a failure in communication and understanding led to tragedy will be examined more closely in the rest of this section.

Events Outside China

The PRC's economic reform measures came to a halt with the dismissal of Hu Yaobang as the CCP's Secretary General in 1987. Hu clearly had become too free-thinking and liberal for many of the diehard Party stalwarts. Deng Xiaoping, with the help of Hu, and his successor, Zhao, had helped rehabilitate and call back to power many leading CCP members from the wilderness and the dungeons of the Cultural Revolution. A host of domestic and foreign developments, some fortuitous, some by design, conspired to make 1989 a stopping point. A decade had gone by since the diplomatic recognition of the PRC by the United States. This was accompanied by the U.S. severance of diplomatic relations with the Republic of China (ROC). The open break of formal diplomatic relations with a World War II ally by the United States was politically like a signal to many China watchers in the world that the PRC's policy of "economic reform and openness" had paid off for China, albeit only in a very narrow sense.

At the same time, since some of Deng's supporters who wanted to abandon Maoism in its extreme manifestations had never been in favor of too much "openness" to Western influence, they were becoming progressively more apprehensive. They feared that further progress in economic reform was about to move China closer and closer to political liberalization. Deng's decision to incarcerate Wei Jingsheng, therefore, was a sign that he wished to pause and reassess the situation in view of the changing international milieu as well as the new circumstances the PRC faced at home.

The greater presence of Westerners in mainland China and of PRC nationals (including numerous students) in the West had increasingly created new opportunities for direct personal contact and influence. Increased official American and other Western presence in Beijing was accompanied by growing Sino-Western intellectual, academic and multifaceted social contacts that were stimulating to participants on both sides. What led to hopeful expectations of positive change in the PRC by Chinese and Western intellectuals unfortunately, however, could be perceived as warnings of a gathering storm by the CCP authorities. We are probably correct in thinking, with a large dose of hindsight, that such a difference in perception existed sharply in the late 1980s.

During this very period when the Reagan Administration was busily engaged in rebuilding military strength, and especially the development of a space defense program against missile attack—dubbed "Star Wars" by many who questioned its practicality and usefulness—the Soviet Union, under a new Secretary General of the Soviet Communist Party (CPSU), Mikhail Gorbachev, was becoming progressively oppressed by the inefficient domestic economy, the harsh consequences of armed intervention in Afghanistan, and the growing burden of holding together a restive Eastern Europe in subjugation. News of actual or potential unrest in Eastern Europe at this juncture could not but instill a growing sense of insecurity in Beijing. It so happened that Deng, Chen Yun and some others then in Beijing's decision-making circles were among those who had met in nightly sessions with Mao thirty years earlier (in 1956) to review the situation in places like Budapest and Poland in Stalin's Europe-under-siege. Future students of Chinese history and of Russian and Eastern European affairs will have to provide a more comprehensive account of what took place in exchange between the several communist party leaderships in the 1980s, in comparison with the same in 1956.

By mid-1989, Gorbachev had arranged to visit Beijing for the purpose of normalizing relations between the two communist parties as a first official step in mending fences between the two states. Since such an event would be a major news-making occasion for the world's top journalists and TV cameramen, their presence in Beijing was bound to be a must. For the leaders in the PRC, requests for visas to Beijing for the occasion could hardly be refused. To some of the PRC's elderly leaders who could well remember how the top officials of the young Chinese communist regime had always to go to the Kremlin for "inspection" and "approval" by Stalin, Gorbachev's having to "come to call" in Beijing might seem especially gratifying. From the perspective of those in the PRC who wished to make their desires for reform known to the world, the anticipated Gorbachev state visit also would be a most welcome opportunity.

Events before June 4, 1989

Against this background, the student movement before midsummer 1989 grew inexorably into a mighty storm that erupted in the tragedy of June 4. How it did so can be better understood if we trace its chronological development from the date of Hu Yaobang's death on April 15th. Hu's sudden death from heart attack was an occasion that triggered an emotional outpouring from those Chinese whose hope and conscience had been awakened with excitement and longing, especially among college students.[1]

1. Student demonstrations were tolerated during the mourning period. Hu's death gave the protesters this unique opportunity to get together for "collective action," free from Public Security's immediate intervention.

The chronological review can be divided into two parts, with the activities around the date of Hu's death (April 15) as a divider. Several events before mid-April may be singled out for analysis. First, on January 6, 1989 Fang Lizhi, a renowned Chinese astrophysicist who had been a rare example of an outspoken Chinese intellectual from the PRC and who had been compared to Soviet physicist Andrei Sakharov in this respect,[2] wrote a personal letter to Deng Xiaoping appealing for the release of Wei Jingsheng. On the night of February 26, the PRC's Public Security succeeded in blocking Fang's attendance at the farewell dinner given by President George Bush before the latter's departure from Beijing after an official visit.[3] On March 1, a statement by students in both Beijing University and Qinghua University castigating Deng Xiaoping appeared in public, although details surrounding this anti-Deng document are hard to come by. At any rate, it was clear that the "counterrevolutionary Wei Jingsheng" would not soon be pardoned.[4]

The events mentioned above up through the first quarter of 1989 linked the name of Wei Jingsheng to requests for his release

---

2. Fang Lizhi, internationally known astrophysicist, was an outspoken advocate of freedom of thought and expression in the PRC. In early 1989, he wrote to Deng Xiaoping a public letter, recommending that the imprisoned Wei Jingsheng and other political prisoners be released on the occasion of the 40th anniversary of the PRC and the 70th anniversary of pre-communist China's May Fourth Movement of 1919, not to mention the bicentennial of the French Revolution in 1789. Fang's letter of January 6 was followed by petitions to the National People's Congress, the CCP Central Committee, and various PRC institutions and political personages. These were signed by actors, academics, writers and other top Chinese intellectuals. For his own account of this period see Fang Lizhi, *Bringing Down the Great Wall* (New York: Alfred A. Knopf, 1991). The texts and signatories (including Wang Ganchang of PRC atomic bomb fame) of two of the above-mentioned petitions can be found in the same volume.

3. Fang Lizhi and Mrs. Fang (Li Shuxian, herself a physicist) were invited by President George Bush to a farewell party during the latter's visit to Beijing. They were deliberately prevented by the PRC's Public Security personnel from attending. Fang's absence caused a delay of the official dinner and was therefore especially noted by the assembled guests and the foreign press. For details, see a vivid account by Orville Schell in *Mandate of Heaven* (New York: Simon and Schuster, 1994), pp. 39-42.

4. For the various petitions headed by Bei Dao, Chen Jün and others to which the Ministry of Justice in effect replied collectively, see Part III, "Chronicles of the Democracy Movement," in *The Truth of Fire and Blood: A Documentary* (a limited publication of the Institute for the Study of Chinese Communist Problems, Taipei, 1989). In addition to this monumental tome, a fairly complete coverage of all day-by-day events during the period between April 15 and June 24, 1989, together with reference materials in full documentation, can also be found in the two-volume documentary, *Daily Reports on the Movement for Democracy in China* or *Minyun Jishi* (Chinese title), (Albany, CA.: August 1989).

from various quarters in China, as well as to official Washington. Outwardly, however, the PRC was still somewhat ambivalent in dealing with the United States. Beijing's Public Security arm was defiant in dealing with PRC citizens—even a prominent scientist like Fang Lizhi—and it was not at all shy in announcing its intentions about how it would deal with Wei Jingsheng. When one U.S. citizen became too persistent in requesting reconsideration by the Chinese official establishment of the issue of pardoning dissidents,[5] it nevertheless contented itself with just sending the "trouble-maker" home. On the side of the students, the slogans used in their loud protests were focused on official corruption, governmental bureaucracy and demand for democracy. In general, the students were still relatively circumspect, trying to avoid making direct personal attacks by name on Deng and those close to him. A radical change of tone came only in the last week of April after the week of mourning for Hu Yaobang had ended.[6]

The first blow was struck by Deng Xiaoping himself on or about April 24, 1989, via an editorial of the official *People's Daily* two days later. Deng designated the continuing student protests and demonstrations as "subversive, counterrevolutionary turmoil." He had apparently told a meeting of the Politburo's Standing Committee of his views, which he also shared with such CCP elders as Li Xiannian, Chen Yun, Yang Shangkun and Peng Zhen. Deng made it clear that the students had been influenced by developments in the Soviet Union, Yugoslavia and Hungary and that the demonstra-

---

5. Chinese Americans like Chen Jün who participated in demanding Wei Jingsheng's release while in the PRC were at the time expelled from the country. (Chen Jün's appeal was forwarded to the National People's Congress on February 29, 1989.) But Wei would "never be pardoned" according to Cai Cheng of the Ministry of Justice. See *The Truth of Fire and Blood*, *id.*, p. III. 1, on March 28, 1989.

6. Although Hu Yaobang was dismissed from his official position as the nominal head of the CCP, he remained nevertheless a party member in good standing. To mourn his passing was not an offense. Hence to do so in groups, even at Tiananmen Square, would not constitute a subversive plot against the State, especially during the week or ten days immediately after Hu's death. In any case, the students' open complaints about the CCP's governance during the month of April 1989 were focused on "anti-corruption," "anti-bureaucracy" and "for democracy." None of these slogans was really contrary to the communist authorities' precepts. Before the massive demonstrations after April 30, the name of Deng Xiaoping was mentioned derogatively only once—in a Beijing University Students' Public Proclamation to the Chinese People. Nor was the Deng family name dragged into any openly questionable commercial dealing until Deng Zifang's name appeared as a consultant of the Kuanghua Corporation of Hong Kong on May 1, 1989 in conjunction with a public statement of the students addressed to the CCP. (*The Truth of Fire and Blood*, *id.*, 1989, p. III. 17)

tions were manipulated by a hidden hand, because they had gone far beyond a purely students' movement. He thought, however, that only a small number of industrial workers and others in the society were perhaps affected, and that the farmers were still outside the circle. Thus Deng showed that he was wary of any further geographical expansion and participation. Yet it was precisely such an expansion in these dimensions that the demonstrators now tried to promote.[7]

The Month of May—Moving Away from Peaceful Change

Between the end of April and the dawn of June 4, 1989, when the Tiananmen massacre took place, the month of May was filled with frenetic activities on both sides of what might have been an unprecedented political change in the PRC. On the one side, the demonstrating students accelerated the process of gathering support from the rest of the country, drawing world-wide attention and sympathy at the same time. In their favor was, first and foremost, the historic date of May Fourth, which the Chinese academic community ever since 1919 had regarded as the memorial day of the continuing drive for academic freedom and political reform. It provided the occasion for a powerful call to the country's intellectuals to come to the aid of their members in the capital.

The second factor in their favor, which was really a double-edged sword, was the impending Gorbachev visit to Beijing on May 17-18, during which neither side of the gathering forces would wish to see open violence. On the other side, for this very reason, the authorities were extraordinarily patient, first waiting to see whether a violent conflict could be at the last minute avoided, and then to be fully prepared should conflict be unavoidable.

If we assume that Deng Xiaoping really believed in his own judgment on the protest movement as subversion, he would need the necessary troops on hand for its suppression. The waiting period prior to Gorbachev's arrival would serve two purposes: It would allow the hidden enemies of the regime to show their hand; it would allow time for the selection and movement of the needed troops. (In this respect, Deng would be re-enacting Mao's tactics during the 1956-57 period when dealing with China's intellectuals a generation

---

7. At this point one should recall Mao Zedong's comments on the 1956 East European uprisings and compare them with Deng's premonitions in 1989. Further comparisons can be made between what Soviet troops did in Eastern Europe for Stalin with what PLA forces did for the CCP under Deng's leadership.

earlier.)[8] If there was a plan, it apparently worked. A few selected items of circumstantial evidence are listed below.

The number of students demonstrating in Beijing grew in scale, reportedly reaching 400,000 strong by April 21, 1989, the day before Deng's declaration of the student movement as a "counterrevolution." On May 17, a monumental, well-organized demonstration, now reported at one-million strong, took place in Beijing, apparently with semi-official consent. There were participants even from government agencies; there were factory workers and members of the military. Sympathetic demonstrations were reported from other cities on the same day, from as far as Lanzhou in the Northwest, Shenyang in the Northeast, and Guangzhou in the South, not to mention Shanghai. This reported geographical expansion peaked on May 17-18 to include 25 cities. By May 20, reports of support of the student movement had been received from Inner Mongolia and Ningxia, a base area of the PRC's nuclear R&D. It was also on that same day when martial law was declared in Beijing.

One might surmise that by then, the necessary military preparations for the suppression of "counterrevolution" had also been completed. It seems that the troops used in the Beijing suppression campaign came from five of the PRC's ten Military Districts and consisted of elements from fourteen army groups and one airborne army, totalling according to one source up to 350,000 men.[9] While a small number of the military forces had been stationed in the Beijing area all along, most were brought to the environs of Beijing on May 19-June 3. None apparently had arrived before May 18. In short, they had been held at the ready but were not brought into Beijing—on call but not literally in the city—until the Gorbachev visit was over. On the other hand, Deng Xiaoping, who ordered the mobilization of the task force, must have done so almost immediately after he had convinced himself that he had a counterrevolutionary insurgency to quell. In the CCP lexicon, the organizers of the student movement were enemies of the regime against whom the "dictatorship of the proletariat" had every right to use force.

A Televised Massacre

Instructions were issued by the Martial Law Command of the Beijing Municipality on June 3 to all city residents, enjoining them

---

8. We refer here to Mao's handling of the short-lived "One Hundred Flowers" movement in early 1957.

9. See *The Truth of Fire and Blood*, *supra* note 4, 1989, pp. V. 128-30.

to stay home and to avoid Tiananmen Square and its environs. Fully armed troops and contingents of the Armed Police were ordered to clear and occupy the Square early on June 4 local time. The armed forces, supported by gunfire and tanks, were let loose on the Square's unarmed occupants, who were caught in the swoop although a more organized portion of the Square's occupants managed to evacuate in the nick of time. (Many new student arrivals from out of town who probably had nowhere to stay overnight were thus among the victims.) The troops cleared the Square of human bodies, remains and other debris with fire so that no clear body count of the victims was possible. As a result, widely disparate estimates of the numbers of dead and injured have been passed down to this day, varying with the reporting dates, sources, and geographical coverage. For instance, based on the reports of Beijing's major hospitals, the Chinese Red Cross gave out on June 6 a total of 2,600 dead from among the victims of the massacre, based on data they had collected.[10] The International Red Cross, reporting on June 8, issued much higher figures: namely, over 5,000 soldiers and more than 2,000 civilians were injured; the dead count exceeded 7,000.[11] A BBC report of the same date mentioned a total of 7,000 dead, including at least 1,000 soldiers.[12] According to the spokesman of the State Council in an official report, dated June 16: dead (including both soldiers and civilians), approximately 300; injured soldiers, over 5,000; injured civilians, over 2,000.[13] As of July 1, 1989, the Hongkong *Zheng-ming* magazine estimates for the week of June 3-9 inclusive were: students and other civilians killed, 10,400; injured, 28,790.[14]

It is impossible to say whether a real popular uprising would have taken place if the PLA had not perpetrated its final act of violence. But in bringing about such a brutal ending of the students' and civilians' protests, Deng and his cohorts demonstrated beyond a doubt that they were Mao Zedong's true followers. They did what Mao would have had the East European Communists do in quelling the uprisings the latter faced in the mid-1950s, and what Mao's

---

10. *The Truth of Fire and Blood*, *id.*, 1989, pp. V. 130-32.
11. *Ibid.*
12. *Ibid.*
13. *Ibid.*
14. Also quoted in *The Truth of Fire and Blood*, *id.*, 1989, p. V. 131.

troops had actually done a few years earlier in many places when the PLA took over from their opponents after the Civil War.[15]

The June 4, 1989 massacre was, however, exceptional and unprecedented in two respects. First, the dastardly act was broadcast by satellite TV world-wide. There could be no denying the fact that the large-scale massacre had indeed occurred. The PRC authorities could not really deny it as they had done before; nor could those outside China who were the CCP's habitual apologizers ignore or dismiss it by keeping silent. Henceforth, both groups could only hope that the world, including the Chinese themselves, will forget. For those in China who have long recall, they cannot escape the memory that their predecessors at Tiananmen had applauded and welcomed Mao as a savior. If Mao was granted a mandate to rule China forty years earlier, should the citizens of the PRC another decade later, say, in the year 2000, or some other date, still believe the CCP's current leaders? Can a second mandate be once more given to the CCP? Deng believed that he or his successors might indeed be able to win the people's trust. Will he? Or, in view of his advanced age, will they?

Aftermath of the Massacre

The aftermath of the June 4 massacre can be enumerated along several lines of analysis. First, in terms of domestic politics, the CCP faction led by Deng that dominated the decision to use force had remembered well Mao's criticism of the resolution of the Hungarian case in 1956. Mao had attributed the Hungarian uprising to the local CP's failure to liquidate the opposition elements thoroughly when the communists took over control initially at the end of World War II. Accordingly, Deng's directive of action after the massacre in 1989 was to pursue the opposition to the bitter end. This approach was decided upon possibly even before Zhao Ziyang went to persuade the students to stop their hunger strike.

---

15. See Yuan-li Wu (ed.) *et al.*, *Human Rights in the People's Republic of China* (Boulder, CO: Westview Press, 1988) especially Appendix A, "A Statistical Analysis of Judicial Practice," pp. 297-315, where the numbers of persons killed or otherwise punished, including confinement in hard labor camps during Mao's unending series of political campaigns, are analyzed. The existence of these victims was rarely a topic of wide concern outside China largely because of the absence of news reporting, which reporters and other non-Chinese at Tiananmen provided in June 1989. This silence was broken wide open by Hongda Harry Wu in *The Chinese Gulag* (Boulder, CO: Westview Press, 1992). The latest of the same author's works is *Troublemaker: One Man's Crusade Against China's Cruelty* (New York, NY: Random House, 1996).

However, the hardliners were of course aware of the existence of a sizable opposition within the CCP establishment eager and willing to pursue economic as well as political reform even at substantial personal risk to themselves. This is why many protest participants succeeded in escaping the government's pursuit and, in some cases, even fleeing the country. The students had sympathizers within the government and party establishment. Here we are reminded of certain parallels in the pre-1949 Civil War period when the shoe was on the other foot.

Of course, CCP hardliners who had been opposed to "reform" or to Deng's way of handling it might have thought that they could go back to the "early Mao" (First Five-Year Plan) or "latter-day Hua" (1977-79) period of PRC economic policy and plan. Deng and the economic reform advocates, however, had enough sense to try to retain the purely technically reformist aspects of economic reform, shorn of the liberal aspects of political philosophy and institutional rearrangements. Thus, already as early as June 16, 1989,[16] while speaking before the inner leadership, Deng exhorted his listeners to focus on a few popular actions that would placate the reform supporters, including more "reform and openness," the further development of Special Economic Zones, tax and other concessions to draw foreign investors, going into profit-making business "by ourselves" (namely, through the CCP and the state itself), and striking hard against "ten to twenty" (that is, a small number of) notoriously corrupt officials. He would like to speed up the economy to an annual real growth rate of seven percent or at least six percent, including railroads, electricity and various infrastructure development. "Wherever opportunities appear, seize them." "Do not hesitate and let slip lucky breaks." Above all, said Deng to his supporters, do not waste time trying to fix responsibility for the affair (meaning the Tiananmen fiasco), settlement of which could be easily postponed for two to three years.

In foreign affairs, the immediate task after the massacre was to recover the international standing the PRC had lost. In one stroke the country was placed in the category of a pariah state. Export controls were placed by many countries on goods of a strategic nature going to the PRC; high-level official visits that had been planned were either cancelled or postponed; considerations of loans

---

16. Deng Xiaoping's speech of June 16, 1989, the essence of which was summarized above, may be found in greater detail in Volume II of *Daily Reports on the Movement for Democracy on China*, April 15-June 24, 1989, pp. 889-93.

and other forms of assistance were held up; and applications for admission to the General Agreement on Tariffs and Trade (GATT), and later to the new WTO (World Trade Organization), were slowed. An extreme example was the annual renewal of the PRC's most-favored-nation (MFN) status in exporting goods to the United States by virtue of a special waiver granted by the U.S. president.[17] Trade disputes with the United States in particular now continued on a non-stop basis around charges of dumping, counterfeiting, violations of patents, disregard of intellectual property rights, offenses against nuclear weapons and technology proliferation, sale of long-distance missiles under the control of the international missile control regime, and non-improvement of the status of human rights in the PRC.[18] All these charges, encouraged by human rights concerns in many of the PRC's trading partners, have dogged the footsteps of the PRC year after year since June 1989.

---

17. Under the U.S. Trade Act of 1975, imports from countries that did not satisfy certain conditions would not enjoy most-favored-nation status, unless a waiver was granted by the President. Not being a "most-favored nation" (MFN) meant a nation's export to the United States would be subject to much higher import tariffs, which presumably would raise the prices of its goods on the U.S. market, reduce sales, and lower the foreign exchange earnings of that country, i.e., the PRC in this case. When the law was passed, granting or withholding MFN was meant as a leverage against the Soviet Union and its policy to bar the emigration of Soviet Jews. In the PRC case, the condition has been extended to other aspects of human rights. However, before the June 4, 1989 massacre, a Presidential waiver was usually granted. After June 1989, the waiver became a subject of annual Congressional debate, and serious cleavage often appeared between Congress and the Administration. Frequently the scenario was a fight between Congress and the White House, usually ending with the Presidential waiver being passed, but subjected to conditions that necessitated some observable improvement in the human rights condition of China in the following year. Since as a rule no improvement would happen, the same sequence of events would repeat itself until 1994 when President Clinton called upon Congress to "delink" human rights with MFN by promising to engage the PRC on the former issue separately. However, since the human rights situation in the PRC deteriorated even further in 1995, the "delinking" itself may well become an issue in future years.

18. Of all these issues, PRC activities in nuclear and missile technology proliferation have been the most important ones in the field of security. The most important trade issue is the PRC's disregard of intellectual property, counterfeiting of foreign products in violation of agreements on intellectual property because of the absence of any serious technical obstacles to counterfeiting based on "software." The human rights issue in merchandise trade has focused principally on the prohibition under U. S. law of importing goods produced by inmates of the PRC's numerous forced labor camps and similar institutions that double as business firms and their active engagement in foreign trade and participation in subcontracting through the state sector and often through enterprises controlled by the military or the public security agencies.

The net effect of these impediments to PRC trade did not quantitatively affect the growth of the country's trade for very long, but they have affected its importation of certain high-tech products. In particular, sanctions on Chinese exports constitute a potential risk to the country's ability to earn foreign exchange from its trade surplus, which is derived largely from its trade with the United States. Without an assured inward flow of foreign exchange, foreign investors could not but be concerned about loan repayment by the PRC and the foreign firms' ability to repatriate earnings from long-term investments. Thus, Deng's assurance to foreign businessmen that the policy of "reform and openness" would continue after June 1989 was simply not automatically accepted at its face value, quite apart from any revulsion foreign businessmen might feel toward the PRC's use of brute force against its own citizens and innocent human beings.

The PRC tried to overcome these psychological-political obstacles through public relations campaigns, including holding the 1990 Asian Games in Beijing and the 1995 UN Women's Conference at Huairou (outside Beijing). But it was only in 1993-94, after reports of high economic growth attributable to foreign capital inflow—but accompanied by high inflation and ubiquitous corruption—that the PRC could be regarded as having moved partially out of the post-1989 economic morass.

It took a personal tour by Deng in 1992 to the Special Economic Zones to reaffirm his economic policy of openness before the foreign investors and potential Chinese businessmen would take Deng at his word. Unfortunately, their being persuaded to try to make money in China did not automatically put the PRC on the path of steady economic development as a system of market economy. From mid-1989 to mid-1994 when President Clinton officially severed the linkage between the PRC's MFN status and improvement of China's human rights condition, a whole half-decade was irretrievably lost. Institution-building for reform, which did not take place during this wasted time, was probably the most serious loss.[19]

---

19. A most important but time-consuming factor in determining whether a developing country can successfully reach a stage of self-sustained growth is whether the necessary institutions for successful entrepreneurship and human behavior can be developed in time during the first stage of high growth and capital accumulation. Legal codes, accounting principles, self-constraints predicated on ethics and moral education concerning business and social relations, thrift and all the institutional developments that contribute to the orderly movement of factors of production must be cultivated by the development process itself. These principles were described by economist Douglass

II. PICKING UP AFTER 1989

Unfinished Agenda: Reform of the State Sector

It took some politicians in democratic countries in the West quite a few years before they could deal with Li Peng and other top PRC officials at the "national leadership" level without suffering grievous political damage in the eyes of their own electorates at home. The popular aversion created in June 1989 by unvarnished TV reporting of the bloody slaughter at Tiananmen was too hard to erase, perhaps especially in the minds of those in the West who before had been sympathetic to China and ready to condone the CCP's misdeeds. Li in particular was alleged to be the person whose hands were blood-stained from ordering the troops to fire on the students.

In reality, Deng Xiaoping could hardly deny the fact that he alone was instrumental in ordering the generals to move the troops to Beijing to protect the regime and its leaders. To be fair, the troops were called upon to protect not just a few leaders in Zhongnanhai, but also the vested interests of an entire thick layer of bureaucratic and party members led by Deng, Chen Yun and Yao Yilin before the latter two's death in 1994, in economic philosophy and privilege. Many of these people and their families and supporters were to be found in state-owned enterprises that should come under restructuring in economic reform. Hence what to do with these enterprises was, in the minds of the leaders now in power, no less urgent a matter for future resolution than it was on the agenda of the reformists before June 1989.

The protesters in Beijing were only targeting some of the effects of reform and attempts by opportunists to take advantage of its slow advance and to bypass its demand for adjustments. Furthermore, certain elements of the military who displayed loyalty to the CCP demanded reward, and their demand had to be heeded. How to reward them was another concern of top priority. We shall see how these two matters were actually connected. Finally, how Mao's Romanian go-between with the West had been toppled by a military defection had also become quite well-known.[20]

North in a lecture at the Channing House (Palo Alto) in 1996, recapitulating the ideas advanced in his Nobel Prize-winning work in 1993.

20. An account of Ceausescu's death during the Romanian revolt in December 1989 appeared in a Chinese language publication (together with photographs) in Hongkong in 1990. Ceausescu's name was mentioned in the Beijing meeting between Deng and Gorbachev as a go-between not long before the latter's visit to Beijing in

The state-sector firms were originally the principal source of revenue to the CCP and the central authorities. The heavy commercial losses they incurred in the decade of reform, however, produced a serious fiscal burden, partly because of changes in output prices and cost, and partly because of their low-quality products and lack of competitiveness on the freer market. The political bosses of some state firms want to keep control of major resources in their own hands so as better to ensure the continuation of pet projects, not the least of which may be certain construction schemes (for instance, in hydro-power) and specific heavy industry and high-tech enterprises in the arms industry. Since the Chinese policy-makers, whether or not they are communists, are mercantilists at heart, protection of these industries from *privatization* is essential although "marketization" as such would be acceptable even to some of the diehard CCP interests (especially if they personally can become beneficiaries).

However, a distinction must be made between the pure economic reformers who advocate marketization, and ultimately also privatization for the sake of efficiency, and those who like marketization but will resist privatization most strenuously for reasons of retaining political control of the government, which requires the command of adequate resources. Western observers, including advisers from foreign lending agencies, may not always be cognizant of this distinction, still less of the real undisclosed reasons and personal connections between state firms and government officials. However, as we shall see later, if privatization takes place in a manner that makes certain favored private interests take over the firms concerned, that would be a different story.

If the above reasoning is correct, one can more readily understand why certain measures in the resumption of economic reform have been stressed, after 1989, especially during the Eighth Five-Year Plan (1991-95), while others have been treated with ambivalence. Of the 100,000 state firms the PRC supposedly owns, an increasing number have become loss-makers.[21] Since those firms

---

May 1989. The Romanian's fate probably contributed to the PRC leaders' perception of themselves being under siege. See Liu Chixia, *Lomania Baojun Fumieji* [*The Overthrow of the Romanian Tyrant*] (Hongkong: Paihsin Shuyuan, 1990). Gorbachev's own account of his visit to Beijing appears in Mikhail Gorbachev, *Zhizn'i Reformy* [*Life and Reform*] (Moscow: Novoste, 1995), Vol. 2, pp. 435-47.

21. See Willy Wo-lap Lam, *China after Deng Xiaoping: The Power Struggle in Beijing Since Tiananmen* (Singapore: John Wiley & Sons, 1995); in particular, Chapter 2, pp. 51-134 and Chapter 4, pp. 193-238.

account for a large proportion of industrial employment and production respectively, to close them down would greatly reduce employment and nominal GNP. The employment and income effects and their impact on social welfare would be magnified because housing, education, health and other benefits are as a rule tied to the unit of employment (*danwei*), that is, they are "company paid."

On the other hand, the sustained losses of recent years reflect the poor product quality and low productivity of the firms, including those owned by the military. At this time, without upgrading, capital accumulated in the past would be gradually whittled away. At the same time, privatization by selling off existing plants before appropriate adjustments of their asset structure and reevaluation would have the effect of enriching private buyers at the expense of the State. The State's attitude in this connection might well then depend upon who the successor beneficiaries would be after Deng.

Enterprise Groups

According to the decisions of the Eighth Plenum of the Thirteenth Central Committee in December 1991, attempts have been made to form groups of state firms so that the amalgamation of smaller entities under unified control might create more efficient organizations. One can visualize how engineers acting as economic planners who disregard problems both of valuation and of ownership rights could think of making available to the single board of directors of a larger firm physical assets that are technically complementary to one another and belong to different owners for use in specific lines of products. Such mergers and asset transfers were commonplace in the early years of Maoist rule under the then program of nationalization and confiscation directed by Chen Yun and others in the State Planning Commission. Similar practice was probably quite common in the period of forced construction of the Third Line plants.

However, while picking up again this approach today might succeed in reducing the total number of state-owned firms, thereby casting aside some large loss-makers, such an approach may actually hamper future efforts at privatization through sale, or formation of joint enterprises with private interests, especially foreign private investors. The latter interests would be particularly discouraged by the valuation problem unless their objective is to acquire clearly defined specific assets. On the other hand, if the objective of some nimble-footed domestic conspirators is to stall efforts of privatization not under their particular control, a purposeful mixing-up of assets previously belonging to separate entities, even in the absence of other nefarious accounting procedures, might just be a suitable device to adopt.

Reportedly, following the Thirteenth CCP Congress, official thinking has envisaged the creation and expansion in future development plans of new state enterprise groups at lower levels of government, along with establishing perhaps 100 such groups for a start to stimulate the development of the economy in general.[22] In this connection, one should be mindful of the fact that because of the country's size, lower level governments in mainland China could easily preside over populations counted in six to seven digits, with corresponding market sizes. Conglomerate firms of such size are not typical firms of "perfect competition" assumed in Western microeconomics texts.[23]

The PRC's "marketization" concepts in a "socialist commodity market economy" have never been fully and clearly defined by the country's potential policy-makers. Deng Xiaoping himself would in all probability disdain to do so. The lacuna leaves a great deal of room for speculation on the relative size of enterprises in the state sector which real policy-makers would deem desirable if they ever thought about such mundane matters. After 1989, Deng's concern through 1994-95 was about promoting economic growth and keeping the CCP in the saddle of power to 2000. The CCP must therefore develop a firm assurance of revenue for the central government and a clearer formula of revenue-sharing among different levels of government, as well as a system of expenditure control.

Vice Premier Zhu Rongji, the current economic planner, recognizes the need for financial control and the much-needed institution-building for the restructuring of financial institutions, e.g., the establishment of stock markets first in Shanghai and Shenzhen, foreign exchange "swap centers" (exchange markets with the kinds of participants restricted, for instance, to foreign traders), and commodity and futures markets.

---

22. A study completed in mid-1992 on the role of the plan in the 90s by the World Bank contains a comprehensive overview of the reform measures envisaged. See also the outline of the formulation of the Ninth Five-Year Plan, 1996-2000 (in Chinese) on economic and social development published in the *Guangming Ribao*, Beijing, June 10, 1995. Because of the delay in resuming economic reform after 1989, the contents of the Ninth Plan is largely similar to that of the Eighth Plan.

23. Li Peng's report on government work at the Fifth Session of the Seventh National People's Congress on March 20, 1992 seemed to have this approach in mind.

However, these developments are still essentially in the nature of learning and experimentation, and the rules of transparency and competition on an equal footing by large and small firms alike—i.e., without favoritism and corruption—are obviously still lacking. Li Peng's remarks, officially published in October 1995 as a "recommendation" to the National People's Congress for the Ninth Plan (1996-2000), really repeat the program of the Eighth Plan period. The principal points were still those (described in the preceding paragraphs) intended for the Eighth Plan.

If the effort to rescue firms in the state sector is successful soon, the resultant larger earnings reaching the central treasury will help relieve the various pressures on Zhongnanhai. But the success of the rescue effort has to be predicated upon changes in managerial behavior and efficiency both (1) in the firms themselves and (2) in their related supplier and buyer relations, including the financing and regulatory agencies. This last condition requires that there be (a) generally accepted competitive behavior, (b) statutes governing competition that are honestly enforced, (c) macro-economic financial agencies independent of the central and local fiscal organs of the government, and (d) a growing popular acceptance of the rule of law. Rampant corruption and inflation must be stamped out quickly and stay so. The rule of law in inter-business relations and between business and government (as well as the CCP) must above all be firmly established. Can one honestly believe that conditions (a) through (d) can be brought about quickly?

Without delving further into these general points, let us turn to several final issues: the development of present-day rural China, the inflow of external (non-Chinese and Taiwan) capital and technology, and the PLA's peculiar role as a supplier of capital and entrepreneurship at home and abroad.

More on Ownership and Market Entry

As mentioned in Chapter VII, by using the disguised unemployed farm labor, as well as labor seeking higher earnings, the TVEs have shown how they can become a rapidly growing sector for economic development. In the pre-communist 1930s, such businesses were generally side-line occupations, pursued by farm households and workshops. However, capital shortage was a definite constraint then, although attempts were made before the outbreak of the war with Japan in July 1937 to expand rural credit through branch banking by the then Bank of China, the Agricultural Bank of China and some commercial banks.

But the products of prewar Chinese cottage industry were also unable to compete with either domestic factory manufactures or imports (e.g., home spun cloth against the cotton textiles of domestic as well as foreign mills) or rapeseed oil from native oil presses against imported kerosene for rural home lighting. By the late 1980s, the TVEs had become competitors with state-owned enterprises for bank credit whereas private and small collectively-owned enterprises in the economically open regions (in or adjacent to such centers as Shanghai, Wenzhou, Shenzhen, etc.) have themselves turned to exporting rather than trying to ward off import competition. To them, there is not only a technological gap to overcome but, at times, a deliberate policy against them for the protection of the less efficient state sector. Some TVEs also may be owned partly by local governments and private entities.

The CCP has already given up many ideological shibboleths, especially after Deng's *Nanxun* [Southern Inspection Tour] in 1992. What other sacrosanct matters remain to be defended? Are they the vital political and economic vested interests which would become insecure without political power? Is the formation of more efficient "state enterprise groups" a prerequisite?

To put the above questions more simply, if a state firm is unable to compete with a private enterprise, one way out would be to close it down under the little-tried bankruptcy law, as would often happen in a genuine market system. If for political reasons a state firm must not be allowed to close, then it must be made more efficient. A merger may, but does not necessarily, accomplish this objective. But simply making the size of state firms larger could militate against the entry of new firms. The result is similar to discriminating against non-state firms like some of the TVEs before. Still another way, which has already been tried, is to continue supporting the inefficient firm, now under the guise of a new large state enterprise group, with bank credit. This method has, however, proved to be inflationary before and is not a solution. Perhaps foreign firms and joint ventures with inefficient state firms can act as the missing link providing the new enterprise with drive, capital and technology. But what kind of hybrid economic actors will that create if we contemplate the politico-social consequences? Why would foreign firms oblige?

External Economic Relations, Mercantilism and Non-Transparency of the PRC Reform Policy

The violent suppression of the protest at Tiananmen and in the country as a whole raised the question at one time after 1989 whether the PRC would turn completely inward. However, several years later, it was clear that any change was primarily political. But the PRC's approach to external economic policy continues to be a modified form of mercantilism, not the kind of liberal economic thinking the West might have hoped.

The growth of the PRC's foreign trade after 1989 has been regarded by many as one of the positive manifestations of its economic progress. With the recent expansion of the country's exports and capital inflow in the mid-1990s, the PRC has become increasingly regarded by the outside world as a very large potential market, the more so by those who look only at the current Chinese population of 1.2 billion, visit only the bustling SEZs and marvel at the officially reported two-digit annual nominal growth rates of the PRC's GNP, without questioning whether the official statistics proffered are for the entire country and honestly discounted for inflation and substandard products included as a part of working capital in inventory.[24]

Ideologically and politically, Western governments are enticed in every conceivable way to lend to a country that claims to be building an open, market economy at full speed even though the latter is to be a "socialist" market system not yet fully defined. The same governments, especially if their countries' trade deficits are high, also share their own export industries' interest to expand exports. Hence, there has been a coalition of Western official and business interests and selected PRC government interests to increase Western exports to the PRC. At the same time, for high consumption and high-import-economies like the United States, both consumers and import-businesses also wish to expand imports from the PRC. Of course, other domestic interests (both businesses and labor) are against such Chinese goods and making their importation easier.

After 1989, the opponents of PRC imports on macro-economic as well as private business grounds have coalesced with human rights advocates and those concerned about PRC behavior from the perspective of arms control and international security. In the United States, such crisis-crossing personal and national concerns

24. For a discussion on the statistics of growth rates see the next section.

THE PRC'S EXPORTS AND IMPORTS

Billions of U.S. dollars

	Export (X)	Import (M)	X-M (Balance)
1980	18.2	19.9	–1.7
1981	22.0	22.0	0.0
1982	22.3	19.3	3.0
1983	22.2	21.4	0.8
1984	26.1	27.4	–1.3
1985	27.3	42.2	–14.9
1986	30.9	42.9	–12.0
1987	39.4	43.2	–3.8
1988	47.5	55.3	–7.8
1989	52.5	59.1	–6.6
1990	62.1	53.3	8.8
1991	71.9	63.8	8.1
1992	84.9	84.5	0.4
1993	91.8	103.9	–12.1
1994	121.0	115.7	5.3

Source: PRC Customs Statistics.

about business and moral values have produced continuous conflicts. From 1990 until May 1994, the continued granting to the PRC of most-favored-nation status vis-à-vis import tariffs was year after year tied to a vigorous debate on Beijing's human rights record. Removal of this linkage was finally ordered by the Clinton administration in spite of its own espousal during the 1992 presidential campaign of punishing Beijing for the CCP leadership's open show of contempt for human life. Perhaps there was a real expectation that Beijing's foreign trade policy would be more relaxed, its human rights record would at least not deteriorate, and its foreign policy promises would be more believable. So far, however, none of these hopes has materialized. More important for this chapter are certain indications of the PRC's contradictory policy in handling foreign economic relations in this phase of its economic reform.

A careful examination of the PRC's foreign economic relations and trade negotiation history would show that almost every measure one could think of to advance a country's one-sided economic advantage has been tried by the PRC from the time it declared its policy of "openness." For the entire decade of the 1980s, it practised dumping; it continued to implement a protectionist commercial policy without standardizing its rules in the whole country; it often did not even bother to publish laws that it expected foreign business partners to observe; it used multiple exchange rate manipulation from time to time to gain a larger market share; it applied for accession to GATT/WTO in the 1980s and 1990s and then, after grudgingly promising to observe certain of the Agreement partners' terms, it declared its readiness to put a stop to the process unless its basic mercantilist and "infant industry" stand would be accepted by other nations; it engaged in counterfeiting foreign traded goods and disregarded agreements to protect "intellectual property."

It has no respect for international agreements on nonproliferation and control regimes of nuclear and other weapons of mass destruction and their technologies, engaging in uncontrolled foreign sales. It has used forced labor by political and other prisoners in making goods for foreign export while exacting political punishment and suffering from its vast dissident population.

What does such a basic stand imply? To put the matter simply and boldly, it is that the PRC wishes to enjoy the preferential status of a developing nation while being accepted as a superpower. It is ready to exercise sovereign rights in national economic and general policy, which it will define as it sees fit. Yet at the same time it continues to exhibit an abhorrent behavior in dealing with others on contractual matters in disregard of generally accepted standards of law and behavior in a civil society. When cornered, it takes refuge in its own concept of "sovereignty," thumbing its nose at everybody else. Why is this so? Do PRC leaders really expect help and approval of the world by building a "socialist society with [such] Chinese characteristics" ?

The Military in Business

A principal point of interest is that an important part of the state sector of the PRC's economy consists of enterprises that are owned directly or indirectly by the PLA or its agents 100 percent, or they are owned jointly with others, not excluding private foreign interests. It has been openly reported[25] that there are 50,000 such firms. This is a rather peculiar feature to readers outside the PRC. If these firms are at all comparable to the 100,000 state firms in size on the average, they could represent up to one half of the number of the state owned firms. Is that believable? At this point, it would

25. Willy Lam, *supra* note 21, pp. 193-202.

be useful to recapitulate some of the characteristics of this segment of the state sector.

Historically, when the Chinese communist troops were holding out in their guerrilla bases, they used to produce their own provisions and crude weapons. Since 1949, forced labor contingents and their armed guards have often been dispatched to places like Qinghai and Xinjiang for construction work and other productive activities, including making goods for export. It should surprise no one if factories under the control of the military are today directed to produce goods for domestic civilian use as well as the export market. But for outside observers, if not for their human rights concern, such a restructuring of production might even elicit approval from non-Chinese advisers who do not know the entire picture.

Second, long before the partial redirection of the military-owned firms to producing for the civilian economy, the PLA had established at one time up to eight ministries of machine production. At the time, a principal purpose was to conceal the size of defense spending and to camouflage the true identity of the PRC principals when dealing with others nations. One more step was taken under Deng's policy of "economic reform and openness." Parts of these ministries were simply reorganized into state enterprises, often under the management of the same military or civilian heads. These enterprises have continued to produce both for the domestic market and for export. Some well-known names like Norinco, Polytechnologies and New Era, for example, are quite openly active on the world's arms trade circuits.[26] However, when the corporate name is changed, especially through mergers and joint ventures at various stages of metamorphoses, an outsider would not recognize the original identity of a firm, especially if he would rather not know.[27]

Third, there is no reason to assume that such PLA enterprises are necessarily efficiently operated, although they could be. Jiang Zemin reportedly gave the $30 billion revenue earned by these

---

26. See Karl W. Eissenberry, *Explaining and Influencing Chinese Arms Transfers*, McNair Paper 36 (Washington, D.C.: National Defense University, 1995).

27. The Rex International Development Company was one such firm registered in Hongkong with NORINCO as the majority stockholder. See Thomas M. H. Chan (ed.), *Directory of Companies with PRC Capital* (Hongkong: CFRD Consultant), p. 265. See also Chi Wang, "Power Structure and Key Political Players in China," in Joint Economic Committee, *China's Economic Dilemmas In the 1990s: the Problems of Reforms, Modernization, and Interdependence*, 102nd Congress, 1st Session, April 1991, U. S. Government Printing Office, pp. 29-47. For relatives of high-level CCP cadres in State sector firms, see especially Appendix A, pp. 41-47.

firms for the PRC treasury in one year as the reason why he did not object to the PLA's going into business on a large scale.[28]

Fourth, one can easily ascertain that family members of the PRC's nomenclatura are among the top-level employees of some of these state sector firms. If ordinary Chinese entrepreneurs do not dare to complain about unfair competition from the state, one doubts that visiting foreigner economists will. Reports on the application of the contract responsibility system to public assets owned by the military in outright business operations are quite common (for instance, military-operated hotels and transport companies). From this, it is but another step to have the military-operated weapons establishments form foreign trade companies to export arms, from everyday assault guns to sophisticated missiles and weapons of mass destruction. The same firms or their subsidiaries can also produce for the civilian market.

PLA enterprises and enterprise groups can therefore be intertwined inextricably in a complicated "military-industrial complex." That such a category of state-owned enterprises or groups (perhaps one should speak rather in the plural) have existed for some time is never disputed. How large they are in the state sector in value terms in production, how numerous are the numbers in employment, how much they earn and cost in relation to the national budget and GDP estimates have never been documented. Whether these economic interest groups can veto fundamental decisions on economic reform policy, even foreign policy, one cannot tell. Too much is still shrouded in secrecy. One can only presume that quite apart from considerations of national security, this is why *nontransparency* will remain a long-lasting characteristic of the PRC's economy and present a challenge to future China historians looking into the many misfortunes of the human race and of our century.

In practice, since the arms industry may need an export market to survive and may still suffer from critical structural gaps before the PRC can boast of a comprehensive, basically self-sufficient and self-sustained defense industry, building up a modern defense system is a key factor in economic reform. Since the modernization of defense has always been one of the CCP's goals little-mentioned in public, and since defense expenditure has been on the rise, it is necessary not to overlook defense as a principal part of national expenditure, and as an area affecting the progress of economic reform.

28. Willy Lam, *supra* note 21, p. 227.

The defense complex cannot be separated from the fortunes of the state-owned sector.

III. LOOKING AT ECONOMIC AND POLITICAL REFORM TOGETHER

Simplified Conception of Modernization through Reform—Employing the Unemployed

A serious economic problem confronting the PRC authorities that cannot be concealed from casual observers is the massive humanity in the cities and the throngs of people from the farm looking for jobs in the cities or returning for home visits. They are a part of the mobile portion of mainland China's unemployed and are counted in at least the tens of millions. In addition, there are many who remain on the farm but whose absence from farm work would be of little consequence to production, except perhaps in the busy season, allowing for adjustments of work in the household and employing additional help from casual labor. This is the disguised unemployed portion of the PRC's total unemployment. Some readers of this volume will recall that disguised unemployment was a chronic economic problem in pre-World War II China, especially in the more densely populated provinces on the eastern and southeastern seaboard and in some areas of the South-central and Southwest regions like Sichuan. This is why even in provinces where major economic centers and the new SEZs are located, there are large concentrations of the population mired in poverty. Since the mainland Chinese population now numbers 1.2 billion plus after having been under 600 million when the First Five-Year Plan began, one can well imagine how large total disguised plus open unemployment must be even though non-agricultural employment has greatly expanded.

Hence, one major goal of economic growth in mainland China must be the creation of gainful employment for the unemployed labor force. The TVEs, as mentioned earlier, have been one very positive factor in economic reform so far. However, just as the prewar cottage industry could not compete with the technically more advanced factory products and generally higher quality imports then, the same could happen today. The present global economic situation, however, differs from the prewar state of affairs in two respects.

First, as long as the large U.S. consumer market appears insatiable, TVEs producing to satisfy export demand can be expanded with the help of cheap domestic labor. From the CCP's perspective, one drawback may be the expansion of private enterprise at the expense of the state enterprises competing for the same inputs or capital. Some PRC policy-makers may dislike such a development. Accordingly, the authorities may choose to stave off the trend of indirect privatization. If Western firms enter the PRC market and enjoy low-cost Chinese labor, they may even be able to do better than Chinese firms on the PRC's *domestic market* as long as native competitors have a serious technological handicap. All these considerations could weigh heavily against a CCP leadership thinking in mercantilist terms. Such a leadership would wish to maximize net foreign exchange earnings while allowing the country's "infant industry" to grow. Whenever they have been able to get away with it, they have shown no compunction to use forced labor for this purpose.[29]

Restructuring the State Sector

Second, the crux of the PRC's economic transformation, in the final analysis, consists of the restructuring of the present state sector in non-agriculture, to enable the enterprises in it to produce more things that the population really wants, and to limit the resources used to produce what the leaders in the CCP think the people want. This general goal can be achieved only by substituting for the commands and impractical and incomplete plans a flexible market-price mechanism which will be followed by producers, consumers, and government agents alike. But so far the conduct and behavior of all these "actors" appear to be inconsistent and confused because there have been inconsistent rules of behavior and incomplete and disparate regulations haphazardly drawn up. There are missing institutions and enormous regional disparities.

As mentioned before, for individuals and firms to know how they should behave in a nonpersonal market system and for others dealing with them to know what to expect, one needs business, among other things, laws, legal codes and accounting standards, all of which are very slow in coming. The period of learning has been inordinately long. As of 1996, at virtually the end of the Eighth Five-Year Plan and fifteen years after announcement of economic reform and reaffirmation of the goal of modernization, an outside observer cannot yet be sure that there is a full-fledged reform program without ambiguity. Many unresolved issues today were tasks

29. See Harry Wu, *supra* note 15.

which Chen Yizi and other reformers were about to embark on already a decade ago.

But Gradualism Not a Panacea

Learning what to do takes time. But if the necessary learning is not pushed as fast as possible and if there is no understanding of the need for urgency, delay may serve only to encourage aberrant social behavior that sidetracks reform, leading to a marketized society insensitive in operation and dominated by bureaucratic capital, corruption and privilege.

We need to name only a few economic parameters that are too often taken as constants but in fact do change—imperceptibly in the short run, but dramatically over a decade or longer. Among these are the continued growth of the population, the diminution of available non-human resources and their continued decline through misuse and environmental pollution, and the corrosive effect on the social fabric of prolonged and pervasive corruption, gross economic inequality and social inequity. To stave off such disastrous trends, the PRC as a whole, leaders and the common people alike, will have to examine some of the views they espouse and the values they really uphold. The critical choices they still have are few indeed.

First, if the slow change of the economic system through reform fails to offset the net negative effect of the population growth aggravated by resource decline, additional means must be found to speed up the inflow of external financing. Awareness of such a situation would require greater concessions to the West and/or to Taiwan (and Hongkong). Cutting down the geographical area and excluding a part of the total population for which the national authority would be economically fully responsible until later on might be another way out. However, to do so without dismembering the country would require acquiescence to a radical political and constitutional change and a well thought out agenda.

Those who must wait for their turn to become rich, in Deng Xiaoping's terms, must be assured of help from those who enjoy higher priority in becoming rich. Those who wish to continue to rule both groups must subject themselves to a limited timetable. Still another radical decision could be subsumed under the heading of "arms reduction"—namely, an offer to reduce the country's nuclear weapons material under international agreement in exchange for the assured supply of low cost international funding to speed up the development of the underdeveloped poor regions of continental China.

Alternatively, if the PRC leaders believe that population growth and resource decline will not constitute a dire threat to the "trickling down" beneficial effect of gradualism in economic reform, then they may decide to do nothing or very little beyond their present effort. In the latter case, they will sooner or later find themselves engulfed in a rising tide of discontent, which will be fanned by inflation into an economic fire storm. In such a calamity, there will be a heavy political cost to pay, and the present leaders and their successors can hardly hope to stay out of the storm.

If the state firms continue to make losses and are held up with new bank credit and the government nevertheless survives, then the latter must be in the "fortunate" position of being a recipient of either external capital or largesse, or it can exercise enough leverage against some unsuspecting benefactors who have become susceptible to Beijing's economic pressure. Which of the underlying assumptions of these alternative circumstances are realistic remains to be seen.

IV. WHY "NON-TRANSPARENCY"

Introduction

A fundamental problem in determining the actual facts or numbers in the PRC, be it the amount of production of a particular commodity or its price—especially the numerical values of any measurable variable—is that the measuring unit may be subject to unannounced change from time to time. The standardization of weights and measures, a step that is absolutely necessary for economic development and modernization in any country, was also one of the first steps pre-communist China's economic administrators took, for instance, when they unified coinage and for the first time minted the standard silver dollar.

In the context of contemporary China's economic development, it is essential that an increase (or decrease) of such things as production, income, foreign trade and payroll of a given value, and a given percent rate of change in relation to some base period always means the same thing. Otherwise one cannot be sure that the same numerical figure of anything at one time means the same thing at another time. Absent such a reliable yardstick as a measure of change over time, one can hardly engage in meaningful economic calculations. This is true both for the PRC's fledgling businessmen in the post-Hua reform era and for planners and administrators.

Unfortunately, in one respect, the PRC has a serious built-in bias that favors reports of large increases in output, national product or income and foreign trade, and favorable decreases in cost. The policy-makers are convinced that a growing market in China will attract foreign capital; they have a vested interest in reporting high GNP growth, high foreign trade figures and foreign exchange resources, and high production reports. Second, since PRC planners are deathly afraid of inflation, having been frightened both by post-World War II hyperinflation and high inflation in Deng's reform period, they try to report low rates of inflation. If high real growth and low inflation are hard to come by, they are tempted to doctor the figures or to "modify" the measuring yardsticks in order to obtain higher production or lower inflation statistics. In due course, the policy-makers may become duped themselves.

Following is an array of the sources of some measurement errors that may be embedded in some PRC official reports even if they were not deliberately falsified data.

Measuring Growth: Gross Values of Production versus Value-Added—An Accounting Problem

Among many Western concepts imported by the PRC in recent years that have gradually replaced Soviet concepts are "gross national product" and related macro-economic terms. The latter concepts are regarded as more appropriate for international comparison and a more accurate measurement of the end-result of resource use obtained from the value produced net of the resources used up in the process (except the value of invested capital for the production process but used up in production, i.e., "capital depreciation" is usually not subtracted.)[30] Thus the size of this end-result depends both upon the gross value produced and the value destroyed during production. Hence this is a "value-added" concept. It measures also the efficiency of the production effort.

However, using the value-added concept presupposes some knowledge of accounting and the existence of bookkeeping records. During the recent period of "economic reform" the TVEs are a sec-

30. In Western practice in national income accounting largely because over a relatively short accounting period the depreciation of durable assets by profit-making businesses can be quite flexible. Disregarding it is one way of avoiding a controversial factor that can cloud comparisons of what purports to be a net value-added.

tor of rapid growth. Whether such enterprises can always distinguish between "value added" and "value of production" raises doubt in one's mind. The problem of course is not confined to the TVEs.

A Question of Sampling and Sample Size

Because of the country's size, the long neglect of the social sciences under the Mao regime and in the first few years after Mao's death, plus the fact that many technically trained workers were in exile over long periods, there has been a great shortage of trained staff in the growing number of urban centers. Quite apart from the frequently changing economic policies, new policies have often been introduced on an experimental basis in a small number of localities. (Even the end-of-the-century's Ninth Five-Year Plan is still speaking of establishing only a limited number of urban centers in China's vast less-developed hinterland.) Given the lack of trained statistical personnel and the non-existence of a reliable historical data base, one should not therefore be surprised if production, trade, employment and such aggregate as well as specific data by trade or industry are derived from relatively small samples (i.e., in relation to the country's size) and through extrapolation.

Past experience in the late 1950s during the mass movements to collectivize and amalgamate industry, trade and handicraft workshops and the resultant gross errors in classification suggest that the plausibility and reliability of deriving statistics for large groups could be based on questionable assumptions and projections. The entire country is long due for some large-scale painstaking surveys. Reports occasionally seep out from the PRC indicating that thoughtful administrators and academics have started to contemplate this need. In the meantime, there is another source of potentially large discrepancies between officially disclosed data and reality.

Measuring the National Product and Price Fluctuation

Apparently there were knowledgeable, technical people interested in more accurate and meaningful measurements of overall production and output by sector. This is necessary for a better idea about growth over time and for purposes of international comparison, a task that intrigues many outside China. For purely economic and business purposes alone, such comparisons have become of wider concern ever since the PRC became a member of the World Bank and IMF in 1980. For politicians in the PRC, some no doubt still remember Mao Zedong's ambition in the 1950s to overtake the United Kingdom economically first. Under present circumstances, now that the Soviet Union is no more for the time being at least, the next moving targets for the PRC remain to be clearly identified. So far, the PRC has made no official announcement of its target country to overtake. (One would assume that it will ultimately be the United States.)

The PRC's State Statistical Commission (or Bureau) was aware of the need to adjust its gross production estimates to allow for the increase in commodity items and new products, as well as the relative changes in supply and inventory even before the recent concern about market price fluctuations. Ever since the inauguration of the First Five-Year Plan (1953-57) changes in the price base from the initial year of 1952 took place in 1958, 1971 and 1980. An advisory group was invited from the World Bank in late 1990 to offer recommendations for reforming the statistical system after a close look.

According to visitors from the PRC who had access to the survey team's fairly candid report of 1991, it seems that there are several kinds of very serious problems: overestimation of the output series, with increasing effect in the more recent years; statistics not really reflecting changes in certain variables, such as retail price indexes which they purport to measure; and, political concerns obstructing radical adjustments of seriously flawed statistics and their time series. The fundamental problems that require time to correct include shortages of trained personnel and such more technical issues as the use of initial year figures as weights that exaggerate later years' real growth, the effect of increases in new products when economic change accelerates and when new products command higher prices, and the use of current prices for "constant prices." An example of misleading price indexation is the apparent inclusion of prices fixed by the government by fiat (e.g., certain farm products sold in government stores) in the composition of an index intended to measure price change. The staff working in planning and reporting departments who worry about fulfilling plan targets may juggle figures of productions, sale and inventory change so that they will supply statistics required by their superiors.

If the critics' comment in the 1991 report is accurate, which there is little reason to doubt, then the basic problem is really political. One can envisage a situation in which a hapless person has decided to tell no more lies but finds it hard to tell the truth in a way that is incontrovertibly credible. Above all, he would have to be really strongly motivated to change his ways. Unfortunately, discussion in the preceding chapters has shown that the CCP authorities' primary concern is to stay in power. For this purpose, they hold on to the belief that the world must be convinced that the PRC's economic outlook will be, and its past performance has been, truly as rosy as they themselves have painted it and that they never lie.[31]

Since the attraction of foreign investment is a primary purpose of PRC policy in the 1990s, an official practice seems to have been the inclusion of all foreign currency deposits (whether or not they are owned by non-residents) as Chinese foreign assets. These of course may in fact be an addition to the PRC's foreign exchange liabilities at the same time. One should expect this problem to become quite serious after the reversion of Hongkong to China on July 1, 1997.[32]

Developing Tools of Economic Analysis

While the Tiananmen crisis of 1989 greatly disrupted the rediscovery and development of institutions instrumental in the operation of a market economy, not all the R&D work begun earlier for the purpose of a better understanding of the PRC economy was stopped. Among such activities, one important accomplishment was the publication in October 1990 of a 1987 Input-Output (I-O) Table of the Chinese economy. While similar work had been pursued earlier both in the PRC and abroad, including the employment of foreign consultants, the 1987 table was an ambitious effort undertaken by the State Statistical Bureau in 1986. This so-called "I-O Table" (China model) comprised 117 sectors of production (100 subsectors of material production plus 17 non-material subsectors), divided as follows:

31. A final question for future students of Chinese state enterprises may be noted at this juncture. That is, if state sector enterprises pile up losses continuously, at some point the net equity will become nil. If they continue to produce, with the loss covered by bank credit or subsidy, can one convert the negative equity from the losses into "good will" in order to offset it at the time of sale to a new investor?

32. This long suspected practice was disclosed by official PRC sources in *Ming Pao*, Hongkong, and subsequently quoted in Taipei's *Central Daily News*, August 1, 1996, p. 4.

NUMBER OF SUBSECTORS

Agriculture	6
Industry	83
Transport and Communications	6
Commerce	4
Construction	1
Subtotal, Material Production	100
Non-material Production	17
Total Subsectors	117

According to the Bureau, detailed and broadscale surveys undertaken involved 500,000 individual enterprises and other respondents, plus sampling among 80,000 urban and rural households. The "China model" designation of the final I-O Table apparently was meant to tell users that both Western practice and the previous Soviet concept of "material product" were incorporated in the compilation, thus enabling the derivation of data sets respectively from one system to another. With the publication of the results and their wider dissemination, and understanding of both their usefulness and limitation, PRC authorities should henceforth possess a better ability to avoid both production bottlenecks and to analyze some of the effects of macro-economic fiscal and monetary policies.

In addition, with a new census for the 1982 year with the assistance of foreign census specialists and using computer computation of detailed tables, the PRC is now also more in command of its own demographic facts.

The overall national product and income data, the input-output structure of the economy and the demographic profile of the population in detail have, perhaps for the first time in Chinese history, placed a wide-range of technical tools in the hands of the PRC leadership to try to govern the country in a pragmatic and realistic manner. These statistical tools, no more and no less than the high-tech labs in subatomic-particle physics, are really policy-neutral. They can be employed for either good or evil but they have not done away with the need for choice.

CHAPTER IX

EXTERNAL RELATIONS AND NATIONAL POLICY GOALS: THE PRC BETWEEN TWO SUPERPOWERS (1949-1964)

I. INTRODUCTION

Chapters I through VIII have focused on the PRC's domestic policies aimed at the transformation of the country's economic system and political structure. We now turn to an examination of its external policy. The term "external policy" has been chosen deliberately because we propose to discuss at the end of this series of chapters issues presented by both Hong Kong and Taiwan. Using the word "external" would obviate any controversy over the question of national sovereignty and the "one China" issue. We shall begin with a few general remarks, using the term "external" or "foreign" in a broad sense.

The Policy Makers and Foreign Policy Implementation

In the first place, we should bear in mind that to Mao Zedong the PRC's foreign (or external) policy was an integral part of overall policy. Since Mao Zedong's goal was first to seize and then to maintain power, foreign policy was to advance this objective. However, inasmuch as Mao knew little about the world outside China, he had to leave the implementation of his ideas largely to others—in this case, to Zhou Enlai. For among the batch of Chinese work-study students who went to France and were later recruited into the ranks of the international Communists,[1] Zhou was the one who probably knew most about the West. But Mao always saw himself, during the early period of the CCP's internal power struggles, from the Long March on, as the indisputable leader of the party; he was therefore also the final decision-maker on external policy. This position of authority was never disputed by Zhou Enlai after Tsunyi, which is why Zhou's own position as Premier in turn was never threatened by Mao.

---

1. See Chapter XIII on Mao-Zhou relations.

When Zhou Enlai was Mao's representative in Chungking, as well as in Yanan, during World War II, he became the focal point of foreign contacts with the CCP mainly because he knew how to explain matters in a manner acceptable to Western ears. After 1945, he very naturally became the CCP's chief negotiator during talks brokered by General Marshall to explore the possibility of peace through coalition with the Kuomintang (KMT). From 1949 on for a whole decade Zhou Enlai headed both the State Council and the Foreign Ministry. Although Chen Yi took over the PRC's foreign affairs portfolio in February 1959,[2] Zhou remained effectively in charge. Zhou's overall control was somewhat diminished only during the Cultural Revolution period.

However, Zhou never really deviated from Mao's views on important matters, including the treatment of Peng Dehuai (1959), Liu Shaoqi (1967-68) and Lin Biao (1971), to mention three outstanding cases. Since Zhou was always meticulous in anticipating Mao's wishes, and followed Mao's orders quite literally, he was able to survive Mao's caprice and the overall paranoia at the latter's court, virtually to his own dying day. Hence it would be fair to say that the PRC's foreign policy from 1949 to 1976 was in essence that of both Zhou and Mao.[3] But Zhou was definitely the experienced diplomat who could manage the details which Mao definitely could not. All the same, when final decisions of major importance had to be made, Mao called the shots. This would seem to be true in matters related to relations with both the United States and the Soviet Union.

Historical Goals

The PRC's foreign policy issues can be divided according to the country's historical goals, the CCP's communist ideology and its practical experience. As pointed out at the very beginning of this volume, China's experience with foreign countries starting from the Opium War consisted of a string of military defeats, the resultant loss of large expanses of territory to Western countries as well as to Tsarist Russia and Japan, national humiliation and a deep sense of

---

2. One wonders whether Zhou was simply over-burdened by work or wished to give himself a little more room between Mao and the increasing problems that might develop between Mao and Khrushchev. This is a point of interest future students of Sino-Soviet relations might wish to explore.

3. Zhou was always the one who implemented policy and facilitated its realization. When he had more leeway, it was either because Mao was otherwise preoccupied or because Mao had knowingly given Zhou with a wider range of freedom.

national inferiority. Consequently, reversing its self-image has in itself become a national goal in foreign affairs that seems to this day to be very widely shared by the Chinese public. From 1949 to this writing, this goal has consisted of three parts: militarily, to be second to none; territorially, to settle all border disputes with neighbors and to regain "territorial integrity" (including Taiwan); and, emotionally, to win back self-esteem, which is often identified with foreign respect. One should note that to recover self-esteem depends in the final analysis upon the Chinese themselves, that is, more than how they are treated by others from the latter's perspective.

In practice, as we shall see below, it was not always easy for PRC leaders, as well as the Chinese public, even technically highly educated persons, to draw dividing lines between (1) sufficient military strength and over-expansion of the military and chauvinistic bravura and (2) self-esteem by virtue of obvious achievements, which no one anywhere could or would try to deny, and arrogance that demands purely status symbols to be accorded and recognized by others because of the high value placed by the Chinese themselves on "form" and "face."

As for territorial integrity, it cannot be separated as a national goal from either the history of China or its geography. Needless to say, a central objective is to gain control over Taiwan. However, Korea, Hongkong, Thailand, Vietnam, Burma, India, Tibet and the former Soviet Union all posed issues of border delineation in varying degrees of dispute. Historically, the United Kingdom and France were involved with some of those Asian countries and areas that involved either political or economic interests they wished to regain after World War II. At the same time, the PRC has both economic and political interests which it wishes to wrest from the "imperialist powers," including inflows of capital and technology for its own modernization. Until 1971, it wanted the votes of UN members susceptible to U.S., British and French influence to gain entry to the world organization and its affiliates for the sake of status, pride, legitimacy and leverage in international affairs.

Its consistent policy of trying to bar the Republic of China (ROC) government on Taiwan from every level of international recognition as an independent national government, not to mention legal representation as at least a part of China, is an expression of complex subconscious emotions no less than a legalistic stance. (As a matter of fact, this was what the Nationalists through the 1960s insisted on with equal vehemence after their withdrawal to Taiwan from the Chinese mainland.) The PRC's relationships with the Soviet Union and the United States possess strong ideological, security and economic overtones also because of their pre-1949 complex relations with the CCP as a group of armed insurgents.

At this point, one should bear in mind the obvious fact that a country's foreign policy at any time is inevitably affected by what it was in the previous period(s). Even if Mao's government had had a totally free choice of foreign policy as a new government, that freedom was bound to be constrained by the international context at the end of World War II. The United States was in 1949 still allied to the ROC government, providing the latter with military assistance for the reoccupation of Manchuria. The Chinese Communist forces were in turn receiving both military equipment and training from the Soviet forces entering Manchuria, initially under the terms of the Yalta agreement. What both Stalin and the United States eventually chose to do in 1949 was at least partially determined by how they respectively thought the two sides of the Chinese Civil War were going to fare in the conflict, as well as how much aid either side would require from its ally. That the Soviet Union could not make up its mind until very late was probably in part responsible for its order to have the Soviet ambassador in Nanking follow the ROC's government to Canton during the Nationalists' evacuation. However, after the Soviet meetings at the Chinese Communists' headquarters in Xibaibo (near Shijiazhuang) and in Moscow[4] and the successful crossing of the Yangtze by Mao's forces, the choices open to Stalin were quite clear. On the other side, Mao's choices were even more restricted.

For all these complex issues, the most far-reaching decision in effect since 1949 was the Chinese Communists' effort to build up its own military capability through Soviet support and, later, to acquire its own atomic weapons. The remainder of the chapter will be devoted to this topic and the evolutionary change leading finally to the triangular U.S.-Soviet-PRC relationship. However, to do so intelligently, we need first to deal with the Korean War. We shall return to the issue of borders and territory in Chapter XI.[5]

---

4. Looking back at events during this period, the meeting between the Soviet and Chinese CP leaders near Shijiazhuang and the earlier meeting in Moscow, which Mao had requested but could not attend in person, were probably the turning point in persuading Stalin to shift to the full support of the CCP and cut off recognition of the Chinese Nationalists.

5. For a very interesting discussion on the PRC's changing relations with the Soviet Union and the United States respectively, focusing on the alternative emphasis on

II. WAS IT NECESSARY TO "LEAN TO ONE SIDE"?

The PRC's single-minded pursuit of becoming militarily second-to-none in the world does not in fact preclude varying degrees of flexibility in dealing with either "imperialist" or "class" enemies diplomatically. For, according to the CCP, a precondition for China to become second-to-none in military power is for the Communists to stay in power within the country. This is what Mao and, after him, Deng Xiaoping, meant when they spoke of establishing a "dictatorship of the proletariat" with the Communist Party as its vanguard. Maintaining political control of the country therefore is a *sine qua non* of making the country militarily second-to-none. Hence, flexibility in dealing with those who would otherwise be enemies is doctrinally permissible and, pragmatically speaking, even necessary, if not being willing to do so at a given time and place would jeopardize the CCP's power base. This was also explained in a statement by Mao to J. Leighton Stuart, the last U.S. ambassador to Nationalist China before 1949, when replying to a tentative inquiry from Stuart to the CCP leaders on future Communist Chinese relations with the West. At that time, Nanking, seat of the Nationalist government, had already fallen but Ambassador Stuart, erstwhile missionary educator in China and president of Yenching University, had remained behind.

In a long memorandum delivered to the U.S. ambassador on July 9, 1949 through Ch'en Ming-shu,[6] the CCP tried hard to distinguish its "party *line*" from its "national *position*" or "*policy.*" The contents of Mao's message to Stuart were handed to the latter's emissary on or before June 24, 1949, a week prior to the publication of Mao's essay "On the People's Democratic Dictatorship." In this essay was Mao's celebrated statement on the PRC's foreign policy of "leaning to one side," the one side being the Soviet Union. Leaning toward the Soviet Union was a "party line," whereas developing appropriate relations with certain capitalist countries could well be a "national policy or position" that by implication was subject to negotiation. On the other hand, a party "line" is defined by a value system, together with a perceived long-term national goal or interest, and an ideology. On the other hand, a national position is usu-

---

"ideology" and "nationalism" and their relative importance as policy determinants in comparison with other factors, see Lowell Dittmer, *Sino-Soviet Normalization and Its International Implications*, (Seattle, Washington: University of Washington Press, 1992).

6. See Yu-ming Shaw, *An American Missionary in China: John Leighton Stuart and Chinese-American Relations* (Cambridge, MA: East Asian Studies Center, Harvard University, 1992), pp. 250-65.

ally dictated by realistic and sometimes undesirable but unavoidable circumstances—hopefully only short-term national or political interests are involved. In this sense, the Mao-Zhou rapprochement with the United States in 1972 and the post-Hua policy of "openness" and [economic] "reform" under Deng were really further variations of the same position. The "national position" can shift with radically changing external circumstances. Its minimum goal perhaps is for the CCP to stay in power while an upper bound to its national goal has never been defined.[7]

III. AN UNSTABLE SINO-SOVIET RELATIONSHIP

Serving a Costly Apprenticeship under Stalin

As we have seen in Chapter II, Mao and the CCP owed a great deal to Stalin and the Soviet Union in first gaining an upper hand in Manchuria and in the CCP's ultimate victory in the post-World War II Chinese Civil War. The Chinese people also paid dearly for this aid. The Soviet Union regained what the Tsars had seized from the Manchus, including control of the Chinese Changchun Railway connecting southern Manchuria and the Trans-Siberian Railway in the Soviet Far East, as well as the naval and commercial shipping facilities of Port Arthur-Dairen (Lushun-Dalian), not to mention much of the industrial assets built with Japanese investment in Manchuria to which the Soviet troops helped themselves.[8] These economic links served to bind the new Chinese communist state to the Soviet Union already so closely that one could hardly imagine what the United States could conceivably have offered as a result of Stuart's or anyone else's initiative.[9]

Since nothing could have persuaded Mao in the summer of 1949 to reorient his position toward the United States, the die had been cast. The Soviet Union's position was also confirmed after Mikoyan's trip to Xibaibo, the CCP's provisional headquarters. Thereafter Mao seemed to be concentrating on his plans to declare formally the founding of a new central government on October 1. The new PRC was then immediately recognized by the Kremlin the next day. A year later, the PRC's entry into the Korean War against

---

7. The nearest to such a statement is the usual public disclaimer on the PRC's desire to achieve regional hegemony, still less global hegemony.

8. Plus the metallic ores of Xinjiang in northwest China under the 1950 treaty.

9. Any such move would have had to be accompanied by American diplomatic recognition of Mao. It is doubtful that aside from foreign policy and security considerations domestic U.S. political conditions then would have permitted such a move.

U.S. forces under UN command effectively drew a firm line separating the United States from the PRC in the international arena for two decades.

The rest of this chapter will provide a more detailed account of how the PRC first negotiated with the Soviet Union, then entered the war as "volunteers" allied to Kim Il Sung and finally fought at heavy losses as a surrogate of the Soviet Union, just as Stalin wanted.

Following Liu Shaoqi's return in August from Moscow where he had gone in search of Soviet aid and Mao's return from his own trip in early 1950 to try to cement what Liu had begun, Mao apparently thought that he might be able to embark upon a series of campaigns aiming first at the Zhoushan islands, off the coast of Zhejiang, then Quemoy, and finally Taiwan.[10] When he ordered preparations for landing operations, Taiwan was uppermost on his mind. In the meantime, Kim Il Sung was busy planning to reunify the Korean peninsula by attacking South Korea across the 38th parallel.[11] Kim's assessment, apparently based on inaccurate, exaggerated reports from his underground agents and sympathizers in the South, was that these South Korean fifth columnists would rise in arms and within a month occupy the entire Korean peninsula.

It is not clear whether both Mao and Stalin were persuaded by Kim's proposal. But there were other reasons to enhance their optimism. For one thing, Mao himself had recently been successful in taking over nearly all of China against what many thought were overwhelming odds. Both President Truman and Secretary of State Dean Acheson had clearly implied in their public statements that Korea was out of the American defense perimeter. It is entirely possible that under the circumstances, Mao did not think that Kim's operation would interfere with his designs on Taiwan. He might even have believed that both South Korea and Taiwan could be taken over by the communist camp in one sweep.

From the Soviet point of view, should Kim's military reunification of Korea succeed, assuming that he would remain faithful to the Soviet Union, several advantages would ensue. In defensive terms, the Soviet Union's shelter belt of satellite nations would be

---

10. See Sergei N. Goncharov, John W. Lewis and Xue Litai, *Uncertain Partners: Stalin, Mao and the Korean War* (Stanford, CA.: Stanford University Press, 1993), Chapter 5, especially pp. 148-49, including the footnotes quoted therein. See also Li Lianqin, *Zhou Enlai, Da Waijiaojia* [*Zhou Enlai, the Great Diplomat*] (Hongkong: Cosmos Books, 1994).

11. See *ibid.*

extended at its eastern or Asian end. From an expansionist point of view, the Korean Peninsula could, in the future, serve as a jumping board to Japan and to the chain of Japanese islands. (Four of these the Soviet Union had already occupied.) But these geopolitical benefits would also entail certain costs. The potential adversary of the Soviet Union in Europe was the United States, supplemented by the other Western European powers. Adding another satellite in Asia could add to the burdens of the United States. But it could also increase the burden on the Soviet Union itself. Moreover, Kim's adventure could go awry, necessitating the direct intervention of Soviet forces to the rescue. All these risks could, however, be significantly reduced if the PRC could play the role for the Soviets. This is why when the PRC sent its military into Korea as Chinese "volunteers," both conditions would be fulfilled.

What Did the PRC Learn from Its Intervention in the Korean War?

At the beginning, the Korean War could well have been viewed by the PRC as a Kim Il Sung adventure of little import to China. Already in 1948 the PRC had responded to Kim's request for aid by sending back to Kim ethnic Korean troops armed by the Chinese in Manchuria. Once the United States had responded vigorously to Kim's invasion, however, the PRC's eventual full participation in the war began to take on a different aspect. Could such a decision have been made light-heartedly? Several matters can be disposed of quickly.

First, since Mao's own real objective was to seize Taiwan, keeping Stalin on his side would serve a long-term strategic interest, because participating in a *limited* campaign in Korea might earn Mao a larger reward in military and technical aid later on. The proviso was that the Korean fighting be limited and of short duration.

Second, after the initial phase of Kim's successful drive to the south, when the UN forces finally were reduced to holding on to the Pusan perimeter, the PRC may have begun to wonder whether the United States had more ambitious plans in mind. The thought of an emerging larger threat to the industrial and hydro-power facilities on the Yalu and its adjacent territory, as well as to the coastal areas to the south, no doubt arose. Accordingly, a new Northeast military command was formed in the PRC and large numbers of troops in more remote parts of the country were placed at various stages of readiness. These defense preparations also made it much easier for Mao to make his final decision to enter the fray. In a sense, therefore, the final decision was really made by gradual accretion.

Third, one conventional theory of the PRC intervention would place the entire burden of explanation on the fact that UN forces had not stopped at the 38th parallel, heeding Zhou Enlai's warning both in a speech to the PRC's Political Consultative Conference and through the Indian Ambassador in Beijing.[12]

Recent publications based partly on Soviet and Chinese sources and interviews in the two countries have focused on PRC-Soviet negotiations and the fundamental assumptions underlying PRC decision-making. Both Mao and Zhou may have shared the belief that it was an unchanging U.S. policy, in consequence of America's capitalist ideology, to overthrow the communist regime in China. Sooner or later, therefore, the PRC would have to fight the United States, perhaps over Taiwan, possibly in Indochina, or more immediately in Korea.[13] They apparently concluded it was better to do so in Korea than in either of the other two places.

However, even if a U.S.-PRC war was inevitable, the short-run consequence to the PRC could have been too much to bear. The PRC would have to assume further: (1) that Soviet aid would be adequate regardless of the degree of escalation of the war; and, (2) that the United States would not deliberately expand the war to China. Of course, even in a limited war effort on the part of the United States and limited aid by the Soviet Union, the PRC forces in Korea would have to fight well and be prepared for heavy losses.

On the first point, according to the sources now available, the Soviet Union was prepared to supply and help train at least twenty PRC divisions, but it was most reluctant to provide air support. Moreover, choice of the term "Chinese volunteers" was made in

---

12. This was also Zhou Enlai's official explanation for public consumption. See *Zhou Enlai Waijiao Hedong Dashiji, 1949-1975* [*A Chronicle of Zhou Enlai's Major Diplomatic Activities*], hereafter cited as *The Zhou Enlai Chronicle*. This was complied by Foreign Affairs Research Office of the PRC's Ministry of Foreign Affairs, (Beijing: World Knowledge Publishers, 1993). This is a day-to-day account of Zhou's diplomatic activities which occasionally contains a surprising amount of detail. But the Li Lianqin book advances the theory that the decision to fight was based on the belief in the inevitability of war with the United States. Thus deciding to fight in Korea was really choosing a preferred battlefield. Li, *supra* note 10, pp. 163-207.

13. As this chapter will show, the United States really had no intention of prolonging the fighting in Korea. The same can be said of Vietnam where the United States tried not to intervene militarily during the 1950s. The first U.S. armed intervention was evidently undertaken without thinking through all the steps that both sides might have to follow.

conformity with Stalin's wish to avoid the term "war" or "national armed forces." Corresponding to this Soviet concern, the U.S. use of the term "police action" had the same effect. It could be construed as an indication of American official intention under the Truman Administration to keep the conflict within bounds. The fact that industrial centers in coastal China were not attacked by Western forces after the PRC's entry into the war was regarded by the PRC as another sign of U.S. restraint. An even clearer sign was General Douglas MacArthur's dismissal because of his known advocacy of carrying the war into China.

Recent histories of this period that clearly intended to portray Zhou Enlai as a master diplomat have reported how Zhou conveyed the Chinese Politburo's resolution to Stalin to the effect that the "volunteer" army was already on its way to the Korean front on October 9, 1950, ahead of the arrival of the promised Soviet planes. This was a master stroke that made Mao in Stalin's own eyes look like a truly reliable and faithful convert. A cynic might, however, regard such a ploy as playing on the old Georgian's vanity. There was of course a risk involved. But Stalin also had his reputation as a reliable ally and protector to maintain; at any rate, the ploy worked to Mao's advantage. In a sense Mao's seemingly "volunteering" to do Stalin's bidding was a gift to the latter for having told Mao about Gao Gang's unauthorized disclosure of the presence of viewpoints in the CCP leadership that were unfavorable to lining up with the Soviet Union.

Mixing Fighting with Talking

"*Da da, tan tan*" is a phrase in vernacular Chinese often used to describe the style of the Chinese Communists' negotiations with an adversary. The first half of the expression means "fight a bit" while the second half means "talk a bit" rather than "negotiate." Since talking is often a prerequisite of negotiation, it often can be a prelude to serious negotiation, but may serve no other purpose than to reduce active fighting and/or to prolong the "waiting period" so as to wear the adversary down and secure better terms. The adversary may be simply impatient or fail to understand the history of Communist Chinese practice in negotiations. The Korean War negotiations offer a text book case of this "*da da, tan tan*" technique.[14]

---

14. A common Communist Chinese practice in a cease-fire negotiation was to demand a troop withdrawal by the other side first or to attack while negotiating.

Roughly speaking, one can probably delineate the entire period from 1951, when Kim Il Sung and Peng Dehuai sent their joint replies agreeing with the UN commander, General Matthew Ridgeway, to the signing of the Korean armistice in July 1953 into two sub-periods, using the 1952 U.S. presidential election in November as a convenient dividing line. Shortly after Eisenhower's election, the President-elect went to Korea as he had promised during the campaign. Not long afterwards, it was quite clear that the new President was seriously weighing the need for a new initiative in Korea. The realistic choice was not between continuing the stalemate and finding a more conciliatory outcome acceptable to the PRC—and to the Soviet Union—but one from among various alternatives of increasing the stakes the PRC would have to put up. Among the latter alternatives were use of more powerful weapons, blockade, and bombing and shelling of key industrial and transportation centers. The first sub-period took more than a year and was punctuated by sporadic fighting with heavy casualties on both sides. On the Chinese side, the first sub-period could be more aptly described as "fighting-and-talking" while the second sub-period was shorter in time, consisting of more realistic negotiations.

Focusing our attention on the Chinese side, it would seem to us that by the second half of 1951, the PRC leaders had finally accepted the conclusion that the "Chinese volunteers" could not realistically hope to eject the U.S. troops from Korea by force. But they still hoped initially to outlast their adversary through talking-and-fighting. Unfortunately for them, the U.S. adversary was not quite ready to "fold" even then. Moreover, neither the U.S. allies nor U.S. domestic conditions favored a quick American withdrawal, both for strategic and for political reasons. The U.S. negotiators too had been willing to "fight-and-talk" and were no longer as naive and impatient as Mao and Zhou had hoped they would be.

Then, by the time Eisenhower became President and John Foster Dulles his Secretary of State, their impatience in prolonged wrangling by PRC negotiators about whether Chinese or North Koreans taken prisoner during the fighting would be free to go to Taiwan or South Korea when released instead of being forcibly repatriated to Communist controlled China or North Korea, became obvious. The PRC now found itself in a most unenviable position because of the implied American pressure of escalation. They finally had to give up their original, seemingly implacable position.[15]

The Soviet Union in its turn was probably quite pleased about the conclusion of the 1953 armistice. Although it may have endorsed the PRC's 1951 position of trying to win at the negotiation table, by the time of the final negotiations in 1953, Stalin had died and the new leadership might have wished to have more time to rethink the consequences of what had turned out to be a Korean misadventure.

Testing Both the U.S. and the Soviet Union in the Taiwan Strait

A final attempt was made by Zhou Enlai to keep alive and prolong the discussion on Korea's future and the PRC's desired withdrawal of U.S. troops from South Korea in a different arena. This happened when with Soviet help, the Korean issue was placed alongside that of the Indochina conflict then going on between France and the Bao Dai government it sponsored on the one side and insurgents led by Ho Chi Minh and his followers on the other. The Geneva Conference, which U.S. Secretary of State John Foster Dulles was unable to hold off, mostly because of the political inability of France either to give up its post-World War II colonial pretensions or to bring enough military force to bear in order to win, was opened in mid-1954. It soon offered a great platform to Zhou Enlai for his brand of diplomacy. We shall return to this topic in the next section.

But Dulles was at least successful in stonewalling. From the very beginning of the meetings, he made it quite clear that the United States was not about to resume, in the Geneva setting, making itself the target of an interminable harangue of being "against peace" in Korea or "for colonialism" in Indochina. The Korean phase of the Geneva Conference came to an end after only 16 sessions. Zhou Enlai repeatedly accused Dulles of being determined to "sabotage" the conference, or, in plainer language, being unwilling to do Zhou's bidding by reopening the Korean conflict as an international political issue.[16]

Dulles was of course preoccupied with establishing a wall of containment to keep communist influence within the territories of

15. As a matter of fact, President Syngman Rhee came to the rescue by unilaterally releasing North Korean prisoners-of-war held in POW camps under his control. Many Chinese prisoners later elected to be repatriated to Taiwan.

16. *The Zhou Enlai Chronicle*, *supra* note 12, pp. 56-59.

the then Sino-Soviet alliance through a series of interlocking bilateral and multinational defense pacts, with the United States serving as the pivot. In the China area, after the Korean armistice, a bilateral Mutual Defense Treaty with the Republic of China, which President Carter abrogated only 25 years later, was a measure which the PRC leaders doubtless found most painful to swallow. But even before the ink was dry on the Korean armistice, the PRC had begun again to probe in the direction of Taiwan, testing both U.S. and Soviet intentions.

The 1954 Taiwan Strait Crisis

The Korean armistice was signed on July 7, 1953. Almost immediately the PRC proceeded to test the Eisenhower Administration on the Taiwan issue. President Truman had ordered the U.S. Seventh Fleet to protect Taiwan when the Korean War broke out in June 1950. Now that fighting had ceased in Korea, would Taiwan again become a target of opportunity? Understandably, Mao was anxious to know the answer to this question, especially because he had been seriously considering invading Taiwan before the war's outbreak in Korea. According to Ike's own account,[17] Quemoy was shelled heavily at 1:45 PM (Eastern Daylight Time) on September 3, 1954. Report of the shelling and a second report predicting an impending assault by PRC forces on the island itself as early as the next day reached the President, then at Denver. This brought on the first post-Korea and post-Geneva Taiwan Strait crisis.

As a matter of fact, the first real attack on islands off the China coast took place only on November 1 when the Ta-chens and other small islands were bombed by PRC planes. Then, according to Eisenhower's memoirs,[18] an amphibious attack by nearly 4,000 troops was launched by the PRC, overwhelming 1,000 Nationalist irregulars defending I-chiang-shan, a small island seven miles north of the Ta-chens. This took place in spite of the conclusion of the text of the Mutual Defense Treaty between the United States and the Republic of China. The timing of the PRC military build-up and the attack on the Ta-chens and I-chiang-shan were fair indications of the PRC's deliberate testing of Eisenhower's policy.

Amidst arguments in the U.S. Senate, Eisenhower's final response to these PRC moves consisted of a series of steps. First, the

17. Dwight D. Eisenhower, *Mandate for Change, 1952-1956* (Garden City, NY: Doubleday, 1963), Chapter XIX, pp. 459-483.
18. *Ibid.*

Formosa Resolution was adopted by the Senate on January 28, 1955 on top of the Security Treaty which was signed by the President two weeks later. The Formosa Resolution "authorized" the President to employ the armed forces of the United States as he deemed necessary for the specific purpose of securing and protecting Taiwan and the Pescadores and of *such related positions and territories* of that area now in friendly hands and for *the taking* of *such other measures* as he judged to be required or appropriate in assuring their defense. After the passage of the Resolution, Eisenhower further instructed the Pacific Fleet to assist the Chinese Nationalists in evacuating the Ta-chens at President Chiang Kai-shek's request, with his agreement, for purely military reasons.[19]

The above detailed description is meant to show how the so-called "Formosa Doctrine" was crafted to delimit the obligations under the Mutual Defense Treaty, openly granting the President sufficient flexibility, while making it clear to potential adversaries that the President did in fact possess the constitutional power to act in a very timely manner. Of course, the case Eisenhower had was probably unique, because he had the undisputed confidence of the public at the time that he would defend U.S. interest as he saw it but would not indulge in any unnecessary show of military force. At any rate,[20] the 1954-55 Taiwan Strait crisis subsided; Zhou Enlai and Mao clearly took the broad hint.

A Second Taiwan Strait Crisis

In February 1955 while John Foster Dulles was in Bangkok[21] attending the first SEATO (Southeast Asia Treaty Organization) Council meeting, President Eisenhower cabled to confirm the understanding Dulles had that the United States would assist Chiang Kai-shek to defend Quemoy and Matsu logistically, but would participate more directly if convinced that the attack was "militarily a part" of a larger campaign aimed at Taiwan. Dulles, in turn, on March 10, 1955, voiced the opinion in his report on the Manila

19. In a message to John Foster Dulles, who was then in Bangkok at the first SEATO meeting, Eisenhower said on February 21, 1955, that U.S. participation in the defence of Taiwan and the related areas would be more direct if the Presidential decision on the situation warranted it. It seems that this was meant to let the PRC know that such Presidential determination under the terms of the Formosa Resolution would be more prompt than the PRC might otherwise deem possible. At the same time, the decision would be made only by Eisenhower himself. *Id.*, p. 474.

20. Dwight D. Eisenhower, *Mandate for Change, supra* note 17, pp. 470-74.

21. *Ibid.*

Council meeting that an effective U.S. defense of Quemoy and Matsu would require resort to nuclear weapons. On the PRC side, given the experience of its negotiations with the United States in Korea, it would seem logical that rational CCP leaders were likely to have come to the same conclusion.

However, there can never be 100 percent certainty on such an assessment by the PRC. It was always possible to dismiss such an interpretation of U.S. policy as a sophisticated American poker play. Mao could bolster his own confidence by repeating the bombastic statement for foreign and domestic consumption that the "Chinese volunteers" had fought the world's strongest military power to a standstill, without mentioning the limited use by the United States of its total strength. He could tell his followers that the United States was really a "paper tiger."

The PRC's own propaganda machine and that of its fellow travelers had daily trumpeted the theme of an irresistible tide of the Chinese people's wish to oppose American militarism so that he might even be persuaded himself of the genuine invincibility of his "just cause." Balancing the risks of a more adventurous test of U.S. intentions against the incessant inner push to become master of all China by conquering Taiwan was a crude realistic question, namely, whether the U.S.-Soviet nuclear balance might one day tilt decisively in the Soviet's favor. The event that may have triggered the Soviet and PRC perception of such a change could well be the successful launching of the Soviet Sputnik at year-end 1957 and the world-wide, including U.S., astonishment and in some quarters near-panic.

During the four-year period (1954-58) between the two Taiwan Strait crises, there was a significant increase in the strategic missile strength of the Soviet Union. Of this the White House was perfectly aware.[22] However, within Washington's political circles and in the United States as a whole, two other events also exerted considerable influence on the media and public opinion. Perhaps the White House at first did not give sufficient attention to the psychological impact of these events. They were the appearance of the so-called Gaither report on the relative position of U.S. national security and alleged shortcomings of the U.S. defense posture and the successful

---

22. Dwight D. Eisenhower, *Waging Peace, 1956-1961* (Garden City, NY: Doubleday, 1965), Chapter XII, "the Troubled Islands Again," pp. 296-303. See also William Bragg Ewald, *Eisenhower, the President, Crucial Days, 1951-1960* (Englewood Cliffs, NJ: Prentice-Hall, 1981), Chapter XVI, July 12, 1956, "The Road Not Taken," pp. 283-97.

launching of two Soviet earth-circling satellites. The first satellite, immediately known world-wide as Sputnik (an accompanying traveler), testified to the existence of Soviet rockets capable of producing large thrusts and, therefore, of lifting heavy rockets and their payload out of the atmosphere, quickly interpreted by the U.S. public as well as elsewhere as the possible existence of a comparatively advanced stage of Soviet nuclear missiles.

Second, by extension, a suspicion began to grow in the minds of some policy-makers and politicians that the United States may inadvertently have fallen behind its principal communist adversary in all spheres of science, weaponry and strategic preparedness. That the earlier appearance of the Sputnik was essentially a result of the separation in U.S. government planning of the defense program from the civilian earth-satellite project in the international geophysical-year program, and, according to Eisenhower, the details of the two programs' budgeting were not generally known.[23] It was also true, according to Eisenhower's own account, that the effect of original budgetary parsimony, which had reduced the R&D funding of long-range missiles after World War II, had already been substantially reversed by 1956.

However, these facts and explanations were of no effect on either Nikita Khrushchev or Mao Zedong, especially in their self-congratulatory mood. As mentioned in Chapter V above,[24] Mao in the first half of 1958 was still in his seventh-heaven euphoria as the infallible leader after silencing all critics in the "Anti-Rightist" campaign of 1957 and before Peng Dehuai's shocking revelations of 1959 on the agricultural and steel production disasters of the Great Leap. Khrushchev, having finally overcome political opponents like Malenkov and Molotov, dismissed Marshal Zhukov as Defense Minister and took over the premiership himself in October 1957. He was understandably anxious to consolidate his newly won domestic position and therefore in need of some demonstrable reinforcing success abroad. Therefore, given his style of bluster and bombast, his boast of overtaking the United States militarily or even economically before long was for him not a particularly unusual hyperbole.[25] One could well imagine how Mao, in his own characteristic timing, might try to put Khrushchev's exaggerated

23. See *ibid.*

24. See Sections I and II in Chapter V.

25. See, for instance, Strobe Talbott (tran. and ed.), *Khrushchev Remembers* (Boston, MA.: Little Brown, 1970), pp. 516-519, on catching up with and surpassing the West in nuclear weaponry. See also Chapter 14 on Khrushchev's view of Mao Zedong.

claims of technological and military superiority over the United States to a real test. It may be that Mao really did not know better.

On August 3, 1958, Eisenhower had Secretary Dulles, in response to an inquiry from the Chairman of the House Foreign Affairs Committee about U.S. policy toward the offshore islands in the event of a PRC attempt to seize them, issue a well-publicized statement that it would be "hazardous" for anyone to think that such an act could be "considered" or "held to be a limited operation." Instead, it would constitute a "threat to the peace of the area."[26] This was an indirect allusion to the Formosa Resolution. As events would have it, August 23 turned out to be the first day when the PRC fired 20,000 rounds of artillery at Quemoy. A daily average of 8,000 rounds of artillery fire then followed, plus strafing by PRC planes and a blockade to close off the island from Nationalist supply ships.

Several developments then quickly followed, demonstrating rather clearly how the U.S.-PRC "dialogue" unfolded. A statement by Secretary Dulles was issued on September 4, 1958, with Eisenhower's approval, repeating in essence the Formosa Doctrine, while stressing that the President retained the authority under U.S. law to determine personally whether any action against the offshore islands was a prelude to an attack on Taiwan. At the same time, the statement expressed the hope that the PRC would not act against the world's eager desire for peace. Then, on September 6, Zhou Enlai stated on radio that the PRC was ready to resume talks with the United States at the ambassadorial level, which had been suspended two years earlier.

Resumption of these talks originated from a U.S. proposal of July 28, before the start of the bombardment. Then on September 7, U.S. naval vessels successfully escorted Nationalist supply convoys to Quemoy, effectively breaking the Communist blockade. The U.S. naval vessels, however, were in international waters off the China coast. On September 11, the U.S. President went on TV to give an account of the events of the crisis since mid-August. He said that there should not be appeasement of the aggressor but that in his belief there would be no war. Finally, on October 5, the PRC defense minister reduced the daily bombardment, first by stopping for a week at a time, and finally firing on Nationalist convoys only every other day.[27]

---

26. Dwight D. Eisenhower, *Waging Peace*, *supra* note 22, p. 296.
27. *Id.*, Chapter XII, pp. 296-304.

During the entire period, military aid was given to the Chinese Nationalists in terms of equipment for landing supplies using amphibious trucks, together with techniques of counterbattery artillery firing. The PRC-U.S. "dialogue" was made more effective only through actual fighting as a demonstration of the will and ability to resist.

While full information from the PRC side on this episode is still wanting as of the summer of 1996, published material since the death of Mao is enough for us to construct a plausible conjecture of what was then happening between the Soviet Union and the PRC. As we have already pointed out, Khrushchev at the end of 1957 had only just consolidated his own position against the potential and actual opposition of Stalin's other close political and military supporters like Molotov and Zhukov. It would only be natural for him now to turn to the Soviet Union's largest neighbor, the PRC, and Stalin's professed loyal follower, Mao, for a review of the Asian aspect of Stalin's policy.

Khrushchev was undoubtedly aware of Mao's disapproval of de-Stalinization no less than Mao's penchant for risky adventures, however imaginative and grandiose they might be, during the 1954-55 Taiwan Strait crisis and earlier in the Korean War and during the armistice negotiations. Although at the end of 1957 the details of Mao's plans on agricultural collectivization through the communes and the hare-brained scheme of a Great Leap in steel and grain production were still at an emerging stage in Mao's own mind, Khrushchev, having gathered considerable experience regarding Soviet agriculture as well as industrial development, had to be deeply interested in Mao's ideas.

Besides, there was unfinished business between the two countries. The "Chinese volunteers" were still in Korea. Their withdrawal, if timed concurrently with that of U.S. troops, could constitute a proposal to be wrapped up in a larger peace offensive. As far as the two communist countries were concerned, the PRC request for Soviet technical aid and equipment for the Chinese Second Five-Year Plan, modified to include the nuclear industry sector (with personnel training), as discussed in the Eighth CCP Congress and its follow-up proposals, could not be far from the desk of the First Secretary of the CPSU Central Committee. Khrushchev's own interest in collective agriculture and large state farms inevitably would be aroused by Mao's new ideas.

All these topics, not to mention the until then joint strategy of the two countries vis-à-vis the capitalist West would more than fill the crowded agenda for a full-dress conference. Although no agenda was published, Mao and Khrushchev met in four sessions from the afternoon of July 31 to noon, August 3, 1958, when a communiqué was signed.[28]

One can only speculate on what exactly transpired at these sessions. As mentioned above, less than three weeks after the Khrushchev visit, the heavy artillery bombardment of Quemoy began and on September 5 the Soviet counselor in Beijing paid Zhou Enlai an evening visit, apparently bearing a hurried inquiry whether Zhou would receive Foreign Minister Gromyko in an unscheduled call. The purpose of the Gromyko visit was quite transparent inasmuch as Zhou reportedly explained to the Soviet diplomat the PRC's view of the issue between Taiwan and the United States and what Beijing's policy and intentions were. He added that the PRC's firing on the offshore islands was not to liberate Taiwan by force, but to punish KMT troops and to stop the United States from trying to create "two Chinas." Zhou's final words at this impromptu meeting were intended to soothe the distraught Gromyko with the assurance that should the PRC's firing lead to "trouble," China alone would bear the consequences. She would not drag the Soviet Union down with her.[29]

Gromyko met with Zhou and Mao himself on the next day, September 6. Subsequently, in his memoirs,[30] Gromyko wrote that Mao said to him during this visit that one could induce U.S. forces offshore to land on the coast and draw them inland, whereupon the Soviet Union could "give them everything it had." This remark, continued Gromyko, greatly alarmed him and he promptly reported it back to Khrushchev. From the PRC side, we learn much later[31] that Khrushchev wrote to Mao at least twice—on September 27 and October 4. The first letter was apparently dated two days after the first resumed U.S.-PRC ambassadorial meeting. The second letter was written one day before the temporary muzzling of guns on October 5 on orders of the PRC command for one week as mentioned above. A second U.S.-PRC ambassadorial meeting had

---

28. *The Zhou Enlai Chronicle*, *supra* note 12, p. 293.

29. *Id.*, p. 242.

30. In his 1980 book, *Memories* (translated by Harold Shukman, London: Hutchinson, 1989), p. 251, Andrei Gromyko expressed astonishment at Mao's nonchalant attitude in suggesting the Soviet countermeasure of using nuclear weapons on Chinese soil after having drawn American forces deep into the interior.

31. *The Zhou Enlai Chronicle*, *supra* note 12, p. 245. See also Gromyko, *id.*, p. 251.

taken place on September 30. For more details, we shall have to wait for the opening of Chinese or Soviet files in the future.

The handling of the Second Quemoy Crisis by the three parties sufficiently revealed to each how the other two parties would probably behave in like circumstances until the power balance should again change. First, both the United States and the Soviet Union saw each other as needing to act with restraint to prevent a widening war. Khrushchev probably concluded that Mao was not easily controllable. Depending upon what threat Khrushchev used against Mao this time, he might have to rethink the aid the Soviet Union was then giving to the PRC, especially in nuclear weapons development. To the United States, the growing difficulty of handling the PRC and especially Mao was becoming progressively more evident.

As far as the PRC was concerned, Mao succeeded in learning in the summer of 1958 that both the Soviet Union and the United States were not willing to go to war with each other or to become embroiled in serious fighting with the PRC. Thus Mao did not have to be seriously concerned about being attacked by an external opponent at a moment of his own weakness, all too imminent, for the Great Leap's failure became increasingly evident to Mao himself in 1960-61.[32]

IV. THE SINO-SOVIET BREACH

Although Mao's seeming disregard of a potential clash between PRC and U.S. forces over Taiwan in 1958 might look to Soviet eyes like playing with fire unnecessarily, Khrushchev took no immediate action against Mao. Actually Zhou Enlai flew to Moscow on January 24, 1959, at the head of the PRC delegation to attend the 21st Congress of the CPSU.[33] Two weeks later, apparently after very lengthy discussion, he and Khrushchev signed an Expanded Sino-Soviet Agreement of Economic Cooperation at the Kremlin. There was as yet no outward sign of a breach between the two partners. However, a radical change was brewing.

In June of 1959, high officials from the Soviet industrial sector were in Beijing and some Soviet advisers were officially received by Zhou before their home leave for the summer.[34] The Foreign Ministry reported rather cryptically that they and the host talked about the Great Leap which, as we now know, was still in full swing,

---

32. See Chapters IV and V above.
33. *The Zhou Enlai Chronicle*, *supra* note 12, pp. 257-58.
34. *Ibid.*

although signs of shortage and economic disruption were beginning to appear. According to Bo Ibo's 1993 publication about this period (1959), capital investment in heavy industry and steel production were then being pushed at the expense of the economic plan and the customary Soviet plan managers' practice of maintaining proper material balances and ratios of accumulation and investment to current production. In the agricultural sector, compulsory grain requisition was reaching progressively higher proportions of production without providing enough supply for the urban population. The grain inventory was at the same time being depleted.[35] In the absence of information from Soviet files on China for this period, we can nevertheless surmise what some of the Soviet specialists on home leave in summer 1959 and other Soviet officials probably had to say in their reports on what they had been able to observe in person in the PRC. One should also bear in mind Khrushchev's personal experience in the Ukraine.

The infamous Lushan Conference, which ended with the resuscitated frenzy of the second phase of the Great Leap and the downfall of Mao's critic, Marshal Peng Dehuai of Korea fame, took place in July.[36] Since Peng had gathered data on the Great Leap disaster after returning from a trip in Eastern Europe, it was within reason for Mao to suspect that Khrushchev and Peng had been in contact.

Khrushchev was himself again in Beijing at the beginning of October 1959.[37] Between October 2 and 4, the two sides were engaged in heated discussion; Zhou conferred further with Suslov and Gromyko after he, in the company of both Mao and Liu Shaoqi, had seen Khrushchev off. From subsequent events we can be reasonably certain that the exchange was most acrimonious on both sides. The PRC Foreign Ministry's published record showed that the Soviet ambassador was received by Zhou in the evening of November 11 to relay an important message.[38] His instructions were to tell Zhou that as a result of Khrushchev's discussions in Beijing in October the Soviet leaders had now concluded that they were en-

---

35. Bo Ibo, *Ruogan Zhongda Juece yu Shijan di Huigu* [*Many Major Decisions and Events in Retrospect*] (Beijing: CCP Central Party School Publishers, 1993), Vol. II, pp. 884-87.

36. *The Zhou Enlai Chronicle* was silent on Zhou's diplomatic activities between June 27 and August 20, 1959. Zhou received the Soviet aid personnel on June 20 and was engaged in a discussion on the Great Leap. Presumably, like many other party leaders he was summoned to the Lushan conference during the missing period. See *The Zhou Enlai Chronicle*, *supra* note 12, p. 258.

37. *Id.*, p. 262.

38. *Id.*, p. 267.

tirely in agreement with the CCP principals. Even in regard to some individual matters, the differences too had vanished following the full discussion. Accordingly, said the ambassador, the Soviet side had destroyed the record of the October meeting! Zhou's reply in return was that the contents of the previous exchange had also been withheld from dissemination to the Chinese Party's rank and file and that after the full discussion in October both sides could now really understand each other's respective views.

What were some of the contents of the October discussion on which the two parties could agree in principle, but which they would nevertheless wish not to disseminate too widely? One such matter no doubt concerned what each side thought about the "inevitability of war" between the "socialist countries" and the "imperialist" and "capitalist" West. But even if such a war was ideologically going to be inevitable in the end, differences could still exist on how best to prepare for it. Or, if such a war was deemed avoidable, there could still be genuine differences on how best to avoid it. There were obviously very practical reasons for not publicizing the existence of such real differences and their rationale. Besides, Khrushchev was then concerned about whether or not, and how, to pursue détente with the West, especially with the United States. He had just returned from Camp David in September and could be thinking of the next summit with Eisenhower.[39]

As for the special issues over which, as averred by Zhou Enlai on November 11, 1959, the two sides still had differences but which they now better understood than before Khrushchev's October visit to Beijing, a full list might well include the future of Soviet aid on the PRC's nuclear program, not just the issue of a radio communications facility for Soviet submarines on patrol in the Pacific. Was the group of returning Soviet experts "on home leave" already the first contingent of experts being withdrawn? Was the hurried dispatch on November 11 to Zhou Enlai's office an attempt to forestall all the CCP's possible use of its record from the October meeting of some embarrassing Soviet statements among other "fraternal parties" and to put the Chinese off-guard on further with-

39. See Gordon H. Chang's excellent analysis, *Friends and Enemies: The United States, China and the Soviet Union, 1948-1972* (Stanford, CA: Stanford University Press, 1990), especially Chapter 7 and the draft Herter letter (p. 212).

drawals of Soviet aid which officially ended only in mid-year 1960?[40]

It is now common knowledge, according to PRC sources, that the Soviet Union had decided by 1959 to stall the PRC's effort to become a member of the nuclear club. This decision had, however, come far too late. The first PRC nuclear test took place on October 16, 1964; Khrushchev's China policy failure was doubtless among the principal reasons for which he was overthrown by his dissatisfied erstwhile supporters and opponents in the CPSU. As matters turned out, Khrushchev fell barely two days before the PRC's nuclear test.

V. SPECIAL VULNERABILITIES OF A NASCENT NUCLEAR CLUB MEMBER

On October 19, 1970, Zhou Enlai told the visiting American journalist Edgar Snow and Mrs. Snow during a meeting in the evening about the nearly perfect coincidences of Khrushchev's fall from power and the first PRC nuclear test at Lop Nor.[41] The published record of Zhou's day-to-day activities did not completely conceal his slightly triumphant tone even as he disclaimed the CCP's intimate knowledge of the Soviet Union's domestic political situation. Zhou also more than hinted at Khrushchev's withdrawal of technical aid in mid-1959 and the latter's denunciation of the original Soviet promise to offer more concrete help in the Chinese nuclear program. There's no doubt that Khrushchev's failure to stop the PRC's emerging nuclear development played a much more serious role in shaping the background of subsequent Sino-Soviet relations under Brezhnev than anyone could have foreseen.

The PRC's official position on its own effort to acquire a nuclear capability has always focused on the attempt—a natural PRC desire—to frustrate the superpowers' wish to hold on to their nuclear "monopoly." Logically, one should of course ask what the so-called monopolists would do once their "monopoly" were broken. Would they not try to regain their monopoly? If so, how?

Various studies based on declassified U.S. sources, as well as tidbits of information from the Soviet side,[42] point unmistakably to

---

40. Zhou gave 1959 as the date of Soviet aid withdrawal in all subsequent references to this subject, indicating thereby what must have been really a peremptory termination of aid, especially in nuclear weapons development.

41. *The Zhou Enlai Chronicle*, *supra* note 12, p. 568.

42. See Gordon H. Chang, *supra* note 39. Chang also mentioned Arkady N. Shevchenko in whose *Breaking with Moscow* (New York, NY: Alfred A. Knopf, 1985)

two such efforts under contemplation during the 1960s, one close to the beginning of the decade, and one other toward its end. The first case was linked to JFK's interest in exploring Soviet thoughts about stopping the PRC's nuclear program before its final materialization. Apparently the U.S. estimate would put the date of the first PRC test perhaps a year earlier than 1964. Kennedy's thoughts seemed to be closely linked to the nuclear test-ban discussion of that period. The second time the idea of a joint U.S.-Soviet effort surfaced was toward the end of the 1960s, originating from the Soviet side. To date details are still lacking. That either side, if solicited, might not wish to respond to such a proposition from the other would be quite understandable. Khrushchev in 1963 was apparently politically insecure enough to wish to lay himself open to accusations from his communist colleagues, both in the Soviet Union and abroad —not just the Maoists—to do the "imperialists'" bidding. At the end of the 1960s, President Nixon was possibly beginning to ponder how best to "reopen" China.

However, it was by no means clear how much PRC leaders fully appreciated in 1964 what the PRC's successful bomb test really meant to themselves or what the long-term consequences might be.

---

there was a passing mention of discussions in 1969 by Soviet officials of a nuclear strike against PRC targets (p. 286).

CHAPTER X

EXTERNAL RELATIONS AND NATIONAL POLICY GOALS: COUNTER-CONTAINMENT AND OPPORTUNISM

I. BORDER SECURITY BEFORE AND AFTER THE SINO-SOVIET BREACH

Territorial Integrity: Border Security and the 1954 Geneva Conference

Conceptually, if one thinks of the national border of a country as an imaginary line, one can stand on either side of the line and look alternately in opposite directions. In the case of Dulles's policy of containment of communism during the Eisenhower Administration (1953-60), the American objective was to establish a string of defensive alliances enveloping the Soviet Union and the PRC, supported by U.S. and allied bases projecting military power. In Asia, this military power was pointed toward China. From the Soviet and Chinese points of view, where such a containing wall did not yet exist, their policy obviously should strive to prevent its erection. Conversely, wherever a breach in the ring of containment occurred, or appeared likely, that particular segment would serve as a point from which the forces being contained might strive to break loose and fan out. To CCP leaders of the first generation like both Mao and Zhou, who were also seasoned warriors in the armed revolution, these ideas should have been quite commonplace.

Thus, had the Korean War ended in a Kim Il Sung victory, a communist-controlled Korean peninsula could have served as a dagger pointing at Japan. In this respect, the Vietnam and Korean Wars, albeit in different decades, could be regarded in the same way. Until the Geneva Conference of summer 1954, the West could still entertain the hope of keeping the Indochina states outside communist control. Through the 1950s there was at least a faint possibility of dividing the former French colony of Vietnam into two parts. In fact, even through the 1960s and up to 1973 when the United States and communist North Vietnam signed an armistice, it was primarily a U.S. and South Vietnamese hope to draw a stable dividing line between a communist North and a non-communist South. But neither the terrain nor the particular contestants in Indochina were like those in Korea.[1] In particular, during the early years of fighting in Indochina, the French troops were unable to draw upon the requisite material and moral support from Paris as American and South Korean troops had been able to from the United States during the first phase of the Korean War.

From the perspective of this book, the conflict in Indochina at the stage of the 1954 Geneva Conference was particularly suitable as a textbook illustration of the PRC's multifaceted foreign policy and of how Zhou Enlai tried to implement it with élan. Zhou's success at Geneva during the first "post-Korea" summer was, to tell the truth, really quite exceptional. However, it was by no means a complete success for Zhou.

A Mixed Result in Geneva

First, one of the PRC's main purposes at Geneva was to use the simmering Indochinese conflict as an occasion to fan the flames of a "revolutionary war of national liberation" against the French. If successful, this PRC effort, with help from Moscow and other communist parties, could serve the purpose of creating a breach in Dulles' wall of containment. If unsuccessful, from the Communist Chinese point of view, a friendly communist regime led by Ho Chi Minh might nevertheless create a buffer for the PRC and indirectly for its then Soviet ally, ready to be exploited on some future occasion.

A secondary purpose for both communist countries at Geneva was to reopen the Korean issue in spite of the armistice a year earlier in case the prize that eluded them in 1953 on the battlefield and at Panmunjom might fortuitously be seized in the conference halls of Geneva.[2]

However, in regard to Korea, if Zhou Enlai had any real hope of reopening the political issue on "mutual force withdrawals," so as to induce the Americans to withdraw U.S. forces from any Asian territory, his hopes were dashed completely by Dulles from the outset. Contemporary press comments on a silent Dulles-Zhou en-

1. The jungles of Indochina were more suitable for guerrilla warfare than Korea. U.S. trained local troops, with air, ground and naval forces from the United States, were apparently less effective in Vietnam than they were in Korea.

2. There were other nations in Geneva which the communist twosome wished either to lobby or to undermine. With the aid of available Soviet files, future historians may be able to look more closely at the Soviet role.

counter recorded the American's seeming personal disdain and insult toward Zhou Enlai at an opening reception when he refused to grasp Zhou's outstretched hand. The press invariably attributed it to the U.S. diplomat's over-zealous anti-communism.

However, according to Leonard Mosley, quoting Rod O'Connor, an aide close to Dulles, this treatment of Zhou by Dulles could be interpreted differently.[3] It had the desired effect of shutting off the Korean issue as a profitable subject for any discussion with the United States, and effectively stopped Zhou cold, which would have been most difficult to do otherwise. Mosley quoted O'Connor's comment on Dulles's ability to fend off people to whom he did not wish to speak.

The Geneva Conference began on April 26, 1954; the last and 15th plenary session scheduled, *pro forma*, to discuss the Korean issue, took place on June 15, effectively ending the Korean phase of the conference. In his talks in Geneva, Zhou Enlai repeated many times his by now customary denunciation of U.S. efforts to impose its ideas on peoples in Asia against their will. At the last meeting, he again insisted on withdrawal of foreign military forces from Korea as a prerequisite for solving the Korean problem. The PRC reluctantly gave up the hope of further wrangling in mid-June but the outcome had been determined already two months earlier through the U.S. refusal to be an active participant in the Korean portion of the meeting.

On the subject of Indochina, however, Zhou and his allies were successful. But their success was really an outcome of the French military defeat at Dienbienphu while the Geneva Conference was still on. Zhou, acting in effect as spokesman for both the PRC and Ho Chi Minh, pushed the Communist Chinese position, which to a France then desperately looking for a way out of the Southeast Asian quagmire might have appeared both reasonable and acceptable. Zhou intimated to Bidault, the French foreign minister, that although there was the common phenomenon of fighting in Laos, Cambodia and Vietnam, he (Zhou) really had no objection to stopping the fighting by adopting different solutions for the three separate cases. If Laos and Cambodia wished to stay within the French Union, he did not see why they could not, each in its own way.[4]

---

3. See Leonard Mosley, *Dulles: A Biography of Eleanor, Allen and John Foster Dulles and Their Family Network* (New York: The Dial Press/James Wade, 1978), pp. 353-55.

4. *Zhou Enlai Waijiao Hedong Dashiji, 1949-1975* [*A Chronicle of Zhou Enlai's Major Diplomatic Activities*], hereafter cited as *The Zhou Enlai Chronicle*. This was

However, for Vietnam he would have liked to see the Bao Dai government move closer to its local Laotian communist opponents. The PRC position, Zhou emphasized, was not to see U.S. military bases established everywhere. (He was deliberately being divisive toward the two Western powers.) Blaming the fruitless discussion in the Korean phase of the Conference on the United States, which he said he had anticipated, he now claimed a strong desire to see the return of peace to Indochina in two steps.

First, he would segregate and redeploy the several contending forces to their respective designated areas. He would engage in political discussion and carry out elections later on. These ideas were Zhou's principal themes with which he lobbied Eden, Bidault and Mendès-France, respectively the U.K. prime minister and the foreign minister and prime minister of France. Zhou approached the Indian U.N. representative, Krishna Menon, and other delegation heads in Geneva in the same manner. He virtually lectured the delegates from the Indochinese states in the same vein. However, throughout the second and Indochina part of the conference, the U.S. delegation had already received its instructions from Dulles not to become a party to the final Declaration of July 21, 1954 that was signed by France, the U.K., the PRC, the Soviet Union and the three Indochinese countries.[5] This solution for Indochina in 1954 could be regarded as an interim partial success for Zhou Enlai.

Broadening the PRC's Diplomatic Horizon: From Peace to Conflict with India

The PRC's relations with Vietnam during the mid-1950s were somewhat peripheral to a complex struggle between the United States and the Soviet Union for hegemony. When one became more powerful in the eyes of the other, an effort would be made by the other to correct the tilt. Thus the contest would continue both locally and from one region of the world to another. In Asia, the two countries' relations with each other proceeded in a manner best understood only in the context of the Vietnam war, in which the United States and communist Vietnamese troops faced one another

---

compiled by Foreign Affairs Research Office of the PRC's Ministry of Foreign Affairs, (Beijing: World Knowledge Publishers, 1993), pp. 56-96.

5. India, Canada and Poland were invited to be the members of a Supervisory Commission on the troop arrangements agreed to by the principals. The United States deliberately stayed out of the Indochina combat to avoid having to help pull the French colonial chestnut out of the fire.

while the forces of the two communist powers were only indirectly involved. But more about the PRC and Vietnam later.

The next partial success for Zhou in his policy to secure the PRC's border during the 1950s had to do with India, following the military occupation of Tibet. It was again only an interim solution. This success was marked by an agreement with India in June 1954, which unfortunately was also to seal for the balance of the Mao regime the fate of Tibet. But the Agreement lapsed in 1963 and India refused to renew it.

From the PRC's point of view at the time, India had become free and independent only a few years before the establishment of the communist government in China. Many Indian intellectuals and politicians were sympathetic to the concepts of economic planning and socialism, having themselves been influenced by the same socialist ideals, as had many pre-communist intellectuals of China. Ideologically, therefore, India and the PRC should not possess inherent "contradictions"—communist jargon for conflicts—beyond reconciliation through peaceful negotiation. To Zhou Enlai, therefore, if there were real difficulties between the two countries, they would concern commercial and political interests having little to do with India's long-term foreign policy. If this was what Zhou more or less expected, he was destined to be disillusioned.

During the 1950s, the PRC was quite without friends in the world outside the Soviet Bloc countries. India was, however, in favor of transferring China's seat in the UN to the PRC. It often acted as a conduit of PRC views to the West and vice versa and the West quickly caught on. India was very important to the PRC politically in those days. For a time because of Nehru, India was courted by the West; Churchill called Nehru the "light of Asia."[6] When India sometimes acted as a sponsor of the PRC, Zhou Enlai took full advantage of every such opportunity. Since both the PRC and India professed to be anti-imperialist, outside observers had good reason to expect the friendly relationship to continue longer than it did.

On a personal level, Nehru was India's prime minister, a disciple of the Mahatma, and the latter's natural and generally acknowledged political heir. He shared many Indians' bitter experience of imprisonment in British jails. It is impossible to say, in the hypothetical situation of an undiminished British will and capacity to

---

6. Winston Churchill's letter to Nehru of June 30, 1955, included in Sarvepalli Gopal, *Jawaharlal Nehru, A Biography* (Cambridge, MA: Harvard University Press, 1979), Vol. 2, p. 257.

hold on to the empire in India successfully in the face of Japan's invasion, what might then have happened to Gandhi's policy of civil disobedience and the independence of India, not to mention the fate of the Congress Party and Nehru.

In the real world, Nehru's politics put him at the head of independent India as the proponent of a policy of nonalignment. The policy of nonalignment, that is, not joining any military alliance, was based on Nehru's belief that it would enable India to give first priority to economic development and spend much less on the military. At the same time, Nehru's policy of nonalignment, together with his being the pacifist Gandhi's disciple, also made it very hard for him ideologically, and for his government politically, to raise military spending. Nehru therefore was at a disadvantage in dealing with a person like Zhou Enlai who was a Leninist at heart, although an exceptionally capable diplomat and negotiator. Nehru was not a pacifist, according to Gopal, but a pacificist who really believed that peaceful means, patience and perseverance could in the end resolve seemingly unbridgeable disputes.[7]

Nehru's close long-time personal friend, Krishna Menon, who held the defense portfolio and was India's UN representative in the critical years before the Sino-Indian border war of 1962, leaned always toward the PRC virtually to the bitter end. Menon influenced both Nehru and Zhou on their respective views each about the fundamental character of the other and of the other's government and people; unfortunately he was mistaken in both instances.

At any rate, to the outside world, the PRC in 1954 represented itself through Zhou as the first underdeveloped country that had fought the United States to a standstill, namely, in Korea. At the same time, Zhou wanted the world to think that the PRC entered the war in Korea only reluctantly because it had to help a smaller neighbor against a powerful, imperialist United States to defend its own territorial integrity. Zhou sought to make the several Southeast Asian countries in Geneva accept this image of China as a peacemaker and a protector of smaller countries for real. He then tried to don the same peacemaker's mask, though modified, in dealing with India. This is the background of actual developments. In short, Zhou was playing a role. The about-face in relationship between the PRC and India within a decade was most revealing because to Zhou it was just a role change.

Consider first the following points.

---

7. *Id.*, Vol. 3, Chapter 10, pp. 204-31.

The border dispute between India and the PRC had been intimately connected with the issue of Tibetan independence, dating back to the days of the Manchus before 1911. Without going into historical details,[8] we can treat 1950 as a starting point.

In early October 1950, when the PRC ambassador to India, Yuan Chung-hsi, was negotiating with a Tibetan delegation sent to India by the Dalai Lama, an attack by 40,000 PLA troops was launched in Eastern Tibet, capturing Chamdo, its main center. At the same time, another PLA force was entering Tibet from Xinjiang in the Northwest, crossing the disputed Aksai Chin border area. Thus, Tibet was virtually surrounded by Chinese troops on three sides, earlier diplomatic exchanges between India and the PRC having been to no avail. In one of the last notes sent to the PRC Foreign Ministry, the Indian ambassador pointed to certain trade and related rights Great Britain had enjoyed in Tibet which India sought to inherit as a matter of historical usage.[9]

In the meantime, in November 1950, apparently upon Indian advice, Tibet applied separately to the UN Secretary-General to intervene against the PRC's "unwarranted aggression." Tibet claimed that it was an independent nation and that its earlier relation with Imperial China was based purely on a shared religion. However, when the Tibetan appeal came before the General Committee of the UN General Assembly, the United Kingdom, probably mindful of its economic interest, especially in Hongkong—for which reason it was the first Western country to recognize the new People's Republic—took the floor first, to speak in favor of deferring decision. Two reasons were advanced. First, the actual conditions on the spot and Tibet's legal status were unclear. Second, an amicable resolution was still possible. The second reason was also based on a statement submitted by the then Indian representative who claimed to have received a note to this effect from the PRC![10]

The proposed shelving of the Tibetan plea to the UN led to a PRC Central Government request for the dispatch of a Tibetan delegation to Beijing for negotiations. The result was the 1951 Agree-

---

8. For details see Chin H. Lu, *The Sino-Indian Border Dispute* (Westport, CT: Greenwood Press, 1986), Chapter 5, pp. 43-59.

9. The rights the British enjoyed included the right to send representatives to Lhasa, Gyantze and Yatung, where they could also station troops, maintain post and telegraph services and rest houses between Sikkim and Gyantze, and to have Indian law apply in lawsuits involving an Indian as defendant.

10. Lu, *supra* note 8, pp. 52-53.

ment that incorporated Tibet into the PRC.[11] A year later, in September 1952, the Indian Government changed the name of its Representative's office at Lhasa to a Consulate General and placed all its trade agencies in Tibet under the latter's jurisdiction, thus lending recognition to Tibet's being a part of the PRC. At the end of December 1953, shortly after the signing of the Korean Armistice and at India's initiative, talks between India and the PRC began for the purpose of settling outstanding differences.

The preamble of an "Agreement between the Republic of India and the PRC on Trade and Intercourse between the Tibet Region of China and India," concluded on April 29, 1954, listed the five principles made famous by Nehru and Zhou Enlai as reflecting the spirit of friendship and equality underlying PRC-Indian relations.[12] As a part of the Agreement, Indian military escorts at Yatung and Gyantze were withdrawn while Indian communication facilities and equipment in Tibet were handed over to the Chinese free of charge as announced by India as a token of good will.

The additional fact that India had also been selected as caretaker of PRC interests in its unfinished affairs with non-communist countries in both Korea and Indochina made India's relations with Beijing doubly manifest. One could hardly envisage a closer outward relationship of mutual respect and trust between the PRC and India or between Zhou Enlai and Nehru. Thus everything seemed to be settled except one, namely, the border issue.

II. CHANGES IN THE INTERNATIONAL ENVIRONMENT

The Geneva Conference of 1954 was a major landmark in Zhou Enlai's diplomacy both from the PRC's point of view and from foreign perspectives, not the least from that of the United States. Zhou was able to trade on the PRC's military record both in mainland China and in Korea and on his own diplomatic perform-

---

11. The 1951 Agreement on Measures for the Peaceful Liberation of Tibet between the Central People's Government and the Tibetan Government represented a typical treaty of annexation. Had the situation been reversed, the PRC would have called it an "unequal treaty." The first major provisions contained a declaration by the Tibetan people to return to the "big family of the PRC"; it was followed by promise of the Tibetan government to help the PLA enter Tibet and then have the Tibetan forces incorporated into the PLA. The Central Government would then be in charge of all of Tibet's foreign affairs. A second part of the Agreement then promised Tibet local autonomy, non-interference in local cultural affairs, religious and economic practices and, finally, exemption from the institutional "reforms" implemented elsewhere in China. See Lu, *id.*, p. 54.

12. *Ibid.*

ance. All this was largely for the benefit of those countries not yet familiar with the "Zhou Enlai phenomenon." But in addition, Geneva was also an unusual site for an astute politician to develop and size up new opportunities. The present section will show what some of these new opportunities were and how Zhou sought to exploit them.

PRC Foreign Policy Behavior on the Sino-Indian Border

Zhou Enlai took time off from the Geneva Conference from June 24 to July 19, 1954. In the space of one month, he visited India and Burma, talked with Ho Chi Minh for close to a week, and was back for a policy review in Beijing. Earlier, an Agreement with India was reportedly negotiated by Ambassador Pannikar in Beijing under Prime Minister Nehru's direction. According to Nehru's biographer (Gopal), both Krishna Menon and Pannikar exerted considerable influence on Nehru's understanding of Zhou's personality. According to Gopal, quoting from Menon's telegram from New York to Nehru[13], dated June 21, 1954, Zhou was "never evasive" with Menon, he was "extremely shrewd and observant, very Chinese but modern."

While visiting in India, Zhou was studiedly deferential to Nehru and seemed to agree with the latter's idea on making East Asia "an area of peace." He also sought the latter's assistance on meeting U Nu, then head of the government in Burma, as well as India's good offices for improving PRC-Indonesian relations. Nehru, in his turn, spoke highly of Zhou to his chief ministers on July 1, 1954 in connection with Zhou's planned visit to India. How wrong he was about Zhou, Nehru was later to learn, but learn he did.

In the meantime, while in India, Zhou succeeded in convincing his host that a visit to the PRC by Nehru would be in order. This Nehru did in October of the same year. Nehru was more than a little impressed by the million Chinese who turned out to greet him and whose "enthusiasm" seemed to him to posses an element of "spontaneity."[14] Although Nehru raised the question with Zhou that Chinese maps of the bilateral border region showed much territory as Chinese which was traditionally regarded on Indian maps

---

13. Gopal, *supra* note 6, Volume 2, 1979, p.194. Zhou and Menon conferred eight times in Geneva between May 23 and June 13 according to the Chinese record, *The Zhou Enlai Chronicle*, *supra* note 4, for this period.

14. Gopal, *supra* note 6, Volume 2, 1979, p. 227.

as Indian, he (Nehru) nevertheless did not pursue the subject. Zhou's explanation was that the small-scale Chinese maps were from KMT times and that the PRC government had not had time to resurvey. Both sides gave out for public consumption the explanation that given time and the experience of long-term friendly relations between the two countries, these still outstanding minor issues would take care of themselves. Accordingly, there was no mention of the border issue in the 1954 Agreement, and no final joint communiqué at the end of Nehru's Beijing visit was released.[15] For the time being, bilateral differences were glossed over.

A close examination of the 1954 Sino-Indian Agreement would reveal two specific aspects of PRC foreign policy. One aspect had to do with Sino-Indian-Tibetan relations. In this respect, India gave up its rights in Tibet which it thought it had inherited from the British in return for the reciprocal opening of a few trading agencies. But there was no mention of any delineation of the exact border line although both sides knew that such a demarcation was still wanting. Yet subsequent events have shown that both sides actually cared very much about how the boundary would in fact be drawn. Nehru seemed to believe that this would be a relatively simple task between two reasonable men who could be open and above board with each other. Zhou probably thought that Nehru and Menon had already been charmed by him and that Nehru's readiness to concede his bargaining chips without much argument was an indication of India's weakness and its readiness to concede even further.

Two other reasons also played a role: (1) India's domestic politics and public criticism of Krishna Menon in particular[16]; (2) India's concern about Pakistan and fears of a separatist Kashmir and Pakistan's involvement in the matter. In short, on the one hand, Zhou underestimated Nehru's strong innate nationalism and his complex personality—a disciple of Gandhi but a reluctant pacificist who was sufficiently pragmatic to realize that "non-alignment" would prove unpractical after all if there was insufficient military strength in oneself.

---

15. *Id.*, Volume 2, 1979, p. 229. According to a telegram to Nehru from Raghaven, India's ambassador to Beijing, dated October 28, 1956, Zhou told U Nu that he did not raise the border issue with Nehru while he was visiting India because of the latter's intense feelings about the matter, but he had intended to.

16. See, for instance, Kanwar Lal, *Jawaharlal Nehru: Promise and Performance* (Delhi: Arts and Letters, 1970), pp. 226-43, and Sita Ram Goel, *In Defense of Comrade Krishna Menon* (New Dehli: Bharati Sahitya Sadan, 1963).

More generally, although the "five principles," or *panch sheel,* which were incorporated in the preamble of the 1954 Agreement appeared to be pious principles of international behavior that seemed harmless at first sight and therefore acceptable to most, their ultimate impact really depends upon interpretation. The five principles are: (1) mutual respect for each other's territorial integrity and sovereignty; (2) mutual non-aggression; (3) mutual non-interference in each other's internal affairs; (4) equality and benefit; (5) peaceful coexistence.[17]

In general, "sovereignty" requires far more careful analysis than one usually tends to give it. "Non-aggression" leaves undefined the purpose for which force may be used. For instance, is the use of force for self-defense "non-aggression"? "Non-interference in a country's internal affairs" would seem to depend upon how "internal" versus "external" affairs are defined. Throughout PRC history, Zhou Enlai as well as his successors and colleagues have used these terms loosely, changing without compunction their interpretation for the sake of expediency and as an excuse for acting without moral constraint. No one, however, can claim that other nations have not been sufficiently forewarned. That this issue was not brought out by either side, each for its own reasons, seemed to explain why for several years after June 1954 India continued to be very helpful to the PRC. The Bandung Conference in particular served as the "coming-out" party for Zhou Enlai. Nehru's role at Bandung was one of facilitating Zhou's still uncertain steps beyond the PRC's immediate border.

The Bandung Conference—Zhou's Strategic Opportunism

With Nehru's support, Zhou Enlai was invited to the Bandung Conference in April 1955. Billed as the first Afro-Asian conference, the meeting to which the United States and the Soviet Union, not to mention the United Kingdom, were not invited was intended by Nehru, perhaps the primary promoter, as an opportunity to project Afro-Asian nations onto the world stage. The conference afforded Zhou a unique occasion to breach Western—read U.S.—containment free from Soviet watchfulness and chaperonage.

Such an environment was probably best suited to Zhou's background. Zhou went to Bandung with the prestige of his recent diplomatic performance in Geneva, the record of a military stalemate against the United States in Korea, and the latest PRC show of

17. Gopal, *supra* note 6, Volume 2, 1979, p. 180, Note 75.

force in the 1954 Taiwan Strait crisis. He was sponsored by Nehru, the "light of Asia" in Winston Churchill's words.[18] Nehru, who had only recently been in Beijing and thought that Chinese development was well under control by the CCP no doubt gave his Bandung audience the same impression of PRC policy and Zhou's apparent reasonableness and modesty, characteristics the latter had sought studiously to convey himself. Thus Bandung was an opening to several future policy developments for Beijing.

Westward Toward the Suez and Beyond

Chronologically, the PRC scored a breakthrough in the Middle East by establishing diplomatic relations with Egypt, Syria and Yemen in 1956, all within a year after Bandung. Early in 1958, long before the economic disaster of the Great Leap became public knowledge, Iraq switched its diplomatic ties to Beijing from the Nationalists. Morocco and the Sudan also recognized the PRC. The new relationship with Nasser was especially significant because it brought the PRC to the attention of Egypt as a potential source of arms supply in view of the Suez crisis and Egyptian hostility to Great Britain and France. To Zhou Enlai who was always on the look-out for new fissures among other nations, the Suez, control over which would be an invaluable strategic advantage, offered the PRC a new avenue to oil supplies; new strategic opportunities could become accessible ultimately. These were possibilities that the PRC never would have dreamt of earlier. Indeed, who would have imagined that the threat of PRC nuclear weapons export (technology and hardware) to the region in the 1980s and 1990s could start so imperceptibly?

South to Indonesia

Southward down the Indochinese peninsula, the entire Malay Peninsula (from Malaya to Singapore) was in the 1950s still under the influence of active British counter-insurgency efforts.[19] In this respect the British were far more successful in disposing of parts of their prewar empire they could no longer afford to keep than were the French in Indochina. From the PRC's point of view, the Malay Peninsula was a territory for subversion and underground communist activity in the hands of local communists. For activities in the

18. See Lillian Craig Harris, *China Considers the Middle East* (London: I. B. Tauris, 1993), pp.73-76 for a convenient chronology of Chinese-Middle Eastern relations.

19. *Id.*, at Chapters 6 and 7, pp. 95-145.

open, the PRC as a new state at the time of the Geneva Conference was already gradually focusing its attention on Indonesia. To the CCP, U Nu of Burma, Sukarno of Indonesia, and Nehru of India were all in a group of socialists, or quasi-socialists, who could be helpful in the development of the PRC's own foreign policy. Since they were all nationalists and, in PRC and their own eyes "anti-imperialists," they were potential allies. Hence, Asian unity became a generally acceptable concept rather early. Later, it became Afro-Asian unity through the addition of Egypt's Nasser. Besides, the selection of Bandung as a conference site was especially desirable from the PRC's perspective for at least the following reasons:

First, one of the common characteristics of the Southeast Asian countries has been the presence within their national boundaries of large numbers of unintegrated ethnic Chinese residents. Among these Chinese population concentrations were and still are many businessmen who have done well in comparison with the much larger indigenous populations. The ethnic Chinese were objects of envy during the colonial period as well as ready scapegoats to be blamed whenever matters went wrong.[20] Consequently, the local governments were all desirous of adopting new citizenship laws to promote integration and to remove a potential source of intervention from a strong China, whether communist or not, from which their ethnic Chinese subjects might still claim protection in return for sentimental allegiance. The "nationality" problem, therefore, was an outstanding issue between Indonesia and the PRC, resembling the Tibetan border issue in PRC-Indian relations.

Second, it is not clear that Zhou Enlai or other members of the PRC's foreign policy leadership were thinking seriously of a "Greater China" in the 1950s. But one can easily see that Indonesia is geographically in a position to exert more than a little influence on the Malacca Straits just as the Suez could be subject to external pressure from the direction of Aden when it was a British base. If one were to take a very long view, one could even envisage the Suez, the Malacca Straits, and the Taiwan Strait as points on a sea-lane stretching across the Indian Ocean and the South and East China Seas, from Middle Eastern oil producers to an oil-dependent large consumer like Japan.

Besides, the idea of the rims of the South China Sea as an economic sphere was basically a concept of great interest to Japan's

---

20. Yuan-li Wu and Chun-hsi Wu, *Economic Development in Southeast Asia: The Chinese Dimension* (Stanford, CA: The Hoover Institution, 1975).

military overlords and economic expansionists before World War II. Who was to say that members in Beijing's Zhongnanhai would not someday entertain such a vision? Much depends upon for whose benefit such a vision would be intended. At any rate, the idea of a Beijing-Jakarta alliance might have sounded attractive enough to megalomaniacs like Mao Zedong and Sukarno even though it might have seemed far-fetched. An agreement on "nationality" for Chinese residents in Indonesia on the basis of free choice, patriarchal lineage and single nationality was concluded with Indonesia before Zhou Enlai went to Bandung in April 1955.[21]

III. A STRING OF MOSTLY REVERSES

The Sino-Indian War of 1962

None of these principal early protagonists of the PRC's diplomatic cause ended well as a result of their close associations with Beijing. India's Nehru was most helpful to the PRC as the latter's spokesman in the UN in the early 1950s, in favor of seating the communist representative in China's seat and in its somewhat ambivalent support of Tibet's independence aspirations, during the 1954 Geneva Conference on Korea and Indochina; and in the organization of the first Afro-Asian Conference in Bandung which gave Zhou Enlai opportunities to develop ties with newly independent African and Arab states. CCP contacts with the PLO were also established at Bandung while developing relations with Burma's U Nu led to initial contacts, somewhat surprisingly, with Israel.[22] However, while India's Nehru was eminently useful to Zhou and the PRC in branching out in the world, their two countries came to open warfare on the border issue in 1962, although the hostilities were brief.

Thanks to the credulity of both Nehru and Menon, India was ideologically surprised and, possibly for that reason, militarily unprepared. On the other hand, Zhou Enlai was from the very beginning a believer in guaranteeing his winnings through negotiations by preparing well to win in battle. Each side blamed the other for choosing to do battle when the two superpowers were preoccupied with the Cuban missile crisis. One can also argue that Zhou wanted the PRC to demonstrate to the world (perhaps including the CCP's own factions) in 1962 that it could readily take on a militarily weak India in spite of its own economic misfortunes at home in 1960-62.

---

21. *The Zhou Enlai Chronicle*, *supra* note 4, p. 96.
22. Lillian Craig Harris, *supra* note 18, pp. 84-85.

In the end, although the Indians were bested in the field, India was induced to acquire Soviet arms. At the same time, according to the *Times* of London,[23] high altitude U-2 reconnaissance planes (presumably flown by American pilots) were allowed to land and refuel in India on their way to overfly Tibet. Also in early 1964, Nehru allegedly gave the United States permission to install a remote sensing device operated by nuclear battery near a Himalayan peak.[24]

After Nehru's death, Zhou reportedly told a Sri Lankan reporter that Nehru was the most arrogant man he had ever met.[25] Nehru in turn had come to the conclusion that Zhou was a person "not influenced by . . . friendship or obligation," in short, a true communist.[26]

Of course, strategically, Soviet aid to India helped heighten the PRC's concern about India. This in turn would increase the PRC's interest in cultivating the good will of Pakistan. The very chain of reasoning about strategic interest might be responsible for the original PRC decision to build a road to Pakistan across the disputed area on the Aksa Chin border. PRC interest in Kashmir represents another leverage on both India and Pakistan. Geostrategic considerations seemed to be consistently a factor in shaping the PRC's foreign policy under Zhou Enlai.

The 1965 Coup in Indonesia

As mentioned above, the subject of "overseas Chinese" was discussed by the PRC Foreign Ministry with Indonesia's representatives before April 1955. After Bandung, bilateral PRC-Indonesian relations were enhanced in terms of economic and cultural exchanges and official visits.[27] Many Indonesians visited the PRC during 1955-65 in conjunction with the diplomatic activities between the two countries. There were return visits to Indonesia by Marshal Chen Yi, Foreign Minister and Zhou's alter ego at the time. Some

---

23. May 22, 1978, quoted in Gopal, *supra* note 6, Volume 3, 1981, p. 254.

24. *Ibid.* Statement by Indian Prime Minister Morarji Desai, Nehru's successor, April 17, 1978.

25. *The Ceylon Observer*, October 11, 1964. Gopal, *supra* note 6, Volume 3, 1981, p. 271.

26. In a note to C. Rajagopalachari, dated April 28, 1955, Nehru described Zhou as a "hard-headed communist . . . not influenced by such infantile notions as friendship or a sense of obligation" (Gopal, *id.*, Volume 2, 1979, p. 242. fn. 65).

27. *The Zhou Enlai Chronicle*, *supra* note 4, entries for 1960-65, pp. 269-488.

of the Indonesians were from the military, especially the air force.[28] Aidit, head of the Indonesian Communist Party, and his cohort, were also among the notables. From time to time, Mao Zedong, then still deliberately assuming a low political posture before unleashing the fury of his Cultural Revolution, was trotted out to whet the appetite of Sukarno for grandstanding, which he liked to share with Mao.

This was a decade when Indonesia, under Sukarno, was trying to acquire arms from the superpowers as well as from Beijing. Army General Nasution's visit to Moscow and successful arms purchase there, which he boasted to have substantially raised the country's arms capacity, were often noted by the press. The frequent visits of foreign office, military and communist party personnel from both sides were doubtless tied to some of the arms deals. In October 1965, a coup led by an army officer and rebellious troops struck and began two years of severe political unrest. Many top army generals were kidnapped and killed. But the coup was put down by troops under the command of General Suharto, who later became President of Indonesia.

Although the coup was supposed to be against the Sukarno government, Sukarno himself was implicated as was the Communist Party of Indonesia (KPI). By late October, many KPI members and Sukarno's men in and out of government had become targets of arrest, imprisonment and a widespread man-hunt. Altogether some 100,000 victims were reported from many parts of the country; among the victims were Chinese residents alleged to be communist rebels who took part in the coup. Imported PRC arms were said to be in use by the rebels. More thorough studies with the help of PRC official files will be needed to fix responsibility in the future. But an unintended effect of the failed coup was the *suspension* of diplomatic relations with the PRC by Indonesia until long after even the resumption of U.S.-PRC relations! Many innocent Chinese and Indonesians, however, fell victim to the aftermath of the bungled kidnappings and assassinations. Finally, in 1967, a leading PKI official, Njono Bin Sastroedia, Lt. Col. Untung, a battalion commander of Sukarno's security guard, and former Air Vice Marshal Dhani, who as Sukarno's military advisor visited Beijing in 1965, were put on trial.

---

28. For a detailed account of these tangled events see Hal Kosut (ed.), *Indonesia: The Sukarno Years* (New York: Facts on File, 1967), pp. 108-29.

As a byproduct of the political upheaval in Indonesia, Sukarno fell from power in two steps. First, in March 1966 Suharto assumed the real powers previously held by Sukarno, although nominally still serving under the latter. Then, in May 1967 Sukarno was stripped of all of his titles and trappings of power, including the presidential palace he had used since 1945.

The concept of a "Jakarta-Pnom Penh-Hanoi-Beijing-Pyongyang axis" was no more. The "crush Malaysia command" Sukarno established in February 1966 was dissolved as a result of an accord signed by the new Indonesia Foreign Minister Adam Malik and Malaysia's Deputy Prime Minister Abdul Razak in August 1966. The last event dealt a final blow to any dream the PRC might have had of using Indonesia as a bridge to extend communist influence northward up the Malaysian land ridge between the South China Sea and the waters of the Indian Ocean.[29]

Setbacks in the "Intermediate Zone"

Parallel to the failed attempt to build a special PRC-Indonesia connection from the mid-1950s to the mid-1960s, Zhou Enlai's effort to do the same in North Africa also ended in failure. A second Afro-Asian Conference was originally scheduled in midyear 1964. This meeting was to expand further Beijing's diplomatic horizon. Given a measure of domestic economic recovery from the Great Leap years, new developments for an able and sharp-eyed opportunist like Zhou Enlai to exploit should have been possible. However, various untoward events occurred.

In the first place, Ben Bella of Algeria was ousted in a coup and replaced by Boumedienne. Since Algeria was to host the second Afro-Asian Conference, it had to be postponed, at first to 1965. The opposition of Nasser to the PRC's refusal to include the USSR and the turmoil in Indonesia during and after 1965 effectively eliminated a suitable role for Sukarno. The second Bandung-type conference thus never came to pass.[30]

One should point out that as one focuses on the first half of the 1960s, this was the period when Liu Shaoqi-Zhou Enlai held sway in the PRC while Mao had largely withdrawn from managing day-to-day affairs, with the exception of PRC-Soviet relations. Thus Zhou and his second in command, Chen Yi, could not be absolved

---

29. For a discussion of communist activities in Thailand and Malaysia, see Yuan-li Wu, *The Strategic Land Ridge* (Stanford, CA: The Hoover Institution, 1975).

30. See Lillian Craig Harris, *supra* note 18, Chapters 5 and 6, pp. 73-95.

from the policy guffs in South and Southeast Asia and the Arab world.

Insufficient knowledge about the internal political conditions in countries in the area, perfectly understandable for the foreign office personnel of the PRC, contributed to the wrong policy options and local partners. Besides, the PRC was not without active competitors from both the Western powers and the Soviet Union. A general comment on Zhou Enlai's stewardship of PRC foreign policy outside the sphere of the expanding Sino-Soviet conflict might be that Zhou aimed to do too much too quickly. Mao's radical ideas, however innovative, were not matched by the PRC's material and human resources in pursuing foreign policy. Cunning, trickery and opportunism were not enough. Zhou was being just too clever by half. Nehru was disgusted with Zhou's dissimulation and apparent lack of integrity. On the border matter and the construction of the road to Pakistan, Zhou did not understand why anyone should bother with these concepts. As a Leninist, he obviously had no such worries and probably thought that one should not.

IV. TURNING INWARD: A HIATUS OF NORMAL FOREIGN ACTIVITIES

Interruption of Normal Diplomacy

Just when the expansive foreign policy of Zhou Enlai came to a halt in the mid-60s, the entire country seemed to turn inward. Mao Zedong was focusing his full attention on two issues: (1) consolidation of power in his own hands by purging all potential opponents real and imagined; and (2) going all out in combating the post-Khrushchev "revisionist" Soviet Union in all conceivable ways. Since the two tasks absorbed all the energy of the CCP leadership, very little attention could be devoted to normal foreign activity.

One should bear in mind the abnormal, virtually unimaginable conditions under which both party and government officials had to work in the PRC, especially in 1967-69, during the Cultural Revolution. Every cadre was in fear of being investigated in terms of party loyalty. The screening process often occupied all the individual's working time. To our knowledge Zhou Enlai was not subjected to personal investigation but he had to fend off the continuing harassment of his key aides. To prove to the radical Maoists one's loyalty to the Chairman became the most important of one's daily tasks, not one's work assignment. Foreign service officials called back to prove their own loyalty were often not replaced. What might have seemed to be abnormal or even absurd behavior in a foreign country or in dealing with foreign persons was often meant for career evaluation by radical colleagues or secret evaluators at home.

Thus, beginning in 1966 PRC diplomats from around the world were recalled, ostensibly to be examined for their loyalty to Mao's ideas. Huang Hua,[31] the same person who was sent by Zhou in 1949 to see Leighton Stewart in Nanking, was the only PRC ambassador who stayed at his post through the Cultural Revolution. Numerous PRC officials and students were involved in violent and ludicrous actions while abroad in order to demonstrate their doctrinal purity as Maoists. Thus one should write off this period from normal PRC diplomatic activity as if it had never been. Rather one should concentrate on several activities designed to weaken or harass the Soviet Union in its continuing contest with the PRC.

Verbal Attacks

First, verbal attacks on the Soviet Communist Party, denouncing its "revisionism" or doctrinal impurity were mounted. This was carried on both through the CCP media and at international communist and communist-affiliated conferences. The purpose of these activities was to undermine the Soviet party's standing while enhancing that of the CCP and Mao. The approach was most useful only as long as Mao was alive, that is, before 1976. It was useful to the PRC only as long as the latter continued to maintain the inevitability of revolution by class struggle and the effectiveness of guerrilla warfare in revolution.

Competition Through Military and Economic Aid

During 1955-71 both the Soviet Union and the PRC used military and economic aid as an inducement to less developed countries to win political friendship, sympathy and occasionally economic *quid pro quo*, or to create difficulties for competitors.[32] Pakistan and Tanzania were the largest military aid recipients from the PRC. Among others were Uganda and Somalia, Congo (Brazzaville), Guinea, Mali, Ceylon, Indonesia, Iraq and South Yemen. In general the Soviet Union was more successful; the delivery of PRC aid was often less reliable.

---

31. *Id.*, Chapters 6 and 7, pp. 95-145.

32. The Hoover Institution, *Communist Military Assistance to Non-Communist Developing Countries*, 1973.

Outright Military Confrontation on the Sino-Soviet Border

Militarily the most significant conflict on the Sino-Soviet border probably occurred at Damansky Island on the Manchurian border. Elsewhere there were similar engagements. Since the PRC was weaker than the USSR, its willingness to engage in such conflicts, like the fighting in Korea, was in part to demonstrate its readiness to fight and perhaps to exact a price the opponent might be reluctant to pay.

Thus, by the end of the 1960s, Soviet-PRC relations were approaching a point when no obvious, peaceful solution to an increasingly worsening situation appeared to be readily available. The way out was not yet at hand.

CHAPTER XI

EXTERNAL RELATIONS AND NATIONAL POLICY GOALS: TOWARD RESTRUCTURING

I. THE PRC'S CHANGING PERCEPTION OF THREAT

Diminishing Soviet Reliability

In 1954, when both Zhou Enlai and Molotov were at the Geneva Conference and still working as allies in a joint effort to frustrate the U.S. policy to contain the Sino-Soviet communist bloc, both Moscow and Beijing viewed the United States as the worst capitalist enemy. However, by mid-1959, barely six years after Stalin's death, Beijing had for a time already begun to think of the Soviet Union as an unreliable ally. In Chinese eyes, Moscow had reneged on its promise to help a loyal "fraternal" communist country that fought a costly war in Korea—in effect, as a surrogate of the Soviet Union. Furthermore, twice in the 1950s (1954 and 1958) the Soviet Union had been unwilling to lend substantive military support to Beijing in the latter's campaign against Taiwan for fear of being drawn into direct armed conflict with the United States.[1] Beijing had thought, especially after Sputnik (1957), that Soviet military power was much stronger than Moscow seemed to think itself. After the 1962 Cuban crisis, when the PRC saw the Soviet Union backing down in the face of an open American challenge, Beijing probably lowered its estimate of Soviet power another notch. Moscow may have become truly a "paper tiger," to use Mao's colorful expression, to be "*despised strategically*."

Under these conditions, it would be quite natural for the CCP to vent its displeasure with the CPSU for failing to live up to the obligations fellow communists theoretically owed to one another. The inter-party dispute was first couched in doctrinal terms so that each side accused the other of schism.[2] But as arguments heated up

---

1. Dulles had apparently discounted the possibility of saving the French tenuous hold on Indochina and was quite unwilling to allow the PRC to reopen the political harangue at Panmunjom. He was then focusing on the formation of SEATO.

2. See Strobe Talbott (tran. and ed.), *Khrushchev Remembers* (Boston, MA: Little, Brown & Co., 1970), pp. 471-79, for Khrushchev's short account of the open schism

and tempers became frayed, the quarrel in ideology became one between two armed nation-states. The international environment began to change radically. Two questions must have gnawed on the minds of PRC top leaders, demanding to be answered. First, what might the Soviet Union do under Brezhnev? Second, what could the PRC do in return? After all, the PRC was the weaker of the two. It could not ignore the far superior Soviet military power in a *tactical* sense. The PRC was always mindful of the difference between its strategic superiority (i.e., in its own view) and its tactical weakness.

Soviet Border Defense and the "Brezhnev Doctrine"

Given the enormously long Sino-Soviet border from Manchuria all the way across Central Asia, Chinese raids from across the border could be more than a nuisance from the Kremlin's point of view. Fortification of border defense, stationing of strategic and tactical nuclear weapons at convenient locations, and some redeployment of additional conventional forces would appear logical, particularly to military and Party leaders like Brezhnev and his supporters.[3] The accelerated completion of a second trans-Siberian rail link from European USSR to the Pacific coast would seem to be another obvious priority. All these heavy military and related investments would have to be made over and above strategic nuclear and naval constructions which became an aftermath of the Cuban crisis that made catching-up with American nuclear superiority an urgent need to the Soviet military.[4] Given all these very costly options, one can well imagine that the Brezhnev leadership was almost bound to encounter enormous difficulty and be reluctant to come to a hard decision on the renegade PRC. The result would very naturally be to do things to keep various options open—i.e., to temporize and postpone making a final irretrievable decision.

It would have been very hard for the Soviet Union to make a rational choice of going to war with the PRC, abstracting from whatever legal, ideological, political, economic, moral, or humanis-

---

from his perspective from 1960 on. The vehemence of the PRC's ideological attack as contained in a series of articles in *Honqi* (*Red Flag*) probably reflected Mao's contempt for Khrushchev, believing that the latter would not dare to take really stronger military measures against him at that time.

3. Such a response in military terms would seem to be the kind of natural reaction Stalin's more hard-line successors might make.

4. For a discussion of this topic by the present author, see Yuan-li Wu, *U.S. Policy and Strategic Interests in the Western Pacific* (New York, NY: Crane Russak, 1975).

tic considerations existed. There was one very simple reason. That is, from a selfish, amoral and purely military point of view, it would have been impossible to find a strategy that could guarantee for Soviet war planners an "end of the war" scenario noticeably better than the condition before its start. A military victory followed by a peaceful settlement satisfactory to both sides would have been unlikely. Occupation of the PRC or some of its principal strategic points, given continued Chinese guerrilla opposition, would have been costly in the extreme. The Japanese invasion of China and America's experience in Vietnam up to that time were examples that could not be ignored.[5] However, might the PRC be frightened to a point that it would shift to a more peaceable policy? Could there be a change in PRC leadership, replacing Mao and his radical associates by a more amenable individual or group? The last point could well have been discussed in the Kremlin.

The period between April 1969, when Lin Biao was officially designated at the Ninth Party Congress as Mao's heir apparent, and September 1971, when Lin died, must have been crucial from both Soviet and PRC perspectives. If the Kremlin wished to try to plot against Mao with Lin's help, willingly or unwillingly, the post-April 1969 period might have appeared especially suitable. Given Mao's paranoia, he too might well have thought so. Militarily, if any action against the PRC was contemplated at this time at all,[6] use of tactical nuclear weapons, whether or not in a specific operation on the PRC's nuclear installations, should not be excluded. Such a threat could look quite real in Chinese eyes, even though, as mentioned previously, such a hypothetical approach would not be an optimal strategy, or even a realistic one, from the Soviet point of view. In spite of Mao's penchant to take enormous risks with Chinese lives occasionally, from his point of view, the mere possibility of a "stupid" or accidental attack ought to be taken seriously. One would assume that this would be Zhou Enlai's thinking.

In this respect, one should bear in mind that a visit by Kosygin on his return flight from Hanoi to attend Ho Chih Minh's funeral gave Zhou Enlai an opportunity to look for a mutually acceptable way of reducing the growing tension between the two erstwhile communist allies. But Zhou's conclusion from the discussions initi-

---

5. This was a topic of discussion in 1979 between the author and a Soviet strategy research scholar during a Moscow visit.

6. See Chapter X above.

ated by this brief encounter was disappointing.[7] Brezhnev seemed to remain as inflexible in his hardline policy as Khrushchev had been in his time.

Given this latest encounter, one can imagine why the five Warsaw Pact nations' invasion of Czechoslovakia in August the year before (1968) in the name of communist international solidarity must have looked even more threatening to Beijing after the Kosygin visit in 1969.

The PRC was not a small, non-nuclear country like Czechoslovakia. However, the Kremlin might have had another thought—the same idea could have passed through Mao's mind. What if a Soviet military incursion were accompanied by an uprising in China? Had not Lin Biao just been appointed as Mao's successor by the CCP? Did not the PRC authorities subsequently accuse Lin of instigating an abortive coup? In any case, the beginning of a radical realignment of both domestic and foreign policies by more than one country was soon to occur. A most important event in these circumstances was a rapprochement between the PRC and the United States.

II. EVENTS LEADING TO THE 1971-72 U.S.-PRC RAPPROCHEMENT

The Damansky Island Incident

The Sino-Soviet border situation reflected one historical fact: namely, that it was last drawn under what would be called by the PRC as well as all its predecessor governments an "unequal treaty," which none would wish to recognize. While the PRC was not opposed to negotiations as a way of fixing the border anew, its standpat position was to denounce the old frontier first before engaging in new discussions. This was the position it took on the McMahon Line. The Soviet Union too, like India, was not averse to discussing the border issue except that it did not wish to begin by abandoning the original border line.

Inasmuch as during the early and mid-1960s the border had become heavily defended, it was not surprising that both deliberate and unintentional skirmishes would occur. One of the most widely reported incidents occurred on March 2, 1969, at Damansky Island

7. This meeting between Zhou and Kosygin took place at the VIP meeting room of Beijing Airport when Kosygin was on his way back from Ho Chi Minh's funeral in Hanoi on Sept. 11, 1969.

(Chen Pao in Chinese) on the Ussuri River in Manchuria.[8] A second incident in which the Soviets apparently had the upper hand then followed on the 15th of the same month. These clashes ended in talks in May at Khabarovsk without a prior Soviet acknowledgment of the invalidity of the old "unequal" treaty. A one-year agreement for navigation on the Ussuri was then signed in mid-August.

Given the example of the Soviet armed intervention in Czechoslovakia in 1968 and the veiled Soviet threats to lay waste to PRC nuclear and missile facilities in northwestern China,[9] Soviet military pressure was apparently being put on the Chinese rather seriously. There were additional incidents accompanying the negotiations. The Chinese, on their part, were not totally clear as to what the real Soviet intent was. The internal political situation in the PRC was still somewhat ambivalent. Liu Shaoqi, the former head of state, had been drummed out of the Party on trumped-up charges going back to the 1930s. Lin Biao, as Mao's deputy, was in charge of the nation's military, responsible for defense in the event of any real attack by Brezhnev's legions.

Mao, still the top strategist and Party chairman who could never be wrong and had finally beaten down all doubters in the Cultural Revolution, was not about to tolerate anyone, especially his deputy, who might question his judgment. When Kosygin conferred with Zhou Enlai at the Beijing airport in September 1969, barely six months after the Damansky clash and on the heels of the Khabarovsk talks, the Russian apparently suggested that the PRC join the Soviet Union at a conference for the development of a common political line for the international communist movement.

In such circumstances, Zhou could only mouth Mao's dicta as a provisional refusal. According to Zhou, he had to tell Kosygin that Mao had mentioned the experience of the Cominform long ago when the existence of a single agency under Moscow's control failed to produce a united policy. Documents drafted by the world's communist and workers' parties did not produce anything useful. The world's communists had long ago reached a point when each national party had to develop its own agenda. Each should there-

---

8. See, for instance, Thomas W. Robinson's summary account, *The Sino-Soviet Border Dispute: Background, Development, and the March 1969 Clashes*, Rand Report RM-6171-PR , Santa Monica, August 1970.

9. See *id.*, p. 73.

fore continue to do the same and test its ability to be a vanguard of revolution.[10]

According to Robert A. Jones, Romanian communists had developed great sensitivity in judging the degree to which they could safely distance themselves from Soviet wishes without undue risk.[11] It was the kind of Romanian "selective cooperation" of 1970-71 rather than "militant nationalism" of 1966-69 that was probably passed on to the PRC leadership in a series of meetings on June 9-11, 1970 when a Romanian Executive Committee of the country's CP Central Committee was closeted with Zhou's group in Beijing. This time Mao also met with the entire group from Bucharest on the last day of the sessions.[12]

A Digression on Domestic Policy

The Romanians' role in the development of PRC policy at this point, it seems, was to reinforce the several strands of information that had reached Zhou Enlai. It was he who had to decide not only what Mao should know, but also how he (Zhou) should present the message to the Chairman. For it was an especially critical time in the course of Mao's purge of his former associates through the Cultural Revolution.

In April 1969, the Ninth CCP Congress had finally been called. A thirteen-year hiatus after the Eighth Party Congress had ended. Liu Shaoqi had already died in prison during the Cultural Revolution. Mao's political campaign was successful primarily because he had the full support of the Red Guards, who in turn were supported and controlled by Lin's army. Lin was named at the Ninth Congress Deputy Party Chairman as well as the future heir-apparent upon Mao's demise.[13] Putting Lin in such a position automatically made him a target in the eyes of the Jiang Qing faction of CCP radicals. Zhou naturally had to walk gingerly around Mao, Lin and Jiang Qing, not to mention the many agents and informers around all of

---

10. *Zhou Enlai Waijiao Hedong Dashiji, 1949-1975* [*A Chronicle of Zhou Enlai's Major Diplomatic Activities*], hereafter cited as *The Zhou Enlai Chronicle.* This was compiled by Foreign Affairs Research Office of the PRC's Ministry of Foreign Affairs, (Beijing: World Knowledge Publishers, 1993), entry dated September 11, 1969, p. 539.

11. Robert A. Jones, *The Soviet Concept of "Limited Sovereignty" from Lenin to Gorbachev, the Brezhnev Doctrine* (Houndmill, Basingstoke: Macmillan, 1990), p. 160.

12. *The Zhou Enlai Chronicle*, *supra* note 10, pp. 555-56.

13. Naming an heir-apparent in the party constitution was an unprecedented "feudalistic" practice!

them.[14] This probably explained why Zhou had to make Mao realize for himself the serious turn in policy Brezhnev could be about to make. The Romanian visitors no doubt would have liked to line up the PRC with other East European opponents to Brezhnev's big stick approach. For the same reason, Zhou had to temporize and delay. Accepting the Soviet suggestion of border negotiations but limiting the talks at Khabarovsk to river navigation was in line with the approach. Quoting Mao in the airport conference with Kosygin served the same purpose. But more had to be done.

III. A LAST HURRAH: ZHOU ENLAI'S DIPLOMATIC COUP AFTER BANDUNG

The U.S.-PRC Diplomatic Rapprochement

The preparation and execution of the U.S.-PRC rapprochement culminating in President Nixon's 1972 visit to mainland China was no doubt a monumental coup in Zhou Enlai's long diplomatic career. If we regard Kissinger's visit to Beijing on July 7-11, 1971, prelude to President Nixon's February 1972 visit, as the end of a diplomatic *tour de force*, the stage for it was officially set some time before December 1969. On December 12, 1969,[15] at an evening meeting with his Pakistani visitor, Zhou Enlai spoke of the new age of negotiations. He told the ambassador from Karachi that the PRC and the United States had always had a line of communication through the two countries' ambassadors in Warsaw. He noted further that the Warsaw contact was interrupted on January 18, 1968, nearly two years earlier, but that a renewed probe had been made by the United States at a Yugoslav fashion show. Zhou further mentioned the Sino-Soviet border talks at Khabarovsk and referred to the U.S.-Soviet SALT talks (Strategic Arms Limitation Talks) in Helsinki.

He then pooh-poohed the usefulness of these long talks, as if feigning disinterest in engaging in them and by implication the es-

---

14. Reference should be made to the critical 1949 exchange between U.S. Ambassador Stewart and Zhou, Mao and Ye Jianying through the intermediary of Chen Mingshu. In *The Zhou Enlai Chronicle, supra* note 10, Zhou, however, referred to the intermediary as Lo Longji, a democrat and fellow traveler who later became a target of Mao's 1957 Anti-Rightist campaign. The message was not made public by Lo until several years later, according to Zhou. Lo feared that the message was untimely, said Zhou. Mao's essay on "leaning to one side" having been published, Lo was afraid of being regarded as a "rightist." That was probably Zhou's fear himself. See Chapter IX, end of Section II. Is it possible that Zhou actually held up the Stuart message himself?

15. *The Zhou Enlai Chronicle, supra* note 10, p. 546.

tablishment of another channel of communication which one might assume the ambassador was at that time suggesting. However, Zhou continued, the United States of course could employ any one of these channels without creating still another. Since Zhou well understood the usefulness of a "back-channel," the existence of which could be readily denied, he had in fact answered the Pakistani envoy in the affirmative while protecting himself against potential domestic political enemies who might accuse him of insufficient radical backbone in the face of a superpower's exploratory gesture.

If we count the date of this conversation on December 12, 1969 as the time of the curtain's rise, and Kissinger's arrival in Beijing on July 7, 1971 as the time of the curtain's fall, there was a period of a little over 19 months. During this interval, the following directly related events took place in succession. First, on November 21, 1970, Ceausescu of Romania sent his deputy to see Zhou Enlai, conveying a message from U.S. President Nixon and Secretary Rogers stating that the United States sought normalization of relations with the PRC so as to improve and develop economic, scientific, and technical relations. To that end the United States would be prepared to engage in negotiations anywhere, through whatever channel, and at any time. Zhou's reply was that Taiwan was the key problem between the PRC and the United States because Taiwan was "an inalienable part of China" and that if Mr. Nixon really had the desire and method to resolve this problem, the PRC would welcome his special representative, including Nixon himself.

Second, the above statement was a formal message because it apparently was given to the Romanian in Washington by Mr. Nixon together with then Secretary of State Rogers. As a matter of fact, another similar but slightly more informal verbal message from Mr. Nixon had been delivered to Beijing several days earlier, having come from Pakistan. In response to this earlier U.S. message delivered on November 14, 1970 via President Yahya Khan to Zhou in a private talk (Yahya Khan had arrived on a state visit), Zhou stated that the Taiwan issue was the crux of the problem the PRC had with the United Sates and that it had been outstanding for fifteen years. If Nixon had a solution, said Zhou, he (Nixon) could send someone to negotiate. This answer from Zhou was positive and was confirmed by Zhou's reply via Ceausescu's messenger. It also betrayed no eagerness on Zhou's part.[16]

16. On January 14, 1971, the Pakistani Ambassador visited Zhou; the Romanian ambassador called on Zhou on January 26. Confirmation of the delivery of the

Third, having thus assured himself of genuine U.S. intentions, Zhou "went public" on the PRC's intention to deal with the United States when he spoke with the American table tennis team invited to the PRC, asking the visitors upon returning home to convey greetings of the Chinese "to the American people."

Fourth, as a step further, Zhou then met with selected American newsmen on June 21, 1971. The Kissinger sessions with PRC leaders then took place on July 7 to 11, 1971.

Two additional events—doubtless connected to those enumerated above— were a five-hour conversation between Zhou and the Soviet ambassador on March 21, 1971 and a call on Zhou on June 12, 1971 by the Yugoslav Foreign Minister. The last event was unmistakably a sign of reconciliation, not only with Yugoslavia, but indirectly also with the Soviet Union. After all, Yugoslavia had served as a whipping boy for the "revisionist" Soviet Union in the CCP-CPSU polemics for nearly a decade.

We shall have to wait for the opening of more PRC or Soviet files before we can be sure of what went on during the 5-hour dialogue between Zhou and the Soviet ambassador on March 21, 1971. At any rate, no open warfare occurred between the two former communist partners in that year. In view of the Yugoslav's call on Zhou nearly three months after the Russo-Chinese dialogue, it would seem that the worst of the tensions in Moscow, Beijing and Washington stirred up by the U.S.-PRC rapprochement were being somewhat dissipated.

Diplomatic Gains of the PRC

Kissinger and his staff made two more trips, in 1971 and 1972, before accompanying Nixon to Beijing in February 1972. The Shanghai Communiqué, however, only acknowledged the fact that both sides of the Taiwan Strait claimed that there was only one China and that the United States would not dispute the fact of those claims, nor did it say that Taiwan was a part of the PRC. Zhou also claimed that the United States was thinking in terms of two stages of improving bilateral relations: first, by establishing liaison offices on both sides and then during Nixon's second term, by moving further, which in Chinese minds could mean full recognition. Since Nixon resigned before completing his second term, full recognition at the expense of the Chinese Nationalists was left to

---

messages was presumably the principal purpose in both cases. *The Zhou Enlai Chronicle*, *id.*, pp. 571-72 and 577.

Mr. Carter in 1978. The severance of relations with the Nationalists in 1979, however, stopped short of being complete only as a result of the Congressional passage of the Taiwan Relations Act (the TRA).

Substantial gains were made by the PRC as a result of the "normalization" of relations with the United States. Already in October 1971 when Mr. Kissinger went to Beijing a second time, his timing coincided with the annual voting in the UN on the issue of Chinese representation in that organization. The indication, through this timing, that the United States might be about to change its China policy could well have encouraged some nations to switch their votes in favor of seating the PRC. As a result, the matter did not qualify as an "important question" by UN rules and the PRC won, thus becoming a member of the Security Council with veto power. This belied Zhou Enlai's own dictum, "what one cannot win on the battlefield one cannot win by negotiation."[17] Zhou did himself one better!

Zhou was now able to pursue the unfinished task of winning additional diplomatic recognition from other nations than the United States. For establishing relations with the PRC, Prime Minister Tanaka of Japan was ready to accept Zhou's condition of derecognizing the Republic of China on Taiwan. The United Kingdom, first among the Western powers in recognizing the PRC many years earlier, finally withdrew its remaining consulate from Taiwan. Numerous other nations then severed relations with the Nationalists at the PRC's demand.

Incomplete Gains in the 1970s

The PRC's failure to win total victory on the Taiwan issue in 1971 and later again in 1979 was clearly a setback. The long-term outcome will depend upon how the future China will develop after its next potentially convulsive "dynastic change" after Deng Xiaoping's departure from the post-Mao Chinese scene.

To begin with, we have to bear in mind that the rapprochement between the United States and the PRC came about as a result of the convergence of three conditions on the world scene. First, the Soviet Union was compelled, in its distorted view, to proclaim a doctrine of intervention in order to keep control of deviant communist regimes in the larger empire Stalin had built. From the PRC's

---

17. *The Zhou Enlai Chronicle*, *id.*, p. 663, from Zhou's comments on the 1973 U.S.-North Vietnam armistice agreement on February 2, 1973.

perspective, this attitude appeared threatening enough for it to seek a realignment of its relations with the two superpowers.

Second, the Soviet Union hesitated to attack the PRC because the latter was too populous and too large a country to be easily defeated by conventional means, followed by military occupation or by Soviet domination, at a sustainable cost. On the other hand, use of nuclear weapons could trigger PRC retaliation by kind even though such a nuclear exchange could be grossly destructive or even suicidal to the Chinese.

Finally, the United States, sensing the above Soviet dilemma and the coincidental PRC fear and that it might welcome a restructuring of its relations with both the United States and the Soviet Union, made a bold offer that made possible exactly the adjustments required. The United States sought the benefit of extricating itself from the costly Vietnam War by obtaining both PRC and Soviet acquiescence. It offered the PRC the economic and political benefits of normalization at the cost of the Chinese Nationalists, short of the latter's total abandonment, and at the cost of South Vietnam (lessened by "Vietnamization" and an offer of timely military assistance in the event of renewed attack by the Communists from the North).

Unfortunately, the conditions on the American domestic front did not permit the requisite support being given to South Vietnam in 1975 when the 1973 cease-fire was violated. The promised assistance did not materialize. At the same time, the diplomatic victory awarded to Beijing did not come at a time when the PRC could immediately implement an economic modernization program which Deng Xiaoping was to try to carry out only well after 1978, and again to renew in 1992.[18]

The strategic considerations that made the U.S.-PRC rapprochement possible did not automatically make a viable PRC economy an assured outcome. No one could have foreseen all this. The PRC's internal economy was still in a mess, Deng Xiaoping's post-Mao economic reform was still ten years away. Even the Cultural Revolution was not yet entirely over. Hence the economic possibilities Western and Japanese businessmen thought forthcoming were still far off, whereas misuse of funds and resources made available by the West after "normalization" led essentially to waste and a premature debt burden, some large disappointments and many new economic risks. On the other hand, the Chinese Nation-

---

18. See Chapters VII and VIII.

alists, though politically made a pariah, were given a period of stability which enabled the Taiwan economy to develop to a stage that fifteen years later it could in some respects be either a potential economic rival or a partner of the Chinese mainland. Given the respite they received, the Nationalists under Chiang Ching-kuo began their shift to a progressively more conciliatory stance toward the PRC in 1987, making Taiwan a potentially welcome source of external capital the PRC sorely needs. Thus a partial failure in 1972 could turn out to be a blessing in the 1990s.

IV. SOVIET RESPONSES TO THE PRC-U.S. RAPPROCHEMENT

No Soviet Thumb-Twisting

The comings and goings of high officials between Beijing and the capitals of the United States, Pakistan, Romania and the USSR in the years starting in 1969 through the early 1970s testified to the radical policy shifts on the part of Mao Zedong and Zhou Enlai. The initiatives were taken principally by Washington and Beijing as we have tried to show in the previous section, thanks to the details we now have on Zhou Enlai's diplomatic activities. But it would be a mistake to think that the Soviet Union simply sat idly by and took everything lying down. In this connection, while we suffer from the still closed official files, speculation on the basis of a few known facts, however scanty, enables us to point to two sets of developments.

There probably was an early Soviet probe to see whether the Mao regime could be subverted from within. Not much information is available in the public domain because the Soviet probe may not have been serious, possibly because it was never thoroughly thought through and was abandoned halfway. However, the timing of what little information has become available since 1995 suggests that Soviet thoughts were probably connected with the Lin Biao affair in September 1971. Lin Biao's death put an end to whatever plot might have been hatched in the Kremlin.

Second, following the Vietnam armistice in 1973 and the occupation of South Vietnam by the forces of the Communist North in 1975, there was nearly a decade of political instability and warfare in Indochina. It was only after the collapse of the Soviet Union itself in 1991 that the Sino-Vietnamese border of the PRC acquired a semblance of quiescence and semi-stability. Actually, there was a short outburst of hot war in the early months of 1979 between PRC and Vietnamese forces. The PLA's not too glorious experience in that encounter in turn has had some lasting consequences.

The Victor Louis Affair in 1968-71

In November 1970, Victor E. Louis, a free-lance journalist ostensibly writing for a London evening paper, went to Taiwan and managed to interview the then ROC Defense Minister Chiang Ching-kuo as well as the Minister of Economic Affairs and other high officials handling public information.[19] During his stay in Taiwan, Louis kept in touch with the late Jimmy Wei, veteran Nationalist newsman and a close friend of the Defense Minister. Louis was known to hold a Soviet passport which did not fail to catch the attention of journalists and some serious China-watchers.

The Victor Louis initiative could well have been a factor of impact on Soviet-PRC relations during the critical period before the crash of Lin Biao's Trident plane in September 1971. For, according to Wei's diary, Victor Louis's discussions with the Nationalist Chinese touched upon the hypothetical possibility of a Soviet official declaration of neutrality in the event of the "resumption" of Nationalist and CCP armed conflict, accompanied by active Soviet military involvement in attacks on PRC coastal military bases and the destruction of PRC nuclear facilities at Lop Nor. The ensuing intermittent discussions between the emissaries of the two sides in the following months suggested that the Soviet Union had an interest in setting up an alternative non-Maoist Chinese communist regime for at least a portion of the Chinese mainland that could "cooperate" or "co-exist" with the Taiwan-based ROC.

On behalf ostensibly of the Soviet Union or at least the KGB, Louis pressed the Nationalists for information on the latter's specific interest in the kinds of Soviet weapons that might be supplied to Taiwan for such a "joint venture." The Nationalist side, according to the Wei diary, pressed Louis to ask his principals for a serious decision on post-Mao Soviet-ROC relations in such a hypothetical event. Apparently no further discussion developed out of these intermittent contacts Victor Louis first initiated in Tokyo.

---

19. Victor Louis's contact with Taiwan was not a secret, because he initiated it through the International Press Club in Tokyo. The many meetings he had with Taiwan personages between October 1968 and November 1970 when the contact was broken off were the topic of the personal diary of journalist Jimmy Wei. Extracts of the Wei diary were published in a Special Supplement of Taipei's *World Journal* on May 21-26, 1995. The diary material was given to the *Journal* several years after Wei's death by his daughter.

Both the Damansky Island clash and the Khabarosk discussion on border issues seemed to have had an effect on the schedule of the sustained bilateral discussions after Victor Louis's visit to Taipei. But the chain of events begun by the Pakistani and Romanian messengers and information about their activities could very well have cooled Soviet interest in pushing ahead on what would have been a risky exploit at best. However, one cannot but wonder whether Soviet intentions behind Victor Louis's proposition was in any way another part of the mystery of Lin Biao's alleged flight. Nor can one rule out the possibility that the Soviet Union's intention was to create dissension between the PRC military and the ever suspicious Mao Zedong.

A Soviet Effort to Contain China from Vietnam?

While the Victor Louis effort lasted too short a time and was murky in detail, a far better reported facet of Soviet activities in conjunction with the U.S.-PRC rapprochement had to do with events in Indochina after the evacuation of American military presence from Vietnam. They deserve our attention because of their more far-reaching consequences in later years.

In the first place, some geopolitical factors should be borne in mind. The U.S.-PRC rapprochement presented the Soviet Union with the potential threat of a two-front war in the minds of its security planners because of the existence of the NATO alliance and the unreliable PRC. Given a potentially hostile PRC, one can imagine why the new U.S.-PRC connection conjured up in the Soviet mind the ghost of the Berlin-Tokyo axis of World War II and the late 1930s.

Given its sizable population, the fact that the Vietnamese Communist Party is one of the largest in Asia after the Chinese party, and the degree of training, battle experience and modern equipment acquired during the long Vietnam war, a Communist-controlled united Vietnam could have been a valuable ally to the Soviet Union in any future Sino-Soviet confrontation. In geopolitical terms, a Soviet-Vietnamese alliance could present the PRC with a two-front hostile combination as well.

Second, from the PRC's perspective, given its foreign policy goal of breaking out of hostile encirclement, a Vietnam-USSR alliance could have served as the framework of a Soviet policy to contain China. Such a situation would have been tantamount to the defeat of Zhou Enlai's long-term foreign policy going back to the Dienbienphu defeat of French troops in 1954. As in many another

Southeast Asian country, native Vietnamese political and economic interest groups have invariably been concerned about the ethnic Chinese among them. The search for energy resources to support the country's future development and expansion has made the off-shore oil and natural gas deposits in areas around the Spratly, Paracel and adjacent islands a center of contention with the PRC and other Southeast Asian nations. The Tonkin Gulf had already been an occasional battleground involving Vietnamese forces.

In these circumstances, problems of border demarcation on land between Vietnam and the PRC was really the least of all points of actual and likely conflict between the two sides. As long as Ho Chi Minh was alive, the Communist Party of Vietnam was mindful of his leadership and the help China (actually including the Chinese Nationalists) had provided him in the early years of the anti-colonial movement.

Ho's death provided the occasion for Kosygin's stop in Beijing, for the eventful discussion with Zhou Enlai, on the return leg of the Russian's visit to Saigon to attend Ho's funeral. With Ho gone, leadership changes within the Vietnamese Communist Party, the relative capacity of the Soviet Union to provide continuous military and economic support to Vietnam, in contrast to the PRC's economic deterioration and political instability in the same period, resulted in the ascendancy of Soviet influence. Under these circumstances the Soviet-Vietnamese Treaty of Friendship and Mutual Cooperation was signed in November, 1978.

Although by then Zhou Enlai had died, his successors in the PRC Foreign Ministry were nevertheless able, with some cooperation from Sihanouk, to use Cambodia as an indirect restraint on Vietnam's effort to extend its potential influence against the PRC in favor of the Soviet Union. This contribution to their Soviet ally was demonstrated by an air and ground attack on Cambodia in December 1978. According to Nguyen Van Cahn,[20] 180,000 Vietnamese troops were at one time deployed in the occupation of Cambodia in support of Heng Samrin's government, not to mention another 6,000-men strong force in Laos. The infiltration of Thailand by Vietnamese agents in the guise of refugees also took place during this period. But Chinese intervention on the other side was instrumental in keeping the pot of Indochina boiling for the next decade.

---

20. Nguyen Van Cahn, *Vietnam under Communism, 1975-1982* (Stanford, CA: Hoover Institution Press, 1983), pp. 60-68 and 227-44.

A final show of force by the PRC, immediately after the return of Deng Xiaoping from Washington, through the short military confrontation between the PLA and Vietnam's forces in early 1979, marked the last phase of the PRC's hard-line response to fend off Soviet expansionism in the direction of Southeast Asia and the South China Sea. The ups and downs of indirect thrusting and parrying between the PRC and the former USSR continued until the dissolution of the latter in 1991, the normalization of PRC-Vietnam relations in November of the same year and the UN-held elections in Cambodia in 1993.[21] The last two events, one might say with some justification, would not have happened, but for the collapse of the Soviet Union.

As Gorbachev mentioned correctly, his 1989 visit to Beijing would have been a triumphal conclusion of normalization of Sino-Soviet relations that had begun to go precipitately downhill in the 1960s. In a more limited sense, from the PRC's perspective, the Chinese effort to bring about the security of China's land border, one of the country's historical foreign policy goals, seemed to have definitely been reached in June 1989. Of course, the assurance of national security has several stages.

At this writing (1996), continental China appears to be free from real external threat. The return of Hongkong and Macao to become parts of a single Chinese nation has already been assured by international agreement and is within reach before the end of this century. Only the Chinese economy is not yet sufficiently developed to a point of self-sustainable growth for all of its 1.2 billion plus people. Two indispensable ingredients of the missing factor are capital and technology, often embodied in physical capital and highly skilled human labor. Will the PRC's external policy be appropriate for this purpose?

---

21. See Carlyle A. Thayer, *Beyond Indochina* (Oxford: Oxford University Press, 1995), Adelphi Papers No. 297, for a broad survey of conditions in Indochina as a whole after 1975 through 1993. Many references are given by Thayer that deserve the reader's attention. For the earlier years (1975-82) in Vietnam see Nguyen Van Cahn, *supra* note 20.

CHAPTER XII

EXTERNAL RELATIONS AND NATIONAL POLICY GOALS: SOURCES OF CAPITAL AND LEARNING TO KNOW ONE'S NEIGHBORS

I. SELECTED SOURCES OF EXTERNAL CAPITAL AND CONDITIONS OF INFLOW—JAPAN

The *net inflow* of external capital into the country and its effective use in conjunction with domestic savings will in the long run turn out to be the key determinant of the success or failure of the PRC's economic development. We stress the phrase "net inflow" because external capital brought into the country must be offset by the normal outflow, together with capital flight, if any, of PRC capital for safekeeping or investment abroad during the same period. In addition, foreign exchange and other short-term monetary instruments brought into the country could conceivably be taken out again (on occasion, even by money smugglers, who may or may not double as smugglers of goods). Some of the same funds, once smuggled abroad, using some off-shore financial centers as intermediary, could later be reinvested back in the PRC! Hence it is the net inflow that counts.

We must also stress the term "effective use." While the incoming capital may be invested to produce real goods and services for the general public, it also may be devoted to the production and use by consumers of goods that serve what critics would call conspicuous and wasteful consumption. From a technical, purely economic point of view, the kinds of goods and services produced by external investment in China should not be judged in such value terms. But whether external investors tend to encourage conspicuous consumption or not is often a controversial issue in the eyes of the social critic. Hence we must not ignore the political and social circumstances and outcomes of the investment flow.

The purpose of this chapter is to examine whether the PRC's external policy in the post-Hua period has contributed rationally and effectively to the enhancement of external capital inflow and its effective employment by looking at three special cases: Japan, Hongkong and Taiwan. (We use the term "external" not "foreign" so as to include at this point in history both Hongkong and Taiwan because they are certainly external to mainland China whether one considers them "foreign" or not.) We have selected these special sources of supply of external capital because they touch on all the important aspects of the PRC's foreign economic policy in general and are illustrative of the kinds of difficult problems the PRC must resolve effectively both from the economic point of view and politically in consonance with the country's national goals in the long run.

Experience with Japan after World War II

Nationalist General Ho Ying-ch'in, who represented the Republic of China as one of the victorious allies of World War II, was present at the ceremony to accept the surrender of Japan in 1945. Twenty-seven years later, in 1972, Japan switched full diplomatic relations from Taipei to Beijing. The paths traversed by both Japan and the two Chinese sides were inordinately torturous; the twin Sino-Japanese relationships were characterized by many instances of pretense and make-belief on both sides. For those readers who are unfamiliar with the history of contemporary Sino-Japanese relations, the following brief account will serve to highlight the evolution of this relationship. It will help explain the main purpose of this section of our discussion of the PRC's external policy, its modernization efforts, and the issues encountered in dealing with Japan.

First, when a peace treaty was finally signed between Nationalist China and Japan in Taipei, the ROC, unlike other nations in Asia which had been invaded by Japan and managed nevertheless to survive under Japanese occupation, waived the demand for reparations. Japanese forces and civilians in occupied China were almost immediately repatriated back to Japan. This treatment differed sharply from that meted out by the Soviet Union, whose troops entered Manchuria in the last moments of the war. The difference in treatment was intended by Nationalist China to provide a basis for a new start in its postwar relations with Japan. During the Korean War and until the U.S.-PRC rapprochement, Taipei was the China officially recognized by Japan while trade with Communist China was carried on by Japan only as an exception to the official relationship between Tokyo and Taipei. Japan also had to observe the decisions of the Coordinating Committee (COCOM) in Paris which coordinated control over Western (and Japanese) export restrictions of trade in strategic goods and advanced technologies with all Communist countries, including the PRC.

However, while Japan had little choice but to observe ostensibly the rules imposed by COCOM controls, it regarded its own foreign trade expansion as a matter of fundamental national interest and did its utmost to promote this national goal. Japan's home islands were dependent upon imports from abroad. Before World War II, the supply of goods produced at home could be augmented by imports from her colonies, including Korea and Taiwan (then known as Formosa in the West) and Manchuria (a Tokyo-sponsored dependency since 1931). Now that the colonies had been taken away, imports had to be paid for with exports. Hence, Japan had every intention to develop exports and to accumulate an export surplus in order to build up foreign investments anew. Japan obviously hoped to use the PRC and Taiwan as markets and sources of supply as before the war.

Accordingly, in dealing with the PRC, Japan invented a series of new concepts and novel institutions in order to permit trading with the Chinese mainland without upsetting the existing political relationship with Taiwan under a principle of "separating economics from politics."[1] Behind such a cloak of political expediency acceptable to all parties, small-scale trade by private Japanese traders proclaiming their special friendship for the PRC and the Chinese people began even before the early 1960s. This trade was sanctioned officially after a talk between Zhou Enlai and Ikeda Hayato in August 1960. Continuing official negotiations between Liao Chengzhi and Takasaki Tatsunosuke (one time minister of MITI and head of a Japanese firm in Manchuria before 1945) led to an agreement fixing such two-way bilateral trade at an average annual volume of $100 million between 1960-62. Inasmuch as Japan's exports could under this arrangement be financed by the Export-Import Bank of Japan, the payments arrangement, known as "memorandum trade," was a significant advantage from the point of view of the PRC then pressed for foreign exchange. Because of strong objections by Washington and Taipei, however, the Japanese Government was finally prevailed upon to have Yoshida Shigeru, the former Prime Minister, write a letter addressed to Taiwan stat-

1. See Chae-Jin Lee, *China and Japan: New Economic Policy* (Stanford: Hoover Press, 1984), pp. 5-6.

ing that despite the new arrangement there was no real change in Japan's policy on the two Chinas.[2]

Trade Fluctuations

One point worth noting had to do with the vicissitudes of Sino-Japanese trade during this period and how they should be interpreted. A superficial examination of trade statistics in the light of the PRC's public actions would offer one interpretation. A closer look at the PRC's political and economic developments during the same period in conjunction with our earlier account about the Great Leap and the Lushan Conference of 1959 would, however, present a distinctly different interpretation.

According to the data of the Japan-China Economic Association cited by Chae-Jin Lee,[3] the PRC's imports from Japan dropped sharply from $19.6 million in 1950 to $5.8 million in 1951 and $0.6 million in 1952. The corresponding value then rose from $4.5 million in 1953 back to $19.1 million in 1954. PRC exports to Japan followed the same V-shaped curve after having risen from a trough of $54.9 million during the Korean War in 1951 (no figure given for 1950) to $69.9 million in 1952, and $199.3 million in 1953. It traced a roller-coaster path during the next decade and a half. The swing in 1951-54 clearly reflected the fighting in Korea and Japan's conduct as a wartime base of the U.S. in the Korean War. However, according to Lee, Zhou Enlai suspended all economic and cultural exchanges with Japan along with private agreements on trade, fisheries and *steel export* deliberately as a show of outrage at Prime Minister Kishi's refusal to accept Zhou's political demands, and bilateral trade again slumped in 1959 through 1961, recovering only in 1962.

It is questionable that the PRC could have done anything else during these years when trade with Japan had to be curbed because

---

2. The historical Yoshida letter presenting Japan's real governmental position but in the form of a private communication to the Nationalist Republic of China was meant to be kept secret, because as a private communication, it presumably should not have represented the Japanese government's official position or have official status. Its official status in the eyes of the ROC, which demanded a retraction of Japan's giving assistance to the PRC economically through an official Japanese agency, was essentially derived from Yoshida's position as the first postwar prime minister of Japan whose special status was in some sense "sanctified" by the emperor. See Chang Ch'ün, *Wo yü Jih-pen Ch'i-shih-nien* [*Japan and I Over Seven Decades*] (Taipei: Research Council of Sino-Japanese Relations, 1980).

3. Chae-Jin Lee, *supra* note 1, p. 4.

of the PRC's domestic economic collapse. Beijing's inability to keep up its promised steel export to Japan was a plain give-away of the true reason, namely, the collapse of modern steel production and available export as a result of the economic disaster of the Great Leap years and the nuclear bomb drive which followed, one upon the other. Yet, (not unexpectedly) Zhou was skillful enough to pretend that the consequence of Mao's economic mistakes was solely a political retaliatory gesture in Communist Chinese negotiations with Japan.

Lessons from Japan's Project Loans and a Long-Term Trade Agreement

The Yoshida letter of May 1964 was a low watermark in PRC-Japanese trade. Then, when the Vietnam War finally ground to an end in the early 1970s, Japan's diplomatic relations with the PRC took a sharp turn for the better. Following President Nixon's radical change in U.S. China policy, which led to the entry of the PRC into the UN Security Council in November 1971, Japan quickly extended full diplomatic relations to Beijing in September 1972, more than six years ahead of the United States. According to some of his critics, the new Japanese Prime Minister Tanaka Kakuei who succeeded Sato Eisaku, perhaps tried to do one better than the United States in this respect in order to curry favor with the PRC, hoping thereby to steal several steps ahead of its U.S. and NATO competitors in what looked like a monstrously large China market to many people. Leading Japanese businessmen in the Tokyo as well as Kansai region were eagerly anticipating this bonanza to fall upon them very soon.[4]

On January 5, 1974, Japanese Foreign Minister Ohira Masayoshi met with Mao Zedong and Wang Hongwen (erstwhile textile worker but then CCP Deputy Chairman) after signing a main bilateral official trade agreement in the post-World War II period.[5] Four more years later, on February 16, 1978 a Long-Term Trade (1978-85) Agreement was concluded between the PRC and Japan, marking what both sides believed to be the beginning of a new era of bilateral economic relations. Actual developments turned out to be quite a bit more turbulent than either side had expected. Those historical dates are a useful reference and reminder for later foreign entrants to the Chinese market.

---

4. Chae-Jin Lee, *id.*, pp. 8-10.
5. Chae-Jin Lee, *id.*, pp. 15-21.

As pointed out earlier in Chapters VI and VII, Hua Guofeng's short tenure as CCP chairman was partly a result of his own poverty in new ideas that would have enabled him to strike out in a different direction from the approach laid down by Mao. A fundamental mistake Mao committed in his day was his blind trust in the use of unskilled labor through a sheer increase in scale, i.e., the numbers of workers mobilized. Hua, however, was no less mistaken in thinking that substitution of modern technology and machinery in individual plants for peasant workers and traditional methods of production would by itself accomplish miracles where Mao had failed. Hua was to learn a bitter lesson through the failure of the Baoshan steel project, which apparently gave his political opponents (Chen Yun in particular) the knock-out argument against him. In part, however, the over-eagerness of Japanese businessmen after the signing of the long-term trade agreement also had the effect of making the availability of capital and technology seem too easy to some PRC planners. Some might say that this perception made the PRC's economic failure during the Hua period virtually inevitable. (Here one is reminded of the early overwhelming enthusiasm in the West after 1979 and again after Deng's "southern tour" in 1992.)

Given Hua Guofeng's desire to modernize and expand Chinese industry quickly, the construction of a new steel center at Baoshan near Shanghai was a pivotal pilot project.[6] PRC planners and metallurgical specialists, very likely influenced by what they had learned about grandiose Soviet projects, thought of the "Baogang" plan, i.e., Baoshan steel, initially with enthusiasm. The Chinese officials were greatly impressed with Nippon Steel, the primary Japanese contractor and negotiator, including the company's technical prowess and standing in Japanese industry. They in turn tried very hard to tell their Japanese counterpart how they wanted to acquire the utmost in modern, state-of-the-art technology comparable to some used by top firms in Japan that they had seen. The PRC wanted the best but had no idea that what was technically the latest and the best in a given set of economic and technical circumstances might not at all be the most appropriate elsewhere. At the same time, being proud of their new political status as their own masters, they insisted on their right to make the final choice, including quite innocently the right to make their own mistakes.

---

6. Chae-Jin Lee, *id.*, pp. 30-75.

In effect, the Baogang project apparently went into construction without a really comprehensive feasibility plan and engineering study of the entire project, perhaps without even the assurance of the mutual compatibility of the component parts of the entire project. A list of the many component parts in the two stages of the entire Baoshan project showed that, when the first stage was already well along, the cost analysis and subsidiary sub-contract negotiation of the component plants had not yet begun.[7] Wholesale open criticism of the Baogang project was launched by Chen Yun after Chen's return to power, and the criticism was backed by Deng Xiaoping in the background. This maneuver had the political effect of speeding Hua Guofeng's fall.

Under these conditions, mutual recrimination naturally followed. Some Chinese probably thought that Japanese businessmen like Nippon Steel had been less than frank in dealing with their Chinese "friends." However, a more objective observer might note that a truly frank dialogue between the two sides could not have been easily established. While PRC representatives might have outwardly behaved in a humble manner, they probably would have been offended if they had been dealt with really matter-of-factly. On the opposite side, some Japanese might have thought of their Chinese partners as more than a little ineffectual and incompetent, but they would not have wished to offend by being too frank. As a result, when an impasse finally developed, the Chinese thought of the Japanese as duplicitous. Yet a more fitting comment should be that neither side was really noticeably less duplicitous than the other when it came to negotiations on matters of self-interest.[8]

On large development projects like the Baoshan Steel case, the unexpected large cost increase in the course of the negotiations would not have occurred if a thorough feasibility study had been conducted earlier. The history of the series of surprises, disputes, threatened and actual contract cancellations, when viewed collectively and objectively, would actually represent potential findings at various stages of a good feasibility study and project modeling. Haste and lack of experience were the real reasons for the problems encountered. The Chinese were apparently afraid of be-

---

7. Chae-Jin Lee, *id.*, Table 11, pp. 42-43.

8. Cf. Ezra Vogel, "Japanese Visions for the 1990s" and "Japan's Global Economic Activity," in *Continuous Issues and Policy Choices in U.S.-Japan Relations*, Proceedings of the Harvard Faculty Study Group on U.S.-Japan Relations, 1990-92, chaired by Joseph S. Nye, Susan J. Phars, and Ezra Vogel (Cambridge, MA: The Center for International Affairs, Harvard University, 1993), pp. 56-70 and 94-103.

ing taken for a ride when they started to deal with the Japanese. The latter, on the other hand, were too eager not to miss the PRC's business. In the end, the Baoshan project had to be cut down in size. The project also turned out to be too delayed from the point of view of the renewed attempt at accelerated development; the entire development program was as a whole over-concentrated on capital-intensive heavy industry.

One can only speculate on what PRC planners and non-Japanese foreign businessmen learned from the Baoshan fiasco. Several tentative general observations appear warranted on the basis of these and other similar developments. First, use of multi-lateral and open bidding apparently came about already at the end of the Baoshan negotiations. Second, the division of off-shore oil exploration contracts by separate geographical regions involving different international oil companies may have been partly influenced by the Baoshan experience. Third, the PRC may have become more convinced than before that while offers of foreign capital may appear numerous to begin with, it is not easy to translate such offers into real large-scale projects. Finally, the Baoshan experience doubtless also taught PRC planners that unless dependable sources of foreign exchange income can be developed, to rely upon export credit offered by international bank loans or credit from particular foreign national lending agencies can be unduly burdensome and subject to gross uncertainty and cost, in view of the exchange rate fluctuations of particular currencies, like the appreciation of the yen.

Following the establishment of diplomatic relations in 1972, trade relations between the PRC and Japan expanded rapidly. The stepped-up increase in oil prices by OPEC (Organization of Petroleum Exporting Countries), and the consequent rise of other prices in the industrial countries in general produced a widespread increase in the prices of many goods in world trade. The PRC's export of crude oil and oil products contributed to increasing world interest in the country's offshore and onshore oil deposits. The CCP's decision to establish SEZs also led to a very large increase in the country's external trade.

PRC exports to Japan in 1992 had risen to US$11.7 billion in comparison with US$13.7 billion of exports from Japan.[9] The

9. For trade and investment data, the Taiwan Bureau of Foreign Trade regularly publishes monthly trade statistics and studies, as does the PRC's State Statistical Bureau. Readers should use the data for individual countries with care. Some countries give trade data on goods by origin and final destination; others use country of consignment and loading/unloading for purposes of classification by country. U.S.-PRC trade

PRC's world trade figures rose accordingly. The problems encountered by other non-Japanese foreign businessmen have been essentially similar to those Japan has had over the years. The United States, however, has taken over the role Japan had in being the target of the PRC's wrath, and has spearheaded the endless negotiations on trade disputes.

II. HONGKONG AND TAIWAN

Background of PRC-Hongkong and PRC-Taiwan Relations

In light of the above, the 1982 U.K.-PRC negotiations and the Sino-British Agreement signed in 1984 on the retrocession of Hongkong (including the Kowloon Leased Territories) have assumed great importance for the PRC, Hongkong and the British. The Agreement stipulated that Hongkong would revert to Chinese sovereignty on July 1, 1997, to be henceforth known as a Special Administrative District (SAD) for fifty years. Thus, at one stroke of the pen, all the physical fixed assets and immovable tangible goods in Hongkong at that date would find themselves located in the expanded PRC territory and subject to the latter's physical control.

Whatever was mobile at the time of the agreement, of course, could be moved away between the agreement date and mid-1997. This would apply to a part of the local labor force (the technically skilled workers and professionals), who might desire emigration and could find places to go. Ownership of the immovables can be shifted through sale to foreign owners and re-registration of ownership in foreign lands under non-PRC laws.

Since under the 1982 agreement the PRC promised not to disturb the accustomed mode of life of Hongkong residents, and private business would be permitted to operate in Hongkong as before for another half century after the reversion, one can envisage how a set of promising conditions for all parties appeared to be fully assured. A number of monumental benefits would accrue to the PRC in terms of access to capital and the availability of a skilled labor force and the Hongkong SAD's access to the world's markets. At that time, since the promised benefits of the PRC's economic reform would be to Chinese advantage no less than to that of Hongkong residents and non-Chinese third parties, it was easy to

---

figures vary greatly for this reason alone. U.S. imports from the PRC, based on origin, are much larger than PRC statistics of exports to the United States by virtue of Chinese omission of goods trans-shipped via Hongkong which the PRC regards as exports to Hongkong.

assume that the rosy prospects of the post-1997 period would be fairly safe. But as Chapter VIII has already shown, the skeptics of the mid-1980s turned out to be right. However, let us turn to a look at the Taiwan case first.

PRC-Taiwan Relations

Taiwan is important to the PRC for a number of different reasons. First, like Hongkong and ethnic Chinese communities in other Asian nations in Southeast Asia—Singapore is another example—Taiwan is a source of capital for investment in the PRC. Second, like Hongkong (and Macao), Taiwan is a special political target of the PRC. Hongkong was ceded to the British under the Treaty of Nanking following the Manchu dynasty's defeat at the end of the Opium War. (The New Territories on the mainland Kowloon side across the Hongkong harbor were turned over to the British under a 99-year lease that determined the 1997 date of retrocession.)

Therefore the return of Hongkong to Chinese sovereignty has immense sentimental and historical value for many Chinese nationals on both sides of the Taiwan Strait. Hongkong's loss to Great Britain as the latter's probably most prosperous remaining Crown Colony correspondingly has a sentimental and historical value to Britons, because Hongkong probably would not have reached its present world status if it had not been under British administration at the end of World War II in view of the turbulence in China during the Chinese civil war. But for the British political presence and control over Hongkong then, the colony could not have served as a haven for mainland China's businessmen, political dissidents and refugees. This special function of Hongkong to China, as well as to other adjacent Asian lands ever since the second half of the 19th century, resembles that of neutral Switzerland to Europe.

On the other hand, but for the hard-working Chinese and other Asian immigrants and the large inflow of Chinese and non-Chinese entrepreneurs, skilled workers and capital, the Hongkong economy could never have developed into the global economic center and free port that it has become today. As an international financial center, it would not have come into existence but for the combination of mercantile and financial capabilities and wiliness that seem to characterize the British, Chinese and other international financial talents that have congregated there.

Like Hongkong, Taiwan's economic progress during the post-1949 period has been a product of its population's hard work and sacrifice, but a major portion of the population consists of refugees from the Chinese mainland and their offspring who immigrated to the island around 1949 to escape Communist rule. Although the PRC now claims both Hongkong and Taiwan as parts of long lost territories, Taiwan has been under the rule of the Nationalist Republic of China since 1945. Besides, even the Chinese mainland was mostly under the control of the Nationalist government now on Taiwan until 1949.

President Lee Teng-hui of the Republic of China now on Taiwan was elected in a free and contested election to become the first elected president (March 1996) in Chinese history. He won the hard fought election with a 54 percent majority when 70 percent of the eligible voters went to the polls. He had succeeded the late Chiang Ching-kuo in a peaceful and orderly manner as provided by the constitution when Chiang died. Hence for Beijing to claim both Taiwan and Hongkong as its territory purely as historical facts is to ignore some very important political as well as legal issues. Mao Zedong's one-sided declaration at Tiananmen on October 1, 1949 at least should require a popular reconfirmation of a kind that would substantiate a mandate freely given by the people concerned.

Interestingly enough, just as the free elections that have taken place in Taiwan have conferred a special political aura on top of its earlier success in economic development, Hongkong has also instituted a series of colony-wide and local district elections since 1984 to increase the degree of representativeness of its government so that by mid-1997 the last British crown colony in Asia might pass into history as a largely democratic society that is both politically and economically free. This development would make Hongkong a second example of a Chinese community in Asia combining substantial political freedom with economic progress.

Political Obstacles to the Inflow of Hongkong and Taiwan Capital

As a matter of fact, the inflow of capital from Hongkong into China has always been taking place over the years. Subsequent to the initiation of economic reform under Hu Yaobang and Zhao Ziyang, external investments from Taiwan also went into the PRC, at first only indirectly via Hongkong, but later quite openly with official approval after a process of application and registration with the ROC Ministry of Economic Affairs. Both Taiwan and the PRC have also set up their respective intermediary organizations, separate from the respective governments proper, to handle discussions of bi-coastal practical matters. But as of this writing (1996 summer), two sets of disturbing events have occurred that again have given rise to new controversies. They are both political and economic. Let us consider the political issues affecting Hongkong first.

A question that arose early in Hongkong's legal minds had to do with legal standards after 1997 governing civil and criminal cases, rules of procedure, and the appeal process. A crucial point is whether the House of Lords would still be the court of final appeal. Raising such a question actually presupposes that there would be an orderly process through the courts; it also betrays the suspicion harbored by Hongkong's China watchers that *habeas corpus* could be on the way out long before mid-2047 (1997 plus 50 years).

Second, June 4, 1989 turned out to be a watershed in mutual perceptions by the PRC and Hongkong of each other. Hongkong residents watched in dismay the televised massacre at Tiananmen. Spontaneous demonstrations occurred en masse in support of the China demonstrators. Hongkong, by virtue of its geography, has since served as a gateway of many dissidents and their ideas to and from the PRC.

In 1995-96, as the fateful mid-1997 date approached, the PRC took upon itself to announce that the elected legislature of Hongkong would cease to function from July 1, 1997, before the expiration of its term of office, and proceeded to appoint a new provisional assembly to produce a substitute in its place.

In the case of Taiwan, the PRC has concentrated its attack on the alleged inclination of the ROC government under President Lee Teng-hui to aim at establishing a separatist regime, although "Taiwan independence" is actually only a plank of the platform of the Democratic Progressive Party (DPP). Lee is the head of Kuomintang (KMT), a party which transferred its headquarters to the island with Chiang Kai-shek and which has been continually in office in Taiwan since 1949. As mentioned above, Lee is the first popularly elected president of the ROC in China's history. In order to show its grave displeasure and desire to influence the outcome of the election on March 23, 1996, the PLA staged military maneuvers and fired nuclear-capable missiles (with dummy warheads) immediately outside the two principal harbors at both ends of the Taiwan island. These firings had been preceded by staging similar missile tests in August 1995 on target areas more remote from the island itself.

A second event which had the effect of discouraging ordinary visitors to mainland China from Taiwan occurred more than a year before the 1996 election when an entire tour group from Taiwan was robbed and killed at a lake resort in Zhejiang. There were other instances of lack of personal security for Taiwan businessmen on the mainland as well as instances of unreliable treatment of Taiwan investors.

The preceding examples illustrated how it could be rather difficult for Taiwan and Hongkong investors to enjoy both private security of property and personal safety in the PRC. Taiwan businessmen have been pressing for a bilateral agreement on protecting Taiwan investors on the mainland. One wonders, however, how anyone can guarantee that such an agreement on paper can really be enforced or what appeal process will be set up for broken official and personal promises.

Two additional puzzles need to be solved concerning the PRC's economic diplomacy. First, can the PRC really and truly understand what it takes to keep both Taiwan and Hongkong economically viable so that they in turn will be positive and willing contributors to the mainland's development? Second, can those conditions be maintained? Let's look at some of these conditions one by one.

III. PRIVACY, ECONOMIC FREEDOM AND INSTITUTION-BUILDING

Privacy and an International Financial Center

Let us consider for a moment what a private businessman in a highly competitive market and ruled by a government he does not fully trust would most value in the banking institution he deals with. He probably would want most to see that the bank was absolutely discreet, a discreetness that would guarantee him privacy in regard to all his transactions involving the bank. He would like to keep knowledge about his transactions entirely to himself, away from the eyes of "third parties." The "third parties" in question would include: (1) government authorities and their agents where the bank is located; (2) those of the businessman's own government and the latter's agents if they are not the same as in (1); (3) other curious third parties. At the same time, this privacy must be accompanied by total trustworthiness demonstrated through experience over a long period of time, reinforced by law and ethical standards in business practice.

In Hongkong's case, businesses as well as individuals will have to operate under incomplete and new legal institutions. Some of the financial institutions and their personnel will be inexperienced in the manner in which rules on privacy are to be observed. Many "third parties" may be actively attempting to undermine such new privacy concepts as might exist, because the PRC authorities are themselves unfamiliar with these concepts and, even more, because agents serving different masters in the PRC, not to mention still others unconnected with the PRC, could also be operating in the area.

Given these conditions, would it be too surprising if financial transactions are steered away from Hongkong once whispers of inappropriate acts breaching privacy begin to be bruited?

Total Freedom of Movement of People and Communication

Needless to say privacy and security in financial transaction cannot be separated from freedom to travel and freedom of information and communication (electronic and print). Immediately after the signing of the 1982 UK-PRC agreement, there was a sharp increase in the demand for passports and foreign visas that would permit residents (especially former mainland China immigrants) to leave Hongkong for non-Chinese destinations overseas.[10] In 1996, shortly before the expiration of the date at the end of April for Hongkong-born residents to apply for overseas British passports that other countries are expected by the applicants to honor in granting entry visas in the future, there was a spectacular rush for such applications. Fear of tighter control and ad hoc PRC intervention has become a concern in the local and international news media. In earlier years elsewhere, e.g., in Taiwan, national control of radio communication was an obstacle making free private international banking virtually impossible.

Failure to Learn from Europe's Experience in Economic Union

We can easily see how institutional and behavioral differences will inevitably alter the ways in which business in the two areas will operate after a merger. The experience members of the post-World War II European Common Market, a Customs Union, have had in developing a greater degree of economic integration shows how domestic economic instability in any one member country can be transmitted to another. Domestic adjustments to soften the economic impact of one's own economic and/or political instability are painful, which prompts the political leaders of the country in ques-

---

10. For detailed accounts on Hongkong see the *Far Eastern Economic Review*, Hongkong, 1982 *et. seq*. For a short background, see *The Future of Hongkong Toward 1997 and Beyond*, by Hungdah Chiu, Y. C. Jao, and Yuan-li Wu, co-editors (New York: Praeger, 1987).

tion to try to adopt measures to pass on the adverse impact to a neighbor, especially if the neighbor is small and unable to resist. This situation is most likely to occur between Hongkong and the PRC after mid-1997.

A PRC wracked by inflation could seek to reduce prices with legitimate imports from Hongkong. Smuggling from Hongkong could rise illegally. Imports from the outside world could cause the Hongkong currency to depreciate and adversely affect the ability of the Hongkong residents to import for their own use. Or, Hongkong authorities may be instructed to draw down its own exchange reserves, or to engage in economic contraction. Conversely, a free-wheeling Hongkong could act in a manner making an economic policy of stable growth on the mainland more difficult by providing opportunities to subvert laws aimed at curbing uncontrolled free market activities, described by mainland critics as speculative and corrupting influences. One can develop other illustrations.

In order to minimize such disputes, prior discussion and agreement on staged economic integration, proceeding by limited measures over a long period, will be necessary. This is of course the approach members of the European Union have tried to follow. But the PRC does not seem to understand the nature of the problems. It seems to think that one can proceed to solve economic problems by ignoring the need to achieve a basic political understanding first, an understanding on "burdens" and "opportunity-sharing" in a broad sense. In the case of Hongkong, the minimum political understanding was already articulated in the 1982 agreement, but the PRC has since tried to rewrite the agreement unilaterally.

In the case of PRC-Taiwan relations, there seems to be a latent desire on both sides to proceed with developing economic relations while bypassing political issues. However, as the present section has tried to indicate, in the absence of a minimum political understanding to live and let live, "economic integration" can hardly begin beyond watchful trading in goods and services.[11]

Non-Transparency of Business Relations with the PRC

According to the Customs returns of both Hongkong and Taiwan, Taiwan's exports to the PRC rose from US$9.7 billion in 1992,

11. "Toward Union?" by Wang Ping and Yuan-li Wu, unpublished paper, Conference on China's Future Constitution, sponsored by the Foundation for China in the Twenty-first Century, California, 1995.

the year when Deng Xiaoping called for the continuation of "economic openness," to US$17.9 billion in 1995, the last year for which data are now (1996 summer) available. Taiwan's imports from the PRC rose from US$0.75 billion in 1992 to US$3.1 billion in 1995. At first glance, these figures suggest that trade can go on, perhaps even flourish for some businesses, without any prior political agreement satisfactory to both sides. Some readers may wonder whether this implies that economic exchange between Taiwan and the PRC can actually proceed separately from political agreement.

Aside from problems of statistical accuracy and valuation methods, the Taiwan-PRC trade statistics at best can only measure the direction of movement of goods between the two areas and imply the existence of payment obligations. The obligation to pay by one side to another implies that buyers of certain goods and services on one side (e.g., Taiwan) need to pay sellers on the others side (e.g., the PRC), but this is not tantamount to saying that the payers/buyers are necessarily Taiwan nationals or have their abode in Taiwan. The business firms involved could very well be third country-registered firms or citizens and have the diplomatic protection of other countries. During the post-World War II period, ethnic Chinese migration has created numerous multinational firms jointly or individually owned by ethnic Chinese and non-Chinese interests. The result is that the personal loyalty of individuals and businessman has absolutely no bearing on the national distribution of trade or investment by origin or destination. We are in fact confronted with a perfect example of statistical non-transparency, another topic future historians may wish to unravel.

IV. RESTRUCTURING ZHOU ENLAI'S DIPLOMATIC LEGACY?

A Historical Perspective

The panoramic view of the PRC's external relations examined in Chapters IX, X, XI and XII focuses on the restitution of what PRC leaders have thought China rightfully deserved but was taken away by other nations. They have therefore almost unceasingly tried to strengthen the nation's military power and with it the "righting" of "wrongs" inflicted on China by "foreign imperialists." They seem to be constantly afraid that undeserved inequities threaten the country and "unequal treaties" are always lurking around the corner, diminishing the PRC's "territorial integrity," "sovereignty" and "national respect." They demand "equality of treatment" by occasionally, deliberately as it were, denying it to others. PRC diplomats often carry an aura of innocence, humility and reasonableness, alternating with harshness and arrogance.

PRC foreign policy-makers often make their choice among available policy options on the basis of what is feasible, that is, what they can get away with, and what the immediately foregoing historical situation, as perceived by the Party leadership in power, appears to be expedient. Truth and humanity, not to say civility, and good faith be damned. Because of the many years of "revolutionary experience" against stronger foes, seasoned PRC diplomats usually can persevere longer than their counterparts from democratic countries or new nations. Since they usually do not take into account the costs of their policy to those outside the immediate party circles, they quite often can last longer both on the battlefield and at the negotiation table. Their memory too lasts longer and is selective enough to serve their interest.

The above description, however harsh and unflattering, seems to be Zhou's own image of what PRC foreign policy and its diplomats should be. Zhou Enlai implemented the PRC's foreign policy under Mao's overall direction virtually from 1949 to 1974-1975. It was only in the last two to three years of Mao's life that Zhou perhaps had less to worry about Mao's direct intervention. Even in the few years between 1960 and 1965 when Liu Shaoqi and his supporters made the political mistake of trying to sideline Mao—that is, in Mao's eyes—Zhou took great care not to do so and thereby succeeded in surviving the first waves of Mao's attack during the Cultural Revolution.

Dealing with Stalin and the Soviet Union

The first strategic objective of the PRC's foreign policy was to secure as much military equipment and technology—the more advanced, that is, within the PRC's capacity to absorb, the better—as the Soviet Union was able and willing to supply, and as soon as possible. To do so, Mao, Zhou and the others acted toward Stalin as if they genuinely thought Stalin was always the leader of the communist international movement. Through them the PRC appeared more than willing, and even honored, to play second fiddle to Stalin and his Soviet Union. Mao flattered Stalin in particular by asking for ideological guidance—for instance, by sending someone to Beijing who could offer guidance in the editing of Mao's own writings from the point of view of the teachings of Marx, Lenin and Stalin. The PRC leaders showed that they were willing to throw Chinese forces into the Korean War against superior enemy forces even without Soviet air cover in order to obtain all the support, by air and otherwise, and training they thought they could really acquire.

Although the final decision to do so was undoubtedly Mao's, Zhou's execution of this strategy was certainly convincing. The decision to go to the negotiation table in Panmunjom suited both the PRC and the Soviet Union and probably marked the height of Sino-Soviet cooperation. The economic and technical aid the PRC subsequently obtained from Moscow was a concrete reward at a cost paid with Chinese lives.

Both in 1954 and 1958, by instigating the two Taiwan Strait crises, Mao, through Zhou, was hoping to secure some gratuitous gain at the expense of Taiwan and simultaneously testing Soviet and U.S. willingness each to help its Chinese ally at some risk to itself. They received confirmation of probably their independent appraisals that neither was willing to risk war.

In 1962, following the apparent Soviet concession in the Cuban crisis, both Mao and Zhou probably came to the conclusion that the Soviet Union was the weaker of the two superpowers. However, the Soviet Union continued to be the one super-power that could help the PRC build up its military, and the exploitation of Soviet military know-how continued. Apparently the PRC was more successful than the Soviets had thought possible in acquiring nuclear capability. Perhaps the Soviet Union was just not alert enough.

At some point toward the mid-1960s, Mao became aware of the dangers of Soviet military intervention in the face of the mounting ideological quarrels the Maoists had started. Zhou became now the one to design an ideological and political defense by trying to construct a defensive "soft" alliance of Asian-African and, hopefully, Latin-American countries to deter any open military actions against the PRC. It is in this respect that the final phase of Zhou's diplomatic effort was primarily focused.

Characteristics of Zhou Enlai's Diplomacy in the Non-Soviet World

Several outstanding characteristics of Zhou Enlai's approach to foreign policy in dealing with the non-communist countries may be outlined as follows.

It seems that according to Zhou, the primary tactic in dealing with Western countries was to be divisive as regards the United States and others by pointing out: (1) how those countries' self interest really did not coincide with that of the United States; (2) how the PRC's aims were really quite limited (talking about "territorial integrity," "sovereignty" over Taiwan and the like); and, (3) how the PRC and the other countries could really develop much better relations but for the unreasonable, selfish and arrogant superpower behavior of the United States (be it through Dulles or American capitalist interest, or "war mongers" in general). A minimum objective was to improve relations through reducing relations with Taiwan or, in later years, by demanding full diplomatic recognition of the PRC outright (as in the case of Japan in 1972). The same divisive technique was applied to France and the U.K. from the Geneva Conference on. (This is the same tactic in PRC-U.S. trade talks and in diminishing Taiwan's international contacts.)

On various occasions, while talking to revolutionary regimes, Zhou Enlai was not taciturn in advising younger revolutionaries and insurgents on tactics, drawing upon his experience in China. A refrain often repeated was that revolutions should be carried on by stages. A limited demand during negotiations is never the final demand. For most African countries seeking independence his advice was to think in terms of a national democratic revolution first. To speak of land reform and peasant ownership would alienate farm proprietors. To talk of expropriation by workers would frighten the capitalists. Such simple slogans, useful perhaps in doctrine and ideology, would increase the ranks of one's opponents and therefore become self-defeating. He referred to the CCP's experience in talking about a national democratic revolution in Chungking (then still Chongqing), shelving the goal of socialization only after seizing and consolidating political power.[12]

All this explanation on revolution's tactics does, however, raise a question when it comes from a diplomat who espouses *panch sheel*, in talking with Nehru, including the denial of exporting revolution to undermine other nations while at the same time promoting the sale of arms and weapons technology to rogue states and insurgents in Asia, Africa, Latin America and the Middle East. In the 1990s, the PRC has continued to export sophisticated weapons and nuclear technology. If what one will say or do tomorrow may directly contradict what one promises today, what is the value of today's promise or agreement to others? Even from the PRC's purely selfish point of view, such a policy that is based purely on short-term expediency may soon run out of usefulness, that is, unless of course one or more of the following few conditions prevail: (1) the opponent is downright stupid; (2) he has a very short mem-

12. See Chapter II above.

ory; (3) he is unaware of the PRC's record and does not know the facts. (The facts will be covered up and obscured. Herein lies the advantage of "non-transparency."); or, (4) his real interest is not involved; the victim is a third party!

Zhou Enlai views diplomacy as a part of warfare, of political struggle. When he was in Chungking during the war with Japan, he was recruiting for the CCP. He could not but be aware of what would happen later to some of those he successfully recruited, during the Anti-Rightist movement when forced labor (*laogai*) camps were filled, or during the Cultural Revolution, or during other numerous purges and drives. Of the PRC, Mao and the PRC's foreign policy, the French writer and philosopher André Malraux said to Mr. Nixon in 1972 before the President's departure for China: "China's foreign policy is a brilliant lie . . . . The Chinese . . . believe only in China. Only in China!"[13] However, one might add, "China," as leaders like Mao and Zhou see it, has no meaning. It has no permanence, no absolute value, only a day-to-day transient identity. "I the leader am China" is what a Chinese Communist leader in effect says.

In 1996, Zhou Enlai is long gone. But the Mao-Zhou diplomacy lingers on. Is a restructuring possible? Is a restructuring not necessary?

---

13. Richard Nixon, *The Memoirs of Richard Nixon* (New York: Gosset and Dunlap, 1978), p. 557.

CHAPTER XIII

CHARACTER AND BEHAVIOR: COMMUNIST OR CHINESE?

I. WHAT KIND OF PEOPLE WERE THE COMMUNIST LEADERS?

Characteristics of the Top Leadership and CCP Followers

China has changed in many ways during the half century after World War II. However, in 1996, no fewer problems exist and seem to defy solution than before. Although the portrait of the PRC's founding father Mao Zedong still hangs over Tiananmen, the historical Avenue of Perpetual Peace must now share its vista with popular American eateries bearing the names of non-Chinese, private entrepreneurs. While the government office that gave McDonald's and Kentucky Fried Chicken their licenses to open shop may have thought of their presence as symbols of post-Mao openness or "glasnost," students of contemporary Chinese history may instead be struck by a surprising degree of incongruence.[1]

Mao Zedong was born into a farm family in 1893. As a teenager working on his father's farm, he was already a rebel. With relatively little formal education, he entered a teachers' training institute in Hunan, graduating at the age of 24. Through a favorite teacher in Hunan who had joined the faculty of the University of Peking in 1918, Mao found employment as an assistant at the university library.[2] His assiduous reading in Chinese history of rebellions and dynastic statecraft, later continued in the former imperial quarters of Zhongnanhai, probably gave Mao the background to rival any tyrant in Chinese history or any scholar of Chinese imperial dynasties and Machiavellian politics.

At the end of World War I, when many young Chinese went to France in a work-study program, including a large number of the

---

1. One may well wonder whether a combination of the post-Mao brand of authoritarianism and semi-market economy is represented here. Perhaps this is "communism Chinese style," for lack of a better expression.

2. See Kao I-ko, *Mao Tse-tung yü Chou En-lai* [*Mao Zedong and Zhou Enlai*] (Taipei: K'oning Publishers, 1993), pp. 11-13.

CCP's "first generation" leaders, Mao reportedly gave up an opportunity to join them.[3] Already known then through his journalistic efforts, Mao stayed with his chosen activity in organizing the rural unemployed and writing on changing China. His ineptitude in any foreign language may have been another consideration. His theory of peasant revolution through the artificial classification of classes and violent class struggle was a product of this period.

Historically, a Chinese person who went through recognized examinations administered by the state and was awarded the appropriate scholastic titles would become a candidate for appointment to government office. Even in present-day China the entry level of employment is often affected, if not determined, by the highest academic degree earned by the applicant if the person is not otherwise disqualified. Not possessing such a recognized rank at his time, Mao was excluded from the group of rank-conscious "intellectuals." Mao also was not a "returned student" from the ranks of the radical students from abroad. Many communists were inducted into the party in the Soviet Union or in Western Europe after World War I. Whether or not Mao was in fact discriminated against for this reason, it would be quite plausible if he himself had this suspicion.

Mao, therefore, was a "marginal man,"[4] both as an intellectual and a communist revolutionary. In his own eyes, he was probably an unrecognized prophet of his time. However, inasmuch as he was successful, he could later afford to treat those who might have looked upon themselves as his betters quite poorly (Guo Moruo was a singular exception of renown). One wonders whether this warped psychology at least in part explains Mao's contempt for the traditional Chinese intellectual.

It can be argued that a revolutionary leader who defies the existing social and political order, as well as its institutions and representative individuals, tends to be a marginal person who is excluded in fact or in his own imagination from groups of importance to which his belonging should have been a birthright. Conversely, such a marginal person already possesses some of the necessary characteristics of a rebel. But there are other prerequisites, for the person

---

3. There are a number of biographical studies on Mao, among which one Ph.D. thesis by Esther Kuo entitled *Mao Tse-tung as a Political Leader* (Eugene, OR: University of Oregon, unpublished edition) is especially worth reading.

4. On the marginalization of Chinese intellectuals, see Yü Ying-shih, "Chung-kuo Chih-shih Fen-tze ti Pienyuan-hua" [The Marginalization of Chinese Intellectuals] in *Erh-shih-i Shih-chi* [*The Twenty-first Century*] (Hongkong: The Chinese University, November, 1991), pp. 16-25.

might otherwise simply end up as an outcast. The potential revolutionary leader must also be able to command a large enough following to constitute a dedicated and weighty opposition to the established order. If the established authority is weak, or is inept in the use of force, even a poorly armed rebellion can go a long way. Otherwise, foreign help will be needed. In the CCP case, conscious and deliberate aid was extended from the Soviet Union, albeit not without great hesitation at times. Elsewhere, as in the West, assistance was more indirect and often unwittingly provided.

Although he had many able and educated assistants, Mao's mass support came first from the poor and unemployed peasants. His personal participation in peasant revolts dated back to 1927 and earlier when he was a young man in the early 30s. In the initial period of the CCP, he was unlike his competitors who were largely young intellectuals drawn to the Communist Party while abroad or were academics of urban origin. They tended to focus on urban workers and to concentrate on activities against the traditional order in cities, where the establishment was stronger. In urban centers there were foreign concessions under non-Chinese control and additional alien police forces to contend with. Mao's experience in guerrilla war in the countryside thus gave him a better chance to reach the top, surviving the series of Nationalist campaigns from the time the ROC government was firmly established in Nanking in 1927 to the Sian Incident in 1936 on the eve of the pre-World War II Japanese invasion, which was discussed at the beginning of this book.

If the revolutionary leader is a "marginal man" who thinks the existing order must be overthrown, he will not be in favor of incremental reform. He will not be burdened by psychological and conventional barriers which must first be crossed. This is why the series of mass movements from "land reform" to the "Great Proletarian Revolution" were so ruthless, inhuman and thoroughgoing that they deliberately tried to erase pre-PRC institutions—not just the non-Communist political and social opposition, but also all pre-PRC values, traditions, and cultural traits that offended Mao. Yet, in the end, like Hung Hsiu Ch'uan, Mao too fell victim to the imperial delusions of traditional China.

Why Did the Followers Support Such a Leader?

Mao and others who led Chinese peasants in armed revolts against Nationalist government forces in the 1930s and in wartime and post-World War II China, as well as against local warlord-type regimes only nominally under the central government, probably should be regarded more as individual groups of desperate peasants in revolt rather than a unified force of armed opposition tightly bound by ideology. The desire to take up arms against Japan and a conviction that the Nationalist government was unwilling or unable to do so was in many cases the primary reason why young men and women, many of them students, went to Yanan or other guerrilla areas to join the Communists. This popular conviction was partly inflamed by CCP recruiting propaganda.

In the late 1930s and early 1940s, as the war dragged on and inflation and shortages worsened, the supporters of the war effort and the Nationalists became progressively more disheartened. The CCP under Mao with the able assistance of Zhou Enlai and their lieutenants, who were then ensconced in Chungking itself as CCP representatives, succeeded in expanding its own following. The party heavily camouflaged its ultimate goals, while preparing itself for the post-World War II national drive to power, as we first described in Chapter II.

In short, Mao attracted his followers from different population groups, in addition to the very poor peasants, who joined him or other operating communist cell clusters in successive periods from, let us say, the Sian Incident (1936) to 1949 for a variety of reasons. During the pre-Sian Incident period, the core of the armed opposition probably consisted of Mao's ragtag peasant army, plus provincial forces driven out of Manchuria by the Japanese, and "returned" cadres inducted in Moscow and Western European countries, many from the original work-study group, or, like Chi Ch'ao-ting, from the United States. Among them notably were Zhou Enlai and Deng Xiaoping, who became best known in the West only in more recent years. There were a number of military men who later played key roles in the PRC's accelerated drive to develop modern weaponry, including the atomic bomb, such as Marshal Nie Rongzhen, who was Zhou's contemporary in Europe and also a Whampoa Military Academy man.

In the "pre-Sian Incident" period, when active guerrilla warfare was the principal method of survival and continuing operation, including base building, the peasant army recruited with the help of violent "land reform" was a product of Mao's ideology in practice. For Mao's brand of class warfare in land redistribution was simply unrestrained violence. This would be entirely in conformity with the idea of total social restructuring by a marginal-man type leader devoid of all inhibition and regard for existing institutions and mores.

Later, during the early 1940s and in Chungking and other Nationalist controlled areas, Zhou was to head the effort of recruiting sympathizers, many of whom still later joined the pilgrimage from Hongkong to the CCP headquarters near Shijiazhuang. Mao had toned down his earlier ideas to the level of "new democracy" and "coalition government." This Chungking episode was in a sense a trial run for Zhou Enlai's "reasonable," "moderate," and analytical but nonetheless Machiavellian approach in diplomacy which he later practiced in person at Nanking in 1947 and at Geneva, Bandung and Zhongnanhai from 1954 to 1972.

Supporting Mao to the End—Why?

Among Mao's very able aides and steadfast—outwardly at any rate—supporters were technocrats. One would hazard a guess that they were nationalists, possibly chauvinists who wanted to be a party to the open eradication of the humiliation of military defeats suffered in foreign hands from the mid-19th century on. They wanted to be personally involved in building China's military power to a status second to none, as we have mentioned from the very beginning of this book. Within this broad category of technocrats, a small group of scientists and engineers in the early period of communist rule was trained in Western countries during and toward the end of World War II. Others studied later in the Soviet Union when Sino-Soviet relations were friendly. Their numbers were greatly augmented in conjunction with the drive under Nie Rongzhen for the weapons and related industrial development program.

Outside the military sector, a managerial group including party "elders" like Chen Yun and Li Fuchun were also trained in Soviet methods of economic planning and management. After the collapse of the Soviet Union in 1991, we have seen to what extent the Soviet economy was mismanaged. We can understand how few good enterprise managers and economists the PRC was really able to develop from 1949 to 1973 with Soviet help. It was only when institutions of higher education were reopened after the "Cultural Revolution" and when Western educated individuals began to return after the U.S. diplomatic recognition of the PRC in the 1970s that things began to change.

A third group of persons responsible for Mao's long tenure in Zhongnanhai was the Party cell organizations at the grass root (including the committees controlling and informing on urban households) woven into the police, intelligence and security systems whose heads had assistance and support from corresponding Soviet organizations.[5]

The methods of social control employed by Mao to consolidate political power, as explained in the first part of this volume, owed their success to two factors: (1) The employment of mass movements each directed at a separate target group constituted a comprehensive network hard for individuals in different targeted groups simultaneously to escape; and (2) the use of unconventional, utterly ruthless, uninhibited methods, which many thought unbelievable at the beginning, and were therefore utterly taken by surprise. Implementation of these two groups of policies one after another during 1949-57[6] made armed opposition very hard to organize soon after 1950. Unarmed opposition by intellectuals and the more educated strata was wiped out by the end of 1957 with the suppression (including physical liquidation) of "rightists" and the aid of ubiquitous forced labor camps. These controls were especially effective against non-communists who had no previous experience of how the CCP operated.

Reluctance and Delay of the Potential Opposition

It was not always possible to oppose Mao's armed supporters and party cadres once an official campaign had begun because of the progressively tightening control network and its ruthlessness. But sporadic revolts definitely occurred when the collectivization and communization campaigns began, according to escapees. On the whole, however, why was Mao able to manipulate the CCP for so long? This question has to be answered.

First, when the Chinese population became dissatisfied with the wartime and post-World War II conditions of the country and the CCP offered an apparently plausible future, the people were too eager to believe and asked too few questions.

Second, once power was in the CCP's hands, individuals who might not actually believe what they were told would go along with the authorities because they were reluctant to oppose authority as a matter of habit. They still sought favor from their bosses, more power, some material benefits, perhaps just a slightly better life.

---

5. A number of books have appeared on the PRC's intelligence system in recent years. See, for instance, John Byron and Robert Pack, *The Claws of the Dragon* (New York: Simon and Schuster, 1993).

6. See Yuan-li Wu (ed.) *et al.*, *Human Rights in the People's Republic of China* (Boulders, Co.: Westview Press, 1988).

Above all, the people had been thoroughly disarmed and cowed. The real activists had been eliminated in one way or another. Many potential ones had been placed in forced labor camps.

Third, even among those who were sure that the party or even Mao was wrong, they might have preferred to be silent so as not to be an early victim. By means of delay one might be lucky enough to avoid a greater misfortune.

Finally, there were those who did not know that there was a better way than what they were told or who really did not understand the difference. Of course, they would continue to go along with the party as long as there existed enough supporters in its armed contingents to enforce the party's will.

It would seem that there were enough people in the preceding categories who have continued to keep Mao's successors in power even after the Tiananmen massacre of student demonstrators and civilians.

II. A COSTLY DICTATORSHIP

A Path to Dictatorship and the Cost of Corruption

Given the delayed reaction of a target group to the particular set of repressive measures aimed at it, a consequence was the progressive tightening of Mao's control and the concomitant expansion and consolidation of his power. For a time at least, the logic of this progression was even greater difficulty for anyone who tried to oppose him. As a result, the number of sycophants and hangers-on in the CCP would increase; their only role was to sing the Chairman's praise. This phenomenon by itself would again strengthen the Chairman's own conviction, as it would most other dictators long in power, that indeed he could do no wrong. This made him shun advice that might contradict his preconceptions. In passing, we should give Mao credit that he seemed able to reexamine his own mistakes from time to time even though he could not suffer being told by anyone else that he could be wrong without every well-meant advice being given a malicious intent and treated as a sign of conspiracy.

By eliminating actual and potential opponents one by one, Mao as the all-powerful CCP Chairman found himself really alone, with no one left worthy in his eyes of eventually succeeding him, given his own mortality. The last one was Lin Biao, who either very conveniently died after the failure of a plot against Mao or was killed on Mao's orders.[7] Lin, whose position in the PLA led to his selection to control the youthful Red Guards who through the Cultural Revolution provided the last mass movement Mao employed against his former colleagues in the CCP, was the opponent who could have successfully turned against him.

At this point one should not overlook two historically characteristic features of the Mao regime that really are more lasting than the Mao dictatorship. First, there was the megalomania of Mao, the personality cult, and after Mao the search for a substitute to a personified national pride. Second, there was no natural process of political succession when a dictator or even a mere Chairman of the CCP was to leave for good as "paramount leader".

From a Modern Genghis Khan to Demi-God

Mao Zedong was an accomplished writer of classical Chinese poetry and, as we mentioned in Chapter III, occasionally chose to express himself through this literary medium. One of these verses was reportedly penned in February 1936, the year of the Sian Incident before the outbreak of the Japanese invasion in July 1937 and the CCP agreement with the Nationalists jointly to resist Japan. Another poem deserving special mention was penned by Mao in April 1949 after the PLA's capture of Nanking and less than half a year before Mao was to declare the inauguration of the PRC at Tiananmen. One should call the reader's attention to both verses because as a poet Mao was less reserved in revealing his true emotions.

Let us repeat here what we first mentioned in Chapter III.

In the 1936 verse Mao talked about some of the exceptional emperors in Chinese history but did not regard any of them as worthy of standing at the pinnacle of the Chinese Olympus. Neither the First Emperor of the Chin Dynasty who conquered the six warring independent states and unified the then much smaller China nor Wu Ti of the Han Dynasty who extended Chinese influence westward toward central Asia could, in Mao's mind, really compared with him. Mao even looked down upon Genghis Khan, who reached as far as Central Europe, for Genghis was really handicapped by a very limited range of capabilities. Mao said then quite clearly that the mountain top still awaited the coming of the true hero.

---

7. See Chapters III and VI *supra*.

Mao's 1949 poem was very explicit in another way. He swore that he would not pause after the seizure of Nanking but would continue to pursue "the tottering foe." Thus crossing the Taiwan Strait was to be included in his plans. These plans then had no place for a peace of compromise and stability.

Although the cult of personality was a device promoted by Lin Biao to curry Mao's favor, it was one far from being frowned upon by Mao himself. By the time Mao felt compelled to turn on his long-time comrades, both he and his radical supporters (loosely speaking, the Gang of Four faction), Mao found, were incapable of mobilizing the masses working through the Party bureaucracy. He was compelled to fall back on the Red Guards because of their emotional immaturity and ignorance. Like the Boxers of the Manchu period when they were mobilized through superstitious groups, the teenagers and young adults were mobilized really in a like manner, by promoting Mao as a demi-god, with chanting and recitation of meaningless praises of Mao. The "personality-cult" was literally a new "folk religion" which promoted Mao to a demi-god and anyone Mao anointed to a lower-level deity.

The semi-superstitious dictatorship created in this manner gave Mao, the guerrilla-rebel turned demi-god, all the earthly goods, material benefits and honors, making him an emperor of a dynasty for one generation. Lord Acton's axiom that power corrupts and that absolute power corrupts absolutely remains true but became an incomplete description of the Mao dynasty. The Mao regime did develop into a dictatorship in his life time. As we have already speculated in Chapter VIII, it might yet metamorphose into another dictatorship of a different stripe. But the Mao "dynasty" had no way of creating a process of succession by inheritance. There was no politically acceptable process to select a real successor. (The same lack is apparent in the 1990s on the threshold of the post-Deng Xiaoping period.)

Guo Moruo's Advice to a Rebel-Turned-Emperor

One revealing incident might cast light on Mao and through him on both the continuity of Chinese culture and its violent historical changes by fits and starts. Mao tried to change the Chinese person and Chinese culture certainly. He was not entirely successful even in changing himself. But the PRC after Mao was certainly unlike the PRC before 1949 or before Mao's death in 1976. The following events should be related in this connection.

Guo Moruo, historian, essayist and poet who became head of the PRC's Academy of Sciences in 1949 and simultaneously director of its Social Science Division, was one of the few intellectuals who retained Mao's high regard through the decades.[8] Guo published in Shanghai in October 1945 a monograph to commemorate the third century of the fall of the Ming Dynasty and the entry of the troops of Li Zicheng into Peking, which led to the suicide of the reigning Ming emperor and the subsequent conquest by the Manchu troops of all China. Guo's story described the very short duration of Li's tenure in Peking and his subsequent defeat by the former Ming general, Wu Sangui, who had defected to the Manchus. Guo attributed Li's fiasco to allowing his chief aides to go wild on wine, women, looting and collection of money in the capital after the unexpectedly easy victory over the dispirited Ming troops who were supposed to be defending the city while Wu's main Ming forces were in the front at Shanhaiguan, fending off the Manchu columns.

A second reason for Li Zichen's fiasco was his failure to induce the Ming's main strength to come to terms with him through General Wu. Instead, one of Li's generals had seized Wu's old father as well as Wu's girl friend. The result was the Ming general's defection leading to the establishment in China of an alien dynasty.

The Guo Moruo monograph was interpreted by part of the press after its first appearance in 1944 as a satire on Chiang Kai-shek. However, although Mao always compared his own farm rebel origin to that of Li Zichen, Chiang was in 1944 by no means in such straits as the Ming emperor. It so happens that the Guo tract went into a second printing in March 1946 in Peking and at least the new version presumably was read by Mao. Mao apparently accepted the advice Guo proffered through his monograph and the cities of Beijing and Tianjin were treated in the manner suggested but rejected by the rebel leader three centuries earlier. However, Mao continued to seek the destruction of the KMT enemy under Chiang thereafter.

In his original story, Guo Moruo noted that the rebel leader could have been "feasting on dog-meat stew" in the palace instead of fleeing for his life had he followed the advice to seek a peaceful settlement with General Wu. The phrase "feasting on dog meat" was a reference to a Chinese parable of a hunter killing his hunting

---

8. See Guo Moruo, *Jiasheng Sanbainian Ji* [*In Commemoration of 1664*] (Beijing and Shanghai: Wild Grass Press, 1946).

dog for stew after the hare was killed, for the hound had served its purpose[9]. Mao did finally turn on his partners in revolution during the Cultural Revolution, but the slaughter was not scheduled for the first part of the reign. Nevertheless Mao's behavior resembled that of a Chinese emperor more than many would have thought possible.

Deng Xiaoping's Own Succession and Its Social Implication

If an "heir to the throne" cannot be automatically identified, for instance, through inheritance, the second-generation chief must win recognition on his own merit or he must indirectly owe his position to those who finally choose to support him. This merely moves the chain of reasoning one step further—to the source of power and authority of Caesar's electors and to the rewards expected and received by the latter. To put it differently, if a hereditary communist dictatorship is a contradiction in terms, would a group of large power-holders, i.e., modern warlords and holders of non-military fiefdoms that constitute a modified oligarchy, be a viable alternative in the post-Deng period? In this respect, would the end of Chinese communism be a Chinese plutocracy, with concentrations of power and wealth? Or would it finally evolve into a fascist state?

We must next look at the hundreds of millions of other Chinese on the lower levels of the pyramid.

III. HOW TO CHOOSE WISELY?

Questions about the Chinese Character[10]

Questions about Chinese communist leaders, their aides, their followers and members of the general public in the PRC who sim-

---

9. *Id.*, p. 28.

10. For a review of Max Weber's basic principles on the role of the Protestant ethic in the development of capitalism in the West, readers more at home in English should read Talcott Parsons's translation of Max Weber, *The Protestant Ethic and the Spirit of Capitalism* (New York: Charles Scribner, 1930; 1st British edition by George Allen & Unwin, 1930). R. H. Tawney's Foreword to this edition raises certain issues that deserve thoughtful contemplation, especially because Tawney was later author of *Land and Labor in China* (New York: Octagon Books, 1964) which deals directly with our topic in this study. One might note here on the side that "the spirit of capitalism" and the "capitalist spirit" may be interpreted quite differently in Weber's works. In this respect Tawney and Weber may present such a difference. See Hisao Otsuka, *The Spirit of Capitalism* (Tokyo: Iwanmi Shoten, 1982), translated by Masaomi Kondo. Weber's *The Religion of China, Confucianism and Taoism*, translated by Hans H. Gerth (New York: The Free Press, 1951), focuses on the Chinese aspect. The *Introduction* to this volume by an eminent Chinese sociologist, C. K. Yang, adds a great deal of the research

ply went along with the more vocal ones almost inexorably lead to queries about the character of the Chinese. Some of the same questions have also been raised by those who study Chinese history and are therefore applicable to all persons subject to the influence of Chinese culture, by no means limited to the residents of mainland China.

1. Do Chinese put a lower value on human life? Mao certainly seemed indifferent to human life. He clearly exhibited this characteristic during the Korean War (1951-53), the Great Leap (1958-60), and the Cultural Revolution (especially 1967-68) not to mention the pre-1945 and the 1947-50 years of the revolutionary war and post-World War II Civil War years. This characteristic was shared by many of Mao's followers, albeit no doubt in varying degrees.

2. In this connection, CCP leaders, in facing critics of the PRC's human rights record, have often claimed that because of the country's poverty, its population was more concerned about having enough food than enjoying personal freedom, or even political and economic freedom. The argument is plausible but it is at variance with the position of those who deny that Chinese in general have little value for life as such.

3. Do the Chinese tend to obey authority without question? Mao always challenged authority but always wanted others to bow to his. If we treat Mao as an exception, because he was, in his own words, born to rule, we need to deal with the special issue presented by Mao later. In general, however, questions 1 and 2 can be reconciled by saying that while Chinese as a whole value life no less than non-Chinese, Chinese are more likely to obey authority and the authority could fail to value life. In this case, the original questions (1 & 2) evolve into a different one; namely, is a government made up by Chinese more likely to be indifferent to human life by virtue of the influence of Chinese culture?

4. Some students of Chinese history think that Chinese intellectuals in general tend to emphasize an individual's obligation to the collective, especially the state, and place too little emphasis on a person's own rights to pursue his or her own ends. As a result, the concept of inherent human rights of the individual is sometimes ignored. Furthermore, because the individual's rights can be ignored, they are in fact ignored. Thus, in Chinese history, the individual

---

findings subsequent to Weber's original path-breaking work and is analytically useful as a systematic guide. For more reference on later works see Yü Ying-shih and others in the Notes below.

Chinese intellectual sought to accommodate himself to the outside environment. He did not automatically fight back to assert his rights. While in the long run, such accommodation enabled him to survive, engaging as well as he could in "self-cultivation," the concept of "human rights" is alien to the PRC political tradition, nor are they a part of the pre-Communist Chinese tradition. Non-resistance and accommodation encouraged aggression and even became a deterrent to economic advance. Ironically, survival over long periods of time may also have been made easier.

5. Perhaps the last point could be the plus side; that is, life at bare subsistence can be guaranteed! To repeat, being extremely adaptable and surviving on very little, China time and again managed to survive before it was extinguished by its conquerors who themselves were then corrupted by the Chinese and eventually overthrown by others or by a new generation of Chinese. But lacking the pressure to compete and to innovate was too often the negative force that aborted growth and innovation after reaching a plateau of development.

6. Critics of the Chinese character also say that the average Chinese is too self-centered to extend a hand to another person in need. This is tantamount to repeating a criticism made famous by Sun Yat-sen, founder of the KMT, in his lectures on the Three Principles: that Chinese are like loose grains of sand that never can coalesce to form a solid mass.

7. Western sociologists interested in tracing the human motivation of the development of American and other Western societies have identified Protestant ethic as the inner drive in Western development. Lacking such could help explain the Chinese failure in modernizing industry and commerce. By the same token, Confucianism is blamed for its conservative emphasis on harmony, fear of social destabilization and aversion to enterprise and change.

A Problem of Multiple Dimensions

The more one reads and thinks about the Chinese character, Chinese culture, and Chinese history, the more one becomes uncertain about a cure-all for China's malaise. To the author, a theory of history for China would probably be too simplistic, however elegant. If one looks carefully for concrete cases and in the works of Chinese thinkers over the five thousand plus years, for every feature attributed to the Chinese character as a factor retarding development, one can find another that could in the same time frame have had the opposite effect. As we have seen in this volume, it is a combination of these factors, some interrelated, causally and in time, some totally coincidental and exogenous, that have brought about the Communist episode of the past fifty years.

The Idealized Chinese Character

When we speak of the character of the average Chinese in a general way, we can compare it to what Chinese intellectuals regarded as the idealized personality before Mao's persistent social and psychological engineering after 1949. This is the Confucian *junzi* (*chün-tze*) whom one should strive to be like. Under present circumstances in the PRC we would be at a loss for an answer if we had to come up with a corresponding ideal. But for traditional China, the image of the idealized character, *junzi*, is to all intents and purposes a composite personality characterized by Confucians over many centuries. The particular behavioral features can be gleaned more or less as follows:

1. *Treating all other persons as one would like to be treated oneself by others.* This is essentially the golden rule. It is almost the same both in the Western formulation and in Confucian teaching: "do unto others as you would like others to do unto you" or in the negative form, "do not do unto others as you would not like others to do unto you." These alternative formulations can be found in Ivanhoe's introductory lectures[11] on Confucian "self-cultivation." A more detailed discourse is available to Chinese language readers in Yü Ying-shih's *Modern Explanation of Traditional Chinese Thought.*[12] For those who wish to delve more deeply, an earlier

---

11. There do not seem to be many easily accessible works on Dai Zhen (Tai Chen) in English. Philip J. Ivanhoe's *Confucian Moral Self Cultivation* (New York: Peter Lang, 1993) in the Rockwell Lecture Series, Vol. 3, does contain a short section on Dai, apart from source references in footnotes. See also Liang Ch'i-ch'ao, *Ching-tai Hsüeh-shu Kai-lun* [*A General Treatise on Ch'ing Dynasty Philosophical Studies*], (Shanghai: Commercial Press, 1921). To this author, Hu Shih's volume (in Chinese), *Tai Tung-yüan ti Che-Hsüeh* (Taipei: Commercial Press, 1967) contains a very full historical account of the development of Tai's multi-dimensional thought and includes the original texts of both *Yuan Shan* and the explanatory commentary on Mencius, *Mengtse Tz'e-yi Shucheng*. Readers should note that Tai Chen and Dai Zhen are respectively Wade-Giles and Pinyin transliterations of the same mid-18th century Confucian philosopher-philologist. Tai Tung-yüan was simply Tai's pen name which Hu Shih used in his book, published by the veteran Chinese Commercial Press in its Everyman's Library Series only in 1967.

12. Yü Ying-shih's *Chung-kuo Sse-hsiang Ch'uan-t'ung ti Hsien-tai Ch'üan-shih* [*Modern Explanation of the Tradition of Chinese Thought*] (Taipei: Lienching Publishers, 1987, 2nd edition), consists of a collection of his writings in addition to a substantive introduction. It should be consulted for many facets of China's intellectual history. For

study by the scholar and former ROC ambassador to the United States, Hu Shih, provides a full treatment of the works of Tai Chen (Dai Zhen in Ivanhoe) whom Ivanhoe also quoted without elaboration beyond mentioning the essence of the golden rule above.

Tai Chen, a philosopher as well as philologist, lived in the 18th century (1724-76). Hu Shih's study on Tai was based on the latter's two principal works, a detailed study of Mencius (372-289 B.C.) reinterpreting the latter's thought, drawing on his painstaking philological research, and a summary of Tai's philosophy of human nature, entitled *Yuan Shan* [*The Origin of Goodness*], based largely on Mencius, probably the most energetic and well-known classical Chinese philosopher and teacher after Confucius. In giving the dates of these various thinkers, we point to the historical origins of the altruistic aspects of humanistic thought long before the appearance of Mao's regime in mainland China and the closeness of certain classical Chinese thought to that of the West. Tai Chen's works were written in the mid-18th century. Corresponding to that time period in the West were the American and French Revolutions and the flowering of Western liberal ideas. Hu Shih's Tai Chen study was first drafted in 1934 and completed on August 13, 1936. It was exactly a year later (August 13, 1937) that the first Japanese bombs fell in the Shanghai theater of the Sino-Japanese war, the prelude of World War II in Asia, heralding the developments that made the final emergence of the Communist Chinese regime possible. Yu Ying-shih's 1976 and 1987 studies which China scholars should also read would bring us even closer to the results of contemporary research.

2. *Philosophical distortions of Confucian ideas, rights and obligations.* One feature of Confucianism is the distinct emphasis on interpersonal relationships: the five cardinal relationships of: monarch-subject; father-son; husband-wife; brother-brother; friend-friend. Each one of a pair owes the other an appropriate degree of loyalty, respect, trust and compassion, all of which are derived from human love. Two points inherent in this enumeration are too often forgotten and the result can be a gross distortion, some may say abuse.

---

the purpose of this chapter, four pieces, dealing respectively with Chinese concepts of life after death, the idealized Chinese *chüntze*, Buddhist and Taoist concepts, and the thoughts of Hu Shih are especially instructive. In addition, readers should read Yü's 1976 book, *Lun Tai Chen yü Chang Hsüeh-ch'eng* [*On Tai Chen and Chang Hsüeh-ch'eng*] (Hongkong: Lungmen Book Company, 1976).

First, the mutuality of these individual relationships is in fact always implied. One person's feeling for his sibling invariably implies the reciprocal feeling of the sibling for the first person. The citizen's loyalty to the state (the monarch of Confucius' time) coexists only with the obligation reciprocated by the state toward the citizen. Mencius was totally outspoken in his reply to King Hsüan of Ch'i about the banishment of the last emperor, Chieh, of the Hsia Dynasty and the overthrow of tyrant Tchou of the Shang Dynasty by Chou. According to Mencius, "He who mutilates benevolence is a mutilator, he who cripples rightness is a crippler; and a man who is both a mutilator and a crippler is an 'outcast.' I have indeed heard of the punishment of the outcast Tchou, but I have not heard of any regicide." If Mencius were alive today, his comment on Mao's many acts in China, from Jingangshan to 1976 (not as early as 1957), and on the Tiananmen massacres would scarcely have stopped at a call for the rehabilitation of political scapegoats![13]

If we follow Tai Chen, the satisfaction of human desires forms the basis of proper human action—that is, in determining whether any particular action would be right or wrong. Unlike the teaching of Buddhism, Confucianism does not demand the denial of human pleasure. Hence the state owes the citizen what in the latter's human nature the latter seeks, including both material well-being and non-material rights. Rights and obligations always accompany each other. When one asserts one's right vis-à-vis another, one affirms one's own obligation toward the other, which is the other's right vis-à-vis oneself. Thus Confucianism in its true spirit does not condone dictatorship or even an autocratic, abusive parent. Neither loyalty nor parental discipline can be one-sided only.

In his study on Tai Chen in the early 1930s, Hu Shih cited the record of the Manchu emperor Yongzheng's semi-judicial investigation of a high official under indictment, giving the monarch's own opinion and adding other third party reports as proof of the person's guilt. The sovereign's opinion and the trumped-up charges were patently illogical and fanciful reasonings were advanced to coincide with Yongzhen's statement of the same. The accused official was further required to admit his own guilt because Yongzhen's argument was considered invariably correct. Hu gave this case as an example of how a superior position of power was used as a right to

13. The Chinese translation of Mencius is taken from D. C. Lau, *Mencius*, *Chinese Classics: Chinese-English Series* (Hongkong: The Chinese University Press, 1979 and 1989), Book 1, Part B, p. 39.

truth, which was not a rule based on Confucian teaching of proper interpersonal relationships. Mao Zedong's own practice during the Great Leap and the Cultural Revolution represented a parallel case. The same is true for the practice of writing endless confessions, which is essentially a series of self-incriminations.

A second distortion of Confucian ideas is to give them a narrow interpretation overlooking what Confucius did not explicitly state on particular occasions. Several economists and important architects of Taiwan's economic policies responsible for the ROC's successful development in the post-World War II period have lamented the average citizen's seeming unconcern for the social costs of economic activity, lacking a sense of responsibility to persons outside the family or outside one's acquaintance. They have proposed to add another crucial interpersonal relationship to the five enumerated above: stranger-stranger.[14] Such an obligation to strangers, sometimes described as the "sixth crucial interpersonal relationship," is of course already implied in the golden rule ("do unto others. . .").

3. *Need for an inner drive—Weberian and other.* Let us turn once more to the issue raised by some sociologists: The Weberian proposition that China has been without the benefit of an ascetic Protestant ethic as an inner drive to sustain savings and investment for growth through profit-making. However, this assertion has been proven wrong in many instances in the case of Chinese communities as a whole. The experience of whole nations in Southeast Asia—Malaysia, Thailand and Indonesia, in which ethnic Chinese communities form important groups—since the 1970s and especially since the 1980s, has shown this simplified assertion to be untrue.

Taiwan from the mid-1950s on through 1995 for which data are available offers an even more enduring example over the entire thirty-year period (1965-95). South Korea, strongly influenced by both traditional Confucian and Japanese cultures, presents an equally persuasive example against treating an ascetic Protestant

---

14. In this connection, the reader may wish to examine the works of an outspoken popular Taiwan writer and social critic. See Po Yang, *Ch'ou-lou ti Chung-kuo Jen [The Ugly Chinese*] (Taipei: Hsinkuang Publishers, 1992). Several very useful broad and informative references on Chinese culture and the Chinese character have also appeared in recent years. See, for instance, the two volumes on Chinese thought in *Chung-kuo Wen-hua Hsin-lun* [*New Essays on Chinese Culture Series,* Vol. 1, *Idealism and Reality, 1989,* 6th printing; Vol. 2, *The Way of Heaven and the Way of Man*] (Taipei: Liencching Publishers, 1993, 8th printing), edited by Liu Tai and Huang Chun-chieh. See also Yih-yuan Li and Kuo-shu Yang (eds.*), Symposium on the Character of the Chinese, an Interdisciplinary Approach* (Taipei: Academia Sinica, 1973).

ethic as a necessary driving force of capitalistic economic development.

To assert the existence of a widely shared inner drive, for example, *such as a Protestant ethic*, however, would be more convincing for all the countries we have just listed since World War II. For the pre-World War II period, we are of course aware of the Japanese example. The desire to survive in the face of dire external threat—Taiwan and South Korea for example—may have provided a government-induced as well as common, private driving force. Foreign capital investment for exporting local resources (e.g. oil) and manufactures based on cheap local labor may be an alternative force driving economic growth. A forceful, strong-willed dictator like Mao Zedong could provide the same function of depressing consumption in favor of investment. Even a Mao-style hero like Lei Feng conceivably could have performed a similar function to sustain a continuing process of growth.

The preceding comments are not meant to say that Protestant ethic did not play a role in the growth of Western capitalism. What they mean is that there can be other alternative factors capable of producing alternative economic processes. In Mao's case, in spite of his personal strong will and drive, Mao nevertheless failed in his time. An obvious explanation is that other aspects of his policies, economic and other, were wrong. Moreover, in general terms, the inner drive Mao provided did not work conjointly with the inner drives of the self-interest of Mao's masses. In Confucian terms, and according to Tai Chen's humanistic philosophy, Mao failed to touch the human interest and desires of the populace.

Lacking Religious Sanction?

In the absence of any religious belief in heaven and hellfire, and facing uncertainty after death, do Chinese Communists feel completely free of such sanctions? What do the Chinese Communists truly feel? Perhaps some never think about this question. But why have they decided to provide a common resting place for CCP heroes at Babaoshan (the Eight Precious Jewels Mountain)? Why the preservation of Mao's earthly remains at Tiananmen in addition to his mere memory in some people's minds? Or is the Tiananmen Mao memorial the true equivalent of a holocaust museum which we find in the West after World War II?

Folk religions in China do offer both rewards and sanctions in after-life on the basis of what one does in one's life-time. Some genuine Confucians at heart who do not have formal religious affiliations—who do not even practise ancestral worship—may think that living and dying in accordance with true Confucian ethical principles do not need any additional religious confirmation after death. They will be remembered for having lived a good or evil life, which to them may be sanctification or damnation enough.

Under these circumstances, we cannot say much more about the Chinese character and about how to make as sure as possible that interpersonal relationships in China will not lead to chaos in the future except that the rule of law and a generally accepted code of ethics are among the elements most urgently needed in contemporary PRC society.

Some students of Chinese culture seem to believe that the average Chinese character is malleable. That is to say, we are not entirely powerless in influencing human character through education, for example, and the environment in a broad sense. This seems to be the way in which one has to go in China and from outside China.[15] For ethnic Chinese, their special task may be to remember that a true modern Confucian should not be without the spirit of enterprise, including helping others to attain it. For that is a part of "moral self-cultivation." Decisions made by many Chinese both in the CCP and outside will in their turn determine the future course the post-Deng PRC will follow. The external world and physical environment will play a part, even a very large part, in the choices the future Chinese nation will have. But the choice will be made by Chinese themselves. They now stand at the threshold of momentous decisions making. Hopefully, their decisions will be wise.

---

15. See Donald J. Munro, *The Concept of Man in Contemporary China* (Ann Arbor, Michigan: The University of Michigan Press, 1977).

CHAPTER XIV

AGAIN AT THE CROSSROADS: CONCLUSION

Overview (1947-96)

At this stage of our discourse, let us return to the question why the Chinese Communists apparently received a popular mandate in the ancient capital of Imperial China, Beijing, in 1949 to rule the country only to lose it so utterly and openly in just under 40 years. To answer this question, we must be clear on the significance of certain key dates. Although October 1, 1949 was proclaimed by Mao Zedong as the date of birth of the new People's Republic of China, the year 1957 was really the critical year when the CCP and Mao reached the zenith of control over the Chinese mainland. October 1, 1949 was a date when the Tiananmen mass meeting gave Mao a sense of supreme popularity. It also gave a portion of the Chinese populace the thrill of hope and expectancy, but to others it was the beginning of an enormous fear of the unknown. When Mao unleashed the Anti-Rightist Campaign in 1957, Mao and the CCP had finally attained real dominance and revealed their true colors. From that time on, few non-communist fellow travellers of the CCP could in their innermost conscience still give either Mao personally or the party as a group 100 percent unreserved support. What happened thereafter up through Mao's death in 1976 was bound to make the CCP leadership a great deal short of majority backing even within the Communist Party itself.

Deng Xiaoping returned from his last banishment in 1977 and was still in overall command in 1989. He had been pursuing a generally reformist policy since the early 1980s, reversing many Maoist measures; he began to try to cross the swirling waters dividing the unknown terrain of "socialism with Chinese characteristics" from Mao's man-made wilderness. Deng's lack of success outside the agricultural sector in convincing even those in the CCP who had been rescued from the hands of the radicals in the Cultural Revolution's turbulence was evidenced by his having to feed his own handpicked top aides Hu Yaobang and Zhao Ziyang to the wolves, one after the other.

But the reformers themselves were unable to locate all the necessary stepping stones across the torrents let loose by the reform measures. They did not have a well-defined goal. Little wonder they did not know what concrete policies they should adopt. They suffered from the self-inflicted disadvantage of not having participated in the learning process the non-communist world underwent in the post-World War II years on the futility of the centralist economic planning model which they had blindly followed.

Fortunately for mainland China, Deng did not abandon economic reform altogether. However, the CCP's repute after June 4, 1989 was at the lowest ebb because Deng had failed to deliver what many had, one might say unfairly, expected of his reform. After some hesitations and false starts, Deng finally had to embark on his own "imperial inspection" tour to the South (*nanxun*), where economic reform measures had gone farthest. Deng's tour was equivalent to a reaffirmation of economic reform in general. Hence, after mid-1989, from the resumption of reform in late 1992 to this writing (1996), the reformists have had to pick up their unfinished tasks haltingly. Trying desperately to avoid political pitfalls, they have been awaiting the appearance of clearer guideposts, which they hope will somehow come on the scene together with Deng's eventual successor(s) who have not fully come out from the dark corners of the PRC's political stage in their identifiable regalia.

To repeat, the CCP under Mao had by and large completed its task of transforming the mainland Chinese economic and social system into its socialist image. By then, Mao and the CCP had the requisite political clout to remold the Chinese society and economy and thereby to inflict upon the Chinese nation whatever institutional, human and physical reshaping they saw fit. The final phase of violent and chaotic institutional and organizational remolding then took place during the Cultural Revolution, the process not fully ending until the departure of Lin Biao, the Gang of Four and finally Hua Guofeng.

Beginning with Hu Yaobang and Zhao Ziyang, the Deng regime started to try to mend the PRC economic system and society. Their focus, however, was on the economy, but even the narrow economic focus presented a scope they could not at first imagine. It seems that the CCP authorities of the 1980s generation very conveniently did not own up to the fact that it was their own old revolutionary masters under Mao who had destroyed the institutional and organizational structure under which they had secured the position of total power by 1957. Perhaps they did not fully realize that the pre-1949 Chinese political, social and economic institutional and organizational matrix did not permit the successful modernization of China and the simultaneous repulse of Japan's full-scale military invasion of the country.

However, as we examine today the growing reform agenda of the post-1989 Dengists, it is also increasingly clear that the present-day reformers are largely merely retracing many of the developments which had been begun by their non-communist predecessors in the 1920s and 1930s before the Japanese invasion. For instance, the Moganshan meeting (Chapter VIII) listed on its unfinished agenda the conversion of the Soviet-type People's Bank system from one which functioned entirely as the cashier of the government's Treasury and the controller of the State Planning Commission into an agency with the role of an overall monetary policy-maker and watchdog. The pre-1937 non-communist Chinese economy was precisely at the same stage of system development in the monetary and banking arena to which the post-1989 reform program has returned.

To take another example, the establishment of joint state-private corporations in the 1930s to promote industrial production and foreign trade was already intended to be a means of speeding up development with state aid. They were not, however, intended to be forerunners of a drive to turn the entire economy into one of state capitalism. In fact, one of the critical issues to be resolved, if the Sino-Japanese War had been averted, would have been the introduction of policy measures designed to restructure the Chinese market economy so that it would not allow too much growth of state enterprises, and what the CCP then castigated as bureaucratic capital, and to keep a watchful eye on the distribution of wealth and economic power in the course of development. But the war with Japan could not be averted and the Mao dynasty and the Chinese Communist period of absolute statism became China's real history.

As the PRC reaches the end of the first decade after June 1989, it is obviously in a progressively worsening state of gross disparity in income and wealth between coastal and inland areas, between farmers and urban residents, and between those who are politically well-connected and those who are not. Some Chinese who went through the period of the CCP's rise to power, including Qian Jiaju and others (possibly Deng Xiaoping too) who are now in their 70s and older can surely recall the hue and cry against bureaucratic capital, corruption and inflation before and during 1949. Among them a few must realize that the same phenomena have only increased in scale and vehemence after the turmoil of 1989. A few members of the old pre-1937 generation may even detect many resemblances to the hopes as well as discontent of those days. Yet there remains one vital difference. The PRC today faces no foreign invasion from the east. It does not have to expand its military build-up except by its own choice. Jiang Zeming today does not seem to have an armed insurgent group in the PRC. So why is the reported progress without a spirit of exhilaration? Why do the present leaders seem to feel so insecure and to hesitate before the unknown?

In short, the difficulties confronting today's PRC reformers, like Zhu Rongji and his aides at the top, closely resemble the problems of modernization before but are a great deal worse. We submit that such changes for the worse are positively related to the thoroughness and callousness their political predecessors exhibited in the mass campaigns against opponents and countless innocent noncommunist fellow Chinese and in socializing and collectivizing the war-wrecked Chinese economy in a helter-skelter manner. The Anti-Rightist movement of 1957 was truly the most far-reaching, disastrous coup de grâce. Even after Mao's death, its effects have been aggravated by additional events perpetrated by remnant Maoist successors and militarists in the years down to our time. Why has this been the case?

Institutional Restructuring and Societal Performance

In the first part of this volume, we saw how the CCP tried to liquidate their political opponents and to replace all persons of relative social prominence in both urban and rural areas with their own cadres. Land owners, businessmen, persons having foreign contacts, bankers, shopkeepers and the like—in short, those who were at one time or another active members of the society—were all targeted in successive movements. The victims were generally more educated than their replacements. Associates, relatives and family members close to individuals targeted for elimination were often induced to denounce the victims—e.g., children against parents, wives against husbands, friends against friends—during the campaign to suppress "counterrevolutionaries." Informants from among colleagues and employees were urged to report on business people during the "Three-Antis" and "Five-Antis" campaigns in the 1951-53 period. Academics, teachers, writers and publicists were forced to grind out confessions repeatedly until they could actually put on paper confessions repudiating their own past history in a manner that would satisfy their worst enemies and bring about psychological collapse.

Violence and wantonly destructive behavior were encouraged during the Cultural Revolution to eradicate all traces of a civil society.

When the wholesale socialization of small firms and the cooperativization of China's multitudes of craftsmen and retail merchants were pushed, their traditional business ties were severed and haphazard mergers were ordered without a second thought. Assets and liabilities of individual businesses were left in a tangled mess; contractual relationships were left in an irretrievable state. As a matter of fact, there never has been to our knowledge any conscious official effort to sort out what has happened to private property over the several decades of PRC rule, as West Germany's (and later the reunited Federal Republic's) *Treuhand* has done to prepare for privatization after the collapse of East Germany. A case worth special mention is the amalgamation of commercial banks and other public and semi-public financial institutions from the very beginning of the Communist take-over in Shanghai in the early 1950s, culminating in the wholesale nationalization of large private businesses in Shanghai and other commercial centers.

These activities took place under the CCP leaders of Mao's generation because Mao's party was in a hurry to assume totalitarian control, partly in order to consolidate the power it had seized more firmly in its own hands, without necessarily any rational purpose, and partly to promote the systematic social change its ideology and political conviction dictated as a necessary first step to implement its developmental and military plans. What the CCP and its leaders neglected to consider was the damage all these acts did to the country's institutions, organizations and individuals who must continue to live with given institutions and organizations.

If the institutions and organizations that had existed were destroyed and the knowledgeable persons were killed, what and who would be there to take their place and how would individual persons then act as life went on? Leaders in the CCP seemed never to have thought of the consequences of the destruction of mutual trust, personal integrity and compassion, there being then no law or a generally accepted, dependable code of behavior to fall back upon, except selfish expediency. They have substituted only faith in the Communist Party or its leader. But these new gods do not stay put by themselves.

A Theoretical Digression to the Dynamics of Development Theory

In his effort to alter the existing Chinese society at the end of World War II from the traditional state, as incompletely modified by latter-day Manchu reformers and the May Fourth modernizers of 1919, Mao Zedong radically and ruthlessly disregarded existing Chinese rules of interpersonal conduct and laws which the ROC government in Nanking and its predecessor central governments in the North after the 1911 revolution had been trying to import and copy from Japanese, British and German models. In the economic sphere, Mao and his faithful lieutenants first adopted measures in 1950-52 against the banking and financial system, totally disregarding property rights and conventional practices. The same group was chiefly responsible for restructuring the network of retail and wholesale distribution and service trades in 1950-56, without which economic life cannot function in any large region.

As this and earlier chapters state, they did all the institutional remolding post-haste and haphazardly, first to stop galloping inflation, then to push forward their own vision of "modernizing" the country by following the Stalinist model as they probably perceived it. This second part of the task they knew they could not do unless they forcibly squeezed out of the vast majority of China's peasants and urban population all their accumulated meager savings. Unfortunately, none of these party leaders had been exposed to Western authors who were themselves only beginning to examine more critically the utopian reports on the actual accomplishments of Soviet economic planning and the growing number of theoretical and empirical explorations in the field of economic development, including various non-peaceful experiments in the inter-relationship between land reform as a redistribution of wealth and a nation's economic development efforts.

Some Western economists may recall that it was only in the mid- to late 1940s that Keynesian economic theory began to spread and virtually dominate the field of business cycle theory. It was also during this period that national income theory and its measurement began to merge with economic development theories. Not the least of the post-World War II empirical development of international lending institutions was the growth of the World Bank from its modest start as the International Bank for Reconstruction and Development, a junior twin of the International Monetary Fund, itself a creature of Keynes and Harry White at Bretton Woods.

Economic development in the post-World War II days was commonly associated with the idea of industrialization and, therefore, with the transformation of an agricultural economy by developing industry and other nonagricultural sectors. Hence agrarian reform was often considered a necessary ingredient of modernization. This thought lay behind the self-designation of the CCP as agrarian reformers. Politically, this historical path of intellectual development made theorists who were opposed to the proposition of central planning as an appropriate system for the economic development of underdeveloped countries a suitable target of attack as reactionaries. To question the economic efficiency of socialist economic planning was even in free-thinking Western academic institutions for many years a foolhardy thing to do. It was not until the open dissolution of the Soviet Union politically as an empire in 1991, two years after the breach of the Berlin Wall, that it has become gradually "politically correct" to say that the communist economic system could not accomplish what Marx, Lenin, Stalin and Mao all said it could, each in his own way.

In spite of the 1989 Tiananmen crisis, Deng Xiaoping was obviously still convinced that economic reform shorn of political liberalization remained the preferred way, indeed, the only way for China, that is, at least for the near term. His year-end Southern Inspection tour in 1992 testified to Deng's belief. By sheer coincidence, one presumes, one year after Deng Xiaoping's tour to resuscitate the PRC's economic reform program, which was then running the real risk of becoming moribund, the 1993 Nobel Prize in economics was awarded in Stockholm to Douglass C. North of Washington University, St. Louis, MO.

In his Nobel lecture, December 3, 1993, North advanced his theory on "Economic Reform through Time."[1] On the basis of this theory, one may start from the proposition that economic institutions define at any given time the possibilities of economic activity by individuals and groups (organizations) and the constraints (formal and informal) they must observe. Given the incentives for action within such a scope, the actions then give rise to the outcomes manifested in history. The history may be one of growth if the in-

1. See Douglass C. North, "Economic Performance through Time," *Les Prix Nobel* (Stockholm: Les Prix Nobel, 1993). Readers may wish also to consult the author's monograph (with Richard Y. C. Yin), *Can One Unscramble an Omelet* (Baltimore: Occasional Papers/Reprints Series in Contemporary Asian Studies, 1993-No. 1), which shows how Chinese personal behavior in economic matters has made economic reform extremely time-consuming and hard.

centive system (through, e.g. competition and commerce) is favorable. In the contrary case, if the incentive system, derived from the interaction of the given institutions and organizations, is adverse to positive actions, the outcome, as seen in history, would be one of decline.

Two more propositions can be added. First, the incentive structure usually changes rather slowly. Second, over time and, therefore, from one generation to another, there is a crucial learning process by means of which organizations and actors (both economic and political) learn what is the most productive action to secure the best pay-off. If the interactions between institution and organization produce a favorable incentive system that remains relatively stable, one would expect economically developed countries to continue their favorable growth. In a different case, if a significant improvement in the incentive system favorable to faster growth should occur in a developing country over a period of time, we should expect the country in question to become what some would today call an "emerging economy," such as one of the Asian small or large economic "dragons" of development. In the reverse case, growth could stop, or a decline, slow or precipitate, could set in.

A Delayed Effect of the CCP's Institutional Destruction

The multifaceted destruction of pre-Communist (pre-1949) institutions had the effect of upsetting the incentive framework and implementing mechanism which the Dengist economic reform team under Hu Yaobang and Zhao Ziyang probably tried to structure when they were both in power in the 1980s until the middle of the decade. But the previous destruction of the institution-organizational matrix had been too thorough and too long for a smooth process of economic growth to develop anew quickly. For example, having discarded "rule by law" for many years—not to mention the "rule of law" —the CCP had to re-institute even a criminal law from the very beginning. The bankruptcy law was not put in place in name only among the country's economic statutes until shortly before the second Tiananmen, and has only been sporadically applied. The continuing disputes on patent and copyright piracy with Western countries in the 1990s decade has been an unavoidable consequence of the institutional gap created by the CCP itself.

Restructuring the institutional framework by filling the missing gaps in the capital and producer goods market areas so casually destroyed more than three decades earlier is an effort to undo what the Chinese communists' have done deliberately themselves. In addition, the reformers, among their other tasks, must replace parts of the institution-organizational matrix which came into being under the CCP's own make-shift rules. One of the most burdensome is to replace many welfare, educational and collective-social consumption roles of the *danwei* (the government and enterprise employing unit). This is one of the unsolved problems of reforming the state sector of the economy that has to be resolved.

To relinquish these *danwei* functions without providing a substitute would be politically impossible for the CCP government. To request private business to take over *danwei* roles would be beyond its capability. Somehow the roles must be reduced or assumed by a combination of joint private-public effort by stages. The absence of clearly defined property rights and of accounting principles derived therefrom then constitutes a hopeless drag on development and the market economy.

Even more heart-rending are the lives lost when organizations and enterprises were destroyed. Humanitarian and moral considerations aside, replacement of these human resources will take time in the best of circumstances. Students sent abroad for training and education must be allocated to many fields outside technology, engineering and the natural sciences and must be nurtured for many years to gain experience. After the 1989 repression, the additional worry is whether they would return to China at all. All in all, therefore, the necessarily slow pace of reform implementation is to a large extent a consequence of the CCP's mindless destruction of institutions and its reckless decimation of pre-communist organizations and talents.

When communist and military bureaucrats (and Maoist radicals) were taken in to replace their predecessors, they had to learn (sometimes by osmosis) what the new codes of conduct should be and were. In the course of unceasing intra-CCP infighting—most notably during the Peng Dehuai episode in the Lushan Conference aftermath and the Cultural Revolution period, the frequent changes in personnel and shifts in current policy positions made it exceedingly hard to guess what was the politically-correct stance to assume. The consequences are twofold. In the first place, under the existing incentive system, the highest risk was inevitably associated with innovation while the safest and best policy was to "stay the course," followed by jumping quickly to the superior person's wish as soon as it could be detected, retaining always the possibility of a sudden move toward the "exit." This attitude favored the assembling of "yes men" and bureaucrats following a day-to-day routine, changing only when told to. This meant that one learned not to do anything different. If "zero growth" was not permitted, the "plan fulfillment" would be a safe record when the time came for job evaluation. In the second place, those who could best anticipate the leader's wishes would most likely reach the top fastest.[2] They are the sycophants in every large organization, by no means in the PRC alone or in political organizations only.

The Impact of Soviet-Type Central Planning on Scrambled Institutions and Decimated Personnel

If the incentive system was radically and capriciously revamped and potential actors who might have been knowledgeable and experienced enough to help were killed, exiled, imprisoned or simply so frightened as to be silenced, one would expect a general diminution of economic efficiency and entrepreneurial activity. This was probably the outcome when the PRC's First Five-Year Plan was nominally put in place at the end of the Korean War. As we have tried to show in Chapter V, the attempt to implement the 1953-57 plan and the formulation of the original Second Five-Year Plan took place against such a background of institutional destruction and shrinkage of the available pool of knowledgeable personnel (which the PRC had inherited from the previous regime, augmented by returnees from overseas in the first few years of the 1950s).

The efficiency of Soviet-type economic planning was grossly exaggerated by its practitioners in the Soviet Union and by its advocates in the West in the interwar period. Students of the system from the PRC were learning from this model and were either without actual Western or other theoretical cases for comparison. As a result, we should not expect results greatly better than what the Soviet economy could produce, especially from the point of view of the civilian sector of an economy operating under the assumptions of freedom of choice for both consumers and producers.

At this point, we can do no better than register the hope that future historians of the Chinese economy will be in a position to reanalyze the historical development of the PRC's economic system in the 1953-58 period and look closely into the interaction between

2. See Frederick A. Hayek, *The Road to Serfdom* (London: George Routledge, 1944) and "The Pretense of Knowledge," *The American Economic Review*, December 1989, pp. 100-113.

centralist planning and institutional change. Theoretically, we can, however, remind our readers of the following points.

Like Douglass North's path-breaking research on the direction of long-term economic change in history which won the Nobel Prize in 1993, Hayek's earlier work on the concept of insufficient knowledge for central economic planning belatedly drew the same Nobel recognition in 1974. Hayek's ideas as summarized in his 1974 Nobel essay was based to a large degree on his 1942 work on "Scientism and the Study of Society" in *Economica,* which antedated the first edition (1944) of *The Road to Serfdom* by a little less than two years.[3] Hayek's 1944 publication was, according to the book's inside front cover, dedicated to the "Socialists of All Parties." It was a warning to advocates of central planning on the central plan's inefficiency on the basis of insufficient knowledge, if for no other reason than its socio-political effects, including an explanation of "Why the Worst Get on Top."[4] Had Hayek's Nobel honor come earlier and the title of his Nobel 1974 lecture entitled "The Pretense of Knowledge" appeared sooner, someone might have had an opportunity to call it to the attention of the PRC's policy-makers. But would anyone have listened before 1989? Would anyone have dared to speak of the book's contents after 1957?

An irony of history is that Hayek's 1942 and 1974 works were separated by 32 years, a time span corresponding closely to the 32-year period from 1957 to 1989 noted in the beginning of this chapter. One must not over-emphasize such coincidences. Perhaps the real significance of such a coincidence in timing is that it tells us how important it is for relevant ideas to reach policy-makers in a timely fashion.

Consider the case of Ma Yinchu, a famed demographer-economist who left Nationalist-controlled Shanghai for Hongkong, according to Qian Jiaju's account, in order to join Mao Zedong's forces and to declare his public support of the new regime. He was not able to escape dismissal and banishment by Mao because of his disagreement with Mao's belief in the benefits of unlimited population growth.[5]

Mao's views were advanced without any real thought on many factors. They could be defended only as long as the additional net

---

3. "Scientism and the Study of Society," *Economica*, London School of Economics, Vol. IX, No. 35, August 1942.

4. See *supra* note 2.

5. See Ma Yinchu, *Xin Renkou Lun* [*On Population: A New Theory*] (Beijing: Beijing Publishers, 1979).

increase in output would always exceed in value the corresponding increase in total resources used as a result of demographic growth. Mao simply ignored other policy measures necessary to squeeze out this net increase such as improvement in population quality and additional availability of resources needed to offset environmental deterioration. Many of China's academics, among them many former sympathizers duped by the CCP, thus left the country or were silenced, after the Anti-Rightist campaign. They were no longer there, perhaps not even alive, during the Cultural Revolution period to try to diminish its impact on the regression of the institutional and organizational infrastructure.

Worship of Size

There seems to be an unreasoned lingering admiration, bordering on worship, of size and scale—the alleged mobilization of more than one hundred million peasants on a specific task during the grain production drive in 1958-59, the long-advertised gigantic Yangtze Gorge hydro-project for which millions of Chinese citizens have had to be moved from their homes, the longest railway built across China in a given number of days, and so forth. One is reminded of the Great Wall, a tourist attraction and focus of a historical "size syndrome."

To many, size symbolizes power. This was certainly true in Mao's case. Power can be especially important to some people who do not have it. It is perhaps even more important to a nation that has lost what it believes it once had. A nation and a political leader may wish to excel over and above all others, as Mao Zedong unashamedly affirmed in both speech and verse. Such leaders are likely to be strong and ruthless.[6] Large undertakings usually entail high cost. High cost is less likely to deter really determined, powerful leaders, especially if they themselves do not have to bear the burden, or if they do not appreciate the total real cost and risk. Insufficient knowledge and callousness may both be present. This is a point which psychologists in China will be better able to contemplate and should not fail to address.

All the above tendencies can be found in ample abundance when we look at Mao and many of his followers in their governance of China in the last half-century. However, in the post-Deng period, it may be possible for the PRC's future leadership to undertake an-

---

6. See *supra* note 2. Also Chapter X, "Why the Worst Get on Top," in Hayek, *supra* note 2, at pp. 100-113.

other evaluation of the determining factors of the PRC's development prospects. Such a review during and after the next CCP Congress would be most timely.

Lessons from Ludwig Erhard's Reform in West Germany[7]

In this connection, let us take a quick look at the free market economist Ludwig Erhard's reform of the West German economy, which marked the beginning of the German economic miracle after World War II. Essentially the German program consisted of removing price controls all at once while strictly enforcing macroeconomic controls by restricting the supply of the quantity of money through controlling bank deposit withdrawals. This combination of policy measures implied that relative prices would be free to change and producers and consumers would rearrange resource allocation on the basis of the new flexible prices. This was the successful process initiated by a one-time comprehensive reform that took place in West Germany, which PRC visitors to the Kiel World Economic Institute discussed with their host before the 1989 Tiananmen crisis. The gist of the German explanation, according to Chen Yizi, was virtually the same as related by another German economist, G. Walter, in his subsequent conversation with this author and as reported by the American media.

At the time of the West German economic reform, several potential problems which exist in the PRC today were either not present in occupied Germany or could be readily resolved. The issues were as follows. First, the institution-organization matrix issue raised by Douglass North in relation to long-term growth did not really exist. West German producers and consumers still knew what the laws, codes, and conventions governing behavior were in spite of the wartime physical destruction. They did not have a serious learning problem, and enforcement of these necessary constraints by governmental agents should have been minimal.

Second, inasmuch as West Germany was still under Allied Occupation, Allied forces were present to maintain order while any pain resulting from the hypothetical role of forcible enforcement could be blamed upon the aftermath of the war and, by inference,

---

7. Ludwig Erhard, a founding member with Hayek of the Mont Pèlerin Society, which was organized to promote the free market economy after World War II, was Chancellor of West Germany in 1963-66. He was the promoter of Germany's postwar economic reform. For reference to the successful German reform in comparison with the on-going stumbling PRC effort, see the discussion in Chapters V, VIII and XIV in this volume and the Chen Yi-zi account of an interview with Herbert Giersch of Kiel.

the Occupation. Not the least important was the general understanding by Germans that the Western occupying powers probably wished to relinquish their status as such as soon as they could, certainly not to remain indefinitely against the wishes of the German population.

Third, if shortage of individual goods and special workers should occur, post-World War II economic aid programs were still available to bridge over economic shortfalls with the comprehensive, overall external aid then available.

Comparisons with Conditions in the PRC in 1996

In comparison with conditions in the PRC, as of 1996, it seems that the task of institutional and organizational restructuring in mainland China is still in an early phase of the process, including banking and fiscal reform and foreign trade and exchange policy, which are still caught in a traditional and substantive struggle between mercantilism and free trade. The overall problems of economic regulation and the tolerable degree of concentration of economic power and of economic inequality in the country remain unresolved. Moreover, the political framework for the peaceful resolution of these issues is not in place. Many laws, codes and conventions of economic conduct and organizations and agents for their implementation and enforcement have yet to be set up and tested. All this will take time, and time cannot be shortened; acceleration is impossible without first making a start. It seems that some members in the PRC leadership have been, or are becoming, ready to do so.

As the Tiananmen crisis in 1989 demonstrated, the PRC leadership then sought the PLA's support in order to gain a breather. Since the breather was secured and has already lasted half a decade and the crucial state enterprise sector, and in particular the military sub-sector, have finally become the focus of attention of the leadership, it seems that there is at least a chance of resolution of the real issue. The chance, however, is small.

The "real issue" is whether the military's role in political restructuring and the economic problem of the employment of its vast numbers can be smoothly resolved along with the privatization of some state enterprises, and whether the PLA's original function as the armed tool of the CCP (not the defensive force of a nation-state) can be reconciled with a world seeking, in an unsteady gait, to establish a new order following the collapse of the former expansionist Soviet Union.

Contrary to the fears of some PRC leaders, the outside world is not really seeking to isolate the PRC, still less to contain it. Neither the inflow of investment capital nor the potentially attendant balance of payments requirement would totally defy solution, if the kind of economic development it has unceasingly trumpeted behind a screen of nontransparency, the enthusiasm of Western investors and ethnic Chinese neighbors in spite of the disapprobation of others, and the historically proven aptitude of the Chinese to survive are all true.

However, it is by no means obvious that the task of modernization the Chinese nation has set for itself since 1842 will be successfully fulfilled, or its fulfillment will be clearly in view when the 20th century draws to a close. On the contrary, the PRC is still in danger of revolving around in a historical cycle of being only partially "modernized," but partially stagnating. Perhaps moving "in a tumbling irregular orbit" it will be continuously a danger to itself if not to others.

A Brief Summary: Where the PRC Went Wrong Historically

In the opinion of this writer, the PRC made a number of wrong choices during the last half century. It embraced the Soviet-type economic planning model which could not really promote development in the civilian sector of the economy on the basis of freedom of choice. It was successful in winning popular support by covering up its real intentions. However, it wiped out the existing institutions and liquidated their organizational framework without putting in a functioning social and cultural replacement after seizing power. It aggravated its own task and the plight of the Chinese population by imposing upon the latter extraordinary demands for resources for the production of its own nuclear arsenal and defense constructions against foreign invasion that fortunately for the Chinese did not materialize. The external threats were not entirely imaginary. But the threats were partly the PRC's own making, an outcome of its own external policy in choosing friends and enemies.

What Is to Be Done?

As Karl Popper told his readers in the preface to *The Open Society and Its Enemies* in 1950 (second edition)[8], one idea always leads to another, the continuous flow of ideas never ending. Having

---

8. Karl R. Popper, *The Open Society and Its Enemies*, Vol. 1, "The Spell of Plato" (New Jersey: Princeton University Press, 1962), p. ix.

made what in our view were egregious errors, what can the PRC now do? It is natural to ask this question. But to answer it could require writing at least one more book, if not several, and is certainly beyond the scope of this book. Even more important perhaps is that to be useful the answer should really be given by people from the Chinese mainland themselves. As an outside observer and at this point in our account of events of the last fifty years, we can only offer a short list of new questions, answers to which emanating from the Chinese mainland and from the CCP can be used as tests for prognostication. The more answers can be given in the affirmative, the better will be the prospects of success.

1. *Scale test.* If one cannot successfully undertake a utopian task of thorough restructuring for mainland China as a whole, can one attempt step-by-step changes one at a time? For instance, reform can be instituted in a few selected provinces at a time.
2. *Compensation test.* If a new policy touches on several parties on the mainland (including possibly the central authorities on the mainland) might one institute step-by-step implementation in a manner like the planned changes in the rights and obligations of the European Union? Interprovincial, central-provincial and Taiwan-mainland issues are all in this category. If the incidence of the policy varies from one area to another, will adequate compensatory measures be provided?
3. *Advance time-schedule test.* Will the mainland authorities promise to institute additional reform measures on a preannounced time schedule? Similarly, is there a promised schedule of completion dates for each of the step-by-step measures?
4. *Self-enforcement test.* Will the result of any new policy announcement automatically permit open inspection by the public and by non-Chinese observers? The step-by-step removal of non-transparency and of information blackout and limits to access would be tantamount to the same. These measures would seem to be the initial orientation needed to direct the reformers' thinking.

To add more tests or to provide specifics on what to do had better be left to the future. The most important for the future of the PRC is an open commitment which alone in time can restore trust as a true substitute for what André Malraux called "the beautiful lie" of the PRC under Mao.

All the above four tests have two effects. They can help reconstitute faith for all Chinese in themselves, credibility of PRC officialdom in the eyes of others, and mutual trust among individual Chinese in the process of institution-building to promote long-term sustained growth. No less important is a very pragmatic consideration; namely, if the gradualistic approach to reform and modernization implied here in these tests takes too long, the reformers will be forewarned that the total time required will overrun such things as the unavoidable time constraint represented by resource decimation, environmental decline and the increase in the numbers and reduction of the quality of the population, mentioned in Chapter VIII above. Let us repeat again, these tests must be applied by the Chinese themselves; they are not an imposition forced by others on the Chinese. For the goal of modernization, not just survival, is set by the Chinese for themselves and the prime responsibility for fulfilling this goal is of course theirs, as it has been since Chang Chih-tung's time.

Because of the current interest on the part both of many mainland officials and generally in Taiwan, we add a fifth test among possible mainland initiatives, a special fifth, "Kinship or Tai Chen (Dai Zhen) test." The idea stems from the history of World War II when numerous U.S. personnel were present in England and continental Europe at the time of Nazi Germany's surrender to the Allies. American forces had been sent to Europe to take part in the armed effort to overthrow the Nazis. On V-E day, at the Voice of America end-of-the-War broadcast to Europe by a prominent member of the American press, Templeton Peck, later editor of the *San Francisco Chronicle*, spoke of the wartime comradeship of the two nations and a shared belief in freedom and humanity although, as we all know, the United States became independent of British rule because the original British emigrants wished to be freer than they could have been at home.

This particular episode came to the author's mind in early 1996 while attending a service in memory of that very speech writer of 1945. It so happens that in spring 1996, one half century after the defeat of Hitler, the PRC authorities chose to fire nuclear-capable missiles to Taiwan waters to symbolize their displeasure at the upcoming general presidential election on Taiwan in late March. The PRC made it quite clear that it was against the incumbent ROC president and KMT candidate Lee Teng-hui, who was accused by the CCP of being a candidate for Taiwan independence and separatism in disguise. We add this "kinship test" as a supplemental fifth test for the PRC to employ in judging for itself whether specific new reform measures are desirable or not from the point of view of long-term growth and modernization.

It may be useful to point out that the proposed kinship test can be regarded as a special case of the Dai Zhen test (Chapter XIV), which requires that one apply the test of some action hypothetically to oneself to determine whether one would find the impact a welcome one before applying it to others.

INDEX

G

H

I

J

K

L

M

Q

R

Occasional Papers/Reprints Series in Contemporary Asian Studies

500 West Baltimore Street
Baltimore, Maryland 21201-1786
U.S.A.
(410) 706-3870

(For back issues, new prices effective from October 1, 1991)

1977 Series

No. 1 - 1977 **ISSN 0730-0107** **ISBN 0-942182-00-6**

Chinese Attitude Toward Continental Shelf and Its Implication on Delimiting Seabed in Southeast Asia (Hungdah Chiu), 32 pp. $3.00

No. 2 - 1977 **ISSN 0730-0107** **ISBN 0-942182-01-4**

Income Distribution in the Process of Economic Growth of the Republic of China (Yuan-Li Wu), 45 pp. $3.00

No. 3 - 1977 **ISSN 0730-0107** **ISBN 0-942182-02-2**

The Indonesian Maoists: Doctrines and Perspectives (Justus M. van der Kroef), 31 pp. $3.00

No. 4 - 1977 **ISSN 0730-0107** **ISBN 0-942182-03-0**

Taiwan's Foreign Policy in the 1970s: A Case Study Adaptation and Viability (Thomas J. Bellows), 22 pp. $3.00

No. 5 - 1977 **ISSN 0730-0107** **ISBN 0-942182-04-9**

Asian Political Scientists in North America: Professional and Ethnic Problems (Edited by Chun-tu Hsueh), 148 pp. Index $6.00

No. 6 - 1977 **ISSN 0730-0107** **ISBN 0-942182-05-7**

The Sino-Japanese Fisheries Agreement of 1975: A Comparison with Other North Pacific Fisheries Agreements (Song Yook Hong), 80 pp. $5.00

No. 7 - 1977 **ISSN 0730-0107** **ISBN 0-942182-06-5**

Foreign Trade Contracts Between West German Companies and the People's Republic of China: A Case Study (Robert Heuser), 22 pp. $3.00

No. 8 - 1977 **ISSN 0730-0107** **ISBN 0-942182-07-3**

Reflections on Crime and Punishment in China, with Appended Sentencing Documents (Randle Edwards, Translation of Documents by Randle Edwards and Hungdah Chiu), 67 pp. $3.00

No. 9 - 1977 **ISSN 0730-0107** **ISBN 0-942182-08-1**

Chinese Arts and Literature: A Survey of Recent Trends (Edited by Wai-lim Yip), 126 pp. $5.00

No. 10 - 1977 **ISSN 0730-0107** **ISBN 0-942182-09-X**

Legal Aspects of U.S.-Republic of China Trade and Investment — Proceedings of a Regional Conference of the American Society of International Law (Edited by Hungdah Chiu and David Simon), 217 pp. Index $8.00

No. 11 - 1977 **ISSN 0730-0107** **ISBN 0-942182-10-3**

Asian American Assembly Position Paper: I. A Review of U.S. China Relations, 62 pp. $3.00

No. 12 - 1977 **ISSN 0730-0107** **ISBN 0-942182-11-1**

Asian American Assembly Position Paper: II. A Review of U.S. Employment Policy, 24 pp. $3.00

1978 Series

No. 1 - 1978 (13) **ISSN 0730-0107** **ISBN 0-942182-12-X**

Indian Ocean Politics: An Asian-African Perspective (K.P. Misra), 31 pp. $3.00

No. 2 - 1978 (14) **ISSN 0730-0107** **ISBN 0-942182-13-8**

Normalizing Relations with the People's Republic of China: Problems, Analysis, and Documents (Edited by Hungdah Chiu, with contribution by G. J. Sigur, Robert A. Scalapino, King C. Chen, Eugene A. Theroux, Michael Y.M. Kau, James C. Hsiung and James W. Morley), 207 pp. Index $5.00

No. 3 - 1978 (15) **ISSN 0730-0107** **ISBN 0-942182-14-6**

Growth, Distribution, and Social Change: Essays on the Economy of the Republic of China (Edited by Yuan-li Wu and Kung-chia Yeh), 227 pp. Index $5.00

No. 4 - 1978 (16) **ISSN 0730-0107** **ISBN 0-942182-15-4**

The Societal Objectives of Wealth, Growth, Stability, and Equity in Taiwan (Jan S. Prybyla), 31 pp. $3.00

No. 5 - 1978 (17) **ISSN 0730-0107** **ISBN 0-942182-16-2**

The Role of Law in the People's Republic of China as Reflecting Mao Tse-Tung's Influence (Shao-chuan Leng), 18 pp. $3.00

No. 6 - 1978 (18) **ISSN 0730-0107** **ISBN 0-942182-17-0**

Criminal Punishment in Mainland China: A Study of Some Yunnan Province Documents (Hungdah Chiu), 35 pp. $3.00

No. 7 - 1978 (19) **ISSN 0730-0107** **ISBN 0-942182-18-9**

A Guide to the Study of Japanese Law (Lawrence W. Beer and Hidenori Tomatsu), 45 pp. $4.00

No. 8 - 1978 (20) **ISSN 0730-0107** **ISBN 0-942182-19-7**

The Pueblo, EC-121, and Mayaguez Incidents: Some Continuities and Changes (Robert Simmons), 40 pp. $4.00

No. 9 - 1978 (21) **ISSN 0730-0107** **ISBN 0-942182-20-0**

Two Korea's Unification Policy and Strategy (Yong Soon Yim), 82 pp. Index $4.00

1979 Series

No. 1 - 1979 (22) **ISSN 0730-0107** **ISBN 0-942182-21-9**

Asian Immigrants and Their Status in the U.S. (Edited by Hungdah Chiu), 54 pp. $4.00

No. 2 - 1979 (23) **ISSN 0730-0107** **ISBN 0-942182-22-7**

Social Disorder in Peking After the 1976 Earthquake Revealed by a Chinese Legal Documents (Hungdah Chiu), 20 pp. $4.00

No. 3 - 1979 (24) **ISSN 0730-0107** **ISBN 0-942182-23-5**

The Dragon and the Eagle — A Study of U.S.-People's Republic of China Relations in Civil Air Transport (Jack C. Young), 65 pp. $5.00

No. 4 - 1979 (25) **ISSN 0730-0107** **ISBN 0-942182-24-3**

Chinese Women Writers Today (Edited by Wai-lim Yip and William Tay), 108 pp. $5.00

No. 5 - 1979 (26) **ISSN 0730-0107** **ISBN 0-942182-25-1**

Certain Legal Aspects of Recognizing the People's Republic of China (Hungdah Chiu), 49 pp. $4.00

No. 6 - 1979 (27) **ISSN 0730-0107** **ISBN 0-942182-26-X**

China's Nationalization of Foreign Firms: The Politics of Hostage Capitalism, 1949-1957 (Thomas N. Thompson), 80 pp. Index $5.00

No. 7 - 1979 (28) **ISSN 0730-0107** **ISBN 0-942182-27-8**

U.S. Status of Force Agreement with Asian Countries: Selected Studies (Charles Cochran and Hungdah Chiu), 130 pp. Index $4.00

No. 8 - 1979 (29) **ISSN 0730-0107** **ISBN 0-942182-28-6**

China's Foreign Aid in 1978 (John F. Copper), 45 pp. $4.00

1980 Series

No. 1 - 1980 (30) **ISSN 0730-0107** **ISBN 0-942182-29-4**

The Chinese Connection and Normalization (Edited by Hungdah Chiu and Karen Murphy), 200 pp. Index $7.00

No. 2 - 1980 (31) **ISSN 0730-0107** **ISBN 0-942182-30-8**

The Conceptual Foundations of U.S. China Policy: A Critical Review (James C. Hsiung), 17 pp. $3.00

No. 3 - 1980 (32) **ISSN 0730-0107** **ISBN 0-942182-31-6**

Policy, Proliferation and the Nuclear Proliferation Treaty: U.S. Strategies and South Asian Prospects (Joanne Finegan), 61 pp. $4.00

No. 4 - 1980 (33) **ISSN 0730-0107** **ISBN 0-942182-32-4**

A Comparative Study of Judicial Review Under Nationalist Chinese and American Constitutional Law (Jyh-pin Fa), 200 pp. Index $6.00

No. 5 - 1980 (34) **ISSN 0730-0107** **ISBN 0-942182-33-2**

Certain Problems in Recent Law Reform in the People's Republic of China (Hungdah Chiu), 34 pp. $4.00

No. 6 - 1980 (35) **ISSN 0730-0107** **ISBN 0-942182-34-0**

China's New Criminal & Criminal Procedure Codes (Hungdah Chiu), 16 pp. $3.00

No. 7 - 1980 (36) **ISSN 0730-0107** **ISBN 0-942182-35-9**

China's Foreign Relations: Selected Studies (Edited by F. Gilbert Chan & Ka-che Yip), 115 pp. (out of print) $5.00

No. 8 - 1980 (37) **ISSN 0730-0107** **ISBN 0-942182-36-7**

Annual Review of Selected Books on Contemporary Asian Studies (1979-1980) (Edited by John F. Copper), 45 pp. $4.00

1981 Series

No. 1 - 1981 (38) **ISSN 0730-0107** **ISBN 0-942182-37-5**

Structural Changes in the Organization and Operation of China's Criminal Justice System (Hungdah Chiu), 31 pp. $3.00

No. 2 - 1981 (39) **ISSN 0730-0107** **ISBN 0-942182-38-3**

Readjustment and Reform in the Chinese Economy (Jan S. Prybyla), 58 pp. $3.00

No. 3 - 1981 (40) **ISSN 0730-0107** **ISBN 0-942182-39-1**

Symposium on the Trial of Gang of Four and Its Implication in China (Edited by James C. Hsiung), 118 pp. $5.00

No. 4 - 1981 (41) **ISSN 0730-0107** **ISBN 0-942182-40-5**

China and the Law of the Sea Conference (Hungdah Chiu), 30 pp. $4.00

No. 5 - 1981 (42) **ISSN 0730-0107** **ISBN 0-942182-41-3**

China's Foreign Aid in 1979-80 (John Franklin Copper), 54 pp. $4.00

No. 6 - 1981 (43) **ISSN 0730-0107** **ISBN 0-942182-42-1**

Chinese Regionalism: Yesterday and Today (Franz Michael), 35 pp. $4.00

No. 7 - 1981 (44) **ISSN 0730-0107** **ISBN 0-942182-43-X**

Elite Conflict in the Post-Mao China (Parris H. Chang), 40 pp. $4.00
(Out of print, please order No. 2 - 1983 (55) for a revised version of this issue.)

No. 8 - 1981 (45) **ISSN 0730-0107** **ISBN 0-942182-44-8**

Proceedings of Conference on Multi-system Nations and International Law: International Status of Germany, Korea, and China (Edited by Hungdah Chiu and Robert Downen), 203 pp. Index $8.00

1982 Series

No. 1 - 1982 (46) **ISSN 0730-0107** **ISBN 0-942182-45-6**

Socialist Legalism: Reform and Continuity in Post-Mao People's Republic of China (Hungdah Chiu), 35 pp. $4.00

No. 2 - 1982 (47) **ISSN 0730-0107** **ISBN 0-942182-46-4**

Kampuchea, The Endless Tug of War (Justus M. Van der Kroef), 51 pp. $4.00

No. 3 - 1982 (48) **ISSN 0730-0107** **ISBN 0-942182-47-2**

Social Change on Mainland China and Taiwan, 1949-1980 (Alan P.L. Liu), 55 pp. (out of print) $5.00

No. 4 - 1982 (49) **ISSN 0730-0107** **ISBN 0-942182-48-0**

Taiwan's Security and United States Policy: Executive and Congressional Strategies in 1978-1979 (Michael S. Frost), 39 pp. $4.00

No. 5 - 1982 (50) **ISSN 0730-0107** **ISBN 0-942182-49-9**

Constitutional Revolution in Japanese Law, Society and Politics (Lawrence W. Beer), 35 pp. $4.00

No. 6 - 1982 (51) **ISSN 0730-0107** **ISBN 0-942182-50-2**

Review of Selected Books on Contemporary Asian Studies, 1981-1982 (Edited by David Salem, Roy Werner and Lyushen Shen), 67 pp. $4.00

No. 7 - 1982 (52) **ISSN 0730-0107** **ISBN 0-942182-51-0**

Chinese Law and Justice: Trends Over Three Decades (Hungdah Chiu), 39 pp. $4.00

No. 8 - 1982 (53) **ISSN 0730-0107** **ISBN 0-942182-52-9**

Disarmament and Civilian Control in Japan: A Constitutional Dilemma (Theodore McNelly), 16 pp. $4.00

1983 Series

No. 1 - 1983 (54) **ISSN 0730-0107** **ISBN 0-942182-53-7**

Essays on Sun Yat-sen and the Economic Development of Taiwan (Maria Hsia Chang and A. James Gregor), 60 pp. $3.00

No. 2 - 1983 (55) **ISSN 0730-0107** **ISBN 0-942182-54-5**

Elite Conflict in the Post-Mao China (Revised version of No. 7-1981 (44)) (Parris H. Chang), 48 pp. $3.00

No. 3 - 1983 (56) **ISSN 0730-0107** **ISBN 0-942182-55-3**

Media-Coverage on Taiwan in The People's Republic of China (Jörg-M. Rudolph), 77 pp. $4.00

No. 4 - 1983 (57) **ISSN 0730-0107** **ISBN 0-942182-56-1**

Transit Problems of Three Asian Land-locked Countries: Afghanistan, Nepal and Laos (Martin Ira Glassner), 55 pp. $3.00

No. 5 - 1983 (58) **ISSN 0730-0107** **ISBN 0-942182-57-X**

China's War Against Vietnam: A Military Analysis (King C. Chen), 33 pp. $3.00

No. 6 - 1983 (59) **ISSN 0730-0107** **ISBN 0-942182-58-8**

The People's Republic of China, International Law and Arms Control (David Salem), 325 pp. Index $7.00

(Hardcover edition published in *Maryland Studies in East Asian Law and Politics Series*, No. 3, ISBN 0-942182-59-6) $15.00

1984 Series

No. 1 - 1984 (60) **ISSN 0730-0107** **ISBN 0-942182-60-X**

China's Nuclear Policy: An Overall View (Shao-chuan Leng), 18 pp. $3.00

No. 2 - 1984 (61) **ISSN 0730-0107** **ISBN 0-942182-61-8**

The Communist Party of China: Party Powers and Group Politics from the Third Plenum to the Twelfth Party Congress (Hung-mao Tien), 30 pp. $3.00

No. 3 - 1984 (62) **ISSN 0730-0107** **ISBN 0-942182-62-6**

Legal Problems of Seabed Boundary Delimitation in the East China Sea (Ying-jeou Ma), 308 pp. Index $10.00

(Hardcover edition published in *Maryland Studies in East Asian Law and Politics Series*, No. 4, ISBN 0-942182-63-4) $15.00

No. 4 - 1984 (63) **ISSN 0730-0107** **ISBN 0-942182-64-2**

A New Direction in Japanese Defense Policy: Views from the Liberal Democratic Party Diet Members (Steven Kent Vogel), 63 pp. $3.00

No. 5 - 1984 (64) **ISSN 0730-0107** **ISBN 0-942182-65-0**
(Hardcover) 0-942182-66-9

Taiwan's Elections: Political Development and Democratization in the Republic of China (John F. Copper with George P. Chen), 180 pp. Index (Hardcover $10.00) $5.00

No. 6 - 1984 (65) **ISSN 0730-0107** **ISBN 0-942182-67-7**

Cankao Xiaoxi: Foreign News in the Propaganda System of the People's Republic of China (Jörg-Meinhard Rudolph), 174 pp. Index $5.00

1985 Series

No. 1 - 1985 (66) **ISSN 0730-0107** **ISBN 0-942182-68-5**

The Political Basis of the Economic and Social Development in the Republic of China (Alan P. L. Liu), 22 pp. $3.00

No. 2 - 1985 (67) **ISSN 0730-0107** **ISBN 0-942182-69-3**

The Legal System and Criminal Responsibility of Intellectuals in the People's Republic of China, 1949-1982 (Carlos Wing-hung Lo), 125 pp. Index $5.00

No. 3 - 1985 (68) **ISSN 0730-0107** **ISBN 0-942182-70-7**

Symposium on Hong Kong: 1997 (Edited by Hungdah Chiu), 100 pp. Index (out of print) $4.00

No. 4 - 1985 (69) **ISSN 0730-0107** **ISBN 0-942182-71-5**

The 1982 Chinese Constitution and the Rule of Law (Hungdah Chiu), 18 pp. $3.00

No. 5 - 1985 (70) **ISSN 0730-0107** **ISBN 0-942182-72-3**

Peking's Negotiating Style: A Case study of U.S.-PRC Normalization (Jaw-Ling Joanne Chang), 22 pp. $3.00

No. 6 - 1985 (71) **ISSN 0730-0107** **ISBN 0-942182-73-1**

China's Marine Environmental Protection Law: The Dragon Creeping in Murky Waters (Mitchell A. Silk), 32 pp. $3.00

1986 Series

No. 1 - 1986 (72) **ISSN 0730-0107** **ISBN 0-942182-74-X**

From Tradition to Modernity: A Socio-Historical Interpretation on China's Struggle toward Modernization Since the Mid-19th Century (Wen-hui Tsai), 76 pp. $4.00

No. 2 - 1986 (73) **ISSN 0730-0107** **ISBN 0-942182-75-8**

Peace and Unification in Korea and International Law (Byung-Hwa Lyou), 205 pp. Index. $8.00

No. 3 - 1986 (74) **ISSN 0730-0107** **ISBN 0-942182-76-6**

The Hong Kong Agreement and American Foreign Policy (Hungdah Chiu), 18 pp. $3.00

No. 4 - 1986 (75) **ISSN 0730-0107** **ISBN 0-942182-77-4**

United States-China Normalization: An Evaluation of Foreign Policy Decision Making (Jaw-ling Joanne Chang), copublished with Monograph Series in World Affairs, University of Denver, 246 pp. Index. $8.00

(Hardcover edition published in Maryland Studies in East Asian Law and Politics Series, No. 7. ISBN 0-942182-78-2) $12.00

No. 5 - 1986 (76) **ISSN 0730-0107** **ISBN 0-942182-79-0**

Communications and China's National Integration: An Analysis of *People's Daily* and *Central Daily* on the China Reunification Issue (Shuhua Chang), 205 pp. $8.00

No. 6 - 1986 (77) **ISSN 0730-0107** **ISBN 0-942182-80-4**

Since Aquino: The Philippine Tangle and the United States (Justus M. van der Kroef), 73 pp. $3.00

1987 Series

No. 1 - 1987 (78) **ISSN 0730-0107** **ISBN 0-942182-81-2**

An Analysis of the U.S.-China Nuclear Energy Cooperation Agreement (Benjamin Chin), 40 pp. $3.00

No. 2 - 1987 (79) **ISSN 0730-0107** **ISBN 0-942182-82-0**

Survey of Recent Developments in China (Mainland and Taiwan), 1985-1986 (edited by Hungdah Chiu, with the assistance of Jaw-ling Joanne Chang), 222 pp. Index $8.00

No. 3 - 1987 (80) **ISSN 0730-0107** **ISBN 0-942182-83-9**

Democratizing Transition in Taiwan (Yangsun Chou and Andrew J. Nathan), 24 pp. (out of print) $3.00

No. 4 - 1987 (81) **ISSN 0730-0107** **ISBN 0-942182-84-7**

The Legal Status of the Chinese Communist Party (Robert Heuser), 25 pp. $3.00

No. 5 - 1987 (82) **ISSN 0730-0107** **ISBN 0-942182-85-5**

The Joint Venture and Related Contract Laws of Mainland China and Taiwan: A Comparative Analysis (Clyde D. Stoltenberg and David W. McClure), 54 pp. $4.00

No. 6 - 1987 (83) **ISSN 0730-0107** **ISBN 0-942182-86-3**

Reform in Reverse: Human Rights in the People's Republic of China, 1986/1987 (Ta-Ling Lee and John F. Copper), 150 pp. $8.00

1988 Series

No. 1 - 1988 (84) **ISSN 0730-0107** **ISBN 0-942182-87-1**

Chinese Attitudes Toward International Law in the Post-Mao Era, 1978-1987 (Hungdah Chiu), 41 pp. $3.00

No. 2 - 1988 (85) **ISSN 0730-0107** **ISBN 0-942182-88-X**

Chinese Views on the Sources of International Law (Hungdah Chiu), 20 pp. $3.00

No. 3 - 1988 (86) **ISSN 0730-0107** **ISBN 0-942182-89-8**

People's Republic of China: The Human Rights Exception (Roberta Cohen), 103 pp. (out of print) $5.00

No. 4 - 1988 (87) **ISSN 0730-0107** **ISBN 0-942182-90-1**

Settlement of the Macao Issue: Distinctive Features of Beijing's Negotiating Behavior (with text of 1887 Protocol and 1987 Declaration) (Jaw-ling Joanne Chang), 37 pp. $3.00

No. 5 - 1988 (88) **ISSN 0730-0107** **ISBN 0-942182-91-X**

The Draft Basic Law of Hong Kong: Analysis and Documents (edited by Hungdah Chiu), 153 pp. $5.00

No. 6 - 1988 (89) **ISSN 0730-0107** **ISBN 0-942182-92-8**

Constitutionalism in Asia: Asian Views of the American Influence (edited by Lawrence W. Beer), 210 pp. (out of print) $10.00

1989 Series

No. 1 - 1989 (90) **ISSN 0730-0107** **ISBN 0-925153-00-1**

The Right to a Criminal Appeal in the People's Republic of China (Margaret Y.K. Woo), 43 pp. $3.00

No. 2 - 1989 (91) **ISSN 0730-0107** **ISBN 0-925153-01-X**

The Status of Customary International Law, Treaties, Agreements and Semi-Official or Unofficial Agreements in Chinese Law (Hungdah Chiu), 22 pp. $3.00

No. 3 - 1989 (92) **ISSN 0730-0107** **ISBN 0-925153-02-8**

One Step Forward, One Step Back, Human Rights in the People's Republic of China in 1987/88 (John F. Cooper and Ta-ling Lee), 140 pp. $6.00

No. 4 - 1989 (93) **ISSN 0730-0107** **ISBN 0-925153-03-6**

Tibet: Past and Present (Hungdah Chiu and June Teufel Dreyer), 25 pp. $3.00

No. 5 - 1989 (94) **ISSN 0730-0107** **ISBN 0-925153-04-4**

Chinese Attitude Toward International Law of Human Rights in the Post-Mao Era (Hungdah Chiu), 38 pp. $4.00

No. 6 - 1989 (95) **ISSN 0730-0107** **ISBN 0-925153-05-2**

Tibet to Tiananmen: Chinese Human Rights and United States Foreign Policy (W. Gary Vause), 47 pp. $4.00

1990 Series

No. 1 - 1990 (96) **ISSN 0730-0107** **ISBN 0-925153-06-0**

The International Legal Status of the Republic of China (Hungdah Chiu), 20 pp. (Out of print, please order No. 5-1992 (112) for a revised version of this issue) $3.00

No. 2 - 1990 (97) **ISSN 0730-0107** **ISBN 0-925153-07-9**

Tiananmen: China's Struggle for Democracy—Its Prelude, Development, Aftermath, and Impact (Winston L. Y. Yang and Marsha L. Wagner), 314 pp. Index $8.00

(Hardcover edition published in *Maryland Studies in East Asian Law and Politics Series*, No. 11, ISBN 0-925153-08-7) $14.00

No. 3 - 1990 (98) **ISSN 0730-0107** **ISBN 0-925153-09-5**

Nationality and International Law in Chinese Perspective (Hungdah Chiu), 37 pp. $4.00

No. 4 - 1990 (99) **ISSN 0730-0107** **ISBN 0-925153-10-9**

The Taiwan Relations Act After Ten Years (Lori Fisler Damrosch), 27 pp. $3.00

No. 5 - 1990 (100) **ISSN 0730-0107** **ISBN 0-925153-11-7**

The Taiwan Relations Act and Sino-American Relations (Hungdah Chiu), 34 pp. $4.00

No. 6 - 1990 (101) **ISSN 0730-0107** **ISBN 0-925153-12-5**

Taiwan's Recent Elections: Fulfilling the Democratic Promise (John F. Copper), 174 pp. Index (Out of print) $8.00

1991 Series

No. 1 - 1991 (102) **ISSN 0730-0107** **ISBN 0-925153-13-3**

Legal Aspects of Investment and Trade with the Republic of China (Edited by John T. McDermott, with contributions by Linda F. Powers, Ronald A. Case, Chung-Teh Lee, Jeffrey H. Chen, Cheryl M. Friedman, Hungdah Chiu, K.C. Fan and Douglas T. Hung), 94 pp. $6.00

No. 2 - 1991 (103) **ISSN 0730-0107** **ISBN 0-925153-14-1**

Failure of Democracy Movement: Human Rights in the People's Republic of China, 1988/89 (Ta-ling Lee and John F. Copper), 150 pp. Index $10.00

No. 3 - 1991 (104) **ISSN 0730-0107** **ISBN 0-925153-15-X**

Freedom of Expression: The Continuing Revolution in Japan's Legal Culture (Lawrence W. Beer), 31 pp. $5.00

No. 4 - 1991 (105) **ISSN 0730-0107** **ISBN 0-925153-16-8**

The 1989 US-Republic of China (Taiwan) Fisheries Negotiations (Mark Mon-Chang Hsieh), 84 pp. $6.00

No. 5 - 1991 (106) **ISSN 0730-0107** **ISBN 0-925153-17-6**

Politics of Divided Nations: China, Korea, Germany and Vietnam—Unification, Conflict Resolution and Political Development (Edited by Quansheng Zhao and Robert Sutter), 198 pp. Index (Out of Print) $12.00

No. 6 - 1991 (107) **ISSN 0730-0107** **ISBN 0-925153-18-4**

Lawyers in China: The Past Decade and Beyond (Timothy A. Gelatt), 49 pp. $5.00

1992 Series

No. 1 - 1992 (108) **ISSN 0730-0107** **ISBN 0-925153-19-2**

Judicial Review of Administration in the People's Republic of China (Jyh-pin Fa & Shao-chuan Leng), 37 pp. $5.00

No. 2 - 1992 (109) **ISSN 0730-0107** **ISBN 0-925153-20-6**

China's Ministry of State Security: Coming of Age in the International Arena (Nicholas Eftimiades), 24 pp. $4.00

No. 3 - 1992 (110) **ISSN 0730-0107** **ISBN 0-925153-21-4**

Libel Law and the Press in South Korea: An Update (Kyu Ho Youm), 23 pp. $5.00

No. 4 - 1992 (111) **ISSN 0730-0107** **ISBN 0-925153-22-2**

Tiananmen Aftermath: Human Rights in the People's Republic of China, 1990 (John F. Copper and Ta-ling Lee), 133 pp. Index $15.00

No. 5 - 1992 (112) **ISSN 0730-0107** **ISBN 0-925153-23-0**

The International Legal Status of the Republic of China (Revised version of No. 1-1990 (96)) (Hungdah Chiu), 37 pp. $4.00

No. 6 - 1992 (113) **ISSN 0730-0107** **ISBN 0-925153-24-9**

China's Criminal Justice System and the Trial of Pro-Democracy Dissidents (Hungdah Chiu), 21 pp. $3.00

1993 Series

No. 1 - 1993 (114) **ISSN 0730-0107** **ISBN 0-925153-25-7**

Can One Unscramble an Omelet? China's Economic Reform in Theory and Practice (Yuan-li Wu and Richard Y. C. Yin), 34 pp. $4.00

No. 2 - 1993 (115) **ISSN 0730-0107** **ISBN 0-925153-26-5**

Constitutional Development and Reform in the Republic of China on Taiwan (With Documents) (Hungdah Chiu), 61 pp. $6.00

No. 3 - 1993 (116) **ISSN 0730-0107** **ISBN 0-925153-27-3**

Sheltering for Examination (*Shourong Shencha*) in the Legal System of the People's Republic of China (Tao-tai Hsia and Wendy I. Zeldin), 32 pp. $4.00

No. 4 - 1993 (117) **ISSN 0730-0107** **ISBN 0-925153-28-1**

In Making China Modernized: Comparative Modernization Between Mainland China and Taiwan (Wen-hui Tsai), 281 pp. Index (out of print, please order No. 5 - 1996 for 2nd ed.) $18.00

No. 5 - 1993 (118) **ISSN 0730-0107** **ISBN 0-925153-30-3**

Hong Kong's Transition to 1997: Background, Problems and Prospects (with Documents) (Hungdah Chiu), 106 pp. (out of print) $7.00

No. 6 - 1993 (119) **ISSN 0730-0107** **ISBN 0-925153-31-1**

Koo-Wang Talks and the Prospect of Building Constructive and Stable Relations Across the Taiwan Straits (with Documents) (Hungdah Chiu), 69 pp. $5.00

1994 Series

No. 1 - 1994 (120) **ISSN 0730-0107** **ISBN 0-925153-32-X**

Statutory Encouragement of Investment and Economic Development in the Republic of China on Taiwan (Neil L. Meyers), 72 pp. $7.00

No. 2 - 1994 (121) **ISSN 0730-0107** **ISBN 0-925153-33-8**

Don't Force Us to Lie: The Struggle of Chinese Journalists in the Reform Era (Allison Liu Jernow), 99 pp. $7.00

No. 3 - 1994 (122) **ISSN 0730-0107** **ISBN 0-925153-34-6**

Institutionalizing a New Legal System in Deng's China (Hungdah Chiu), 44 pp. $5.00

No. 4 - 1994 (123) **ISSN 0730-0107** **ISBN 0-925153-35-4**

The Bamboo Gulag: Human Rights in the People's Republic of China, 1991-1992 (Ta-ling Lee & John F. Copper), 281 pp. Index $20.00

No. 5 - 1994 (124) **ISSN 0730-0107** **ISBN 0-925153-36-2**

Taiwan's Legal System and Legal Profession (Hungdah Chiu and Jyh-pin Fa), 22 pp. $3.00

No. 6 - 1994 (125) **ISSN 0730-0107** **ISBN 0-925153-37-0**

Toward Greater Democracy: An Analysis of the Republic of China on Taiwan's Major Elections in the 1990s (Wen-hui Tsai), 40 pp. $6.00

1995 Series

No. 1 - 1995 (126) **ISSN 0730-0107** **ISBN 0-925153-38-9**

Relations between the Republic of China and the Republic of Chile (Herman Gutierrez B. and Lin Chou), 31 pp. $5.00

No. 2 - 1995 (127) **ISSN 0730-0107** **ISBN 0-925153-39-7**

The Tibet Question and the Hong Kong Experience (Barry Sautman and Shiu-hing Lo), 82 pp. $10.00

No. 3 - 1995 (128) **ISSN 0730-0107** **ISBN 0-925153-40-0**

Mass Rape, Enforced Prostitution, and the Japanese Imperial Army: Japan Eschews International Legal Responsibility? (David Boling), 56 pp. $5.00

No. 4 - 1995 (129) **ISSN 0730-0107** **ISBN 0-925153-41-9**

The Role of the Republic of China in the World Economy (Chu-yuan Cheng), 25 pp. $3.00

No. 5 - 1995 (130) **ISSN 0730-0107** **ISBN 0-925153-42-7**

China's Economy After Deng: A Long-Term Perspective (Peter C.Y. Chow), 43 pp. $5.00

No. 6 - 1995 (131) **ISSN 0730-0107** **ISBN 0-925153-43-5**

An Entreprenurial Analysis of Opposition Movements (Ching-chane Hwang), 179 pp. Index $18.00

1996 Series

No. 1 - 1996 (132) **ISSN 0730-0107** **ISBN 0-925153-44-3**

Taiwan's 1995 Legislatiave Yuan Election (John F. Copper), 39 pp. $6.00

No. 2 - 1996 (133) **ISSN 0730-0107** **ISBN 0-925153-45-1**

Russian-Taiwanese Relations: Current State, Problems, and Prospects of Development (Peter M. Ivanov), 76 pp. $10.00

No. 3 - 1996 (134) **ISSN 0730-0107** **ISBN 0-925153-46-x**

Recent Relations between China and Taiwan and Taiwan's Defense Capabilities (Hungdah Chiu & June Teufel Dreyer), 28 pp. $4.00

No. 4 - 1996 (135) **ISSN 0730-0107** **ISBN 0-925153-47-8**

Intellectual Property Protection in the Asian-Pacific Region: A Comparative Study (Paul C. B. Liu & Andy Y. Sun), 183 pp. Index. $25.00
(hardcover edition: ISBN 0-925153-48-6) $32.00

No. 5 - 1996 (136) **ISSN 0730-0107** **ISBN 0-925153-49-4**

In Making China Modernized: Comparative Modernization between Mainland China and Taiwan (2nd ed.) (Wen-hui Tsai), 297 pp. Index. $30.00
(hardcover edition: ISBN 0-925153-50-8) $37.00

No. 6 - 1996 (137) **ISSN 0730-0107** **ISBN 0-925153-51-6**

A Study of the Consular Convention between the United States of America and the People's Republic of China (Stephen Kho), 68 pp. $6.00

1997 Series

No. 1 - 1997 (138) **ISSN 0730-0107** **ISBN 0-925153-52-4**

Tiananmen to Tiananmen, China under Communism 1947-1996 (Yuan-Li Wu), 348 pp. Index $35.00
(hardcover edition: ISBN 0-925153-53-2) $45.00

MARYLAND STUDIES IN EAST ASIAN LAW AND POLITICS SERIES

(The following books are published under the auspices or co-auspices of the East Asian Legal Studies Program of the University of Maryland School of Law. The views expressed in each book reflect only those of the author. All books published in hard cover edition, unless otherwise indicated.)

1. Hungdah Chiu, ***China and the Taiwan Issue***. New York: Praeger Publishers, A Division of Holt, Rinehart and Winston/CBS, Inc., 1979. 295 pp. (Now distributed by the Greenwood Press)
   ISBN No.: 0-03-048911-3 $49.95
2. Hungdah Chiu, ***Agreements of the People's Republic of China, 1966-1980: A Calendar***. New York: Praeger Publishers, A Division of Holt, Rinehart and Winston/CBS, Inc., 1981. 329 pp. (Now distributed by the Greenwood Press)
   ISBN No.: 0-03-059443-X $49.95
3. David Salem, ***The People's Republic of China, International Law and Arms Control***. Baltimore, Maryland: University of Maryland School of Law OPRSCAS*, 1983. 325 pp.
   ISBN No.: 0-942182-59-6 $15.00
4. Ying-jeou Ma, ***Legal Problems of Seabed Boundary Delimitation in the East China Sea***. Baltimore, Maryland: University of Maryland School of Law OPRSCAS, 1984. 308 pp.
   ISBN No.: 0-942182-63-4 $15.00
5. Hungdah Chiu and Shao-chuan Leng, editors, ***China: 70 Years After the 1911 Hsin-hai Revolution***. Charlottesville, Virginia: University Press of Virginia, 1984. 600 pp.
   (Published under the co-auspices of the Committee on Asian Studies, University of Virginia.)
   ISBN No.: 0-8138-1027-7 $35.00
6. Shao-chuan Leng and Hungdah Chiu, ***Criminal Justice in Post-Mao China***. Albany, New York: State University of New York Press, 1985. 325 pp.
   (Published under the co-auspices of Committee on Asian Studies, University of Virginia.)
   ISBN No. 0-87395-950-7 (hardcover) $74.50
   ISBN No. 0-87395-948-5 (paperback) $24.95

---

* Occasional Papers/Reprints Series in Contemporary Asian Studies, Inc., 500 West Baltimore St., Baltimore, Maryland 21201-1786. (Tel. (410) 706-3870).

7. Jaw-ling Joanne Chang, ***United States-China Normalization: An Evaluation of Foreign Policy Decision Making.*** Baltimore, Maryland: University of Maryland School of Law OPRSCAS, 1986. 246 pp. (Copublished with Monograph Series in World Affairs, University of Denver)
ISBN No. 0-942182-78-2 $12.00

8. Lester Ross and Mitchell A. Silk, ***Environmental Law and Policy in China***. Westport, CT: Greenwood Press (Quorum Books), 1987. 449 pp. $75.00

9. Hungdah Chiu, Y.C. Jao and Yuan-li Wu, editors, ***The Future of Hong Kong: Toward 1997 and Beyond***. Westport, CT: Greenwood Press (Quorum Books), 1987. 262 pp. $55.00

10. Ray S. Cline and Hungdah Chiu, eds., *The United States and Constitutionalism in China*. Washington, D.C.: U.S. Global Strategy Council, 1988. Distributed by OPRSCAS, 166 pp. Paper. $8.00.

11. Winston L.Y. Yang and Marsha L. Wagner, eds., ***Tiananmen: China's Struggle for Democracy—Its Prelude, Development, Aftermath, and Impact***. Baltimore, Maryland: University of Maryland School of Law OPRSCAS, 1990. 314 pp. Index $14.00.

12. Mitchell A. Silk, ed., ***Taiwan Trade and Investment Law***. Hong Kong: Oxford University Press, 1994. 693 pages. ISBN 0-19-585289-3 $59.00.

ORDER FORM

To Occasional Papers/Reprints Series in Contemporary Asian Studies, University of Maryland School of Law, 500 West Baltimore Street, Baltimore, Maryland 21201-1786, U.S.A.
e-mail: hchiu@law.umab.edu

Check One:

❑ Please Send:

No.	*Author*	*Title*	*Copies*

❑ Please start my subscription of the OPRSCAS: Starting year ____________

Subscription price is U.S. $30.00 per year for 6 issues in the U.S. and $35.00 for Canada or overseas (regardless of the price of individual issues).

My check of U.S. $ ______________ is enclosed ______________ copy(s) of invoice/receipt required. (Institution/library may request billing before making payment) (Make checks payable to OPRSCAS) (Please add postage/handling of $2.00 for one copy and $1.00 for each additional copy.)

Please send books to:
Name/Corp./Library:
Address: (Please include zip code)

____

____

____